CLICKING IN

HOT LINKS TO A DIGITAL CULTURE

Printed in the United States of America

Bay Press
115 West Denny Way
Seattle, WA 98119-4205

Library of Congress Cataloging-in-Publication Data

Clicking in: hot links to a digital culture / edited by Lynn Hershman Leeson.
p. cm.
Includes bibliographical references (p. 349).
ISBN 0-941920-42-9 (alk. paper)
1. Computers—Social aspects. 2. Information superhighway—Social aspects.
I. Hershman Leeson, Lynn, 1941-
QA76.9.C66C57 1996
96-14615
303.48'33—dc20
CIP

Editors: Paula Ladenburg, Patricia Draher
Book design: Philip Kovacevich
Cover design: Philip Kovacevich
Proofreader: Sharon Vonasch

Cover art: *Digital Venus*, Lynn Hershman Leeson, 1996.

CLICKING IN

HOT LINKS TO A DIGITAL CULTURE

EDITED BY

Lynn Hershman Leeson

Bay Press
Seattle

Contents

vii LYNN HERSHMAN LEESON *Clicking In* and *Clicking On:* Hot Links to a Digital Culture

PART 1 TERMINAL TREATISE: Manifestos for the Digital Age

5 JOHN PERRY BARLOW A Plain Text on Crypto-Policy
19 MARK LUDWIG Introduction to *The Little Black Book of Computer Viruses*
37 SADIE PLANT Feminisations: Reflections on Women and Virtual Reality

PART 2 THE CONSEQUENCES OF UNTRUTH

43 JARON LANIER Interviewed by Lynn Hershman Leeson
54 R.U. SIRIUS Interviewed by Lynn Hershman Leeson
61 SHELDON RENAN The Net and the Future of Being Fictive

PART 3 COLONIZING VIRTUAL SPACE: The Impact on Community, Identity, and Property

73 ARTHUR H. LESTER Computer Use in Law and Medicine
78 JOICHI AND MIZUKO ITO Interviewed by Lynn Hershman Leeson
105 SANDY STONE Interviewed by Lynn Hershman Leeson
116 SHERRY TURKLE Rethinking Identity Through Virtual Community
123 SADIE PLANT The Future Looms: Weaving Women and Cybernetics
136 CHRISTIAN MÖLLER Organizing Random Chance
140 METTE STRØMFELDT Window Dressing
148 JOHN PERRY BARLOW Selling Wine Without Bottles: The Economy of Mind on the Global Net
173 GUILLERMO GÓMEZ-PEÑA The Virtual Barrio @ the Other Frontier (or The Chicano Interneta)

PART 4 | THE BODY:
Disappearances, Anti-Bodies, Agents, and the Virus

183 LEV MANOVICH The Labor of Perception
194 FLORIAN RÖTZER Attack on the Brain: Reflections on Neurotechnology
210 PATTIE MAES Artificial Life Meets Entertainment: Lifelike Autonomous Agents
222 DIANA GROMALA Pain and Subjectivity in Virtual Reality
238 MARK LUDWIG Virtual Catastrophe: Will Self-Reproducing Software Rule the World?
247 ARTHUR AND MARILOUISE KROKER Code Warriors: Bunkering In and Dumbing Down
258 CATHERINE RICHARDS Fungal Intimacy: The Cyborg in Feminism and Media Art

PART 5 | DIGITAL-SPECIFIC ART

267 RUDOLF FRIELING Hot Spots: Text in Motion and the Textscape of Electronic Media
279 SÖKE DINKLA From Participation to Interaction: Toward the Origins of Interactive Art
291 JEAN GAGNON Dionysus in Wonderland: A Few Musical Metaphors in Techno-Culture
306 ERKKI HUHTAMO Digitalian Treasures, or Glimpses of Art on the CD-ROM Frontier
318 SIMON BIGGS Multimedia, CD-ROM, and the Net
325 LYNN HERSHMAN LEESON Romancing the Anti-Body: Lust and Longing in (Cyber)space
338 SIEGFRIED ZIELINSKI 7 Items on the Net
344 DAVID A. ROSS Radical Software Redux

349 NOTES
362 CONTRIBUTORS
370 CREDITS

Clicking In and *Clicking On*

Hot Links to a Digital Culture

Lynn Hershman Leeson

The Digital Age exploded into existence not with a whimper but a bang. The globe still shakes from its entry. The journey was long, but the impact is immediate. Now, for instance, the breath of an unborn baby can be captured and rendered visible, the Dead Sea Scrolls have been bathed in enhanced color, and Mona Lisa's smile is safely preserved in a GIF file. Throughout the world, many homes are lit by the dim reflection of computer monitors. Illuminated manuscripts and images coax people to recompose reality simply by clicking in. A mutation is taking place before our charged and filtered eyes. It is a dynamic re-vision that has altered every aspect of life as we knew it. This phenomenon is not a fad or a trend, but an evolution.

The intention of this book is to frame the impact and changes that are currently in process. My challenge as an editor has been to detect the rapidly evolving patterns that, because of digital possibilities, are reshaping daily life. The collection's contributors represent diverse disciplines such as cyber-anthropology, architecture, art, biotechnology, genetics, ethics, history, law, psychology, and medicine. Authors are linked by their mutual ability to click in. Their essays and interviews offer unique perspectives on how the Digital Age is affecting culture.

In the past century the introduction of inventions such as the telephone, telegraphy, electricity, and the automobile elicited both fear and excitement. Perhaps this was because they defied existing perceptions of time, information, travel, communication, and community. Once again we are at a critical point in history; cautiously leaning toward the edge of the next millennium. There is no secure ground on which to stand. Belief systems are shifting. Communities once delineated by physical space or geographic territories are now located by connectivity, access and linkage.

My initial investigation of issues presented in this book began while I was producing a video about the consequences of new technology on personal identity. I sought to capture an overview of how digital culture affected both individuals and society. The initial provocations expanded into the interviews, CD-ROM, and essays in this collection. This material has been in a constant and elastic process of transformation. The nature of digital media is also to be in a continual state of interactive reconfiguration.

Clicking In is a collection of essays and interviews by gifted interpreters and translators of the Digital Age. Its digital companion, *Clicking On* is its digital home companion CD-ROM that interprets some of the issues discussed in the book, such as privacy and invisibility. "Venus" disappears into circuit systems as voyeuristic implications are inferred. An image of an open hand becomes a navigational tool, as does a cursor/camera. Finger digits indicate text segments, and the life lines on the palm become paths to sound- and video-bytes from some of the authors.

Imagine this anthology as a kind of browser, a sampling, a partial link to current issues. Rather than seeking to be definitive, I have chosen to find representative ideas from individuals and communities inhabiting electronic spaces. The information that resulted from this process was in a continual state of flux, alternately migrating and emigrating from one space to another. This collection could also be thought of as a thermometer. As digital forces become the lifeblood of culture, the readings will become more accurate.

I do think that the reader will find a core synthesis, a kind of DNA that links widely divergent disciplines such as cyber-anthropology, genetics, digital art, virtual reality, artificial life, and ethics. That the book is divided into five sections should not be taken as suggesting a hierarchy. Digital dynamics confound such an approach. The organization of this book is designed to provide multiple and overlapping perspectives to the digital revolution.

Soon after computer space became public, electronic manifestos began to circulate. Like most manifestos, they were written to promulgate a viewpoint or critique a system. The three contributors in Part One, *Terminal Treatise: Manifestos for the Digital Age*, address separate but significant issues: privacy, computer life-forms, and gender.

Manipulation is a frequent flier in digital space where, in order to be recognized, it is necessary to wear an electronic mask. The mask might simply be a text log-in name (or, in the case of multiple identities, names), but it could also be an image, animation, or code. These representations of the physical made cyber are often ambiguous. Photoshop is but one of the many programs that render suspect the veracity of anything digitally produced. In fact, the only stable entity in digital space may simply be the illusion that a composite reality exists. The seduction of simulation and fictive space make up Part Two, *The Consequences of Untruth.*

Once, not so very long ago, identity was presumed to be a factor of genetics or environment and community suggested compliance to specific value systems. The changing constructions of individuals to connectivity and the digital implications of authorship and intellectual property are the focus of Part Three, *Colonizing Virtual Space: The Impact on Community, Identity, and Property.*

The body is being repositioned neurologically, physically, biologically, and virtually. Part Four, *The Body: Disappearances, Anti-Bodies, Agents, and the Virus,* amplifies some of these changes and broaches new definitions of life itself.

In the mid-seventies, the phrase "site-specific art" was coined. This phrase was applied to an art that incorporated the space it. Part Five, *Digital-Specific Art,* refers to art that can only exist in electronic space. While this genre has historic and conceptual precedents, its presence has raised fundamental questions as to how to collect, exhibit, repair, and archive this art form that is by nature illusive, reproductive, and public.

The RAMifications of the Digital Age are enormous. Presumptions about communities, identity, property, physicality, art, science, and values are being digitally rewritten. A symbiotic relationship to technology exists. It defines culture as culture defines it.I have heard of an exotic plant that is able to thrive only in the ashes of extinguished foliage. Perhaps the smoke of our burning past will enable us to access our self-selected illusions and click in to the blossoming potentials of the Digital Age.

It is important to know that all of the essays in this book arrived virtually, through some kind of electronic means. Many, like those by Sadie Plant, Siegfried Zielinski, and John Perry Barlow, were downloaded from the Internet. The others arrived via e-mail. I am indebted to the many important thinkers and activists working in this field who, because of space constraints, could not be included in this collection. I am grateful to the contributors to this anthology and CD-ROM for their fearless, inspiring, and groundbreaking ideas. The diligence, wit, and perseverance of Fred Dust were essential to the completion of this book as were the inventive and creative impulses of Paul Tompkins, Rosemary Comella, and Easter Bonnifield who helped to develop the CD-ROM design, images, and authoring format. I would like to thank George Leeson for the clarity and alacrity of his critique and James Luna and Guillermo Gómez-Peña for their endurance and patience. Without the faculty research grant from the University of California, the CD-ROM would not have been possible. Paula Ladenburg's commitment and expertise are deeply embedded in these pages.

Most especially, I am grateful to Sally Brunsman and Kimberly Barnett of Bay Press, whose generosity and commitment provided sustaining support throughout the *Clicking In* and *Clicking On* process.

FIGHT ART CENSORSHIP

PART 1 | TERMINAL TREATISE: Manifestos for the Digital Age

LYNN HERSHMAN LEESON
Fight Art Censorship, Phantom Limb Number 5, 1990

A Plain Text on Crypto-Policy

John Perry Barlow

This classic essay from 1993 anticipates the continuing threats to civil liberties by key escrow encryption technology.

The field of cryptography, for centuries accustomed to hermetic isolation within a culture as obscure as its own puzzles, is going public. People who thought algorithms were maybe something you needed to dig rap music are suddenly taking an active interest in the black arts of crypto.

We have the FBI and NSA to thank for this. The FBI was first to arouse public concerns about the future of digital privacy with its injection of language year before last into a major Senate anticrime bill (SB 266) which would have registered the congressional intent that all providers of digitized communications should provide law enforcement with analog access to voice and data transmissions of their subscribers.

When this was quietly yanked in committee, they returned with a proposed bill called Digital Telephony. If passed, it would have essentially called a halt to most American progress in telecommunications until they could be assured of their continued ability to wiretap. Strange but true.

They were never able to find anyone in Congress technologically backward enough to introduce this oddity for them, but they did elevate public awareness of the issues considerably.

The National Security Agency, for all its (unknown but huge) budget, staff, and MIPS (million instructions per second), has about as much real-world political experience as the Order of Trappists and has demonstrated in its management of cryptology export policies the maddening counterproductivity that is the usual companion of inexperience.

The joint bunglings of these two agencies were starting to infuriate a lot of people and institutions who are rarely troubled by Large Governmental Foolishness in the Service of Paranoia. Along with all the usual paranoids, of course.

Then from the NSA's caverns in Fort Meade, Maryland, there slouched a chip called Clipper.

For those of you who just tuned in (or who tuned out early), the Clipper Chip—now called Skipjack owing to a trademark conflict —is a hardware encryption device that NSA designed under Reagan-Bush. In April it was unveiled by the Clinton Administration and proposed for both governmental and public use. Installed in phones or other telecommunications tools, it would turn any conversation into gibberish for all but the speaker and his intended listener, using a secret military algorithm.

Clipper/Skipjack is unique, and controversial, in that it also allows the agents of government to listen under certain circumstances. Each chip contains a key that is split into two parts immediately following manufacture. Each half is then placed in the custody of some trusted institution or "escrow agent."

If, at some subsequent time, some government agency desires to legally listen in on the owner of the communications device in which the chip has been placed, it would present evidence of "lawful authority" to the escrow holders. They will reveal the key pairs, the agency will join them, and begin listening to the subject's unencrypted conversations.

(Apparently there are other agencies besides law enforcement who can legally listen to electronic communications. The government has evaded questions about exactly who will have access to these keys, or for that matter, what, besides a judicial warrant, constitutes the "lawful authority" to which they continually refer.)

Clipper/Skipjack was not well received. The blizzard of anguished ASCII it summoned forth on the Net has been so endlessly voluble and so painstaking in its "How-many-Cray-Years-can-dance-on-the-head-of-a-Clipper-Chip" technical detail that I would guess all but the real cyberpunks are by now data-shocked into listlessness and confusion.

Indeed, I suspect that even many readers of this publication . . . a group with prodigious capacity for assimilating the arid and obscure . . . are starting to long for the days when their knowledge of cryptography and the public policies surrounding it was limited enough to be coherent.

So I almost hesitate to bring the subject up. Yet somewhere amid this racket, decisions are being made that will profoundly affect your future ability to communicate without fear. Those who would sacrifice your liberty for their illusions of public safety are being afforded some refuge by the very din of opposition.

In the hope of restoring both light and heat to the debate, I'm going to summarize previous episodes, state a few conclusions I've drawn about the current techno-political terrain, and recommend positions you might [take]. When I first heard about Clipper/Skipjack, I thought it might not be such a bad idea. This false conclusion was partly due to the reality-distorting character of the location. . . . I was about 50 feet away from the Oval Office at the time . . . but it also seemed like one plausible approach to what may be the bright future of crime in the Virtual Age.

I mean, I can see what the Guardian Class is worried about. The greater part of business is already being transacted in cyberspace. Most of the money is there. At the moment, however, most of the monetary bits in there are being accounted for. Accounting is digital, but cash is not.

It is imaginable that, with the widespread use of digital cash and encrypted monetary exchange on the Global Net, economies the size of America's could appear as nothing but oceans of alphabet soup. Money laundering would no longer be necessary. The payment of taxes might become more or less voluntary. A lot of weird things would happen after that. . . .

I'm pretty comfortable with chaos, but this is not a future I greet without reservation.

So, while I'm not entirely persuaded that we need to give up our future privacy to protect ourselves from drug dealers, terrorists, child molesters, and unnamed military opponents (the Four Horsemen of Fear customarily invoked by our protectors), I can imagine bogeymen whose traffic I'd want visible to authority.

Trouble is, the more one learns about Clipper/Skipjack, the less persuaded he is that it would do much to bring many actual Bad Guys under scrutiny. As proposed, it would be a voluntary standard, spread mainly by the market forces that would arise after the government bought a few tons of these chips for their own "sensitive but unclassified" communications systems. No one would be driven to use it by anything but convenience. In fact, no one with any brains would use it if he were trying to get away with anything.

In fact, the man who claims to have designed Clipper's basic specs, Ray Kramer, Acting Director of the National Institute of Standards and Technology (NIST), recently said, "It's obvious that anyone who uses Clipper for the conduct of organized crime is dumb." No kidding. At least so long as it's voluntary.

Under sober review, there mounted an incredibly long list of reasons to think Clipper/Skipjack might not be a fully-baked idea. In May, after a month of study, the Digital Privacy and Security Working Group, a coalition of some 40 companies and organizations chaired by the Electronic Frontier Foundation (EFF), sent the White House 118 extremely tough questions regarding Clipper, any five of which should have been sufficient to put the kibosh on it.

The members of this group are not a bunch of hysterics. It includes DEC, Hewlett-Packard, IBM, Sun, MCI, Microsoft, Apple, and AT&T (which was also, interestingly enough, the first company to commit to putting Clipper/Skipjack in its own products).

Among the more troubling of their questions:

- Who would the escrow agents be?
- What are Clipper's likely economic impacts, especially in regard to export of American digital products?
- Why is its encryption algorithm secret, and why should the public have confidence in a government-derived algorithm that can't be privately tested?
- Why is Clipper/Skipjack being ramrodded into adoption as a government standard before completion of an overall review of U.S. policies on cryptography?
- Why are the NSA, FBI, and NIST stonewalling Freedom of Information inquiries about Clipper/Skipjack? (In fact, NSA's response has been, essentially, "So? Sue us.")
- Assuming Clipper/Skipjack becomes a standard, what happens if the escrow depositories are compromised?
- Wouldn't these depositories also become targets of opportunity for any criminal or terrorist organization that wanted to disrupt U.S. law enforcement?
- Since the chip transmits its serial number at the beginning of each connection, why wouldn't it render its owner's activities highly visible through traffic analysis (for which government needs no warrant)?

- Why would a foreign customer buy a device that exposed his conversations to examination by the government of the United States?
- Does the deployment and use of the chip possibly violate the first, fourth, and fifth Amendments to the U.S. Constitution?
- In its discussions of Clipper/Skipjack, the government often uses the phrase "lawfully authorized electronic surveillance." What, exactly, do they mean by this?
- Is it appropriate to insert classified technology into either the public communications network or into the general suite of public technology standards?

And so on and so forth. As I say, it was a very long list. On July 29, John D. Podesta, Assistant to the President and White House Staff Secretary (and, interestingly enough, a former legal consultant to EFF and co-chair of the Digital Privacy and Security Working Group), responded to these questions. He actually answered few of them.

Still unnamed, undescribed, and increasingly unimaginable were the escrow agents. Questions about the inviolability of the depositories were met with something like, "Don't worry, they'll be secure. Trust us."

There seemed a lot of that in Podesta's responses. While the government had convened a panel of learned cryptologists to examine the classified Skipjack algorithm, it had failed to inspire much confidence among the crypto-establishment, most of whom were still disinclined to trust anything they couldn't whack at themselves. At the least, most people felt a proper examination would take longer than the month or so the panel got. After all, it took fifteen years to find a hairline fissure in DES (Data Encryption Standard).

But neither Podesta nor any other official explained why it had seemed necessary to use a classified military algorithm for civilian purposes. Nor were the potential economic impacts addressed. Nor were the concerns about traffic analysis laid to rest.

But as Thomas Pynchon once wrote, "If they can get you asking the wrong questions, they don't have to worry about the answers." Neither asked nor answered in all of this was the one question that kept coming back to me: Was this trip really necessary?

For all the debate over the details, few on either side seemed to be approaching the matter from first principles. Were the enshrined threats—drug dealers, terrorists, child molesters, and foreign enemies—sufficiently and presently imperiling to justify fundamentally compromising all future transmitted privacy?

I mean—speaking personally now—it seems to me that America's greatest health risks derive from the drugs that are legal, a position the statistics overwhelmingly support. And then there's terrorism, to which we lost a total of two Americans in 1992, even with the World Trade Center bombing, and only six in 1993. I honestly can't imagine an organized ring of child molesters, but I suppose one or two might be out there. And the last time we got into a shooting match with another nation, we beat them by a kill ratio of about 2300 to 1.

Even if these are real threats, was enhanced wiretap the best way to combat them? Apparently, it hasn't been in the past. Over the last 10 years the average total nationwide number of admissible state and federal wiretaps has numbered less than 800. Wiretap is not at present a major enforcement tool, and is far less efficient than the informants, witnesses, physical evidence, and good old-fashioned detective work they usually rely on.

(It's worth noting that the World Trade Center bombing case unraveled, not through wiretaps, but with the discovery of the axle serial number on the van which held the explosives.)

Despite all these questions, both unasked and unanswered, Clipper continues (at the time of this writing) to sail briskly toward standardhood, the full wind of government bearing her along.

On July 30, NIST issued a request for public comments on its proposal to establish Clipper/Skipjack as a Federal Information Processing Standard (FIPS). All comments are due by September 28, and the government seems unwilling to delay the process despite the lack of an overall guiding policy on crypto. Worse, they are putting a hard sell on Clipper/Skipjack without a clue as to who might be the escrow holders upon whose political acceptability the entire scheme hinges.

Nor have they addressed the central question: Why would a criminal use a key escrow device unless he were either very stupid—in which case he'd be easily caught anyway—or simply had no choice.

All this leads me to an uncharacteristically paranoid conclusion: The Government May Mandate Key Escrow Encryption and Outlaw Other Forms. It is increasingly hard for me to imagine any other purpose for the Clipper/Skipjack operetta if not to prepare the way for the restriction of all private cryptographic uses to a key escrow system. If I were going to move the American people into a condition where they might accept restrictions on their encryption, I would first engineer the widespread deployment of a key escrow system on a voluntary basis, wait for some blind sheik to slip a bomb plot around it, and then say, "Sorry, folks, this ain't enough, it's got to be universal."

Otherwise, why bother? Even its most ardent proponents admit that no intelligent criminal would trust his communications to a key escrow device. On the other hand, if nearly all encrypted traffic were Skipjack-flavored, any transmission encoded by some other algorithm would stick out like a licorice Dot.

In fact, the assumption that cyberspace will roar one day with Skipjack babble lies behind the stated reason for the secrecy for the algorithm. In their Interim Report, the Skipjack review panel puts it this way:

> Disclosure of the algorithm would permit the construction of devices that fail to properly implement the LEAF [Law Enforcement Access Field], while still interoperating with legitimate SKIPJACK devices. Such devices would provide high quality cryptographic security without preserving the law enforcement access capability that distinguishes this cryptographic initiative.

In other words, they don't want devices or software out there that might use the Skipjack algorithm without depositing a key with the escrow holders. (By the way, this claim is open to question. Publishing Skipjack would not necessarily endow anyone with the ability to build an interoperable chip.)

Then there was the conversation I had with a highly-placed official of the National Security Council in which he mused that the French had, after all, outlawed the private use of cryptography, so it weren't as though it couldn't be done. (He didn't suggest that we should also emulate France's policy of conducting espionage on other countries' industries, though widespread international use of Clipper/Skipjack would certainly enhance our ability to do so.)

Be that as it may, France doesn't have a Bill of Rights to violate, though it seems to me that restriction of cryptography in America would violate ours on several counts.

Mandated encryption standards would fly against the First Amendment, which surely protects the manner of our speech as clearly as it protects the content. Whole languages (most of them patois) have arisen on this planet for the purpose of making the speaker unintelligible to authority. I know of no instance where, even in the oppressive colonies where such languages were formed, the slave-owners banned their use.

Furthermore, the encryption software itself is written expression, upon which no ban may be constitutionally imposed. (What, you might ask then, about the constitutionality of restrictions on algorithm export. I'd say they're being allowed only because no one ever got around to testing from that angle.)

The First Amendment also protects freedom of association. On several different occasions, most notably *NAACP v. Alabama ex rel. Patterson* and *Talley v. California*, the courts have ruled that requiring the disclosure of either an organization's membership or the identity of an individual could lead to reprisals, thereby suppressing both association and speech. Certainly in a place like cyberspace where everyone is so generally "visible," no truly private "assembly" can take place without some technical means of hiding the participants.

It also looks to me as if the forced imposition of a key escrow system might violate the Fourth and Fifth Amendments.

The Fourth Amendment prohibits secret searches. Even with a warrant, agents of the government must announce themselves before entering and may not seize property without informing the owner. Wiretaps inhabit a grayish area of the law in that they permit the secret "seizure" of an actual conversation by those actively eavesdropping on it. The law does not permit the subsequent secret seizure of a record of that conversation. Given the nature of electronic communications, an encryption key opens not only the phone line but the filing cabinet.

Finally, the Fifth Amendment protects individuals from being forced to reveal self-incriminating evidence. While no court has ever ruled on the matter vis à vis encryption keys, there seems something involuntarily self-incriminating about being forced to give up your secrets in advance. Which is, essentially, what mandatory key escrow would require you to do.

For all these protections, I keep thinking it would be nice to have a constitution like the one just adopted by our largest possible enemy, Russia. As I understand it, this document explicitly forbids governmental restrictions on the use of cryptography.

For the moment, we have to take our comfort in the fact that our government . . . or at least the parts of it that state their intentions . . . avows both publicly and privately that it has no intention to impose key escrow cryptography as a mandatory standard. It would be, to use Podesta's mild word, "imprudent."

But it's not Podesta or anyone else in the current White House who worries me. Despite their claims to the contrary, I'm not convinced they like Clipper any better than I do. In fact, one of them . . . not Podesta . . . called Clipper "our Bay of Pigs," referring to the ill-fated Cuban invasion cooked up by the CIA under Eisenhower and executed (badly) by a reluctant Kennedy Administration. The comparison may not be invidious.

It's the people I can't see who worry me. These are the people who actually developed Clipper/Skipjack and its classified algorithm, the people who, through export controls, have kept American cryptography largely to themselves, the people who are establishing in secret what the public can or cannot employ to protect its own secrets. They are invisible and silent to all the citizens they purportedly serve save those who sit on the Congressional intelligence committees.

In secret, they are making for us what may be the most important choice that has ever faced American democracy, that is, whether our descendants will lead their private lives with unprecedented mobility and safety from coercion, or whether every move they make, geographic, economic, or amorous, will be visible to anyone who possesses whatever may then constitute "lawful authority."

Who Are the Lawful Authorities?

Over a year ago, when I first fell down the rabbit hole into Cryptoland, I wrote a *Communications* column called "Decrypting the Puzzle Palace." In it, I advanced what I then thought a slightly paranoid thesis, suggesting that the NSA-guided embargoes on robust encryption software had been driven not by their stated justification (keeping good cryptography out of the possession of foreign military adversaries) but rather by restricting its use by domestic civilians.

In the course of writing that piece, I spoke to a number of officials, including former CIA Director Stansfield Turner and former NSA Director Bobby Ray Inman, who assured me that using a military organization to shape domestic policy would be "injudicious" (as Turner put it), but no one could think of any law or regulation that might specifically prohibit the NSA from serving the goals of the Department of Justice.

But since then I've learned a lot about the hazy post-Reagan/Bush lines between law enforcement and intelligence. They started redrawing the map of authority early in their administration with Executive Order 12333, issued on December 4, 1981 (Federal Register No. 46 FR 59941).

This sweeping decree defines the duties and limitations of the various intelligence organizations of the United States and contains the following language:

> 1.4 The Intelligence Community. The agencies within the Intelligence Community shall . . . conduct intelligence activities necessary for the . . . protection of the national security of the United States, including . . .
>
> (c) Collection of information concerning, and the conduct of activities to protect against, intelligence activities directed against the United States, international terrorist and international narcotics activities, and other hostile activities directed against the United States by foreign powers, organizations, persons, and their agents;

Further, Section 2.6 says:

> Assistance to Law Enforcement Authorities. Agencies within the Intelligence Community are authorized to . . . participate in law enforcement activities to investigate or prevent clandestine intelligence activities by foreign powers, or international terrorist or narcotics activities.

In other words, the intelligence community was specifically charged with investigative responsibility for international criminal activities in the areas of drugs and terrorism.

Furthermore, within certain fairly loose guidelines, intelligence organizations are "authorized to collect, retain or disseminate information concerning United States persons" that may include "incidentally obtained information that may indicate involvement in activities that may violate federal, state, local or foreign laws."

Given that the NSA monitors a significant portion of all the electronic communications between the United States and other countries, the opportunities for "incidentally obtaining" information that might incriminate Americans inside America are great.

Furthermore, over the course of the Reagan/Bush administration, the job of fighting the War on Some Drugs gradually spread to every element of the Executive Branch.

Even the Department of Energy is now involved. At an intelligence community conference last winter I heard a proud speech from a DOE official in which he talked about how some of the bomb-designing supercomputers at Los Alamos had been turned to the peaceful purpose of sifting through huge piles of openly available data—newspapers, courthouse records, and so forth—in search of patterns that would expose drug users and traffickers. They are selling their results to a variety of "lawful authorities," ranging from the Southern Command of the U.S. Army to the Panamanian Defense Forces to various county sheriff's departments.

"Fine," you might say, "drug use is a epidemic that merits any cure." But I would be surprised if there's anyone who will read this sentence who has broken no laws whatever. And it's anybody's guess what evidence of other unlawful activities might be "incidentally obtained" by such a wide net as DOE is flinging.

The central focus that drugs and terrorism have assumed within the intelligence agencies was underscored for me by a tour of the central operations room at the CIA. There, in the nerve center of American intelligence, were desks for Asia, Europe, North America, Africa and "Middle East/Terrorism" and "South America/Narcotics." These bogeymen are now the size of continents on the governmental map of peril.

Given this perception of its duties, the NSA's strict opposition to the export of strong cryptographic engines, hard or soft, starts to make more sense. They are not, as I'd feared, so clue-impaired as to think their embargoes are denying any other nation access to good cryptography. (According to an internal Department of Defense analysis of crypto-policy, it recently took 3 minutes and 14 seconds to locate a source code version of DES on the Internet.)

Nor do they really believe these policies are enhancing national security in the traditional, military sense of the word, where the United States is, in any case, already absurdly overmatched to any national adversary, as was proven during the Gulf War.

It's the enemies they can't bomb who have them worried, and they are certainly correct in thinking that the communications of drug traffickers and whatever few terrorists as may actually exist are more open to their perusal than would be the case in a world where even your grandmother's phone conversations were encrypted.

And Clipper or no Clipper, such a world would be closer at hand if manufacturers hadn't known that any device that embodies good encryption would not be fit for export.

But with Clipper/Skipjack, there is a lot that the combined forces of government will be able to do to monitor all aspects of your behavior without getting a warrant. Between the monitoring capacities of the NSA, the great data-sieves of the Department of Energy, and the fact that, in use, each chip would continually broadcast the whereabouts of its owner, the government would soon be able to isolate just about every perpetrator among us.

I assume you're neither a drug user nor a terrorist, but are you ready for this? Is your nose that clean? Can it be prudent to give the government this kind of corrupting power?

I don't think so, but this is what will happen if we continue to allow the secret elements of government to shape domestic policy as though the only American goals that mattered were stopping terrorism (which seems pretty well stopped already) and winning the War on Some Drugs (which no amount of force will ever completely win).

Unfortunately, we are not able to discuss priorities with the people who are setting them, nor do they seem particularly amenable to any form of authority. In a recent discussion with a White House official, I asked for his help in getting the NSA to come out of its bunker and engage in direct and open discussions about crypto-embargoes, key escrow, the Skipjack algorithm, and the other matters of public interest.

"I'll see what we can do," he said.

"But you guys are the government," I protested. "Surely they'll do as you tell them."

"I'll see what we can do," he repeated, offering little optimism.

That was months ago. In the meantime, the NSA has not only remained utterly unforthcoming in public discussions of crypto-policy, they have unlawfully refused to comply with any Freedom of Information Act requests for documents in this area.

It is time for the public to reassert control over their own government. It is time to demand that public policy be made in public by officials with names, faces, and personal accountability.

When and if we are able to actually discuss crypto-policy with the people who are setting it, I have a list of objectives that I hope many of you will share. They are as follows:

- There should be no law restricting any use of cryptography by private citizens.
- There should be no restriction on the export of cryptographic algorithms or any other instruments of cryptography.
- Secret agencies should not be allowed to drive public policies.
- The taxpayer's investment in encryption technology and related mathematical research should be made available for public and scientific use.
- The government should encourage the deployment of widespread encryption.
- While key escrow systems may have purposes, none should be implemented that place the keys in the hands of government.
- Any encryption standard to be implemented by the government should developed in an open and public fashion and should not employ a secret algorithm.

And last, or perhaps, first . . .

- There should be no broadening of governmental access to private communications and records unless there is a public consensus that the risks to safety outweigh the risks to liberty and will be effectively addressed by these means.

If you support these principles, or even if you don't, I hope you will participate in making this a public process. And there are a number of actions you can take in that regard.

If you belong to or work for an organization, you can encourage that organization to join the Digital Privacy and Security Working Group. To do so they should contact EFF's Washington, D.C., office at:

Electronic Frontier Foundation
1001 G Street, NW
Suite 950 East
Washington, DC 20001
202/347-5400
Fax 202/393-5509
eff@eff.org

I also encourage individuals interested in these issues to join EFF, Computer Professionals for Social Responsibility, or one of the related local organizations which have sprung up around the country. For the addresses of groups in your area, contact EFF.

Introduction to *The Little Black Book of Computer Viruses*

Mark Ludwig

This is the first in a series of three books about computer viruses. In these volumes I want to challenge you to think in new ways about viruses, and break down false concepts and wrong ways of thinking, and go on from there to discuss the relevance of computer viruses in today's world. These books are not a call to a witch hunt, or manuals for protecting yourself from viruses. On the contrary, they will teach you how to design viruses, deploy them, and make them better. All three volumes are full of source code for viruses, including both new and well-known viruses.

It is inevitable that these books will offend some people. In fact, I hope they do. They need to. I am convinced that computer viruses are not evil and that programmers have a right to create them, possess them, and experiment with them. That kind of stand will offend a lot of people, no matter how it is presented. Even a purely technical treatment of viruses which simply discussed how to write them and provided some examples would be offensive. The mere thought of a million well-armed hackers out there is enough to drive some bureaucrats mad. These books go beyond a technical treatment, though, to defend the idea that viruses can be useful, interesting, and just plain fun. That is bound to prove even more offensive. Still, the truth is the truth, and it needs to be spoken, even if it is offensive. Morals and ethics cannot be determined by a majority vote, any more than they can be determined by the barrel of a gun or a loud mouth. Might does not make right.

If you turn out to be one of those people who gets offended or upset, or if you find yourself violently disagreeing with something I say, just remember what an athletically minded friend of mine once told me: "No pain, no gain." That was in reference to muscle building, but the principle applies intellectually as well as physically. If someone only listens to people he agrees with, he will never grow and he'll never succeed beyond his little circle of yes-men. On the other hand, a person who listens to different ideas at the risk of offense, and who at least considers that he might be wrong, cannot but gain from it. So if you are offended by something in this book, please be critical—both of the book and of yourself—and don't fall into a rut and let someone else tell you how to think.

From the start I want to stress that I do not advocate anyone's going out and infecting an innocent party's computer system with a malicious virus designed to destroy valuable data or bring their system to a halt. That is not only wrong, it is illegal. If you do that, you could wind up in jail or find yourself being sued for millions. However this does not mean that it is illegal to create a computer virus and experiment with it, even though I know some people wish it was. If you do create a virus, though, be careful with it. Make sure you know it is working properly or you may wipe out your own system by accident. And make sure you don't inadvertently release it into the world, or you may find yourself in a legal jam . . . even if it was just an accident. The guy who loses a year's worth of work may not be so convinced that it was an accident. And soon it may be illegal to infect a computer system (even your own) with a benign virus which does no harm at all. The key word here is *responsibility.* Be responsible. If you do something destructive, be prepared to take responsibility. *The programs included in this book could be dangerous if improperly used. Treat them with the respect you would have for a lethal weapon.*

This first of three volumes is a technical introduction to the basics of writing computer viruses. It discusses what a virus is, and how it does its job, going into the major functional components of the virus, step by step. Several different types of viruses are developed from the ground up, giving the reader practical how-to information for writing viruses. That is also a prerequisite for decoding and understanding any viruses one may run across in his day-to-day computing. Many people think of viruses as sort of a black art. The purpose of this volume is to bring them out of the closet and look at them matter-of-factly, to see them for what they are, technically speaking: computer programs.

The second volume discusses the scientific applications of computer viruses. There is a whole new field of scientific study known as artificial life (AL) research which is opening up as a result of the invention of viruses and related entities. Since computer viruses are functionally similar to living organisms, biology can teach us a lot about them, both how they behave and how to make them better. However computer viruses also have the potential to teach us something about living organisms. We can create and control computer viruses in a way that we cannot yet control living organisms. This allows us to look at life abstractly to learn about what it really is. We may even reflect on such great questions as the beginning and subsequent evolution of life.

The third volume of this series discusses military applications for computer viruses. It is well known that computer viruses can be extremely destructive and that they can be deployed with minimal risk. Military organizations throughout the world know that too, and consider the possibility of viral attack both a very real threat and a very real offensive option. Some high-level officials in various countries already believe their computers have been attacked for political reasons. So the third volume will probe military strategies and real-life attacks, and dig into the development of viral weapon systems, the defeat of antiviral defenses, and so on.

You might be wondering at this point why you should spend time studying these volumes. After all, computer viruses apparently have no commercial value apart from their military applications. Learning how to write them may not make you more employable, or give you new techniques to incorporate into programs. So why waste time with them, unless you need them to sow chaos among your enemies? Let me try to answer that. Ever since computers were invented in the 1940s, there has been a brotherhood of people dedicated to exploring the limitless possibilities of these magnificent machines. This brotherhood has included famous mathematicians and scientists, as well as thousands of unnamed hobbyists who built their own computers, and programmers who love to dig into the heart of their machines. As long as computers have been around, men have dreamed of intelligent machines which would reason and act without being told step by step just what to do. For many years this was purely science fiction. However, the very thought of this possibility drove some to attempt to make it a reality. Thus "artificial intelligence" (AI) was born. Yet AI applications are often driven by commercial interests and tend to be colored by that fact. Typical results are knowledge bases and the like—useful, sometimes exciting, but also geared toward putting the machine to use in a specific way, rather than to exploring it on its own terms.

The computer virus is a radical new approach to this idea of "living machines." Rather than trying to design something which poorly mimics highly complex human behavior, one starts by trying to copy the simplest of living organisms. Simple one-celled organisms don't do very much. The most primitive organisms draw nutrients from the sea in the form of inorganic chemicals, and take energy from the sun, and their only goal, apparently, is to survive and to reproduce. They aren't very intelligent, and it would be tough to argue about their metaphysical aspects like "soul." Yet they do what they were programmed to do, and they do it very effectively. If we were to try to mimic such organisms by building a machine—a little robot—which went around collecting raw materials and putting them together to make another little robot, we would have a very difficult task on our hands. On the other hand, think of a whole new universe—not this physical world, but an electronic one—which exists inside of a computer. Here is the virus's world. Here it can "live" in a sense not too different from that of primitive biological life. The computer virus has the same goal as a living organism—to survive and to reproduce. It has environmental obstacles to overcome, which could "kill" it and render it inoperative. And once it is released, it seems to have a mind of its own. It runs off in its electronic world doing what it was programmed to do. In this sense it is very much alive.

There is no doubt that the beginning of life was an important milestone in the history of the earth. However, if one tries to consider it from the viewpoint of inanimate matter, it is difficult to imagine life as being much more than a nuisance. We usually assume that life is good and that it deserves to be protected. However, one cannot take a step further back and see life as somehow beneficial to the inanimate world. If we consider only the atoms of the universe, what difference does it make if the temperature is 70 degrees Fahrenheit or 20 million? What difference would it make if the earth were covered with radioactive materials? None at all. Whenever we talk about the environment and ecology, we always assume that life is good and that it should be nurtured and preserved. Living organisms universally use the inanimate world with little concern for it, from the smallest cell which freely gathers the nutrients it needs and pollutes the water it swims in, right up to the man who crushes up rocks to refine the metals out of them and build airplanes. Living organisms use the material world as they see fit. Even when people get upset about something like strip-mining, or an oil spill, their point of reference is not that of inanimate nature. It is an entirely selfish concept (with respect to life) that motivates them. The mining mars the beauty of the landscape—a beauty which is in the eye of the (living) beholder—and it makes it uninhabitable. If one did not place a special emphasis on life, one could just as well promote strip-mining as an attempt to return the earth to its prebiotic state!

I say all of this not because I have a bone to pick with ecologists. Rather I want to apply the same reasoning to the world of computer viruses. As long as one uses only financial criteria to evaluate the worth of a computer program, viruses can only be seen as a menace. What do they do besides damage valuable programs and data? They are ruthless in attempting to gain access to the computer system resources, and often the more ruthless they are, the more successful. Yet how does that differ from biological life? If a clump of moss can attack a rock to get some sunshine and grow, it will do so ruthlessly. We call that beautiful. So how different is that from a computer virus attaching itself to a program? If all one is concerned about is the preservation of the inanimate objects (which are ordinary programs) in this electronic world, then of course viruses are a nuisance.

But maybe there is something deeper here. That all depends on what is most important to you, though. It seems that modern culture has degenerated to the point where most men have no higher goals in life than to seek their own personal peace and prosperity. By personal peace, I do not mean freedom from war, but a freedom to think and believe whatever you want without ever being challenged in it. More bluntly, the freedom to live in a fantasy world of your own making. By prosperity, I mean simply an ever-increasing abundance of material possessions. Karl Marx looked at all of mankind and said that the motivating force behind every man is his economic well-being. The result, he said, is that all of history can be interpreted in terms of class struggles—people fighting for economic control. Even though many in our government decry Marx as the father of communism, our nation is trying to squeeze into the straitjacket he has laid out for us.

That is why two of George Bush's most important campaign promises were "four more years of prosperity" and "no new taxes." People vote their wallets, even when they know the politicians are lying through their teeth.

In a society with such values, the computer becomes merely a resource which people use to harness an abundance of information and manipulate it to their advantage. If that is all there is to computers, then computer viruses are a nuisance, and they should be eliminated. Surely there must be some nobler purpose for mankind than to make money, though, even though that may be necessary. Marx may not think so. The government may not think so. And a lot of loud-mouthed people may not think so. Yet great men from every age and every nation testify to the truth that man does have a higher purpose. Should we not be as Socrates, who considered himself ignorant, and who sought Truth and Wisdom, and valued them more highly than silver and gold? And if so, the question that really matters is not how computers can make us wealthy or give us power over others, but how they might make us *wise*. What can we learn about ourselves? about our world? and, yes, maybe even about God? Once we focus on that, computer viruses become very interesting. Might we not understand life a little better if we can create something similar, and study it, and try to understand it? And if we understand life better, will we not understand our lives, and our world better as well?

A word of caution first. Centuries ago, our nation was established on philosophical principles of good government, which were embodied in the Declaration of Independence and the Constitution. As personal peace and prosperity have become more important than principles of good government, the principles have been manipulated and redefined to suit the whims of those who are in power. Government has become less and less sensitive to civil rights, while it has become easy for various political and financial interests to manipulate our leaders to their advantage.

Since people have largely ceased to challenge each other in what they believe, accepting instead the idea that whatever you want to believe is okay, the government can no longer get people to obey the law because everyone believes in a certain set of principles upon which the law is founded. Thus, government must coerce people into obeying it with increasingly harsh penalties for disobedience—

penalties which often fly in the face of long-established civil rights. Furthermore, the government must restrict the average man's ability to seek recourse. For example, it is very common for the government to trample all over long-standing constitutional rights when enforcing the tax code. The IRS routinely forces hundreds of thousands of people to testify against themselves. It routinely puts the burden of proof on the accused, seizes his assets without trial, et cetera.The bottom line is that it is not expedient for the government to collect money from its citizens if it has to prove their tax documents wrong. The whole system would break down in a massive overload. Economically speaking, it is just better to put the burden of proof on the citizen, Bill of Rights or no.

Likewise, to challenge the government on a question of rights is practically impossible, unless your case happens to serve the purposes of some powerful special interest group. In a standard courtroom, one often cannot even bring up the subject of constitutional rights. The only question to be argued is whether or not some particular law was broken. To appeal to the Supreme Court will cost millions, if the politically motivated justices will even condescend to hear the case. So the government becomes practically all-powerful, God walking on earth, to the common man. One man seems to have little recourse but to blindly obey those in power.

When we start talking about computer viruses, we're treading on some ground where certain people want to post a "No Trespassing" sign. The Congress of the United States has considered a "Computer Virus Eradication Act" which would make it a felony to write a virus, or for two willing parties to exchange one. Never mind that the Constitution guarantees freedom of speech and freedom of the press. Never mind that it guarantees the citizens the right to bear *military* arms (and viruses might be so classified). While that law has not passed as of this writing, it may by the time you read this book. If so, I will say without hesitation that it is a miserable tyranny, but one that we can do little about . . . for now.

Some of our leaders may argue that many people are not capable of handling the responsibility of power that comes with understanding computer viruses, just as they argue that people are not able to handle the power of owning assault rifles or machine guns. Perhaps some cannot. But I wonder, are our leaders any better able to handle the much more dangerous weapons of law and limitless might? Obviously they think so, since they are busy trying to centralize all power into their own hands. I disagree. If those in government can handle power, then so can the individual. If the individual cannot, then neither can his representatives, and our end is either tyranny or chaos anyhow. So there is no harm in attempting to restore some small power to the individual.

But remember: truth seekers and wise men have been persecuted by powerful idiots in every age. Although computer viruses may be very interesting and worthwhile, those who take an interest in them may face some serious challenges from base men. So be careful.

Now join with me and take the attitude of early scientists. These explorers wanted to understand how the world worked—and whether it could be turned to a profit mattered little. They were trying to become wiser in what's really important by understanding the world a little better. After all, what value could there be in building a telescope so you could see the moons around Jupiter? Galileo must have seen something in it, and it must have meant enough to him to stand up to the ruling authorities of his day and do it, and talk about it, and encourage others to do it. And to land in prison for it. Today some people are glad he did.

So why not take the same attitude when it comes to creating life on a computer? One has to wonder where it might lead. Could there be a whole new world of electronic life-forms possible, of which computer viruses are only the most rudimentary sort? Perhaps they are the electronic analog of the simplest one-celled creatures, which were only the tiny beginning of life on earth. What would be the electronic equivalent of a flower, or a dog? Where could it lead? The possibilities could be as exciting as the idea of a man actually standing on the moon would have been to Galileo. We just have no idea.

There is something in certain men that simply drives them to explore the unknown. When standing at the edge of a vast ocean upon which no ship has ever sailed, it is difficult not to wonder what lies beyond the horizon even though the rulers of the day tell you you're going to fall off the edge of the world (or they're going to push you off) if you try to find out. Perhaps they are right. Perhaps there is nothing of value out there. Yet other great explorers down through the ages have explored other oceans and succeeded. And one thing is for sure: we'll never know if someone doesn't look. So I would like to invite you to climb aboard this little raft that I have built and go exploring. . . .

The Basics of the Computer Virus

A plethora of negative magazine articles and books have catalyzed a new kind of hypochondria among computer users: an unreasonable fear of computer viruses. This hypochondria is possible because: (a) computers are very complex machines which will often behave in ways which are not obvious to the average user, and (b) computer viruses are still extremely rare. Thus, most computer users have never experienced a computer virus attack. Their only experience has been what they've read about or heard about (and only the worst problems make it into print). This combination of ignorance, inexperience, and fear-provoking reports of danger is the perfect formula for mass hysteria.

Most problems people have with computers are simply their own fault. For example, they accidentally delete all the files in their current directory rather than in another directory, as they intended, or they format the wrong disk. Or perhaps someone routinely does something wrong out of ignorance, like turning the computer off in the middle of a program, causing files to get scrambled. Following close on the heels of these kinds of problems are hardware problems, like a misaligned floppy drive or a hard disk failure. Such routine problems are made worse than necessary when users do not plan for them and fail to back up their work on a regular basis. This stupidity can easily turn a problem that might have cost 300 dollars for a new hard disk into a nightmare which will ultimately cost tens of thousands of dollars. When such a disaster happens, it is human nature to want to find someone or something else to blame, rather than admit it is your own fault. Viruses have proven to be an excellent scapegoat for all kinds of problems.

Of course, there are times when people want to destroy computers. In a time of war, a country may want to hamstring the enemy by destroying its intelligence databases. If an employee is maltreated by his employer, he may want to retaliate, and he may not be able to get legal recourse. One can also imagine a totalitarian state trying to control its citizens' every move with computers, and a group of good men trying to stop it. Although one could smash a computer, or physically destroy its data, one does not always have access to the machine that will be the object of the attack. At other times, one may not be able to perpetrate a physical attack without facing certain discovery and prosecution. While an unprovoked attack, and even revenge, may not be right, people still do choose such avenues (and even a purely defensive attack is sure to be considered wrong by an arrogant aggressor). For the sophisticated programmer, though, physical access to the machine is not necessary to cripple it.

People who have attacked computers and their data have invented several different kinds of programs. Since one must obviously conceal the destructive nature of a program to dupe somebody into executing it, deceptive tricks are an absolute must in this game. The first and oldest trick is the "Trojan horse." The Trojan horse may appear to be a useful program, but it is in fact destructive. It entices you to execute it because it promises to be a worthwhile program for your computer—new and better ways to make your machine more effective—but when you execute the program, surprise! Secondly, destructive code can be hidden as a "logic bomb" inside an otherwise useful program. You use the program on a regular basis, and it works well. Yet, when a certain event occurs, such as a certain date on the system clock, the logic bomb "explodes" and does damage. These programs are designed specifically to destroy computer data, and are usually deployed by their author or a willing associate on a computer system that will be the object of the attack.

There is always a risk to the perpetrator of such destruction. He must somehow deploy destructive code on the target machine without getting caught. If that means he has to put the program on the machine himself, or give it to an unsuspecting user, he is at risk. The risk may be quite small, especially if the perpetrator normally has access to files on the system, but his risk is never zero.

With such considerable risks involved, there is a powerful incentive to develop cunning deployment mechanisms for getting destructive code onto a computer system. Untraceable deployment is a key to avoiding being put on trial for treason, espionage, or vandalism. Among the most sophisticated of computer programmers, the computer virus is the vehicle of choice for deploying destructive code. That is why viruses are almost synonymous with wanton destruction.

However, we must realize that *computer viruses are not inherently destructive.* The essential feature of a computer program that causes it to be classified as a virus is not its ability to destroy data but its ability to gain control of the computer and make a fully functional copy of itself. It can reproduce. When it is executed, it makes one or more copies of itself. Those copies may later be executed, to create still more copies, ad infinitum. Not all computer programs that are destructive are classified as viruses because they do not all reproduce, and not all viruses are destructive because reproduction is not destructive. However, all viruses do reproduce. The idea that computer viruses are always destructive is deeply ingrained in most people's thinking though. The very term "virus" is an inaccurate and emotionally charged epithet. The scientifically correct term for a computer virus is "self-reproducing automaton," or "SRA" for short. This term describes correctly what such a program does, rather than attaching emotional energy to it. We will continue to use the term "virus" throughout this book though, except when we are discussing computer viruses (SRAs) and biological viruses at the same time, and we need to make the difference clear.

If one tries to draw an analogy between the electronic world of programs and bytes inside a computer and the physical world we know, the computer virus is a very close analog to the simplest biological unit of life, a single-celled, photosynthetic organism. Leaving metaphysical questions like "soul" aside, a living organism can be differentiated from nonlife in that it appears to have two goals: (a) to survive, and (b) to reproduce. Although one can raise metaphysical questions just by saying that a living organism has "goals," they certainly seem to, if the onlooker has not been educated out of that way of thinking. And certainly the idea of a goal would apply to a computer program, since it was written by someone with a purpose in mind. So in this sense, a computer virus has the same two goals as a living organism: to survive and to reproduce. The simplest of living organisms depend only on the inanimate, inorganic environment for what they need to achieve their goals. They draw raw materials from their surroundings and use energy from the sun to synthesize whatever chemicals they need to do the job. The organism is not dependent on another form of life which it must somehow eat or attack to continue its existence. In the same way, a computer virus uses the computer system's resources like disk storage and CPU time to achieve its goals. Specifically, it does not attack other self-reproducing automata and "eat" them in a manner similar to a biological virus.

Instead, the computer virus is the simplest unit of life in this electronic world inside the computer. (Of course, it is conceivable that one could write a more sophisticated program which would behave like a biological virus and attack other SRAs.)

Before the advent of personal computers, the electronic domain in which a computer virus might "live" was extremely limited. Computers were rare, and they had many different kinds of CPUs and operating systems. So a tinkerer might have written a virus and let it execute on his system. However, there would have been little danger of it escaping and infecting other machines. It remained under the control of its master. The age of the mass-produced computer opened up a whole new realm for viruses though. The millions of machines all around the world, all with the same basic architecture and operating system, make it possible for a computer virus to escape and begin a life of its own. It can hop from machine to machine, accomplishing the goals programmed into it, with no one to control it and few who can stop it. And so the virus became a viable form of electronic life in the 1980s.

Now one can create self-reproducing automata that are not computer viruses. For example, the famous mathematician John von Neumann invented a self-reproducing automaton "living" in a grid array of cells which has 29 possible states. In theory, this automaton could be modeled on a computer. However, it was not a program that would run directly on any computer known in von Neumann's day. Likewise, one could write a program which simply copied itself to another file. For example "1.COM" could create "2.COM," which would be an exact copy of itself (both program files on an IBM PC-style machine). The problem with such concoctions is viability. Their continued existence is completely dependent on the man at the console. A more sophisticated version of such a program might rely on deceiving that man at the console in order to propagate itself. This program is known as a worm. The computer virus overcomes the roadblock of operator control by hiding itself in other programs. Thus it gains access to the CPU simply because people run programs that it happens to have attached itself to without their knowledge. The ability to attach itself to other programs is what makes the virus a viable electronic life form. That is what puts it in a class by itself. The fact that a computer virus attaches itself to other programs earned it the name "virus." However, that analogy is wrong since the programs it attaches to are not in any sense alive.

Types of Viruses

Computer viruses can be classified into several different types. The first and most common type is the virus which infects any application program. On IBM PCs and clones running under PC-DOS or MS-DOS, most programs and data which do not belong to the operating system itself are stored as files. Each file has a *file name* eight characters long, and an *extent* which is three characters long. A typical file might be called TRUE.TXT, where TRUE is the name and TXT is the extent. The extent normally gives some information about the nature of a file—in this case TRUE.TXT might be a text file. Programs must always have an extent of COM, EXE, or SYS. Under DOS, only files with these extents can be executed by the central processing unit. If the user tries to execute any other type of file, DOS will generate an error and reject the attempt to execute the file.

Since a virus's goal is to get executed by the computer, it must attach itself to a COM, EXE or SYS file. If it attaches to any other file, it may corrupt some data, but it won't normally get executed, and it won't reproduce. Since each of these types of executable files has a different structure, a virus must be designed to attach itself to a particular type of file. A virus designed to attack COM files cannot attack EXE files, and vice versa, and neither can attack SYS files. Of course, one could design a virus that would attack two or even three kinds of files, but it would require a separate reproduction method for each file type.

The next major type of virus seeks to attach itself to a specific file, rather than attacking any file of a given type. Thus, we might call it an application-specific virus. These viruses make use of a detailed knowledge of the files they attack to hide better than would be possible if they were able to infiltrate just any file. For example, they might hide in a data area inside the program rather than lengthening the file. However, in order to do that, the virus must know where the data area is located in the program, and that differs from program to program.

This second type of virus usually concentrates on the files associated to DOS, like COMMAND.COM, since they are on virtually every PC in existence. Regardless of which file such a virus attacks, though, it must be very, very common, or the virus will never be able to find another copy of that file to reproduce in, and so it will not go anywhere. Only with a file like COMMAND.COM would it be possible to begin leaping from machine to machine and travel around the world.

The final type of virus is known as a "boot sector virus." This virus is a further refinement of the application-specific virus, which attacks a specific location on a computer's disk drive, known as the boot sector. The boot sector is the first thing a computer loads into memory from disk and executes when it is turned on. By attacking this area of the disk, the virus can gain control of the computer immediately, every time it is turned on, before any other program can execute. In this way, the virus can execute before any other program or person can detect its existence.

The Functional Elements of a Virus

Every viable computer virus must have at least two basic parts, or subroutines, if it is even to be called a virus. Firstly, it must contain a *search routine*, which locates new files or new areas on disk that are worthwhile targets for infection. This routine will determine how well the virus reproduces, that is, whether it does so quickly or slowly, whether it can infect multiple disks or a single disk, and whether it can infect every portion of a disk or just certain specific areas. As with all programs, there is a size versus functionality tradeoff here. The more sophisticated the search routine is, the more space it will take up. So although an efficient search routine may help a virus to spread faster, it will make the virus bigger, and that is not always so good.

Secondly, every computer virus must contain a routine to copy itself into the area which the search routine locates. The *copy routine* will be just sophisticated enough to do its job without getting caught. The smaller it is, the better. How small it can be will depend on how complex a virus it must copy. For example, a virus which infects only COM files can get by with a much smaller copy routine than a virus which infects EXE files. This is because the EXE file structure is much more complex, so the virus simply needs to do more to attach itself to an EXE file.

While the virus only needs to be able to locate suitable hosts and attach itself to them, it is usually helpful to incorporate some additional features into the virus to avoid detection, either by the computer user or by commercial virus detection software. *Antidetection* routines can either be a part of the search or copy routines, or functionally separate from them. For example, the search routine may be severely limited in scope to avoid detection. A routine which checked every file on every disk drive, without limit, would take a long time and cause enough unusual disk activity that an alert user might become suspicious. Alternatively, an antidetection routine might cause the virus to activate under certain special conditions. For example, it might activate only after a certain date has passed (so the virus could lie dormant for a time).

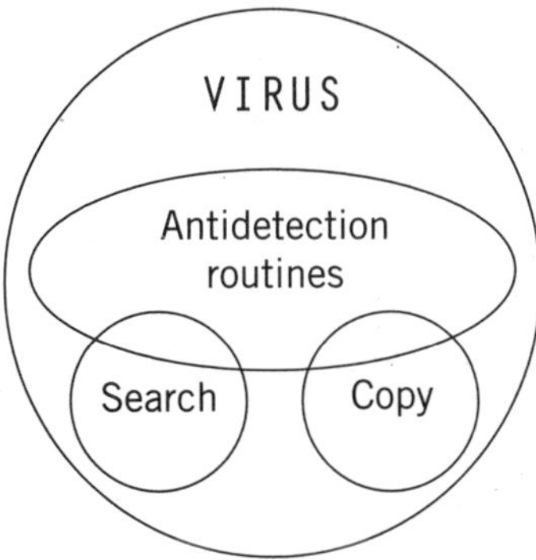

FIG. 1. Functional diagram of a virus.

Alternatively, it might activate only if a key has not been pressed for five minutes (suggesting that the user was not there watching his computer).

Search, copy, and antidetection routines are the only necessary components of a computer virus, and they are the components which we will concentrate on in this volume. Of course, many computer viruses have other routines added in on top of the basic three to stop normal computer operation, to cause destruction, or to play practical jokes. Such routines may give the virus character, but they are not essential to its existence. In fact, such routines are usually very detrimental to the virus's goal of survival and self-reproduction, because they make the fact of the virus's existence known to everybody. If there is just a little more disk activity than expected, probably no one will notice, and the virus will go on its merry way. On the other hand, if the screen to one's favorite program comes up saying "Ha!

Gotcha!" and then the whole computer locks up, with everything on it ruined, most anyone can figure out that they've been the victim of a destructive program. And if they're smart, they'll get expert help to eradicate it right away. The result is that the viruses on that particular system are killed off, either by themselves or by the cleanup crew.

Although it may be the case that anything which is not essential to a virus's survival may prove detrimental, many computer viruses are written primarily to be smart delivery systems of these "other routines." The author is unconcerned about whether the virus gets killed in action when its logic bomb goes off, so long as the bomb gets deployed effectively. The virus then becomes just like a kamikaze pilot, who gives his life to accomplish the mission. Some of these "other routines" have proven to be quite creative. For example, one well-known virus turns a computer into a simulation of a washing machine, complete with graphics and sound. Another makes Friday the 13th truly a bad day by coming to life only on that day and destroying data. Nonetheless, these kinds of routines are more properly the subject of volume three of this series, which discusses the military applications of computer viruses. In this volume we will stick with the basics of designing the reproductive system. And if your real interest is in military applications, just remember that the best logic bomb in the world is useless if you can't deploy it correctly. The delivery system is very, very important. The situation is similar to having an atomic bomb, but not the means to send it halfway around the world in 15 minutes. Sure, you can deploy it, but crossing borders, getting close to the target, and hiding the bomb all pose considerable risks. The effort to develop a rocket is worthwhile.

Tools Needed for Writing Viruses

Viruses are written in *assembly language*. High-level languages like Basic, C, and Pascal have been designed to generate stand-alone programs, but the assumptions made by these languages render them almost useless when writing viruses. They are simply incapable of performing the acrobatics required for a virus to jump from one host program to another. That is not to say that one could not design a high-level language that would do the job, but no one has done so yet. Thus, to create viruses, we must use assembly language. It is just the only way we can get exacting control over all the computer system's resources and use them the way we want to, rather than the way somebody else thinks we should.

If you have not done any programming in an assembler before, I would suggest you get a good tutorial on the subject. I will assume that your knowledge of the technical details of PCs—like file structures, function calls, segmentation, and hardware design—is limited, and I will try to explain such matters carefully at the start. However, I will also assume that you have some knowledge of assembly language—at least at the level where you can understand what some of the basic machine instructions, like *mov ax,bx*, do. If you are not familiar with simple assembly language programming like this, get a tutorial book on the subject. With a little work it will bring you up to speed.

At present, there are three popular assemblers on the market, and you will need one of them to do any work with computer viruses. The first and oldest is Microsoft's Macro Assembler, or MASM for short. It will cost you about a hundred dollars to buy it through a mail-order outlet. The second is Borland's Turbo Assembler, also known as TASM. It goes for about a hundred dollars too. Thirdly, there is A86, which is shareware, and available on many bulletin board systems throughout the country. You can get a copy of it for free by calling up one of these systems and downloading it to your computer with a modem. Alternatively, a number of software houses make it available for about five dollars through the mail. However, if you plan to use A86, the author demands that you pay him almost as much as if you bought one of the other assemblers. He will hold you liable for copyright violation if he can catch you. Personally, I don't think A86 is worth the money. My favorite is TASM, because it does exactly what you tell it to without trying to outsmart you. That is exactly what you want when writing a virus. Anything less can put bugs in your programs even when they are correctly written. Whichever assembler you decide to use, though, the viruses in this book can be compiled by all three. Batch files are provided to perform a correct assembly with each assembler.

If you do not have an assembler, or the resources to buy one, or the inclination to learn assembly language, the viruses are provided in Intel hex format so they can be directly loaded onto your computer in executable form. The program disk also contains compiled, directly executable versions of each virus. However, if you don't understand the assembly language source code, *please don't take these programs and run them.* You're just asking for trouble, like a four-year-old child with a loaded gun.

FEMINISATIONS

Reflections on Women and Virtual Reality

Sadie Plant

the clitoris is a direct line to the matrix—VNS Matrix

Women, he has always said,
are tied to the earth
and too tangled up
with all its messy cycles and flows.

And yet on another invisible hand, women are too artificial for man: a matter of glamour, illusion, a trick. Even her foundations are cosmetic: **she's made up**. Hardly a problem out on the Net, where nature and artifice melt as they meet. No wonder women so quickly become advanced and fearless practitioners of virtual engineering.

Masculine identity has everything to **lose** from this new **technics**. The sperm count falls as the replicants stir and the meat learns how to learn for itself.

Cybernetics is feminisation. When intelligent space emerges alongside the history of women's liberation, no one is responsible. That's the point, the fold in the map, where architects get lost in the pattern. **Self-guiding systems were not in the plan.**

Trace the emergence of cyberspace: through the history of commerce to the point at which **capitalism** begins to come out as a **self-organizing** system; through the history of mediation to the moment of immersion. War is of course the exemplary case: the theater itself becomes cyberspace.

The **construct** cunt activates the program. Viral transmissions appear on the screen. Downloaded images converge with their own engineering. Markets and media; military machines. Intended to serve man's quest for planetary domination and escape from the corruptions of the troublesome meat, the matrix was always having him on. **He** gets the picture as **it** gets in touch.

All that matters turns itself on. Nature has never been waiting for man. Matter is microprocessing: what else do molecules do with themselves? There is no need to soften the edges of the virtual world. The matrix has in any case already hacked into all self-conscious attempts to shape it in man's image of nature and artifice.

Travelers always leave their mark, and what is traversed marks them out in turn. Humanity does not escape its own reprocessings. The technoscapes are **trailers** for future **decompositions** of the **spectacle.** Produced in their own machine codes where zero has long interrupted square one, these trips are as deliciously alien as their own fractal fabrications.

NATURALLY ENOUGH, OUTLAW ZONES ARE COMING.

AUTOMATICALLY.

Part 2 | The Consequences of Untruth

Lynn Hershman Leeson
Seduction, Phantom Limb Number 2, 1990

Jaron Lanier Interview

Lynn Hershman Leeson

JARON LANIER: The name virtual reality is not a good name. But I knew it had some kind of mojo, and I knew that this field needed some kind of mojo. I realized that this field represented more than just another technology fad, that it represented a way of validating the public's mystical love with technology and I wanted to acknowledge that. I thought people would respond to it. And it seemed like using the word reality would do that, even though it has also brought on a lot of nonsense and silliness. I remember when I came into the room with the old VPL group saying "I don't want to call it virtual reality," and Chuck, who was head of software at VPL [the first virtual reality company], said, "I don't like it 'cause you'll have to say VR and it sounds like RV and everybody's going to think of all these retirees tooling around in simulated places."

LYNN HERSHMAN LEESON: What is the most advanced state that virtual reality has reached?

JARON: Probably the best quality virtual worlds are some of the medical ones right now. I'm really happy with how that's going, particularly for surgical simulation. A lot of underlying parts of virtual reality are getting better and better, so I think that in the next year or so there are going to be some really wonderful systems around.

LYNN: Is it possible for people to get so involved with artificial worlds that they become more real than real? Do you think that people can enhance their relationships through this media?

JARON: No, no, I have never seen somebody think of the virtual world as being more real than the physical world. It's really very different. The physical world allows you to be lazy. In other words, you can lie down on a couch and the physical world is still there. The virtual world only exists because of the magic of the way your nervous system makes things real when you interact with them. And the moment you start to space out or become lazy, the reality goes away, and it just turns into a bunch of junk on your head. So that means that people get tired after a while, so you can't really sustain it. You're contributing to the reality of virtual reality, and the physical world stubbornly persists without you for some mysterious reason, which I've always been curious about. But there's another thing too. There's this wonderful phenomenon where when you're inside a virtual world and if you take off the head-mounted display and look around, the physical world takes on a sort of super-real quality where it seems very textured and beautiful, and you notice a lot of details in it because you've gotten used to a simpler world. So there is actually a sensitivity-enhancing effect.

LYNN: And what about the question of relational enhancement? Sandy Stone talked about relationships that people had with each other inside computers where they would disguise themselves in this other persona and they were able to relate and log off or change their identity. Do you find that a phenomenon?

JARON: That's a very interesting question. I think there's a profound question that virtual reality really brings up, which is what is authenticity, not in the world at large, but in one of us, in a human being. What's interesting about a virtual reality interaction is that there's a certain way in which you're actually very naked because the two most expressive components of communication, which are your voice and then the movements of your body, are actually preserved. And your appearance, your body per se, certainly is not preserved. So in a way, the motion of the body, along with the music of the voice, are exposed and become more naked than I think they are in general encounters in the physical world. So I'm not so sure that there's a decrease in authenticity. I think what she's interpreting as hiding might actually not be that at all; it might be a kind of coming out.

LYNN: A different way of communicating.

JARON: Yeah. What is the most authentic form that you can take on nakedly and truly? And would that be a style of changing or a fixed form? What would it be? I'm not sure what the answer to that is, and it's probably different for different people at different times. It's too easy just to say that becoming a virtual creature is hiding, and I don't think that's correct at all.

LYNN: Except that in order to be recognized in electronic worlds, you have to . . . wear a mask of some sort.

JARON: That's not true, because as I mentioned there are really two primary expressive forms that we have with each other; they are the movement of our voice and the movement of our bodies. Now both are easily recognizable. You can recognize somebody's voice on the phone. But the movement of the body is equally recognizable. If you attach little light bulbs to a person and have them wear a dark velvet suit in a dark room so you just see the lights moving, you can still recognize individual people, you can tell if strangers are male or female and how old they are and even what mood they're in. The music of the body and its movement is something we're not as conscious about, but it's every bit as expressive, both individually and generically, as the voice is. And you can't hide it.

LYNN: How did you become involved in this field?

JARON: In virtual reality? Well, that's an interesting question. It certainly wasn't intentional. If I look back on it, I can see reasons why I was heading into it. When I was a kid, I always wanted to transcend the unfair boundaries of the physical world which seemed very frustrating and contrary to the infinity of imagination. I used to build weird things, like I built a Theremin connected to a television that had been rigged as a Lissajous machine so you could move your hands around and make weird patterns on the ceiling. When I was a real little kid, I used to sneak into the Hieronymous Bosch art books in the school and stare at them for hours.

But I got into [virtual reality] when I was trying to build a better way to make programming languages. I was trying to make a better user interface for how you control programming languages and got involved with the idea of a whole sensory interaction to be able to perceive more complicated things more easily. And boy, I sure never expected to be in business. That kind of happened by accident. Some of my programming language work was on the cover of a *Scientific American* magazine issue in the summer of 1984, and when they were going to press they called me and said, "We must have an affiliation because our editorial policy clearly states that the affiliation will follow the author's name." And I said, "Well, I have no affiliation. I'm very proud of it." And they said, "No, no. Our editorial policy clearly states this, you must follow our editorial policy." So I just made up this name on the spot: VPL. And all of a sudden people were calling to see if it wanted investors, and there it was.

LYNN: What do you think will be the practical use for this other than in medical technology? Will regular people be able to use this technology that you helped to pioneer?

JARON: Virtual reality is really the future of the telephone more than anything else. It's not so much the future of computers or televisions or movies or video games. It's the future of the telephone. Virtual reality is the way that people can connect with each other in the most beautiful and intuitive manner, using technology. It'll become a sort of community utility in which dreams are shared and ideas cocreated. I have a little scenario I've been giving lately of what it might be like. So here it goes.

Let's say it's sometime in the future. I don't know when, because it depends on how the economy goes more than anything else. But this could start to happen in 10 to 20 years. You go into your house and you look around, and everything's normal except that there's some new furniture added, but only when you put on these special glasses. Glasses off, and there's no furniture; glasses on, and there's furniture added. And virtual furniture feels real, looks real, it's added in with your other stuff, but it's virtual. One of the items of furniture is a big set of shelves with fish bowls, and if you look in these bowls there aren't fish, instead there are little people running around. If you look in one of the bowls, all the people are in a shopping center trying on clothes and things; and in another one of the bowls, they're attending a physical therapy workshop; and in another one, they're looking at real estate that's available. I don't know if the future's really going to have real estate and shopping centers, but anyway, that's a possibility. They might have a city council hearing where a developer's showing a project that he wants to build, and people are looking at it and flying around in it and stuff.

So you look at all these fish bowls and a few of them have really weird things going on inside, like bizarre parties where people are changing into giant snakes, and what you do is put your hand into one of the bowls, put your head into it, and all of a sudden it starts getting really big, until you're inside it and become one of those people. And those are all groups of people who are joined together and they see you flying in, and that's how it might work. That would be the future telephone.

LYNN: Was the original research for virtual reality funded by the Defense Department for war?

JARON: The truth is that virtual reality was not primarily funded by the military. It depends what you want to count as virtual reality and what you don't. There's a key case in which there was some military money that supported Ivan Sutherland's work from a government agency that's generally associated with military funding, but really not exclusively. And his work, per se, wasn't justified for military purposes. It's true the Air Force did some work in the seventies on it. But so far as I can tell, most of the key elements of the technology have been generated by very creative, passionate people on their own, and the funding has been quite varied. Sometimes the funding has been very low in the early phases, so it was sort of a moot point.

LYNN: You mentioned the body and the voice. But do you feel that while working in these kinds of electronic transmissions and transferences that one detaches from the body in a way?

JARON: No, let's not get lost in a cliché of the body which limits it to what a television camera can see. In other words, you think of a person's body as you see them frontally with clothes on, groomed, and so forth. There's a certain civilized image of what a body is. There is an equally important subjective way of thinking about the body. In this view the body is primarily the sensory motor loop; it's the way that you're able to respond to yourself in the world, and the style of your movements, and the way that you touch against the things in your life, and the people in your life. So if anything, when you can start to modify the sensory motor loop, you become more aware of it. I guess the comparison I might make is that I play the piano, but whenever I play another keyboard instrument, like a harpsichord or a synthesizer, and then go back to the piano, there's a kind of revitalization, because I have a little bit of a different perspective. So if you have a chance to experience your body and the control of it in the form of a grasshopper, and then you come back to being human, I think there is a broadening of experience and an opening of channels in increased sensitivity.

LYNN: Do you see any danger in this field?

JARON: Well, what's funny is that I'm often asked if virtual reality could be dangerous, but I'm always asked in some media, like on the radio or as part of a movie interview or something. And my usual snap answer is that movies are far more dangerous. [*Laughs*] I mean, media is dangerous. If you believe that media is powerful or worthwhile, you have to believe it's potentially dangerous. You can't have power without danger, certainly, unless you're some sort of new age wimpy person. [*Laughs*] But let's try to put this danger in perspective. This type of danger we're talking about is the same danger inherent in any media, which is that when people are malicious. People are sometimes a little nutso, and so forth.

I think the only justification for communication or communication technology or civilization or any of the stuff that we're all engaged in here is a fundamental trust in people and human nature. [Trust], not in all cases certainly, but overall, in general. If you don't have some kind of trust and faith in people, you couldn't ever support the idea of a free press, freedom of speech, right? There's a large-scale love for each other that's embedded in the idea of freedom. So, yeah, I'm definitely convinced that there's going to be real bad schlock in virtual reality. I think the way that virtual reality will degrade is a little bit more toward the direction of schlock than the direction of bad politics or oppression.

But I'm not sure, I mean it depends. You know, with books, there's this huge range of things that you can do. And I'm sure there's just as large a range of things you can do with virtual reality. The justification for having books changes with each new book and so will the justification for each new virtual world.

I will share one idea with you which is that I've proposed that there's no objective justification for technology in areas now except for medicine and natural disasters. Because those are the only two remaining areas where there are human problems that are not brought on by human behavior, right? All the rest of our problems are brought on by ourselves. So therefore, any technology which merely increases human power has to be viewed as probably being a bad technology, since we're powerful enough already. However, communications technologies I think are very much worth exploring because they hold within them the hope of increased empathy.

LYNN: Is this becoming a second language?

JARON: Virtual reality will turn into something that's like a language, but better. But it won't do it for a long time. There will be a time someday, if we all survive, when a whole generation of kids grows up being very familiar with inventing virtual worlds. Just like kids today are familiar with using computers and video games, there will be a generation someday that's used to inventing virtual worlds very quickly. And when they grow up, they'll have this natural facility to improvise the content of reality. They'll be used to a world where they can share virtual spaces with each other at a distance all the time. It'll be normal. And in that society, I think something very special is going to happen, which I call postsymbolic communication. This is an idea of a new type or stratum of communication where people are skilled at, and used to, cocreating shared worlds spontaneously, improvising the content of the objective world. Without limit . . . on an ongoing improvised basis, just the way we improvise conversations with one another now. So that'll be like a conscious shared dreaming. And to me, that's the reason to do all of this. That's the ultimate purpose of it all, to create this wonderful game and exploration; it's a new type of communication.

LYNN: One person mentioned the idea of immortality, that they felt that placing themselves into the computer world allowed them to feel as if they would live forever, and they also thought that it was more ecologically correct because it didn't pollute the environment.

JARON: Yeah, I would disagree with both of those ideas pretty strongly. Or it's not so much that I disagree but I'd express distaste for them. So I'll go through them one by one.

In my mind there's a critical issue for our civilization to face, which is what exactly is our agenda with technology? It used to be clear. The purpose of technology used to be to increase our power so that we wouldn't be under threat all the time. Then it shifted into something different. Once we were powerful enough that we became our own worst problem, then it became our quest for immortality. And I think with that came a kind of retreat from the messiness of the body, the ugliness and the fear of mortality. You'll see that high-tech objects are always designed with this very clean, sort of very anti-biological feeling. You know, it's a clinical aesthetic.

I think there is a desire to become a machine so you don't have to die. The problem with that for me is certainly not that people should like death, because I don't, and only a few Buddhists manage to deal with that. However, what I'm really concerned about is a redefinition of life that sneaks in along with that whole way of thinking. If you redefine life in abstract terms, and stay alive at any cost, and you lose a mystical and organic grounding for what's really valuable about life, you end up with this bland and nerdy culture. And the whole phenomenon of nerdiness and blandness and excessive abstraction, what I call abstraction disease, is something that goes hand in hand with people whose technology myth is one of avoiding dying. You see those things together all the time. For myself, I think it's important that we first acknowledge that the reason we do most technology is that we love it, that it's a cultural pursuit. And I think it's critical that we redefine an agenda for why we love technology that's sustainable.

So for me, the idea of technology being a new way for us to reach each other, a way for us to dream together, for instance, as I discussed with postsymbolic communication, that's a type of adventure that can last hundreds of years. If you think of technology as something making you ever more powerful, it's just something that runs up against a brick wall, somehow, sooner or later. We either blow ourselves up, or we end up with only a finite number of people who can be alive and immortal whose lives turn to shit. I mean, it's just simple logic. It's inevitable that you reach an end point if you think that way. Technology can be an infinite game instead of a finite game.

There are some real contributions that virtual reality can make to ecology. Let me describe the positive first. One of the unique things about our time is that our greatest dangers are utterly invisible to us. For instance, the ecological crisis is something that we don't have evidence of in our everyday lives; things like the ozone hole. So these threats to us can only be understood through media, right? And then the ultimate question becomes, how do you trust the media? How do you know what's real? And that ambiguity, that abstract removal of the threats, is the strangest, most alienating bizarre thing about this time of ours. So I think that new media like virtual reality can play a role in creating a new societal structure in which people are connected to other people who are connected to other people with only a limited number of links so you can personally know somebody who can verify for you things that you need to know about, such as the real status of global warming. And that type of society where you can verify the truth of the world through new types of media connections is absolutely critical to our survival, and that's one of the vital reasons that television has to die as a primary means of information transmittal.

LYNN: And what will replace it?

JARON: Well, what has to replace it is a super-telephone. A society that relies on centralized communication such as television or radio or newspapers cannot survive if the threats to it can only be understood by regular people through those media, because nobody can trust them well enough. So, you have to have a society where communication is more broad-based from individual to individual, so people can build up bonds of trust with specific other people who can tell them the truth of what's going on in the world. And then you can have a society based on truth that can act for its own safety, and I think that could be a really sane society. So new media is vital to our survival. That doesn't necessarily mean virtual reality specifically, but having nonbroadcast media as a primary form of information dispersal is absolutely vital to our survival in the future, and I think virtual reality can play a role in that. That's the main connection.

And then there are some small connections. Virtual reality can help scientists visualize their data better. There's a small possibility that virtual reality can contribute to people being able to work remotely without having to transport themselves to do things. I don't give as much credence to that as some people do because I think there's a lot to be said for physical copresence, and it's hard to replace. I'd much rather have good mass transit systems. The main thing I worry about is a sort of superstitious magical thinking that, somehow, if you do a bunch of high-tech things, other problems get solved automatically. Just because you're using this technology or that technology doesn't do anything to help the ecology. You have to look at the whole system. And, for instance, computers, because they've encouraged people to print a lot, actually might be costing more trees' lives than not. We don't really know. It's hard to analyze. So, I always try to encourage people to not make any easy assumptions about what particular technologies would be more or less ecologically beneficial. I think you have to look at the whole picture and see how it influences the whole pattern of our lives.

LYNN: What you are saying is very optimistic. Even though people have found a way to manipulate and corrupt communication, you assume that people will be more honest in new technology.

JARON: No, I don't think I'm assuming that. I think that people who understand shared threats can work together to avoid those threats. And that's not exactly optimism. And the problem with our society isn't that it's evil or mean-spirited, exactly. It's that it's not connected to the truth. And by the "truth" in this case, I'm just talking about raw truth. In other words, I really think if a figure like a Dan Quayle or one of these country club types of Republican figures, if they were really connected and really got what was going on in some place like South Central Los Angeles, the world would be a different place. But they don't. There's this barrier, and they don't understand it.

And I think the same thing is true for the ecological problems. The problem is that people are connected to reality through the media instead of through direct perception. Of course, what's good about media is that direct perception by itself isn't enough, because people can still perceive whatever they want to and misperceive things directly. But I think that there's this new solution that's possible because of media technology where people can have personal contact with the truth, perhaps through a series of other people.

LYNN: Also, what you said about media and direct perception again brings a confusion about authenticity, because you tend to believe the other more than yourself, which kind of makes your own identity repudiated.

JARON: Yeah, right; I think that's true. It's tricky. One of the things that's really fascinating to me about our times is how these very deep spiritual and epistemological issues are right at the cutting edge of what we need to do to survive. It's an amazing time that way. So, there are such cataclysmic issues afoot right now that it's hard to relax sometimes. That's the only problem; it's easy to worry.

R.U. Sirius Interview

Lynn Hershman Leeson
Introduction by R.U. Sirius

Introduction

I never think about virtual reality. That is, I never spend any time contemplating three-dimensional computer spaces accessible with eye-phones, headphones, and data gloves. Hell. My reality was always virtual. I feel closer to the Beatles than I do to my childhood friends. The rock and roll radio brainwashed me away from the whitebread suburban straightjacket, the go-to-school, get married, get-a-job, die program. Sixties media reprogrammed me to be a dissipated, spoiled consumer of media and commercialized sex objects instead. My best sex is sponsored by Calvin Klein. This is an improvement over reality by a factor of ten.

Virtual Reality™—the actual computer-based technology was, along with smart drugs, the hype of 1989–90. But it was nothing compared to the excitement now surrounding the Net and the Web. The Net and the Web are, in fact, "the real thing." Pity all of those goofy entrepreneurs—those smelly, overweight, clueless guys in red corduroy slacks, sloppily-tucked-in white shirts, eyes wide open in innocence, sitting in some weird technogothic horrorhouse in Berkeley, California, at the feet of some guy who calls himself R.U. Sirius. Forced, no less, to smoke first from the peace pipe before hearing the sage advice, "Yes! Put all your money into virtual reality. Yes, it's where it's at, baby!" And off they went, only to lose the family fortune when the action shifted and Netscape struck paydirt.

What can you say really? The pursuit of three-dimensional immersive experiences continues, of course, right along with the destruction of the formerly working class, the release of Microsoft Windows 95, the tiresome virtual reality of the O.J. trial (the car chase, however, was prime!), the return of cyborg Michael Jackson, the rise of the World Wide Web, and the democratization of heroin. It's virtually exciting times, but somehow being wired *is* being tired and probably means a few hundred more people being fired.

But it ain't me, babe. My virtual ambition knows no bounds. I'm gonna download into the matrix and live forever. Or I'm gonna be the icon-at-large for those who want to crash the machine. Or . . .

Everything in this interview is virtually true.

The Interview

LYNN HERSHMAN LEESON: Were you born with your name?

R.U. SIRIUS: No, my mother called me Ken and she was Mrs. Goffman, actually. So I took the name R.U. Sirius in 1984. I started a psychedelic magazine called *High Performances.*

LYNN: What led you into this?

SIRIUS: A life of crime. I was a Yippie in the early 1970s. I was probably a seventies version of a slacker for the rest of that decade. And I spent a few years trying to work honest jobs and drifted into publishing. It was [through] phone sales that I made my living for a couple of years.

LYNN: So now you're prepared for the 800/900 numbers?

SIRIUS: I'm prepared for the world of virtual communications and sales, of course. Everything is based around sales.

LYNN: In virtual reality or in the world?

SIRIUS: In the world; in the virtual world; in the real world. Everything is advertising.

SIRIUS: Virtual reality right now is a toy that people use to get on the inside of a computer screen; [to] experience a sort of raw cartoony alternative reality that's three-dimensional. It convinces the eyes that you're inside another space, other than [your] physical space. Ultimately it's leading [to a place] where you'll be able to float around in Salvador Dali paintings and lick up the flat clocks, and have them taste like honey, you know. Whatever your imagination can conjure. We're entering a world where the stuff of the mind is manifested using bits and bytes.

LYNN: Do you feel that people [now] particularly need that kind of life-enhancement alternative?

SIRIUS: You've heard of an ecological niche, this would be sort of a psychological, ecological niche. It simply gives the psyche space to expand out into when there's no free space left on earth. It is possible to locate an autonomous ungoverned wild space in cyberspace that you can't locate in the physical realm.

LYNN: It's a pioneering/conquering of territory that's still virgin.

SIRIUS: It's . . . re-virginizing. Great concept: the creation of virgin space. And then the interaction within that space—get in there and fuck it up. That's an advertising slogan for you. Virtual reality: get in there and fuck it up.

LYNN: But do you create the virgin space or do you simply locate it?

SIRIUS: It's space being created by human beings, it's not something really external to us. Technology isn't something that gets laid on us, it's an extension of the human imagination. So it's space that we're creating, which is great, because when we go out and conquer hard space, the interaction of human beings with that hard space is generally pretty destructive.

LYNN: What about image pollution? How do you see this type of new reality . . . alter[ing] how people want to see themselves?

SIRIUS: We're becoming disembodied; we're becoming creatures of media and communication technology. That's just an inevitable process that you can't really judge as good or bad. I see it more or less as being like the polyp to the coral reef or the ant to the anthill. We're somehow designed to create this species brain and nervous system made of information and communications technology. All you can do is try and guide its development and make it interesting and human, or posthuman, but in a human way; sexy and fun rather than just a large-scale accountant's dream. You know, we could be stuck in a future that's like accounting software or something. It's more or less what it's like now. That and violence.

LYNN: How will that affect the way that we relate to each other as live human beings?

SIRIUS: There may be a great deal of alienation from the human flesh. It may seem very strange to actually to get out of your body suit and go out on the street. It could become a very delightful thing suddenly to reexperience nature and reality, like coming down from a psychedelic trip and going out the next day and experiencing the world anew. That's one possibility. In terms of people interacting, one of the fundamental things about virtual reality is that it allows you to share . . . the contents of your mind and your imagination. You're describing to somebody the wild dream that you had last night, and you say, "Do you see what I mean?" and they say, "No." And you say, "Oh, well here." And then they actually see what you mean. So that you have all the tools of saturated communication at your disposal, and you're passing them back and forth. Conceivably it should be possible for human beings to know one another better and better all the time. Whether they want to or not is yet another question.

LYNN: What about the fact that so much of this research has been developed for war technology?

SIRIUS: Well, virtual reality came out of the distant-viewing technologies of NASA and the Defense Department. Nothing that is used for war could be quite as terrifying as weapons already developed before we got into this sphere of virtual reality. We've already had biological and nuclear weapons and stuff like that. This is just more or less peripheral, I would say, to the war games. Certainly a way of abstracting people in the Western world from the results of their actions.

LYNN: Do you think it's possible to fall in love with a computer image?

SIRIUS: I am sure [it's possible]. Look at the people who chase actresses or actors around or the guy who was in love with John Lennon and shot him, or whatever. I'm sure people now write to soap opera fantasy characters; they write to the character rather than writing to the actor, or I'm sure somebody's in love with Bart Simpson. He probably has groupies line up, you know . . . "Where's Bart?"

People have always had myths, they've always had fantasy characters. There's always been a strong relation to fantasy characters. Look at religion. There's people who dedicate their entire lives and sacrifice themselves and their families to a fantasy figure. More people still love Jesus than just about anybody, except R.U. Sirius. We're bigger than Jesus.

Cyberspace translated all of media space, all of the culture that exists in a mass-mediated society. That's really what we're doing. Lots of people are picking up on it; it's a trendy thing. It's a curiosity more than anything else. It's something we can use.

When we were asked to do a TV show proposal by a fairly large television corporation, I sent them a proposal and they said, "No, we want this to be about virtual reality." So I sent it back and called it "Virtual Reality Television." And I took the same script, and I just had a big finger coming into the thing and pressing a button and going into the various aspects of the show by pressing a button. And it was, "Oh, yes. This is it." You know, virtual reality television. It's silly. It'll pass onto something else, probably, soon.

My take is that the edge will move from computer and digital-based stuff into how you mutate things in the real hard world. The next level of fascination is going to be how to actually alter human beings. How can you . . . mutate biologically, starting with the obvious things like plastic surgery and smart drugs and low-level implants and stuff like that, and also, in the external world in terms of wealth and well-being and how we deal with material reality, we're just at the beginning of an economics based on self-replicating systems. Information is first, but you can't really eat information or wear it.

What's happening in the realm of technology, starting with biotechnology and moving very quickly into nano-technology (which the Japanese take very seriously), is basically matter as information; taking it down to the molecular level and being able to, in essence, go to your computer and type out the molecule for building, for creating the consumer product that you want. It comes together and manifests itself, which mimics the way the biological world operates.

LYNN: How is the disembodiment taking place?

SIRIUS: Right now the disembodied being is the collective unconscious of the human system, you know. It is a vast archive. When we get the fiber optics lines in and when you get Project Xanadu completed, where you have a world library that's digital that contains written and visual information, you will have virtual reality machines that convey it. Human beings will become like one big brain where stuff is shooting around. That will probably happen before we leave our physical bodies behind. So who's operating that system? I don't think anybody, any human being, is large enough to be operating that system. It's some kind of strange thing that's calling humanity forward.

LYNN: Do you think there is a feeling of immortality? Are we saving ourselves on computer disks?

SIRIUS: Definitely. Dying should soon be obsolete for anybody who wants to go on; understanding ourselves as patterns of information and then finding a way of preserving that. Plus nano-technology will be a way of actually inserting nano-machines inside the system and cleaning out your arteries. There's a fantastic book, called *The Engines of Creation*, by Eric Drexler, which more or less explores all of the issues of the technology of self-replicating systems, which is the technology of the twenty-first century. There's no reason for the human system not to be able to heal itself and reform itself on an ongoing basis.

LYNN: Or to hurt itself.

SIRIUS: Or to hurt each other, or whatever. The possibilities for germ warfare are enormous. There's always a possibility that we might eliminate ourselves very soon. There is a hole in the ozone layer. It's reached a point where we have something that's so large we can't even cope with it by turning our backs on technology and going back to the woods. It's going to require a techno-fix to deal with the hole in the ozone layer. I think the intelligence of human beings needs to be a focal point; increasing that intelligence and focus, increasing that communication, but also maintaining a sense of humor about it. Cyperpunk could be an army of overly serious, leather-clad, mirrored-sunglassed, resentful computer geeks marching into a bright future. It could be a very dangerous thing.

I think that we're very much in danger of losing the prankster, joker spirit because our times are so serious, and because in a sort of completely connected electronic world of extremely dangerous materials, one mistake can kill everybody. It's hard to keep laughing, but that's really the only way for people to maintain their sanity to deal with the situation.

LYNN: Do you think that our sexual drive is becoming less forceful? If we're going to be immortal, if we're not going to die, what's that . . . ?

SIRIUS: I don't know. I think sex is the only good excuse for embodiment. I think people will try to get as much of it as they can before the body goes out of fashion.

LYNN: What will sex be like without a body?

SIRIUS: I'm not sure. That's the difference between the world which is like an accountant's software and the world that I would like to see. I think that we need to learn to eroticize the brain and the psyche so that when we do move into a postbiological future it has that sense of pleasure for us. We're not just these dry little information machines that are here to process some weird alien situation, or whatever. It should be an enjoyable thing, and to me that means erotic and funny.

LYNN: And who were these aliens that you were thinking about that may have caused us to come to this today?

SIRIUS: Well, of course, there's Sirius, the dog star. I don't really have any particular alien fantasies or contact experiences, but the name R.U. Sirius is an open invitation for somebody to come say, "Yes, I am," and show me the way.

The Net and the Future of Being Fictive

Sheldon Renan

The Evolution of Narrativity—The Way We Tell Stories—Has Suddenly Begun to Pick Up Speed

Narrativity is now like a jet accelerating toward take-off. Perspectives are multiplying. (Story telling) points are beginning to blur. The single consciousness/voice finds itself flying in formation with others.

And content and meaning no longer stay in one place. They are now subject to change—and to be changed by others.

What is happening?

The Net is happening.

The Net is beginning to happen to everything. Including narrativity.

Computer technology began this acceleration. Computers have meant that text, images, and ideas, once so laborious to present and reproduce, could suddenly be formatted, published, and changed with ease.

The computer screen has, in effect, opened the page, opened the text, and opened the narrative structure to deeper involvement by readers.

Sherry Turkle, in her book *Life on the Screen*, cites Richard A. Lanham's *The Electronic Word* to explain how "open-ended screen text subverts traditional fantasies of a master narrative, or definitive reading. . . . The result is 'a body of work active not passive, a canon not frozen in perfection but volatile with contending human motive.'"

Because the silicon technology has become so influential in the way stories are told, it has made the narrative form and practice subject to what is called "Moore's Law." Moore's Law is the recognition (by Intel founder Gordon Moore) that digital speed and capability ramps up continually—doubling every 18 months. It is related to the number of transistors you can get on a chip of a given size.

Narrative space, reach, and reason now follow that same scimitar curve upwards, opening the opportunity for greater complexity and—inevitably—reach.

Today, however, it is The Network and not The Chip that drives change. The chip has become simply ubiquitous and provides fuel for technology's engines, which power new journeys.

The Future of Narrativity Is Stapled to the Future of the Network

The Network is creating conditions that enable new kinds of emotive and fictive spaces—which in turn enable new forms of fiction and new ways of *being fictive.*

The Network creates new relationships between being fictive and being real(ized). Being fictive becomes seen as an integral part of being real. It deepens understanding by creating multiple perspectives, made possible by existing as multiple personas.

More importantly, one does not experience narrativity and being fictive as a bystander—as has been the norm.

On the Net now grow new kinds of social spaces—chat rooms, MUDs (multi-user dungeons), virtual realities, and subject spaces. Physically these spaces and places exist in silicon-based servers, enabled by algorithmic synapses. But in the evolving human matrix, they are the locus of a new social reality.

These new spaces literally create new ways of being. From them are emerging styles of reality which accept, evoke, and embrace being fictive as a natural part of being real. They precipitate the use of multiple personas as means of expanding experience, being, and understanding.

The universes the Network makes possible are also incubators of new fictive forms that over time will challenge past forms of The Telling of The Story.

Another view is that the new forms of narrativity are an inevitable evolution that builds on established forms.

Mimesis, a short history of Judeo-Christian narrativity, was written in the late 1930s by Erich Auerbach. He wrote that as humankind's understanding of existence deepens and becomes more complex, so do the fictive forms through which writers speak.

Auerbach took as his starting point Homer and the *Iliad* and followed fiction 2,000 years forward to Virginia Woolf's telling/evoking/concretizing of *To the Lighthouse*. He shows us the linear epic form evolving to consciousness folded over upon itself. Two dimensions evolving to three.

More dimensions and new forms are on the way.

In the beginning these new forms (as always) appear chaotic, without boundary, empty of art, meaning, and morality. They are "pioneering."

The most striking example is the emergence of MUDs as user-created digital environments. These can be seen simultaneously as another reality and as a jointly constructed narrative form/world/extended story.

A high visibility example of such an environment/narrative structure is Lambda Moo. Physically it exists in a server rumored to sit under the desk of its creator, researcher Pavel Curtis, at Xerox PARC (Palo Alto Research Center). Virtually it exists on the Internet, accessible to all.

Within Lambda Moo, users can create a name, an identity, and a physical (at least described in physical terms) structure in which to dwell. Once established, they can interact with other people (also acting through created identities) who are present and active within this narrative space. Descriptions, interactions, and dialogues are done through text. And the connection, the "überstructure" that makes all this possible, is the Network.

Remembering that the Network is experienced as text, think for a moment of Lambda Moo as a new kind of epic novel with an indefinite horizon—a never-ending story with as many writers as there are readers.

Romantically we like to think of fiction as the work of one mind and one hand. But those who work as professional writers know that creating written products is in fact a collaborative act—

whether it is a book, a movie, or a television soap opera. Even books now considered classics were edited and sometimes even rewritten by editors—not to mention friends, colleagues, and spouses.

In Lambda Moo and the spaces like it, collaborative creation is not secret. It is structure. And it is future, for better and for worse.

The narrative structure, like the universe, is expanding. And communal imagination will become an important element of that expansion.

What will the new fictive forms be like? I will use words from computer architecture.

They will be *scalable.* They will be forms that easily shift from the epic perspective to infinite detail.

They may be *object-oriented.* They may have standard connection points that make them easy to use with other pieces and forms.

They may be *linkable.* Separate works may link up and interconnect.

I was once amazed to discover (I think in the early seventies) that two mystery writers—Richard Stark (a pseudonym of Donald Westlake) and Joe Gores—had conspired to have characters in two separate mystery books, written by the two separate authors, meet in each other's books at the same point in fictional time. They stand on two sides of a doorway and talk for a moment—creating overlapping fictive spaces.

Multiply this by millions of opportunities and occurrences in fictive forms of the future.

Normal dramatic structure will, like time in Einstein's relativity, become deeply compromised, radicalized, and certainly complex.

The new forms will thus be stretchy and throb between the tribal and the anarchic.

The borders between fiction and reality will become increasingly (have already become/have always been) blurred. And fiction will deepen so that one may fall in and never emerge.

There is a Polish movie called *The Saragossa Manuscript.* I saw it once at the Montreal Film Festival in 1964. My memory may have altered it, but in this case, it is appropriate to the plot.

The Saragossa Manuscript is a series of retreats from reality, falling down the stairs of the mind. The characters continually recall something that happened in the past. And the movie continually takes us there.

Somebody in that recollection now remembers something else. Now there is a flashback to the flashback. Somebody in the second flashback tells a dream. And somebody in that dream remembers something that happened to them.

The story only goes backward and downward. The tension builds because soon we have lost the trail of cookie crumbs we left behind us to find our way back. We will never get back.

Of course, Howard Hawks did the same thing more efficiently in *The Big Sleep*. From our feelings in seeing this film and a thousand others, we learn that the movie and the story is always about something else than the story on the surface. The surface is merely the McGuffin, to use a term made popular by Alfred Hitchcock. It is the premise, but not the true experience or the real value.

In the future we will see new "mega-forms" emerge with deeply layered meaning. Fiction will become like a Chinese puzzle, each solution linked and dependent upon the next.

And to what purpose?

The uses of self-enchantment are many. Deepest among them, however, is the need to heal the wounds we have experienced, to succeed where we have failed and, above all, to understand the world compassionately. Implicit in this is the continual redefining of reality. And a requirement of this is The Telling of The Story.

One tells and retells one's own story—and later the stories of others as well—until it comes out right—or at least gains meaning in the reshaping.

This begins when we are still infants. Wishes, dreams, and lies are intertwined to create the path forward for us.

As we grow older, we repeatedly trace the lines of our scars in the dark, as if we could rub them away and make perfect torn pasts. Telling stories to oneself (and later to others) is a way of negotiating understanding and marking existence.

It is, of course, an illusion that we can negotiate existence. We will die despite all we have to say, write, act, and image.

And of course, it is also not an illusion. These dream/prayer/lies/imaginations have power. We ourselves have been shaped by the stories (dreams) (traced scars) (trances created in the dark) of those who wrote, told, and drew them before us.

Narrativity always involves places, pasts, and voices. But it always begins with a single voice.

I was two and often abandoned.

I was eight and "disappeared" by all others in my third grade class. If I sat at a table to eat, they would stand up and leave. If I played in a game, every one else left it. If I stood in a line, it melted away in front of me. I become a ghost.

I was 16 and a forest fire lookout on top of Lookout Mountain in the forests of Oregon. I could see signs of people but always far away—and only through the mediators of binoculars and radios.

Today I am permanently "out of the box," as my corporate clients like to say.

Though I have a deep need to be normal . . . that has made me adept at dressing and speaking as if like others . . . I am marked to myself as being permanently separate.

I am a storyteller.

Today I tell stories as a way of making things come true for companies. They call it strategy. I call it shamanism. It is the power of the storyteller. Certainly my clients would be nervous if they understood how deeply I work to accomplish their goals.

When I "wrote" the rollout of the 486 chip for Intel, the introduction event finished with each attendee finding an envelope under their chair. Inside was an octahedron that sprang into shape in their hands as they pulled it from the envelope. Suddenly four images appeared, projected from four directions down onto the multisided screen each held in their hands.

As they turned the octahedron to capture the images, the images spilled over one another, overlapping, even as they dissolved to other images. The audience could partially affect the flow of images by how they moved the octahedron they held in their hands. This was meant to create a metaphor for the multiple environments that could share the Intel x86 architecture. It also evoked many other things.

When I work on events like this, I travel constantly. Isolated night after night in hotel rooms on the road, I discovered the Network.

On the Network I can talk to someone anonymously at any time. I can be who I need to be at any moment. This somehow soothes my deepest wounds.

I think there are many like me.

On the Net one takes a chat name—and with it the opportunity (used by many) to take a different voice and a different being.

Suddenly I am connected to others, all of us gathered around a thousand electronic fires, in digital caves, in the darkness. Together we begin to weave new social webs. And new ways of being fictive.

Eventually we will—I believe—tell new kinds of stories. Those stories (and forms) will not only grow from chat and e-mail, but also from the new environments we build and the way all things will cross-connect.

Until now this has happened mostly with text. The World Wide Web will change that. It will bring the power of images, sound, and video into the equation.

Xerox PARC has been experimenting with a multimedia MUD that includes video. Video with voice, when bandwidth is free, will become an integrating medium for the Net.

But more important to the future will be the continual growth of the Net—a growth of reach, of population, and of interactivity.

With this growth, certain processes related to art and narrativity, invisible because of the slowness of time, will speed up, become more visible and more volatile.

The evolution of art and narrativity over time can been seen as a transparent dialogue and/or negotiation over the centuries between painters, writers, and dramatists. The subject is the nature of reality and how it should be shown.

There has been, for example, a dialogue as to how a woman should be portrayed. How should a Madonna/mother hold her child?

Artists respond to (knowingly or unknowingly) one another and (knowingly or unknowingly) build on the visions and representations that precede them.

In this discussion, there are few totally new beginnings or completely final endings. Absolute change in narrativity and art is mostly illusionary. De Kooning is part of the same arc or journey as Giotto. He struggles with similar problems. Homer begins an arc that Woolf continues. Shakespeare is on the road to Pinter. Pinter, with his characters that change on stage as we watch them, points the way to Lambda Moo and beyond.

Earlier in the millennium, this dialogue took place slowly and laboriously. It was limited by the speed of production, replication, communication, and travel.

That dialogue and negotiation is beginning to accelerate at a greater speed than we can now comprehend. Perspectives overlap. Dimensions multiply. The probable results are beyond imaginable.

It may, in fact, directly affect and evolve our minds—forcing them, like Gordon Moore's chips, up a steep and ever-climbing curve.

And what those new minds produce will itself grow in density, complexity, and subtlety.

(Think of the fabulous inflammatory richness of the new form of "rap." Think of multilayered imagery imagined through new super-computers that are rapidly becoming ubiquitous. Think of the continually growing capillary of world communication provided by the Net. They are all different vectors resulting from similar forces.)

Certainly we will see a new narrative universe with swirling galaxies full of "intelligent fictive systems." Certainly there will be "bots," software entities with what passes for intelligence that will interact with us and stimulate fiction from us.

We may see the emergence of great artists and leaders—auteurs of the Net—capable of creating a focusing lens for communal fictive being.

We may see a retribalization of social structures through new fictive forms and spaces. We are, in fact, already seeing a self-defined tribalization of certain elements that take on certain online personas (sub, dom, gender crossers, etc.)

Our online identities may become more important to us than our "real life" (RL) identities. Fictive VR may become more useful than personal RL. Being fictive may become a widely accepted practice and means of broadening self-definition. (Think of Carnival and how people use it to ritually transform themselves every year. Think of the *Rocky Horror Picture Show* performances.) We face a future of richer cultures and identities made possible over the Net.

On the other hand, there are dystopian possibilities as well. We may (and almost certainly will) see versions of network-powered fictive kitsch of haunting hollowness. There will be those who prefer the rearview mirror vision of the reactionary narratives like the Oberammergau Passion Play or the Ramona spectacle of Southern California, where people from community audiences play parts that never change or grow over the years.

At worst there is certainly the opportunity for using new fictive forms to manipulate millions through the Net by Hitlers of the future.

The Net is a technological lens which magnifies and extends potential for all that is in the human gene warehouse—dystopian and utopian. But it can provide an extraordinary set of tools and audiences beyond the imagination for the narrative forms of the future.

What the motion picture studio provided in the past, the Net will provide in the future. What, finally, is that?

What, Orson Welles was asked, was it like being able to work with all the then-new tools of a movie studio? Welles replied:

"It's the best toy train set a child could ever have."

PRONTOR-S

Part 3

COLONIZING VIRTUAL SPACE: The Impact on Community, Identity, and Property

Lynn Hershman Leeson
Reach, Phantom Limb Number 3, 1990

Computer Use in Law and Medicine

Arthur H. Lester

Moving at near light speed, the electron at work in computers has facilitated information exchange in both law and medicine, enabling provision of more rapid and accurate professional services to those in need, and has broadened the available information resources for the interested. Before duplicators and other copying devices became available for general use, each profession tended to be limited by local libraries. With the advent of computers, modems, fax communication, CD-ROM libraries, and other communication systems at affordable prices, near-universal access to the data needed to ensure superior services and promote research by those not in university areas is now common. Indeed, the standards of performance expected from local practitioners have changed in light of these new technologies.

Until the availability of modern data processing technology at the local office level, the speed at which legal secretaries could copy documents on a mechanical typewriter, the availability and completeness of a local legal library, and the delivery speed of couriers or the U.S. mail were significant detriments to providing rapid legal services. Courts were, at that time, staffed and operated in a manner that allowed time for manual legal work. While the courts are in the process of change, the new speed of legal data processing overburdens an already stressed system. Not all of these changes, however, are bad and the practice of law in these modern times has led to more certain justice.

In the day-to-day practice of law, modern electronic equipment has also allowed the practitioner to work in an environment often preferable to the standard office while practicing better law. In his or her home, at night, or otherwise physically isolated from the distractions of the office, the modern attorney sends and receives documents by fax or fax-computer, researches using CD-ROM or direct access to legal resources, and communicates through technological tools with virtually every other law office in the country. Hours dedicated to work have become more flexible, enhancing the quality of the attorney's life and that of his or her family. Geography and schedules no longer rule the professional life as they did so recently. These advances allow a single parent to remain productive in the profession through working at home while providing the physical and emotional support the children require during formative years. Jobsharing becomes more possible as work is tasked out to the home professional. Society cannot help but benefit from this change.

Electronic data banks make the latest court opinions and statutory changes available online within hours of release for downloading. Now, whether at home, in the law office, the courtroom, or during travel, the attorney of the nineties has full access to the latest information and documents, allowing preparation for her client's case with precision and in comfort. No longer is an attorney required to take time to travel to a law library to accomplish research and an attorney in any jurisdiction can research the law applicable to any other jurisdiction. With such data banks no farther away than the nearest modem, the California attorney is able to research Massachusetts law for presentation in a federal court in Florida without the great investments of time or funds needed in the past to locate or create the appropriate library. International law is similarly available, enhancing the conduct of transnational business.

For those without this need for immediacy, more limited libraries are available through the use of compact disk legal libraries which are readily available from many commercial publishers. Due to their more static nature, legal information on CD-ROM tends to be more limited than that available through online services and updates are less frequent, usually on a monthly basis. For those with such limited needs, compact disks have replaced rooms full of books and secretarial time needed to insert "pocket parts," besides being less expensive to maintain. Such disks are portable and usable anywhere a computer with CD player is available. This is the only technological limit to this modality of data retrieval. Further, the use of optical scanners allows insertion onto the data bank of an amalgam of information, including the transcript of deposition testimony, illustrations, photographs, technical drawings, and the like.

The proper practice of law requires access to great amounts of diverse information outside the usual legal realm. For example, a personal injury attorney requires knowledge of anatomy, physiology, medical practice standards, and the like. CD-ROM publications in other fields bring the libraries of the world to the attorney's desk. A library can be carried in a briefcase. Whether the user elects to be online or not, in her office and in court she has a distinct advantage because of her access to cases, rules, statutes, constitutional provisions, and texts.

The portable computer has become standard courtroom and conference equipment for many attorneys. Notes are taken for later reference, and cellular communication from computers places the attorney in instant contact with office resources and research teams for unforeseen needs.

While such modern technology is almost universally used, there is an economic cost that becomes significant for the smaller law firm. Clearly, such practitioners are at a disadvantage, but as the price of equipment and services declines, their ability to compete increases. Equal access to information has moved the small firm or rural attorney onto a level playing field with those from more established and urban firms. Attorneys are equally trained and often only the information gap has separated the successful from the remainder.

Legal forms are also available through computer-based resources. Such document availability is important to every attorney since much legal practice involves transactions reduced to writing. Standard forms have usually been tested and developed through litigation, leaving less to litigate when transactions break down. More importantly, clear and tested documents and forms reduce the risk of misinterpretation as to rights and responsibilities, and lawsuits can be avoided. The attorney is able to deliver a product of greater quality and has a more secure ability to properly advise her client. For the client, there is less cost at the inception, less risk in completing a transaction, and less cost in the event of dispute. Courts prefer, and often specify, the use of standard forms in order to lessen documentary ambiguity and the ensuing interpretive problems. Pleading and practice forms also enable the attorney to handle more clients with greater business efficiency, thus enhancing profitability of the practice.

Through computer services such as those provided by the American Bar Association, and through other private services, attorneys communicate and consult, seek and give advice, test ideas, share management problems, and advertise services, all in real time. The legal practitioner is no longer confined to his local market and client services are improved by the availability of a national brain trust.

Electronic espionage is a threat to use of some of the modern data transfer techniques. Just as is true for other businesses, information sought and results obtained, if known by the opponent, can lead to counterpreparation and possible loss for the attorney and client. Interception of data transmission is possible, and is done on occasion, even though it is in violation of the "work-product privilege" currently enjoyed and required by modern legal practice. Confidential communications between client and attorney concerning litigation plans or details of the client's business cannot be fully assured when some computer technology is used and, since not all participants in the legal system can be trusted to follow their ethical requirements, the fear of loss of privacy retards some uses of computers in law.

Medical practice has also changed due to electronic access to and transmission of information. While much of what was stated above concerning online services and use of the computer disks of all types applies also to the practice of medicine, unlike law, patient care is not as dependent upon instant access to knowledge of a new decision. After all, the spleen cannot be moved by legislative or judicial fiat. Notwithstanding this, good patient care requires access to information about new diagnostic techniques and the treatments available, research, medications, and insurance requirements. The modern physician has access to such information through modem communication or CD-ROM, and continuing education courses can be taken via these methods. No longer is the physician so fully dependent on the limited library of a local hospital or medical society, meeting attendance, or the texts and journals he can afford. Online consultation with medical centers has become a standard and "telemedicine" is now being tested and used, allowing medical center experts to participate in the care of patients in remote locations. Patients cannot help but benefit from such data access and transfer, no matter where the care is rendered.

Not only the practicing physician, but also the researcher now has the world's literature available through computer search services, communication networks, e-mail, institutes of higher learning, and centralized medical libraries. Research has become less costly and more efficient since instant and constant access to such information prevents duplication of unproductive endeavors and allows consultation with other experts, as well as enables the results to be tested by independent centers on a more speedy basis. Where incurable epidemics threaten the survival of our society, this takes on great importance.

Modern computers have forever changed the business of medicine. Providers, hospitals, governments, and the insurance industry have become electronically intertwined through the use of medical practice parameters, CPT codes, and DRG (diagnosis related group) criteria for medical care and payments. Electronic transmission and analysis of practice profile data has removed the control of delivery of medical services from the hands of the local providers and has placed it into the hands of third-party payers who, on the basis of collected data, determine the appropriateness of care. A patient can no longer expect to receive services based on decisions made by her and her treating physician.

On a more optimistic note, through the use of computer transfer of data, patients are more protected from unskilled providers. The licensing of a physician occurs at the state level and, until recently, state medical boards rarely communicated with each other. A malpracticing or unethical physician who lost his license in state A easily moved to state B to continue such misdeeds, inflicting harm upon more trusting and unsuspecting patients. Through the use of a federally-run national data bank and through other reporting networks, information concerning lawsuits lost, payments made in settlement of malpractice claims, and significant disciplinary actions are now freely and fully communicated. Since consultation with such data banks is required whenever a physician applies for licensure, renewal of license, and hospital privileges and their renewal, physicians with suspect or actual bad practice records are now denied the ability to continue inflicting harm. "State hopping" no longer occurs to any significant degree.

Medicine and law will never retreat from the gate of information opened by computer-based electronic technology, nor should they. Each professional participant now has the ability to reside in a virtual community not unlike a university center, with free access to information and the ability to exchange ideas, and the ethics and practical aspects of each profession demand that the practitioner remain up-to-date. Clients and patients of these professionals, natural recipients of these benefits, will be better served by those of sufficient modern thought and conscience to make use of computer technology.

Joichi and Mizuko Ito Interview

Lynn Hershman Leeson
Introduction by Joichi and Mizuko Ito

Introduction

Multi-user dungeons (MUDs) are an evolving genre of text-based virtual environment in which users log in, via computer, to participate in what MUDers sometimes call a game but usually consider a communal life. Most MUDs, following the precedent of the first MUDs built at Essex in the early 1980s, are modeled on a fantasy adventure reminiscent of the role-playing game *Dungeons and Dragons.* Diku-MUDs, Aber-MUDs, and LP-MUDs usually involve armor, weapons, gold coins, and the killing of ogres, giants, and sometimes other players. In contrast, MOOs (MUDs, object-oriented), MUSEs (multi-user simulation environments), and TinyMUDs are primarily social, often have a space-age theme, and have little in terms of the adventure game component. MUDs are being reengineered for workplaces, professional communities, and educational contexts by scientists at Xerox PARC (Palo Alto Research Center) and M.I.T., and by educational researchers around the country. There are currently hundreds of MUDs running with thousands of users from around the world. In comparison to other Internet forms of social interaction such as e-mail, Usenet, or Internet Relay Chat (IRC), MUDs are unique in that they provide a rich fantasy environment and multi-user capabilities in real-time interaction. For a cyborg anthropologist, this means fieldsites, populations, mythology, material culture, and sociality.

As a player on a standard combat MUD, what you see on your monitor is text that describes the environment, objects and people in the environment, and actions that you and others perform.

> You are near the center of the little village of Dambarsham. To the north, along Kite Row, you can hear laughter and merry-making. East the road continues into the centre of Dambarsham. A street named Wildman's Walk is south, from which

you can hear a loud "clanking" noise. You quickly come to the conclusion that this is not a quiet little country village. The only peace is to the west, where the road starts to make its way out of Dambarsham.

There are four obvious exits: west, north, south, and east.

> w

This small track leads to Dambarsham, it turns into a road further to the east. A green lawn can be seen in a westerly direction. You notice a Newbie area to the south!

There are three obvious exits: west, east, and south.

Duke Adinar

>say hi Adinar!

You say "hi Adinar!"

Adinar bows gracefully.

Every player constructs a virtual character in the MUD environment, giving it a name, building a home, and acquiring skills, powers, and riches. Higher level MUDers, usually called wizards, lords, or gods, are the supernatural denizens and rulers of the realm, responsible for the actual programming of the environment. They design, in addition to worlds and monsters, the very structures of communication and social organization—action and emotive commands, hierarchical structures, and reward systems.

For those who are invested in these systems, the Net is hardly a space of anonymity and inconsequentiality, but rather is a marked and different social location, albeit one that is decentered from their off-line lives.

I'm conducting an interview with a MUDer friend. She sips a virtual Diet Coke, watching her svelte enchantress figure. Our conversation meanders, but what I am really interested in are her negotiations between her real-life and virtual identities. She describes her online identity as "who I am when I am totally relaxed with you and free to act and be myself." She claims that for her, it is the online presentation of a person that is important to her, not their real-life identities, even for her MUDspouses, and even if she has real-life knowledge of them.

"You don't *care* about their real-life bodies?" I boggle.

"No . . . they could all be 4ft tall and be 30000000 lbs. . . . with warts." I chuckle politely.

> "Would you care if they were projecting a different gender?"
> "Probably not. . . . See . . . I just assume if you are playing a female char that u are a girl, and if you are a convincing enough guy to pull it off, should I get mad???"
> "But what about the real body?" I persist. My friend is patient.
> "To me there is no real body. It's how you describe yourself . . . and how you act (on the Net) that makes up the 'real you.'"

MUDer identity is a shifting field of possibility, the boundary of the self constantly redrawn through computational couplings and decouplings. Nimbly navigating multiple worlds, MUDers are savvy about reshaping the realities they inhabit. The virtual persona is an extension of select aspects of selves, the uninhibited, the altruistic, the superhuman, an identity often considered more authentic because of liberation from the flesh. One of the few female wizzes on my home MUD is a two-time rape survivor IRL (in real life), and "tends to be rather cautious of men in general. But here I can be as confident and flirtatious as I like . . . without fear." An all-powerful lord confides: "My physical appearance isn't good. But here I am my personality. People meet it before they meet the physical me." Identity is continuous but plural; selfhood is more than one person(a).

> I am chatting with the local sheriff, who is explaining to me the complexities of MUD management, his law enforcement duties. One of the rules on a MUD is that each (biologically bounded) person can only run one avatar at a time. Otherwise a number of virtual characters could collectively gain unfair advantage, ganging together to attack a monster or another player. Dispensable adjunct characters could die sacrificial deaths in order to consolidate experience points and treasure
> in a single primary character, creating a monstrous collective organism that defies established subject boundaries.
> "Multiple characters are extremely hard to catch. Something has to set off in your mind—this person, these two are always on together. They call in from the same location. They always run together. You've got to notice that, and when you've got 300 or 400 characters who go on at least once every three or four months, it's real hard to notice those things."

> And when he does catch an offender, the virtual body is difficult to discipline. Even if he kicks the character off the system, there is nothing to prevent the person from logging on repeatedly with anonymous guest characters.
>
> "The more ingenious ones will do things like log on with a program running in the background that tells me, to be impolite, to eat shit and die, because I have had that happen, continuously."
>
> Even if he banishes the entire client computer, "All that generally does on most systems is slow that person down, because most schools have 3-300 IP ports, and I can only banish one port at a time." He sighs deeply.

MUD sociality is both policed and enabled by the peculiar textures and materialities of online interactivity. Different MUDs provide different pleasures, fantasies, capabilities, and features, and different social positions within MUDs provide opportunities for experiencing different social locations. Most MUDers navigate a number of different MUDs with different virtual bodies and distribute their subjectivity across multiple sociotechnical worlds. Some MUDers have confided in me the pleasures and difficulties of gender swapping, and occasionally a story circulates about a chagrined MUDer's discovery of the unexpected biological gender of a MUD intimate. Wizards, who have to act as responsible administrators or coders on their home MUDs, often create player characters on other MUDs to revisit the pleasures of combat and play. Or sometimes they will log onto their home MUD to check out the environment and social scene from the point of view of a low-level player, checking rooms and interface elements that could contain bugs. Unmarked newbie or guest characters also provide opportunities for anonymous lurking, enabling freedom from a socially recognizable virtual body.

Computational embodiment and online ethnography is not without its pitfalls. For one thing, my subjects keep disappearing every time the server is reset or goes down for maintenance. And halfway through my fieldwork, my fieldsite was exiled from its university system and eventually destroyed through a failed backup. Despite the malleability and mutability of the text-based universe, MUD embodiment is absolutely contingent on terminals, servers, bandwidth, and processing power—computer lab space, IP ports, and online lag are persistent features of MUD materiality and the lives of the college students who are the primary inhabitants of MUDspace. MUDs are anathema to many universities because they take up valuable space on computers, slow down network responsiveness, and tie up valuable workstations. They have been banned at various universities across the country, yet they continue to proliferate. Since this interview was conducted, Internet providers have grown exponentially, multimedia MUDs have been launched, and commercial video conferencing has expanded the space of possibility for online communication and the possibilities for virtual embodiment.

The Interview

JOICHI ITO: Should we explain the environment that we're in?

MIZUKO ITO: Yes.

JOICHI: We have an ISDN link to the Internet from our house, which is a good example of a lot of the buzzwords, like telecommuting, and so on. Everything that we'll show you today is public domain software—either public domain or currently being made available for free. There's Network Video Conferencing, Mosaic, which is an Internet document browser and locator, and . . .

LYNN HERSHMAN LEESON: I don't think everybody knows what ISDN stands for.

JOICHI: Okay. ISDN stands for Integrated Services Digital Network. Some people say this is a dumb idea, and some people say it's a good idea, but basically, we have an infrastructure of telephones, using copper wire, and ISDN was, at the time of development, the fastest data rate you could get by converting from analog. Right now, a modem uses audio sounds, like a computer voice, to communicate data communications. Well, what ISDN does is it switches on and off digitals very quickly, so you don't have an analog section in the communication.

An issue is that the fast modems are about half as fast as ISDN now and the higher bandwidth things, like leased-circuit, are getting cheaper, like fiber, and so on and so on, so there's very little space for

SDN, where they're the only solution. But what ISDN is being deployed as is really a way to reuse the current infrastructure to do digital, and it's the best that they can do, and it's basically a telephone company idea. T-1—I'm not sure what it stands for, but it's a unit of data speed that is standard for digital communication. It's 1.5 megabits, so if you go down the scale, 2400 modem is a traditional modem that you can use to read text. 9600 baud is about the slowest speed you would want to do still images, and then ISDN, which is about 64 kilobits, is choppy video like we saw, and then T-1, you can get color video. Then cable TV now is offering in the U.S. 500 megabits, which is like VHS–quality video over the Internet. So that's sort of the bandwidth breakdown, how we're changing—what else?

MIZUKO: MUDs [multi-user dungeons].

JOICHI: MUDs, network games.

MIZUKO: Which Joichi will tell you is our dungeon. Unfortunately, MUDs are all text right now.

JOICHI: CU-SeeMe is a video conferencing package that was developed at Cornell University, and it's a big item right now. It lets you send and receive video on Macintoshes and Unix—but the really important point about CU-SeeMe is that all these people who are using this are using either university, or some kind of Internet access, which is not a metered rate system. This is a very big difference from the telephone. When you're on a phone, you're always worrying about how much is this costing, but the idea about the Net is even if you pay, you pay a flat fee per month, so all the communications that you are doing become part of your environment. So the way that people are using CU-SeeMe is that they have—this guy has the camera pointed at his bookshelf to show he's not in. It's kind of slow right now, but each of these windows that is on the screen is an actual camera image—something going on on the Net, there's John at Cornell, this is SunSITE at Purple Dung . . .

LYNN: What's that name?

JOICHI: They call it SunSITE at Purple Dung, I don't know, it's a virtual name. [*Laughs*] I hope it is. I don't know. This is a mall in

Connecticut, this is Wayne State University, this is Lexington, Kentucky, and here's me, and we're all broadcasting to the Net. Most of these people just have the camera on all day, so if it's an associate, you can see whether they're on the phone and decide whether to call him or not. You can see the traffic on 57th Street; you can see a coffeepot somewhere, and see whether there's coffee in the next room. When you have video or any kind of network in excess is when you start getting new applications. You know, it's when there are people with a lot of free time, who are smart, this is how new applications are getting developed for the Net.

LYNN: What do you do?

JOICHI: What do I do? [*Laughs*] Well, half of it I use for business. I have a virtual company with a bunch of hackers, all younger than me, and we do all of our board meetings on the Net. We talk on the Net, all of the transcripts happen on the Net, and we track everything on the computer. A lot of the kids play with it at home, so tonight we'll have a board meeting, and one kid is going to be in New York, and I'll be here, and the rest of them are going to be in Tokyo. We're going to have the board meeting in a MUD, then we get a transcript of the MUD session, and that becomes our minutes for the board meeting.

LYNN: Are there people on your board, or that you've worked with, that you've never met?

JOICHI: Not in this company. There are a lot of projects that we do where we find the people on the Net, we develop the software on the Net, and it gets distributed on the Net, and you know each other very well, but you've never met. Now, with CU-SeeMe, you can finally see their face and hear their voice, so you have met. It's just that you haven't met physically.

LYNN: Do you think that there may be a change in the free access?

JOICHI: Well, that's one of the biggest issues that phone companies all over the world are grappling with. The phone system was developed when bandwidth was scarce. It's like the rice rationing in Japan. So when you have little bits of data that you're transmitting, you're going to track each bit and charge somebody for it. But now, there's so much bandwidth, so much stuff going on, that it doesn't make sense to do a metered rate system anymore. It makes a lot more sense to say you have access to the global network of telephones, and for 300 dollars a month, or 10 dollars a month, you can call anybody you want as much as you want. That's how the cable company works, and now cable and telephone is converging. John Malone at TCI is saying he will deliver voice over his cable system, so what's going to happen is there's going to be a war to a certain extent in the way that we do billing, because the telephone infrastructure, 30 percent of it or so, is taken up by people who sit there and figure out how much to charge you for each call. There's definitely a structural, and also a cultural, difference between the telephone community and the computer network community.

LYNN: Could you say something about the cultural difference between them?

MIZUKO: Since I'm an anthropologist studying text-based worlds on the Net, there's definitely a certain kind of flattening of context that occurs in the text-based environments. This is changing now that there are things like CU-SeeMe. I think that people feel like they have a little bit more freedom to express certain acts metaphorically that they wouldn't normally do in real life, in their real bodies. It's been interesting for me, because I do meet a lot of people on the Net that I don't meet in real life, that I'll slowly start developing a context for.

For example, there's somebody that I met first through e-mail, then through MUDs, then through phone, and we're going to meet face-to-face soon. It's very different, the parts of the people that emerge in the different contexts. It's not as if people are being disingenuous on the Net, but certainly, with the text-based environment, there's different opportunities for different parts of people to emerge.

LYNN: Speaking from an anthropological vantage point, do you see this changing the way that we view each other, or the environments that we live in?

MIZUKO: I think that the sorts of issues that I've been interested in are what these assorted environments enable people to do because of the decentering from the physical body. There is something very different about it in the sense that a lot of people will talk about how this kind of liberation, or lack of consequence to their physical body, allows them to do certain things. Maybe they can be more flirtatious than they would be normally in real life, because they know that it's not really going to have any physical consequences.

LYNN: Well, it might.

MIZUKO: Yeah, it could eventually. A lot of people have MUD marriages that translate, eventually, into real-life marriages. Sometimes they don't, but a lot of people get married on MUDs, or have multiple marriages on MUDs, and feel more free to experiment with relationships that don't have an immediate, physical referent to them.

LYNN: Can you say what that ceremony is like—getting married on a MUD?

MIZUKO: Usually, they'll do some sort of engagement thing, with rings; they'll create some objects that they can carry around. Then they'll post on the bulletin board, or whatever mechanism the MUD has, that there's going to be an event at such and such a time, and they tell all their friends, and everyone shows up at that time, and they just have a little party.

LYNN: On the computer.

MIZUKO: Yeah, and the church, usually.

JOICHI: You're being very anthropological in saying "they" instead of "we."

MIZUKO: [*Laughs*] Yeah, that distance.

LYNN: Have you ever . . .

MIZUKO: No, I haven't had a MUD marriage. I have attended one MUD wedding, and I've gotten some logs from some other ones, but I haven't participated in that part of the culture that much.

LYNN: Are MUD marriages monogamous?

MIZUKO: I think that's a case where a lot of the kind of commonsensical norms sort of do translate. I think people tend to have a serial monogamy model. On the other hand, there's nothing that would prevent somebody from logging on with a different user name and being married to someone else. So, you don't really know. Because I may be talking to so-and-so, person X, and person Y, and they could be the same person. I would never know.

LYNN: Do you think that contributes to a kind of a schizophrenic positioning?

MIZUKO: Somewhat. Some people like to experiment with different identities and playing with this multiplicity. I think for most people, it's just too hard to maintain a really duplicitous identity.

JOICHI: I remember having several characters and making a point of having them have different writing styles; one guy was forty columns, all uppercase—but when you get sophisticated at spoofing, they come after you and try to check your logs, to see when you've logged on. There's a whole sort of—what do you call that—a subculture, just based on spoofing, and catching people who are spoofing.

LYNN: Who's the "they" that comes after you?

JOICHI: It varies. If you're on a newsgroup, where you're posting messages to several different people, it will be other people in the newsgroup who are being victimized by it. On a MUD, obviously, there are benefits to having two characters, so a lot of MUDs have rules against having multiple characters, so game masters will come after you. In some conferencing systems, they don't care. They like you to have several characters to represent your official opinion and your private opinion, your male opinion, your female opinion. A long time ago, there was a system called The Source, and on The Source, there was a conferencing system called Party, and one of the helpers was named D-Dub. What would happen is you'd get on, and you'd start talking to all these different people, and one by one, you'd realize that they were actually the same person. Then you would go through this crisis, where you thought maybe everybody on this whole system was D-Dub. And then you would realize that only half the people were.

LYNN: But it is sort of like a fingerprint, because you can put on a mask, but eventually, you're going to use the same references, or wording system, no matter how hard you try to wear gloves, or deny it.

MIZUKO: Right. Because most people don't see themselves as really acting out something on a MUD, they just are themselves. So it's hard to always be performing. You know, these are real social spaces that people take very seriously and spend a lot of time on, so if you're always performing, then it's not as fun.

JOICHI: Although you can honestly have several selves.

MIZUKO: That's true, yeah.

JOICHI: I had a couple of selves that I wrote with that had definite point of views. It was important that they were different, and people respected their differences and addressed them differently, and I think as long as it's true, it's okay. If you're doing it just for fun or to cause problems, then it's not good.

LYNN: Can you say again what MUD is, what MUD stands for?

MIZUKO: MUD stands for multi-user dungeon. That's the original name for it. Recently people have been trying to say it stands for multi-user dimension, trying to get away from the *Dungeons and Dragons* metaphor, but that's how it was originally conceived.

JOICHI: Actually conceived at Essex University, by a guy named Richard Bardo, in 1983. When it first started it was just a bunch of hackers hanging out on the games section of the Net. The neat thing was that all the people that were in the MUD could change the MUD. They could change the rules, they could add rooms, add monsters, change their characters, so it was completely dynamic, with no adult supervision at all. The idea was that it kept growing and growing and getting better and better and having open systems and open protocol, and it basically bred. There are now many, many varieties of MUDs all over the world, and they're getting very sophisticated.

MIZUKO: There's a few hundred [MUDs] right now [on the Net]. And there's a lot of different kinds. The original MUD code has been rewritten and appropriated by a lot of different groups. There has never been centralized control, so the sort of ad hoc social structures that come into place are really born out of this fairly—I mean, there definitely is a hierarchy, like you have to have a server, you have to have Internet access, and things like that—but the whole system of MUDs has grown out of this very amorphous network of people. It is a really nice process. As an anthropologist, it's been very interesting.

JOICHI: And from an artificial life point of view, the original code that people write the MUD code in is C—that's the engine that MUD is written on, but around that, you develop all the rooms and the context, and on top of that there are all the players that have developed characters on that MUD. So, if a MUD is shutting down, what will happen is they will "tar" the MUD, which is take the MUD and make it into a file that can be transported to another computer. It gets transported to somebody else, who will be a parent for it for a while. Then it's untarred, and everybody logs in, so the address of the MUD has changed, but the spirit has been able to move from one computer to the other without the users really knowing the difference.

For instance, there's a MUD called *Carrion Fields*, which was losing the computer that it was on. It had hundreds of players, so I volunteered to put it on our system in Tokyo. So temporarily, I have a system with an average of about fifty people logged in all the time, bogging down my computer, but it's kind of like a bee colony. It's like transplanting bee colonies, but they keep nomadic, because people don't like having MUDs on their computers all the time. The thing that's interesting is it's not just a simple matter of code running, rather the whole community moves. They are very, very portable, they can run on any Unix platform anywhere, and they will run the same.

LYNN: You mentioned that the people were younger than you, in your company, and you're young, so do you think this whole system is for younger people to invent, and this literacy has to come to a different generation?

JOICHI: I think that if you look at one generation before me, they didn't really understand the telephone. The telephone was to them an expensive toy. I talk to older people, in Japan for instance, on the telephone, and they say, well, I don't think this is the kind of thing we would like to talk about over the telephone, I think we should meet in person, you know, for some person-to-person discussion. Teenagers, however, can have sex over the phone, right? So the phone has changed from something that looks like a telex to something that looks more like a community environment thing. It's similar on the Net. The older people can use it for e-mail, and for retrieving Congressional reports and things like that, but they really haven't assimilated to the idea of cyberspace as an environment in which you do things—I don't know the English word for this now, *kansei.* What's *kansei?*

MIZUKO: Mmm, sensitivity, or . . .

JOICHI: Something that's emotionally engaging. The other thing is, these kids that I'm working with, these 22- or 23-year-olds, have gone through college with a complete environment always available to them. Most of their social life—not most, but a lot of their social life, happens in the computer. So the sensibility they have about using this medium is completely different from somebody who's grown up with the telephone. I always use the metaphor that you really can't expect a village that doesn't have electricity to come up with plans to regulate consumer electronics. Similarly, I think people who haven't grown up with the idea that bandwidth is cheap, computers are fast, and that games and these new environments are readily available cannot come up with the new ideas as easily as these kids. Most of the people I work with are 22 and 23, and just fresh out of college. Usually, in Tokyo, they are dying because they don't have any more bandwidth.

LYNN: Maybe we can show some things on the monitor?

JOICHI: The software we're showing is CU-SeeMe. It uses another technology called a reflector, which is a site that bounces all of the video coming into it back out again. This is the reflector at Cornell University, and if you look here, this is somebody at Cornell University on 57th Street; this is somebody in Boston.

LYNN: Who is that?

JOICHI: Who is that? I don't know.

LYNN: Why is he on the phone?

JOICHI: Well, one of the main reasons you use this is, before you call them on the telephone, you check to see if they're busy or not. So I see them on the telephone. I wonder if they'll wave to me. And you can type to them. So I'm watching somebody in Syracuse who's on the telephone.

LYNN: Can you do sound?

JOICHI: No, he doesn't have any sound. We'll find somebody else who's not on the telephone. Here's somebody else.

LYNN: Why are they on the phone and not on their computer?

JOICHI: Well, most of these people have cameras pointed into their offices, so people can see whether they're in, on the phone, or meeting with somebody, or busy. It's more of an indicator of their environment, rather than some kind of communication device.

We're running at 64 kilobits right now, but he's running at 14—this is a kind of technology that's feasible over a fast modem. It's black-and-white, the sound is choppy, it's free, and this is sort of a street version of a lot of network video. There are things like network video and multicast, which are built into the little bit higher-end computers, like Indigos and Suns. They eat up about 250 kilobits of bandwidth, but they have much better sound and are color. A lot of universities and big companies, like Xerox PARC, have that kind of environment, so there's network video for the masses and network video for the important people.

LYNN: How do you feel about the fact that you are revealing yourself visually to just anyone who happens to be calling you up and seeing who you are?

JOICHI: It's actually kind of fun. You know, I sometimes leave the camera on to my office all day, so anyone can see what we're doing. You forget about it after a while, but it's kind of neat for people because they see that you're there.

LYNN: Are you ever worried about surveillance, or lack of privacy?

JOICHI: Well, I can always turn it off. I don't have any problem broadcasting my face.

LYNN: Do people find things in your room without your being there?

JOICHI: Yeah, they could find things in my room, they could look at my bookshelf.

MIZUKO: But only what you're pointing at.

JOICHI: Yeah, although now they have a camera that you can control from the outside as well. So you'll be able to pan. Okay, so Bill does not want to talk to us.

Now I'm going to do Mosaic. There's a protocol called the World Wide Web, that was developed at Serne, in Europe. It was originally developed to link to hyper-link documents for physicists. The idea is that you have a document on the Internet, you can click on a word, like "particle physics paper by so-and-so," and that would then go to another computer, get that document, and display it to you. You would be able to link through all kinds of documents dynamically, with pictures and sounds and movies. It was a really simple way for technical people to cross-reference all their information. What's happened now is you can get porno GIFs (graphics interchange format), and commercials about World Cup, and lock-picking guides from M.I.T., or whatever you want. They're all cross-referenced and very easy to find. This is Mosaic, which is a browser through World Wide Web that was developed at National Center for Supercomputer Applications, at University of Illinois, Champaign-Urbana.

LYNN: Do you think that there's much chance for applying the same privacy laws that exist for regular mail to electronic mail and such? We've been talking to people that thought privacy was just pretty much over.

JOICHI: I think we lost the first war with this digital telecommuting bill that just passed in Congress which will let the FBI wiretap, and wiretap is an easier way to get at our e-mail than the postal codes.

Okay, so right now, Mick Philip and I are working on a book, and we have it on the Net, requesting comments from people. So you can either click through the pages, or you can actually type the URL— which is the uniform resource locator, which is just like the telephone number on the Net. I'll type it—this is a long telephone number, but it is the telephone number for a page that Mick Philip, a San Francisco artist, and I are doing. I'm the writer, and he's the artist.

LYNN: How does he know what to do?

JOICHI: Well, we talk a lot, the idea that we have is that there are four basic elements to the aesthetic of technology that's being developed. We divide it up into radical beauty, chaotic harmony, neo-mysticism, and organic technology. For instance, if you click on radical beauty, this will soon have an explanation of what radical beauty is on the right.

LYNN: And when you say you talk to each other a lot, do you mean conventionally, like over the phone, or do you mean online?

JOICHI: A lot of it's e-mail. We get together and meet face-to-face, but we provide a lot of homework for each other before we meet, so a lot of the writing and a lot of the work is theoretically supposed to be done online. Take for example some sample images that he's put together, and clicking on them will bring them up. So actually, anybody on the Internet can see this and start commenting. As we start filling this book out, we'll start incorporating the comments we get from the Net into the book, there'll be a CD-ROM version of the book, which will be a snapshot of what's going on online, and then there'll be a paper edition, which will be very high-quality.

LYNN: How do you define radical beauty?

JOICHI: Radical beauty? Well, what we're working on right now in terms of radical beauty is that radical beauty is sort of an aesthetic that occurs in extremes. There's an intensity in chaos, and a sort of bringing together dichotomies of things. This is something that we're actually working on the definition of right now, so if you have an idea of what radical beauty is, you can post it to our page.

Neo-mysticism is a sort of new mysticism that's developing, based on the convergence of some of the new sciences and older spiritual elements, and in Japan, you find a lot of the super high-tech people going into and reevaluating Buddhism, and so on. Mizuko has a much better understanding of this than I do.

But here's an example: this is the cover of Timothy Leary's *Tibetan Book of the Dead* interpretation called *The Psychedelic Experience.* We redid that to a modern version and cut it on CD, and this was the jacket for that. But anyway, this is another example of how we're working with artists on the Net—the idea is that we're requesting feedback, and the feedback is important, and these are really icons that point to works that will be done. People will still want to buy the works, and it's advertising, and if somebody takes this design, since it's on the Net, everybody knows that these are Mick's now. I think the trick for an artist is to keep getting stuff out on the Net and get credited for it, because people aren't going to steal it anyway, and it's really more like advertising than anything else.

But home pages, getting back to Mosaic, typically have different links to computers all over the place. Let me start with stuff that we have. This is my home page, so this has a list of companies that I'm working for, you can read articles that I've written, and you can go in and see the list of things that I'm interested in right now. What's interesting about this is, I have a list of stuff that I'm interested in. I get messages from people who read this, and, on the Net right now, it's very easy to find out more and more and more about what you already know, because you can find everything. What's hard to find out is who cares about what you know, and what's the bigger picture. So, by publishing your interests on the Net, what you find is you get people saying, well, this has a lot to do with this work I'm doing, so you can go up the ladder instead of down.

LYNN: You started to talk a little bit about privacy, loss of privacy, and those kinds of new dimensions of dilemmas that this media's bringing up . . .

JOICHI: Well, the difficulty with the Net is to try to figure out what is a public space, and what is not a public space. When you look at Mosaic as an interface, when you post a document on Mosaic, my assumption is that it's your home page, it's your front door, you're asking people to come look at it, and it's publicly available. It's something you're doing, it's like a public performance you're doing outside.

But some people think that you're coming in to get information for your computer, and the notion of space, or private space, personal space, and ownership in cyberspace, is a completely new phenomenon that no one really has a handle on. All the people are bringing different metaphors from different fields in and trying to apply it, and there's obviously a lot of friction. This is actually a really big topic, and maybe we should focus on something specific.

LYNN: Well, what about censorship? You talked a little bit about getting flamed, and your definition of getting flamed, and how that affects other people's voices.

JOICHI: Well, there's obviously a very strong Net culture, and I think a lot of people underestimate what the Net culture is. There's an interesting saying that I saw recently on the Net, which said the best way to get information from the Internet is to post the wrong information. There's the idea that the Internet is a living thing, a newsgroup, that's always processing information.

We had an argument recently with a CIA analyst who held that the purest information was where there were all known sources, and you got the information and you analyzed it. And when the analysis was done and you presented the information, it was very secret. The people on the Net hold that if an argument can stand up to all the flames, and all the arguments and discussions in the newsgroup, then it's as close to truth as you can get. So, you see, those are the complete opposites. One, you have a place where it's completely anonymous, and everybody is standing on the strength of their arguments, versus a CIA research project, where everybody is standing on the clearance level and the background and the name that they bring into the deal.

LYNN: Mizuko, could you give me your definition of what "flaming" is, and also of censorship?

MIZUKO: Well, on one hand flaming seems to be just a Net culture pastime, just something to do to make things a little bit more lively. It's a way to keep things going, in a way.

LYNN: But what is it?

MIZUKO: What is it? It's just a sort of inflated verbal fight on the Net, I would say.

JOICHI: I think a lot of how a flame progresses is a factor of the lag time that you have. So when you post a note and everybody has 24 hours to misinterpret it and grow the misinterpretation before you get a chance to make another comment, this is sometimes how flames get out of hand. But on the other hand, having said that, in a chat session where it's real time, you still get similar sorts of flames, it just happens more quickly.

LYNN: Is that because a voice with its inflections isn't heard?

JOICHI: I think that has a lot to do with it. I mean, with a lot of the flames, if you had just put a smiley face at the end, you wouldn't have gotten it. Or, the person who flamed, if he had put a smiley face at the end, it wouldn't have escalated. But, some people genuinely love to flame, so it is a pastime. In the current version of Emax, which is the editor that all the hackers use, you can say "flame," and then it will make a random flame for you, to attach to the end of your Emax message. "You stupid idiot, you don't know what you're talking about, get off the Net!" And it just creates random flames. So, flaming has become such an integral part of people's communication on the Net. It's not as severe as you might think when you first get flamed.

There's maybe three layers of authority that you can have. You should have control over the stuff that gets to you, so everyone should have the right to filter and censor information that gets to them. If they don't want to see messages from feminists, that should be their prerogative. Then there's the moderator of the discussion, who also has the right to start and run a censored conference. But then there's also the administrator of the whole system, like CompuServe or America Online, which I don't think has the right to censor beyond really basic guidelines, and so I think it really depends on where you are. If you're in a MUD, and you're under the reign of a 12-year-old god who can censor anything he wants, it's your choice to be in that space, so you have to follow those rules.

So I think that if you're on the Net, if it's malicious intent, and it's a hack, then obviously they're going to go after him. Censorship, as long as it's well-defined before you get there, is not really a bad thing. I think a good metaphor, that was brought up by Hacking Bay in Temporary Autonomous Zone, is that on earth there was a period where the pirates could go off and start a colony anywhere they wanted to, because there was so much unmapped territory. So, if you didn't like the laws of a country, you could go start your own for a while, and when you got bored, you would close the island down. It's very similar on the Net at this point, where there's an infinite amount of space. If you don't like the culture in one place, if you don't want to be censored, you can go create your own network, and have your own discussions, and do anything you want. I think that there are obviously the backbones and the big systems where I think it should be fairly free, but in the smaller groups, you can set up your own laws, and if you don't like it, go away.

MIZUKO: Yeah, there's an ambiguous distinction between public and private spaces on the Net, and that is where a lot of the issues of privacy, censorship, and power control start breaking down. There's a lot of ruptures because in MUDs, the wizards and gods of the system consider that to be their private space where they're inviting people to come in, whereas the more dominant rhetoric of the Net is one of a democratic medium of equal access. So when a MUD wizard has absolute power over their own MUD and can kick anyone off at will, and you could have a 12-year-old game master that just decides he doesn't like girls, or whatever, just any blatant prejudice he feels like bringing to his MUD, he can, and there's nothing you can do about it. But there is a big question which is, if you have an open socket to the Internet, what does that mean? Where does that boundary between a private and a public space end?

LYNN: How did each of you get interested in this?

MIZUKO: Well, a lot of it for me was through Joichi, because he's older and had been playing with a lot of this stuff. I had been exposed to networking technologies since I was in junior high and have just sort of kept up with it. But you were more involved.

JOICHI: In high school I was at the American school in Japan, so my teachers were so-so, but there was a limit to the resources I had, so I went on to the Net, at the universities, and talked to professors, and found a huge resource of really smart people on the Net. So I did a lot of my studying on the computer, and then I found that there were games, and I discovered MUDs at Essex University, and basically discovered Net culture because I was stuck in Tokyo.

But after that, I met a lot of the people that I met online, a lot of the initial business contacts that I had. I was going to school, and I started doing consulting, and, as the saying goes, on the Net, no one knows if you're a dog. On the Net, no one knows if you're 18, and so if you can write well, and you can make deals, you can start doing business as young as you want. So I was participating in some really interesting discussions at that time. But since then it's just exploded, and now, half of my time, half of my assets are on the Net.

LYNN: Where do you think the center for this kind of mental space exists, meaning the physical center, in terms of the universe. Like, say, in Northern California . . .

JOICHI: There is no center. I think that there are geographical things. There are many different metaphors, but in terms of just the technology, a lot of it started on the east coast, in the Washington, D.C., area, because it was all government stuff, initially. So there's an area called Netplex . . .

LYNN: Did it come out of war?

JOICHI: It came out of the Department of Defense. Most of the people that run the Net are from there. And then it's moved more and more to the west coast, where a lot of the software companies are, and so on. Europe has been doing its own thing.

What I think is that the Net is a huge distribution and communication mechanism for really cool content that comes over the Net. The Japanese networks have a Japanese taste, and there are certain things you can only get in Japan, and when that combines with the insanity from Amsterdam, then you get a completely different thing, and so there really is a lot of presence in all these different types of cooking, you would say, so the Chinese food reigns in this area. There's different countries that have different centers for different types of Net presence.

LYNN: I was just in the south of France, and they compared the Net with Zen Buddhism, and they said that a lot of the people who were users were Zen Buddhists, and it was like a mist that was covering the planet.

JOICHI: Yeah. There's definitely a group consciousness thing to the Net. It's very spiritual in the sense that you're connected all the time. I have a little radio mail thing that I can use to get messages to the Net in five seconds, and get it back. If I'm talking to people who are on the Net, I have a five-second lag time to talk to anyone I want to, so during a meeting, I'm sending e-mail and receiving e-mail, and I'm tapped in to all the brains on the Net that I communicate with, so I have a telepathy, basically, that's going on.

Some of the turnaround has gone from reading your mail once a week, to reading mail every day, to reading your mail every hour, to always being available online. So there are a lot of people who spend half of their consciousness on the Net. There are kids like the Leary newsgroup, which is a newsgroup of Timothy Leary fans, and they communicate on the Net a lot. They take group trips, and they talk about it, and they really feel, after talking to each other, that they have made some kind of spiritual-mental link on the Net.

As sort of a digression, but an interesting story, one of the kids on the Leary list spent all of his energy, really, on the list. He wanted to move to Berkeley, and his parents wanted him to stay in Pennsylvania to go to college. "Because you don't know anybody in Berkeley." And he says, "Well, all my friends on this Leary list are in Berkeley." The mother said, "Well, who do you trust, who loves you more, your family or these weird computer people?" He says, "These weird computer people love me a lot more than you do." And it was an amazing thing, this kid had built up more trust with his friends on the Net, and more communication with them, than he had with his parents. So he's out in Berkeley now.

LYNN: Do you see the flip side of the loss of privacy as maybe increased consciousness, globally?

MIZUKO: Yeah. I mean, the way I like to think of being on the Net is it's kind of this neo-McLuhanesque metaphor of the extensions of agency through these prosthetic devices, like your computer, and your agency, your consciousness, if you want to call it that, or identity, becomes distributed through domains that you normally don't have access to when you're limited to your physical body. So it's a stretching out, and there's a funny fusion, with a lot of different people and content domains that you normally wouldn't have access to. It's a remote access phenomenon that's going on, and there's sort of this giddy sense of freedom around that, but there's also a certain loss of control associated with it, which relates to the privacy issues. If you have an open CU-SeeMe channel all the time, you're broadcasting to hundreds of people, and they own a little piece of you. So, it's an interesting trade-off that goes on, I think, once you start spending more time there.

LYNN: Is it true that certain cultures don't have computer access?

MIZUKO: Yes, and in Japan we find that the physicality of the computer demands a kind of speed at the keyboard, which is very integral to Net culture; being able to have this transparent coupling with your technologies. When you're typing in Japanese on an English keyboard, you can never get the speed that you can if you're typing straight English text.

JOICHI: Yeah, I think the language barrier is going to be the greatest barrier, but on the other hand, there's all this pent-up frustration of the Japanese and the Asian cultures, waiting for multimedia to get on the Net so they can get beyond this. I think that will definitely change how Japanese kids will find ways to communicate. I mean, the fax machine came out in Japan because it was such a pain to write the characters. I think a lot of interesting applications may come out of Japan, just because text is so clunky right now.

LYNN: So, you've got a radio?

JOICHI: Yeah, this is a radio mail, so no matter where I am in the U.S., I am never more than five seconds away from e-mail to the Internet.

LYNN: A lot can happen in five seconds.

JOICHI: Well, I can be in a meeting, and you can ask me a question, and I can send a message to John Markoff at the *New York Times*, and 10 seconds later he can send me a reply, and I can tell you the answer.

LYNN: If he's waiting.

JOICHI: A lot of these people have terminals on the Net, and the thing goes beep-beep. If it's from me, it'll pop up in a certain window that's for me, and if it's an urgent question, they'll reply right away, and you'll get a response right away. It's amazing. Every month, I'm surprised by how much faster the turnaround gets on the Net. It's gotten to the point where if I know somebody is there, and I don't get a reply in, like, 15 minutes, I start getting upset. Because, you know, they can reply while they're on the phone. That means they're not giving me priority. I check my e-mail before I listen to my answering machine now. My e-mail takes a much higher priority than voice communication for me.

LYNN: Can you possibly answer all you get, though? I mean, that's the other side of it.

JOICHI: No, but it's your choice. If I write an article, and I get 200 responses, I can scan 200 responses in an hour or two. It's not that hard. And I can get the interesting ones and respond to them. Those are 200 people who I wouldn't have had contact with otherwise. Filtering is your prerogative. I have a form letter that goes out to people who I don't have time to respond to, and I generally write back to everybody at least once. But it's really your choice. If you have smart technology, there's no need to be overloaded with information.

LYNN: So, do you think a lot of this is about the compression of information?

JOICHI: I think that, sort of from a physics model, we used to live in Newtonian space where meeting people and contacts and things happened at a leisurely pace, so there wasn't that much coincidence, and connections didn't happen that quickly, so you could sort of predict the evolution of your life. But now, you're going into light-speed communication systems, where just contacts and communications and information are going so fast that it's almost nonlinear. So what happens is there's just so much communication, you can get in touch with anybody immediately, so that the time that you always had to wait for the letter to come back doesn't happen any more. Stuff that used to have a time max, and you used to have time to think, you don't have time to think anymore, between responses, so you find yourself thinking more and more in real time, or not even thinking at all, and just channeling.

One of the problems that you get when you're on the Net sometimes is, you stop processing and you just start forwarding. So what happens is, I get a message from somebody, and I go, oh, this guy would know, and I become a router. This guy would know this, this guy would know that. You add value to the Net, and people start sending you more and more interesting stuff, because they always get routed to better stuff. But you end up becoming a router rather than content yourself. Sometimes I don't even read the mail, I just see the keywords, and say this should go to so-and-so. So that's a problem.

MIZUKO: We always joke that Joichi is like a human switchboard, because the amount of content that he starts actually producing is diminishing, but the number of connections that he's making is rising exponentially, so it's been interesting watching that process.

LYNN: What do think the possibility is for machines becoming human, reproducing, and taking over?

JOICHI: There's an interesting article in the paper of Fujitsu about a demonstration of robots. I don't know if you've seen this. They're robots, and they have these very small components, and the robots collect more components and build more of themselves. So as long as you keep throwing in components, then the number of these robots grows exponentially. Obviously, from a theoretical point of view, it's a very trivial thing, but to have actually executed it and done it and showed that it works, is, I think, a neat step forward in that.

LYNN: I'm curious from an anthropological point of view about the implications of the downsides of everybody being online. You know, the question of simulation versus actual physical experiences, and people having their realities in these worlds and not going outside and touching nature, and things like that.

MIZUKO: There's definitely a trade-off equation about the sort of neglect of the physical body that happens with people that are highly involved in electronic communication. Part of my work has been looking at how that electronic space provides for a certain kind of very real, visceral experience that you can't get in the physical world. Now, it's definitely true, though, that it's a trade-off.

The popular myth about MUDers is that they're all people with no social life, and it's kind of sad, isn't it, that they're always on the Net. I think what that story doesn't describe is the fact that these people have very active social lives on the Net, but it does point to the kind of breaks with a lot of what they call their real-life commitments. There's a lot of joking about people being addicted to MUDing, sort of being out of control, requiring that connection to that space and not dealing with their real-world responsibilities, like homework. So, there's a lot of, on one hand, joking, kind of nervous joking, like, oh, get a life, what are you doing on the MUD again, coupled with sort of a real recognition that there's something very compelling about these spaces that make it compelling enough to neglect one's physical body, to not eat for eight hours when you're MUDing.

LYNN: Somebody's doing a documentary called Synthetic Pleasures, which is about people who prefer the artificial world. And I think it was in Japan where they have the ski slopes that are artificial and waterfalls where people would pay to go on a trip to do that, rather than the real one.

MIZUKO: Right.

LYNN: So, do you think that this kind of technology is advancing that kind of simulated world?

MIZUKO: Yeah. I don't know if I would draw a distinction between the real world and the simulated, but there is a way that the electronic environments make certain things concrete that you can't get when you're limited by the normal physical constraints and the biology of the normal body. You can't be a wizard, or you can't concretize those wishes or actions in the physical worlds so there's something very compelling about it, despite the fact that it's very flat, and it's still all text-based. There's something compelling about being able to make an interactive experience out of fantasy environments.

LYNN: Sounds like the MUDs are very vivid, with wizards and gods.

MIZUKO: Yeah, and a lot of them are sort of rendering interactive and social science fiction and fantasy novels. These are very direct translations, like be a character in *Dune* kind of thing. Most of them are more generic medieval metaphor or science fiction metaphor.

JOICHI: Your friend at Xerox PARC, Pavel, is searching and replacing all the "player" references to "user," and he's trying to make MUD an interface for everything on the Net.

LYNN: The language is really critical.

JOICHI: Yeah. Computer words are really funny.

Sandy Stone Interview

Lynn Hershman Leeson

LYNN HERSHMAN LEESON: What did you do at the anthropology conference?

SANDY STONE: I hoped to create a series of provocations, or interruptions about the development of robots and androids before the invention of real machines. This was interesting because, when androids were first developed, they were clockwork devices that looked like people. They did things that people do and they were built in even numbers, men and women or male-like looking things and female-like looking things. They were extremely elaborate mechanisms which worked very well, and they were very popular. It was like a public entertainment. They were shown before the crowned heads of Europe where they did things like play on flutes and play pianos. There was one that played pieces on the piano. You had to crank it from behind, and it performed all of the finger movements. That was what they were very good at. They had hardware and software; the hardware was the frame, and the software was a kind of a "cam" device that contained and coded the information for the motion of the hands and fingers. They had ones that wrote letters, real letters, and ones that danced, though they had to keep one foot in place because there had to be a place for the mechanism to go through. But they were very, very elaborately worked-out.

Then, with the development of real machines, which is to say what we call "true" machines—steam engines, tractors, machines that looked like what they did rather than looking like people looking like what they did—all the androids fell out of popularity. This has been recounted by other people. Andreas Seison did a wonderful report on it. Within a brief period of time all the androids disappeared. It didn't take more than a few years for them to fall completely out of favor, which was rather strange. And then something stranger happened. They reappeared in a transmogrified form in literature—novels, fiction, serialized things in newspapers; and when they reappeared they were frightening and dangerous and disruptive and horrific, and they were also all female.

The thing that a number of us wanted to know, and which is obvious because it hovers in the background all the time, was how come, when there were real machines, suddenly the androids which represented machines became gendered as feminine, were seen as women, and were seen as threatening and disruptive and dangerous. Of course, we know that all of that had to do with the way in which machinery itself was perceived as being threatening and disruptive and dangerous, and so became coded female.

That was provocation number one.

Then I did a quick run on provocation number two, which dealt with how we look at real objects and represent them in very odd ways. I showed Dürer's rhinoceros, which had these big armor plates on it—you can practically see the rivets—and this kind of animal peering out through all of that stuff. Then I showed a picture of a real rhinoceros with its kid; the large family-size model and the fuel-economy model, and they don't have armor plates at all! These things were presumably drawn from life.

Then I showed a slide of locusts drawn from life in the fifteenth century during a plague. A German artist, very good, went out and found these things crawling around eating everything and drew pictures of them, and they didn't look anything like real locusts either, even though he was drawing from an actual object.

So, provocation number two asks how we get from those real things, or a presumably unbiased photographic representation, to these odd fantastic creatures that are presumably drawn from life by good artists.

Then we went on to do the "Habitat" environment. We would show people how men and women are represented in virtual spaces. There are machines in those spaces where you can get sex changes for a certain amount of money; Habitat is a profit-making environment, so you pay money for everything. People can move back and forth between these gendered forms for a few Habitat yen. It's a Japanese system, so it's yen. We know statistically that 20 percent of the people who are online in Habitat are women. By that I mean we can verify by their application forms that they are, as far as we can tell, genetic females who are performing as women in society. We call them women for that purpose. The remainder are men. But in the virtual community 30 percent of the people online are women. What that means is that 10 percent of the men are cross-dressing all the time. And one of the things we look at, of course, is: Why? What do they get out of it?

Well it seems that what they get out of it is, first of all, attention. They are cashing in on the imbalance. Most of the people online are men, and men pay more attention to women than they do to other men, and to a certain extent the women pay more attention to other women than they do to men. So when someone logs on as a woman there's a tremendous swirl of activity. You can see that not only in environments like Habitat, but also in text-based virtual communities where the only kind of interaction is through typing a line of text on the screen. So in all of those things, women, or people who are performing as women, get all the attention.

LYNN: Why are there more men online than women? What does this kind of fantasy relationship to fictional beings do to our sense of relationships?

SANDY: More men [are] online than women because, at this point, technology with a capital T is more interesting to men than it is to women. This is changing.

LYNN: Interesting or available?

SANDY: Both, actually. It is both more interesting and more available. Women as yet don't have the same access to technology that men do. That is slowly changing because more women are becoming interested. Not necessarily from our generation, but I see young women coming up who are bright and sharp and eager, and who have their hands on the technology and will keep their hands on the technology.

One of the things we're observing at the Advanced Communications Technology Laboratory at the University of Texas in the Department of Radio, TV, and Film is how women who gain access to the technology act with regard to it. Do they treat it with the same sort of gendering that men do because, for men, technology by and large is heavily gendered. It's gendered in very classical, traditional ways, meaning that technology is something which is to be conquered, to be rendered submissive; one learns to dominate it, or to extract from it its secrets, either by wooing it or by force. These are things that go back as far as we know. Evelyn Fox Keller first reported on this in a book that she wrote several years ago on, among other things, Sir Francis Bacon and his approach to technology. He vocalized very well the idea that nature was a woman who had to be seized and wooed and her secrets were to be wrested from her by the controlling man. That's the way it's been ever since. We all live in a situation in which that's the case. If you go to engineering schools, you observe the interactions of the engineers, most of whom are men, and you see that they think of the technology in a very gendered way.

We see in looking at virtual environments, for instance, that they are frequently gendered by men as female or feminine. They're seen as things which are penetrated, which one enters, which are enveloping, which are to a certain extent sheltering and shielding, and which can be controlled by the exercise of will. We see those polarities still operating in that space.

But we see some hopeful things as well. In some of the multiple-user domains, which are known as MUDs, or "muds," or "MOOs" [MUDs, object-oriented], or "MUSHes," which are all imaginary environments in which people meet and have social interactions, we see that these things are clearly perceived as social spaces. They have dimensions in the imaginary world, in that people treat them as if they were Cartesian. There are other genders in there, new ones, so the people who are designing those multiple-user domains are to a certain extent aware of these problems—and are trying to give people the opportunity for change—to take up new positions within an expanded gender framework or gender spectrum. We don't yet know what the results of that are. It's hard to know how to place yourself in a spectrum of desire if you are identifying yourself as "it." How do people desire each other when you dismantle a gender framework? I don't know yet, but I'm still watching people doing it. And pretty soon, I hope, we'll have some kind of understanding of what's going on in there and how people are doing it.

LYNN: What is your relationship to the telephone?

SANDY: I became interested in phone sex by working with a phone sex collective. I originally found out about them because I wanted to gather some data about how people talked about desire, how they constructed desire verbally. Well one of the things that immediately became clear when I looked at phone-sex interaction is that phone sex is really about data compression. People are compressing information about physical bodies into very small amounts of space, then they're sending them over wires. The person at the other end gets this very limited amount of information, and does something like adding boiling water, and reconstitutes a very elaborate, very complex image, which is gendered, and which has all of the elements of desire that it takes in order to have a sexual interaction. So, for a while I watched that fairly closely and I got on the line and participated. It was an interesting experience of participant observation.

Afterwards, I had a lot more information about how that kind of compression and construction of desire works than I did before. And the other phone-sex workers had a lot more idea about how computers work because they knew that I was mucking around with computers and they were interested in finding out how computers might be able to help phone-sex work. Well, we came up with some dreams and some fantasies.

LYNN: Like what?

SANDY: Well we designed a hypothetical phone-sex robot that would go online and do phone sex. It would be very cheap. You know, a typical thing about a robot is it was cheap to own and cheap to operate, and collected the money just as fast as the live phone-sex workers did, so the live phone-sex workers could relax and rest, and program their robot, like Mickey Mouse with the broom in *The Sorcerer's Apprentice.* And then it occurred to us all simultaneously, we were sitting around a table with a bottle of Jack Daniels talking about this, and it occurred to us at the same moment that it was so simple that the odds were that someone was already doing it, and we would have no way to know.

That may sound strange, that you might not know, but I've been online with virtual agents, with computer programs that are written for the purpose of acting like a human being within a limited frame, and I've been fooled by them, and I study them. So I'm aware that they can get to be pretty good. This happened to me most recently about three weeks ago. I logged on to a conference on gender change, and we were talking, and when you log on to a new conference and people don't know you, frequently they say, "Hi, I'm so-and-so." I was logged on under the name of Mara at the time, so people said, "Hi Mara, I'm so-and-so," and I said, "Hi" back, and then I started a conversation with one of these people. We talked for maybe three or four minutes about little things. Then I said something and the other person said, "I don't understand that, please type 'HELP' for information," and I said, "What?" And it said "I don't understand that, please type 'HELP' for information," and I realized I was talking to an agent, a "bot." They're called "bots" in the network. I had totally missed it.

LYNN: When you were thinking about the robot for the phone-sex office, did you have a gender in mind? Did most people call and want to talk to women?

SANDY: Originally when I was doing the study, which was actually not that many years ago, most phone-sex was done between heterosexual women and heterosexual men. Most of the heterosexual men, incidentally, were in the Bible Belt, and they called by 800 or 900 numbers to reach these phone-sex workers who could be anywhere in the country. In fact, this group I was studying was in California. Now it's quite different, particularly in a cosmopolitan city like San Francisco or New York, which are the largest phone-sex areas. There are phone-sex workers for all possible persuasions; there are probably even phone-sex workers for transspecies people. We have transgender, and we have transspecies now too. But there are women for women, there are women for men, men for men, men for women, and other configurations as well.

LYNN: Has there been any experience where somebody wanted to meet the fantasy that they were developing?

SANDY: Well, phone-sex workers do that at their own discretion, but usually it's impossible because the person is anonymous or far away. In virtual reality, desire is constructed in exactly the same way, through data compression, tokenization, and then some sort of adding water and expanding. People get very elaborate, well worked-out ideas of what the other person is like. They do that either because the other person sends them specific information which may or may not have anything to do with what they actually look like, or they do it because they imagine that they know [what the other person looks like]. There's a tremendous desire on people's parts to know what the other person looks like, what their life is like. After a while in these social interactions you see this drive to flesh-out the image, to flesh-out what the person looks like, to find out things about what they do in their daily life, and in that sense to construct an imaginary face-to-face interaction as if the person were actually there.

Now, every once in a while people will agree to meet in real life, and sometimes this is a total disaster. They meet, they take one look, they say, "Oh my god!" and they try to drag themselves back into the virtual environment again. Some people succeed in reestablishing the virtual connection with their body representative in the virtual space and go along with that relationship. Some people are never able to do it again. Some people may, they may not know this, but they may make friends again. They may log back under another persona and then they make friends with another persona who turns out to be the same person.

LYNN: What we've experienced through our cultural conditioning seems to be what we want our personal fantasy to be. That can be a very dangerous thing.

SANDY: Yes. It's amazing how often you found that people wound up looking like what you wanted them to look like.

LYNN: Is there a stereotypical way that people want the fantasy to look?

SANDY: There is in phone sex, but there isn't in the virtual communities. That has to do with the different demographics. In the virtual communities more of the people who have access tend to be young, they tend to be computer literate, they tend to be more educated than the average, and they tend to have a certain liberated view. This is not true nationally but it is certainly true in the metropolitan areas; they tend to have a more liberated view of how people should look so there is a wider range of expectations. But in phone sex, if you're not

5 feet 2 inches tall, have red hair, and wear spike heels, you're definitely outside of the norm. So every woman is 5 feet 2 inches, has red hair and spike heels. Now I say "every," I'm exaggerating. There's certainly a spectrum and there's room for choice. I increasingly [notice that] people experiment more in terms of their preference. But a few years ago, if you did phone sex, the odds that you had red hair in your virtual persona were very high.

LYNN: Do you think that virtual relationships are more real than real relationships?

SANDY: The interactions in the virtual space are frequently seen as more real than real. That has to do with the fact that a lot of those people, a lot of the men in particular, who are on the networks are very socially inept. Not all, certainly, but a fair percentage are quite socially inept, and that was why, as it turns out, they got into the line of work in the first place. One of the serious problems that we have in dealing with getting more women into computers and into the fields of engineering, is that there is resistance because there are a lot of men that went there because it was a safe space where there wouldn't be very many women.

LYNN: So building relationships is much safer in a virtual world, more controlled.

SANDY: [That's true] for a lot of reasons. It's safer to make a friendship in a virtual world because when you get nervous you can log off and it's over, and if you're terminally nervous, if you've committed some gaffe which is utterly impossible to recover from, you can log on with a different persona. Then you can befriend that person again, all over again, so you get the opportunity to rehearse social interactions over and over again. You would think that would make people more adept at social interaction off the network, but in fact it doesn't. It doesn't seem to make them any more comfortable in face-to-face interaction.

LYNN: Does this make one less likely to go out in real life?

SANDY: I don't think it does, I don't see that. What I see happening in the Nexus is that it is a wonderful opportunity for new kinds of social interactions for people who have healthy social interactions anyway. It's [also] an opportunity for social interaction that people who are extremely shy or socially maladjusted may never have a chance to do in any other way. So for them it's a positive opportunity, and if they never do any better with social skills off the network, so what, they might never have had those interactions anyway. So this is a real opportunity for them.

LYNN: What is the future of virtual life?

SANDY: Well the sky is the limit with regard to what is going to happen with virtual interaction. In the first place, the networks by which virtual interaction becomes possible are increasing, they're growing at the rate of, depending on who you talk to, either 15 percent or 25 percent a month. Now that rate of growth cannot be sustained indefinitely. Ultimately, we'll be hip-deep in wires, so eventually we reach a saturation point where we've got enough. Everybody in the damn world who has sufficiently high income and who has sufficient access to technology and sufficient desire will be able to get online and participate in one of these virtual communities.

As is currently the case on a somewhat more limited scale, people will be able to have any kind of interaction they can think of. As with the multiple-user domains, they can create rooms for themselves, populate the rooms with furniture, with pictures on the walls, all in the virtual space. They can invite other people in. The other people see the same environment, and they can examine the objects down to whatever detail those objects are assigned attributes. It becomes a very elaborated, textured alternative universe. So there will be a lot of opportunity for alternative world-building; there will be opportunity for new social interactions in those spaces.

What I see now is that people do develop an elaborate social life in the imaginary space; they develop elaborate multiple personalities, all of which are grounded in a single body: theirs. They learn how to manipulate those personalities—take them out of the box, dust them, run them, put them back in the box, put them away, take out another one. It's a much more elaborated, ramified version of what we do every day in our social interactions; you're not the same person when you talk to the milkman that you are when you talk to your lover, unless the milkman happens to be your lover. That's a minor sort of thing that happens on the networks, where people have very carefully worked-out personalities, and that's another sort of opportunity.

Now what does that do for the physical body, does it help the person ultimately who lives in the physical body? We have to live in a physical body, so we live in a society in which power works the physical body, we can't get away from that. Politics works through physical bodies, and everything that we do in our daily lives works through a physical body. Does this enhance that? Not yet. Will it enhance it in the future? Maybe, if people can figure out how to make those connections, if people can figure out how to take the things that they learned in the virtual community and with virtual systems and take that out of there; drag it out of the virtual space into face-to-face daily life, grounded in a biological body that gets sick, that gets AIDS, that dies, that gets hit by cars, that makes love, that ultimately, if you're a women, is the body that reproduces, that produces the new life; all of those things are grounded, they have to be grounded in a physical body so far. So it all ultimately comes back to the physical body and how the things that we see happening, these endless ramifications of virtual communities, come back to help, to assist, to increase the potential of, or to make better the physical body.

That's the question, we don't know yet. But we can hope, and we can try to move people gently, we can nudge people toward the idea that ultimately you have to come out of cyberspace, and you have to eat, and you have to perform other bodily functions, and you have to do other things that you can't do yet in the virtual communities. And in that fact, the fact that you have to come out, lies the whole hope of the thing, that we can take those things and use them here, in this body, to make the world a better place.

LYNN: Was this developed through the war or military industry?

SANDY: A lot of the developments of these technologies are based on the technological advances that were designed originally for the military, and they still are. One of the things that the people who are developing virtual reality systems are becoming aware of is that there is very little money for this except for the military. In the very early days of paleotechnology, the very early days of the development of virtual communities and virtual systems, like four years ago, a lot of people believed that there was going to be funding available for something, and it was clearly so socially oriented that there would be funding available from private sources, that markets would develop in the private sector, that it would be a socially based technology. That has not turned out to be the case. The military is providing most of the funding for the development of virtual systems of all kinds.

A lot of the people who went into the business to develop new techniques and new technologies are very surprised and disheartened by the fact that there hasn't been very much private money developing. They've had to scale back their ideas about what they were doing, and they've had to get rid of some of the people that they had on board, in particular, a lot of the artists. The M.I.T. Media Lab had to get rid of a lot of its artists, the Hit Lab had to get rid of a lot of its artists—people who they felt would do visionary sorts of things with these new technologies. All of those things are closing down and getting narrower. That's partly because we're in a worldwide recession; it's partly because applications for virtual technologies that would bring in bucks have not yet developed. The best application that anybody has come up with so far for a virtual installation is *Virtuality,* which is an arcade game. They have a program called *Pectal Destroyer,* where you can go in and do bang-bang, shoot 'em up, you shoot at other people and eventually, if you don't kill the other person, a big green pterodactyl comes down out of the sky, picks you up, and carries you away. This is the height of technology, the flower of scientific achievement. After years of advancement through the mud and the slime, we have reached the pinnacle of our achievement, and it is a green pterodactyl, and it comes down and carries you away.

Rethinking Identity Through Virtual Community

Sherry Turkle

In online communities known as MUDs or multi-user domains, participants log in from all over the world, each at his or her individual machine, and join communities that exist only through the computer. These are social virtual realities. Participants find themselves in the same "space." They can communicate with each other, talk and meet either in large groups or privately.[1]

You join a MUD through a telnet command to your home computer. When you start, you create a character or several characters. You specify their genders and other physical and psychological attributes. Other participants or "players" can see this description. It becomes your character's self-presentation. On MUDs, created characters need not be human, and there are more than two genders. Beyond this, participants are invited to help build the computer world itself. Using a relatively simple programming language, they can make a "room" in the game space where they are able to set the stage and define the rules. That is, they make objects in the computer world and specify how they work. An 11-year-old player builds a room she calls "the condo." It is beautifully furnished; she has created magical jewelry and makeup for her dressing table. When she visits the condo, she invites her friends, she chats, orders pizza, and flirts. Other participants have more varied social lives. They create characters who have casual and romantic sex, hold jobs, attend rituals and celebrations, fall in love and get married. To say the least, such goings-on are gripping: "This is more real than my real life," says a character who turns out to be a man playing a woman who is pretending to be a man. In MUDs, identity is socially and linguistically constructed.

MUDs are a new genre of collaborative writing, with things in common with performance art, street theater, improvisational theater, Commedia dell'Arte, and script writing. But participants in MUDs become authors not only of text but of themselves. One player says: "You are the character and you are not the character, both at the same time." Another adds: "You are who you pretend to be."

> You can be whoever you want to be. You can completely redefine yourself if you want. You can be the opposite sex. You can be more talkative. You can be less talkative. Whatever. You can just be whoever you want really, whoever you have the capacity to be. You don't have to worry about the slots other people put you in as much. It's easier to change the way people perceive you, because all they've got is what you show them. They don't look at your body and make assumptions. They don't hear your accent and make assumptions. All they see is your words. And MUDs are always there. 24 hours a day you can walk down to the street corner, and there's gonna be a few people there who are interesting to talk to, if you've found the right MUD for you.

In this way, the games provide unparalleled opportunities to play with one's identity and to "try out" new ones. On the screen, the obese can be slender, the beautiful can be plain. The nerdy can be elegant. The anonymity of MUDs (you are known only by the names you gave your characters) provides ample room for individuals to express unexplored "aspects of the self."

Many participants in MUDs work with computers all day at their "regular" jobs. As they play on MUDs, they will periodically put their characters to "sleep," remain logged on to the game, but pursue other activities. From time to time, they return to the game space. In this way, they break up their workdays and experience their lives as a "cycling through" between the real world (known in the parlance of the Internet as real life or "RL") and a series of simulated ones.

This kind of interaction with virtual communities is made possible by the existence of what have come to be called "windows" in modern computing environments. Windows are a way of working with a computer that makes it possible for the machine to place you in several contexts at the same time. As a user, you are attentive to only one of the windows on your screen at any given moment, but in a certain sense, you are a presence in all of them at all times.

The development of the windows metaphor for computer interfaces was a technical innovation motivated by the desire to get people working more efficiently by "cycling through" different applications, but in practice, windows have become a potent metaphor for thinking about the self as a multiple, distributed, "time-sharing" system. The self is no longer simply playing different roles in different settings, something that people experience when, for example, one wakes up as a lover, makes breakfast as a mother, and drives to work as a lawyer. The life practice of windows is of a distributed self that exists in many worlds and plays many roles at the same time. Virtual communities extend the metaphor.

Doug is a Dartmouth College junior majoring in business for whom a MUD represents one window and RL represents another. Doug plays four characters distributed across three different MUDs. One is a seductive woman. One is a macho cowboy type whose self-description stresses that he is a "Marlboros rolled in the tee shirt sleeve kind of guy." Then there is a rabbit of unspecified gender who wanders its MUD introducing people to each other, a character he calls "Carrot." Doug says, "Carrot is so low-key that people let it be around while they are having private conversations. So I think of Carrot as my passive, voyeuristic character." Doug tells me that this "Carrot" has sometimes been mistaken for a "bot," a computer program on the MUD, because its passive, facilitating presence strikes many as the kind of persona of which a robot would be capable.

Doug's fourth and final character is one that he only plays on a FurryMUD (these are MUDs, known as places of sexual experimentation, where all the characters are furry animals). "I'd rather not even talk about that character because its anonymity there is very important to me," Doug says. "Let's just say that on FurryMUDs I feel like a sexual tourist." Doug says that the windows on his computer have enhanced his ability to "turn pieces of my mind on and off."

> I split my mind. I'm getting better at it. I can see myself as being two or three or more. And I just turn on one part of my mind and then another when I go from window to window. . . . And then I'll get a real-time message [that flashes on the screen as soon as it is sent from another system user], and I guess that's RL. It's just one more window.

"RL is just one more window," he repeats, "and it's not usually my best one."

For many people, particularly of college age, "life on the screen" provides what the psychoanalyst Erik Erikson would have called a "psychosocial moratorium," a central element in how Erikson thought about identity development in adolescence. Although the term "moratorium" implies a "time out," what Erikson had in mind was not withdrawal. On the contrary, the adolescent moratorium is a time of intense interaction with people and ideas. It is a time of passionate friendships and experimentation. The moratorium is not on significant experiences but on their consequences. It is a time during which one's actions are not "counted." Freed from consequence, experimentation becomes the norm rather than a brave departure.Consequence-free experimentation facilitates the development of a personal sense of what gives life meaning that Erikson called "identity."

Erikson developed these ideas about the importance of a moratorium during the late 1950s and early 1960s. At that time, the notion corresponded to a common understanding of what "the college years" were about. Today, 30 years later, the idea of the college years as a consequence-free "time out" seems of another era. College is preprofessional, and AIDS has made consequence-free sexual experimentation an impossibility. The years associated with adolescence no longer seem a "time out." But if our culture no longer offers an adolescent moratorium, virtual communities do. It is part of what makes them seem so attractive.

Erikson's ideas about stages did not suggest rigid sequences. His stages describe what people need to achieve before they can easily move ahead to another developmental task. For example, Erikson pointed out that successful intimacy in young adulthood is difficult if one does not come to it with a sense of who one is, the challenge of adolescent identity building. In real life, however, people frequently move on with serious deficits. With incompletely resolved "stages," they simply do the best they can. They use whatever materials they have at hand to get as much as they can of what they have missed. MUDs are dramatic examples of how technology can play a role in these dramas of self-reparation. Time in cyberspace reworks the notions of vacation and moratoria because they may now exist on an always-available window. Players often talk about their real selves as a composite of their characters and talk about their MUD characters as means for working on their RL lives.

Some people, including some mental health clinicians, are tempted to think of life in cyberspace as insignificant, as escape or meaningless diversion. It is not. Our experiences there are serious play. We belittle them at our risk. We must understand the dynamics of virtual experiences both to put them to best use and to foresee who might be in danger. I have observed that those who are able to make the most of their online experiences are those who approach them in a spirit of self-reflection. Without a deep understanding of the many selves that we express in the virtual, we cannot use our experiences there to enrich the real. If we cultivate our awareness of what stands behind our screen personas, we are more likely to succeed in using virtual experience for personal transformation. I believe that increasingly, psychologists will not dismiss exploration of cyberspace as a "waste of time," but encourage patients to discuss their actions there as grist for the therapeutic mill.

For large and small organizations, social virtual realities such as MUDs hold great promise as the meeting spaces and conference centers of tomorrow. For the field of psychology, they encourage new ways of thinking about identity. Identity, after all, refers to the sameness between two qualities—in the case of MUDs, between a person and his or her persona. But in MUDs, one can be many. If identity traditionally implied oneness, MUDs imply multiplicity, heterogeneity, and fragmentation. So "playing in the MUD," playing multiple characters within one MUD or across several MUDs, is part of a larger cultural conversation about the idea of identity as a society of selves.

Through the fragmented selves presented by patients and through theories that stress the decentered subject, contemporary psychology confronts what is left out of theories of a unitary self, sometimes described in terms of a robust, executive ego. Now it must ask, What is the self when it functions as a society? What is the self when it divides its labors among its constituent "alters"? Those burdened by posttraumatic dissociative disorders suffer these questions; I suggest that inhabitants of virtual communities play with them.

Ideas about mind can become a vital cultural presence when they are carried by evocative objects-to-think-with. These objects need not be material. For example, dreams and slips of the tongue were objects-to-think-with that brought psychoanalytic ideas into everyday life. People could play with their own and others' dreams and slips. Today, people are being helped to develop ideas about identity as multiplicity by a new practice of identity as multiplicity in online life. Virtual personas are objects-to-think-with.

When people adopt an online persona, they cross a boundary into highly charged territory. Some feel an uncomfortable sense of fragmentation, some a sense of relief. Some sense the possibilities for self-discovery, even self-transformation. Serena, a 26-year-old graduate student in history, says, "When I log on to a new MUD and I create a character and know I have to start typing my description, I always feel a sense of panic. Like I could find out something I don't want to know." Arlie, a 20-year-old undergraduate, says, "I am always very self-conscious when I create a new character. Usually, I end up creating someone I wouldn't want my parents to know about. It takes me, like, three hours. But that someone is part of me." In these ways and others, many more of us are experimenting with multiplicity than ever before.

With this last comment, I am not implying that life on the screen (whether it be in the form of MUDs, bulletin boards, newsgroups, or chat rooms) is causally implicated in the dramatic increase of people who exhibit symptoms of multiple personality disorder (MPD), or that people on MUDs have MPD, or that cycling through multiple MUDs or multiple channels of Internet Relay Chat (IRC) is like having MPD. What I am saying is that the many manifestations of multiplicity in our culture, including the adoption of online personae, are contributing to a general reconsideration of traditional, unitary notions of identity. Contemporary psychology is being challenged to conceptualize healthy selves which are not unitary but which have flexible aspects to their many aspects. In this context, experiences with virtual community help us in the elaboration of these new visions of self.

The essence of this self is not unitary, nor are its parts stable entities. It is easy to cycle through its aspects, and these are themselves changing through constant communication with each other. The philosopher Daniel Dennett addresses the idea of the flexible self in his "multiple drafts" theory of consciousness. Dennett's notion of multiple drafts is analogous to the experience of several versions of a document open on a computer screen where the user is able to move between them at will. Knowledge of these drafts encourages a respect for the many different versions while it imposes a certain distance from them. What most characterizes the model of a flexible self is that the lines of communication between its various aspects are open. The open communication encourages an attitude of respect for the many within us and the many within others.

The historian and cultural theorist Donna Haraway equates a "split and contradictory self" with a "knowing self." She is optimistic about its possibilities: "The knowing self is partial in all its guises, never finished, whole, simply there and original; it is always constructed and stitched together imperfectly; and *therefore* able to join with another, to see together without claiming to be another."

To come full circle, I see MUDs and other experiences on the Internet as a context for constructions and reconstructions of identity and as a context for the deconstruction of the meaning of identity as "one." These new experiences are the cultural context that supports some beginning efforts in American psychoanalysis to reach for theories of healthy identity whose flexibility, resilience, and capacity for joy comes from having access to its many aspects of self. For example, in the writing of contemporary theorist Philip Bromberg, "good parenting" is not helping a child create a sense of a core self or unitary identity. Rather, the good parent helps the child learn how to negotiate fluid transitions between self states.

In the fall of 1995, I attended a conference at which Bromberg presented these ideas to a group of psychoanalytic colleagues. I was struck by the fact that their most common objection had much in common with the objections raised to the notion of multiple identities on the Internet. In both cases, I heard the same anxiety: What about the body which pulls us back to a sense of oneness, of authenticity, of accountability? What will happen to self-knowledge if it is recast in terms of selves-knowledge? We are all walking on untested ground. Donna Haraway has written of irony that it is "about contradictions that do not resolve into larger wholes . . . about the tension of holding incompatible things together because both or all are necessary and true." The same might be said of the Freudian contribution to contemporary psychological culture. We may be at the end of the Freudian century, but our need for a practical philosophy of self-knowledge that allows for irony, complexity, ambivalence, and multiplicity has never been greater as we struggle to make meaning from our lives on the screen.

The Future Looms

Weaving Women and Cybernetics

Sadie Plant

Ada Lovelace First Weaves Women and Cybernetics Together in the 1840s

It takes another hundred years for this association to cross its runaway threshold, and then there's no stopping them. After the war games of the 1940s, women and machines escape the simple service of man to program their own designs and organize themselves; leaking from the reciprocal isolations of home and office, they melt their networks together in the 1990s.

Cybernetics Is Always Ahead Of Itself

This convergence of woman and machine is reinforced by cyber-feminism, a perspective indebted in this text to the figures of Ada Lovelace and a few ideas from Luce Irigaray, but already running beyond anyone's work and appearing as if from elsewhere, beyond the fabrications of social security systems and patrilineal traditions with which it already collides. The matrix no longer transmits from the past: cyber-feminism is received from the future.

The computer emerges out of the history of weaving, a process often said to be the quintessence of women's work. The loom is the vanguard site of software development, and if Ada Lovelace makes an early encounter between woman and computer, the association between women and software throws back into the mythical origins of history. For Freud, weaving imitates the concealment of the womb: the Greek *hystera;* the Latin matrix. Weaving is woman's compensation for the absence of the penis, the woman of whom, as he famously insists, there is "nothing to be seen." The technique is disdained with her. Yet the development of the computer might itself be described in terms of the introduction of increasing speed, miniaturization, and complexity to the process of weaving, which threads its way to convergence in the global data webs and communication nets of the late twentieth century.

This is the virtual reality which is also the absence of the penis and its power, and already more than the void. The matrix emerges as the processes of an abstract weaving which produces, or fabricates, what man knows as "nature": his materials, the fabrics, the screens on which he projects his own identity, and behind them the abstract matter which comes from the future with cyber-feminism. The matrix makes its own appearance as the surfaces and veils on which its operations are displayed; the impossible elsewhere of cyberspace; the impossible reality of woman.

Queen of Engines

As well as his screens, and as his screens, the computer also becomes the medium of man's communication, carrying his messages like woman once again. As Charles Babbage worked on his computing machines, Ada Lovelace dispersed the codes, conveying his ideas and, as if incidentally, programming the first abstract machine. Means of communication already turning each other on.

Babbage displayed his Difference Engine to the public in 1833, and "Miss Byron, young as she was, understood its working, and saw the great beauty of the invention."[1] Ada had a passion for mathematics at an early age. She was admired and was greatly encouraged by Mary Somerville, a prominent figure in the scientific community with whom she corresponded and, in 1835, attended a series of lectures on Babbage's work at the Mechanics' Institute. Ada was fascinated by the engine and wrote many letters to Babbage imploring him to take advantage of what she considered her brilliant mind. Eventually, and quite unsolicited, she translated a paper by Menabrea on Babbage's Analytical Engine, later adding her own notes at Babbage's suggestion. Babbage was enormously impressed with the translation and, once she had made him promise to "give your mind wholly and undividedly, as a primary object that no engagement is to interfere with, to the consideration of all those matters in which I shall at times require your intellectual assistance & supervision," and not to "slur & hurry things over; or to mislay & allow confusion & mistakes to enter into documents &c,"[2] Ada began to work with him on the machine's development.

Babbage's tendency to flit between obsessions left many of his projects incomplete, but there were also more pressing technical reasons for the unfinished state in which his computing machine was abandoned for a hundred years. It is nevertheless this extraordinary time lag which inspires Bruce Sterling and William Gibson to explore an alternative story, in which Ada lives in a Victorian England already running on the software she designed. The Difference Engine uses her maiden name and takes her into a middle age she never saw: the real woman, Ada Lovelace, died in 1852 while she was still in her thirties.

> The woman brushed aside her veil, with a swift gesture of habit, and Mallory caught his first proper glimpse of her face. She was Ada Byron, the daughter of the Prime Minister. Lady Byron, the Queen of Engines.[3]

The real woman? Cyberpunk is only one confusion: Ada's letters—and indeed her scientific papers—are scattered with suspicions of her own strange relation to humanity. When one of her thwarted admirers declared: "That you are a peculiar—very peculiar—specimen of the feminine race, you are yourself aware,"[4] he could only have been confirming an opinion she already—and rather admiringly—had of herself. "I am proceeding in a track quite peculiar & my own, I believe," she wrote in 1844, and although she was always trapped and sometimes defeated by the duty to be dutiful, she was often convinced of her own immortal genius as a mathematician. Indeed, she worked with a mixture of coyness and confidence; attributes which often extended to terrible losses of self-esteem and megalomaniacal delight in her own brilliance. "That Brain of mine is something more than merely mortal; as time will show,"[5] she wrote. "Before ten years are over, the Devil's in it if I haven't sucked out some of the life blood from the mysteries of this universe, in a way that no purely mortal lips or brains could do."[6]

Ada died in opiated agony in 1852, but her dreams of immortality gave her a strange and fearless intimacy with death. It was instead the constraints of life with which she had to struggle. "I mean to do what I mean to do," she declared, defying her confinement to the familiar roles of wife, mother, and victim of countless "female disorders." By the age of 24 she had three children, of whom she later wrote: "They are to me irksome duties & nothing more."[7] One admirer called her "wayward, wandering . . . deluded." To another, she confided "not only her present distaste for the company of her children but also her growing indifference to her husband, indeed to men in general."[8] As a teenager she was being treated for hysteria (already the wayward matrix, the wandering womb, but it was not until the 1850s that the diagnosis was cancer of the womb), and when she married she was told to bid "adieu to your old companion Ada Byron with all her peculiarities, caprices, and self-seeking; determined that as A.K. you will live for others."[9] But she never did. Scorning public opinion, she nevertheless gambled, took drugs, and flirted to excess. But what she did best was computer programming—the mathematics of the unfamiliar.

Ada Lovelace immediately saw the profound significance of the Analytical Engine, and she went to great lengths to convey the remarkable extent of its capacities in her writing. Although the Analytical Engine had its own limits, it was nevertheless a machine vastly different from the Difference Engine, which can "do nothing but add; and any other processes, not excepting those of simple subtraction, multiplication and division, can be performed by it only just to that extent in which it is possible, by judicious mathematical arrangement and artifices, to reduce them to a series of additions."[10] With the Analytical Engine, however, Babbage had set out to develop a machine capable not merely of adding, but performing the "whole of arithmetic." Such an undertaking required the mechanization not merely of each mathematical operation, but the systematic bases of their functioning, and it was this imperative to transcribe the rules of the game itself which made the Analytical Engine a universal machine. Babbage was a little more modest, describing the Engine as "a machine of the most general nature,"[11] but the underlying point remains: the Analytical Engine would not merely synthesize the data provided by its operator, as the Difference Engine had done, but would incarnate what Ada Lovelace described as the very "science of operations." In her notes on Menabrea's paper, this is the point she stresses most: the Engine, she argues, is the very machinery of analysis, so that "there is no finite line of demarcation which limits the powers" or the applications of the Analytical Engine.[12]

The Difference Engine was "founded on the principle of successive orders of differences,"[13] while the "distinctive characteristic of the Analytical Engine, and that which has rendered it possible to endow mechanism with such extensive faculties as bid fair to make this engine the executive right-hand of abstract algebra, is the introduction of the principle which Jacquard devised for regulating, by means of punched cards, the most complicated patterns in the fabrication of brocaded stuffs." Indeed, Ada considered Jacquard's cards to be the crucial difference between the Difference Engine and the Analytical Engine. "We may say most aptly," she continued, "that the Analytical Engine weaves Algebraical patterns, just as the Jacquard loom weaves flowers and leaves. Here, it seems to us, resides much more of originality than the Difference Engine can be fairly entitled to claim."[14] Ada's reference to the Jacquard loom is more than a metaphor: the Analytical Engine did indeed weave "just as" the loom, operating, in a sense, as the abstracted process of weaving.

BITS OF FLUFF

Weaving has always been a vanguard of machinic development, perhaps because even in its most basic form, the process is one of complexity, always involving the weaving together of several threads into an integrated cloth. It is no coincidence that those Egyptian divinities associated with weaving are also the spirits of intelligence, since "all data recorded in the brain results from the intercrossing of sensations perceived by means of our sense organs, just as the threads are crossed in weaving."[15] Even in the China of 1000 B.C., complex designs "required that about 1,500 different warp threads be lifted in various combinations as the weaving proceeded."[16] With pedals and shuttles, the loom becomes what one historian refers to as the "most complex human engine of them all," a machine which "reduced everything to simple actions: the alternate movement of the feet worked the pedals, raising half the threads of the warp and then the other, while the hands threw the shuttle carrying the thread of the woof."[17] The weaver was integrated into the machinery, bound up with its operations and linked limb-by-limb to the processes. In the Middle Ages, and before the artificial memories of the printed page, squared paper charts were used to store the information necessary to the accurate development of the design, and the punched paper rolls and cards of the eighteenth-century French weavers developed the principles on which Jacquard based his own designs for the automated loom which revolutionized the nineteenth-century textiles industry and continues to guide its contemporary development. Jacquard's machine strung the punch cards together, finally automating the operations of the machine and requiring only a single human hand.

It was of course "bitterly opposed by workers who saw in this migration of control a piece of their bodies literally being transferred to the machine."[18] But this was already the second phase of a migration out to man- and machine-made fabrics. The introduction of manufactured cloth disrupted the marital and familiar relationships of every traditional society on which it impacted. Now "the man had to leave home to make money to buy cloth for his wife" who, moreover, "had ceased to fit the traditional picture of a wife."[19] In China it was said that if "the old loom must be discarded, then 100 other things must be discarded with it, for there are somehow no adequate substitutes."[20]

Weaving is always already entangled with the question of female identity, and all stages of its mechanization bring inevitable disruption to the familiar preindustrial scenes in which woman appears as the weaver. Certainly Freud finds a close association. "It seems," he writes, "that women have made few contributions to the discoveries and inventions in the history of civilization; there is, however, one technique which they may have invented—that of plaiting and weaving." Not content with this observation, Freud is of course characteristically "tempted to guess the unconscious motive for the achievement. Nature herself," he suggests, "would seem to have given the model which this achievement imitates by causing the growth at maturity of the pubic hair that conceals the genitals. The step that remained to be taken lay in making the threads adhere to one another, while on the body they stick into the skin and are only matted together."

This passage comes out of the blue in Freud's lecture on femininity. He even seems surprised at the thought himself: "If you reject this idea as fantastic," he adds, "and regard my belief in the influence of a lack of a penis on the configuration of femininity as an *idée fixe*, I am of course defenseless."[21] He is indeed defenseless, not least because his suggestion that weaving is women's only contribution to "the discoveries and inventions in the history of civilization" gives an incredible power to the feminine he imagines himself to be dismissing once again. For weaving is the fabric of every other discovery and invention, not the least those of Freudian analysis itself. The dream work of condensation is a process of "interweaving," as Freud explains in his analysis of the "Dream of the Botanical Monograph," a dream sufficiently complex to serve as an illustration of the intricate overdetermination in which this weaving results. "Here," he writes, "we find ourselves in a factory of thoughts" where, as in Goethe's "Weaver's Masterpiece," "one treadle stirs a thousand threads" and "over and under shoots the shuttle."[22] Yes, what a contribution to have made! Weaving has been the art and the science of software, which is perhaps less a contribution to Freud's civilization than its virtual termination. Hidden in history as the fabric of his world, weaving threads its way from squared paper to the data nets of artificial memory and machine intelligence.

Babbage owned what Ada described as "a beautiful woven portrait of Jacquard, in the fabrication of which 24,000 cards were required."[23] Woven in silk at about 1,000 threads to the inch, its incredible detail was due to the new loom's ability to store and process information at unprecedented speed and volume. When he began work on the Analytical Engine, it was Jacquard's strings of punch cards on which Babbage based his designs, introducing the possibility of repeating the cards, or what, as Ada wrote, "was technically designated backing the cards in certain groups according to certain laws. The object of this extension is to secure the possibility of bringing any particular card or set of cards into use any number of times successively in the solution of one problem."[24] This was an unprecedented simulation of memory. The cards were selected by the machine as it needed them and effectively functioned as a filing system, allowing the machine to store and draw on its own information.

The Jacquard cards made memory a possibility, so that the Analytical Engine could "possess a library of its own,"[25] but Babbage had become convinced that "nothing but teaching the Engine to foresee and then to act upon that foresight could ever lead me to the object I desired,"[26] and this had to be a library to which the machine could refer both as to its past and its future operations. The punch cards endowed the Analytical Engine with the ability to process information from the future of its own functioning, and Babbage "had devised mechanical means equivalent to memory," as well as "other means equivalent to foresight, and that the Engine itself could act on this foresight."[27]

There is more than one sense in which foresight can be ascribed to the Analytical Engine. When the imperatives of war brought Lovelace's and Babbage's work to the attentions of the Allied military machine, their impact was immense. Her software runs on his hardware to this day. In 1944, Howard Aiken developed Mark 1, what he thought was the first programmable computer, although he had really been beaten by a German civil engineer, Konrad Zuse, who had in fact built such a machine, the Z-3, in 1941. Quite remarkably, in retrospect, the Germans saw little importance in his work, and although the most advanced of his designs, the Z-11, is still in use to this day, the American computer had the greatest impact. Mark 1, or the IBM Automatic Sequence Controlled Calculator, was based on Babbage's designs and itself programmed by another woman, Captain Grace Murray Hopper, often described as the "Ada Lovelace" of Mark 1 and its successors. She wrote the first high-level language compiler, was instrumental in the development of the computer language COBOL, and even introduced the term "bug" to describe soft- or hardware glitches after she found a dead moth interrupting the smooth circuits of Mark 1. Woman as the programmer again.

Runaway Circuits

Cybernetics, the term coined by Norbert Wiener for the study of control and communication in animal and machine, was integral to these wartime computers. Governors and thermostats are basic examples of cybernetic devices which, unlike the linear operations of less complex machines, respond to their environments by looping their own information back on themselves. Postwar cybernetics was the science of this abstract procedure, a nonlinear approach to systems of every scale and variety of hard- and software which nevertheless perpetuated the modernist myth of human control and wanted only the negative feedback of controlled equilibrium. At the end of the century, cyber-feminism's man is inside, not in charge of, circuits which are not so well-behaved; runaway mutations which guide his history to its own termination. Matrix cybernetics runs with the positive feedback of the new world disorder.

The computer is always heading toward the abstract machinery of its own operations and running beyond its intended constraints. Emerging from attempts to produce or reproduce the performance of specific functions, such as addition, it leads to a machinery which can simulate the operations of any machine and also itself; abstract machines which can turn their abstract hands to anything. The Analytical Engine was not yet this advanced; as Ada Lovelace recognized, it had "no pretensions whatever to originate anything. It can do whatever we know how to order it to perform."[28] It was an abstract machine, but its autonomous abilities were confined to its processing capacities: what Babbage, with terminology from the textiles industry, calls the mill, as opposed to the store. Control is dispersed and enters the machinery, but it does not extend to the operations of the entire machine.

Not until the Turing machine is there a further shift onto the software plane so that the mill and the store begin to work together, and "programs that change themselves could be written."[29] An unprecedented dispersal of control, the Turing machine still brings control back to its master program, and it is only really after the introduction of silicon in the 1960s that the decentralized flow of control becomes an issue, eventually allowing for systems in which "control is always captured by whatever production happens to have its conditions satisfied by the current workspace contents."[30] The abstract machine begins at this point to function as a network of "independent software objects," running on horizontal lines of communication without the necessity of dominant points of reference.

This is the strange world to which Ada's programming has led: self-organizing systems, self-arousing machines; systems of control and synthetic intelligence exceeding the commands of some central authority; an unfamiliar agency which has no need of a central will and has already bypassed a subject position.

Past Caring

Human history is the self-narrating story of the drive to resist precisely this move. It pulls itself up from carnal passions to self-control in a journey from the strange fluidities of the material to the self-identification of the soul. Stealth bombers and guided missiles, telecommunications systems and orbiting satellites epitomize this flight. Matter, the womb, is merely an encumbrance; either too inert or dangerously active; woman has never been the subject, the agent of this history, the autonomous being. Not that she is left behind; carefully concealed, she nevertheless continues to function as the ground and possibility of his quests for identity, agency, and self-control. She wears "different veils according to the historic period."[31] Woman has been the natural resource for man's own cultural development. She has provided a mirror for man, his servants and accommodation, his tools and his means of communication, his spectacles and commodities, the possibility of the reproduction of his species and his world. If the repression of the matrix, the veiling of the womb, is integral to this flight, the cybernetic systems which bring the matrix into human history are equally the consequences of a drive for domination and autonomy. Still confident of his own indisputable mastery, man continues to excite and turn these systems on. In so doing he merely encourages his own destruction. Every software development is a migration of control away from man, in whom it has been exercised only as domination, and into the matrix, or cyberspace, "the broad electronic net in which virtual realities are spun."[32]

The matrix weaves itself in a future which has no place for historical man: his agency was always a figment of its loop. Like woman, software systems are used as man's tools, his media, and his weapons; all are developed in the interests of man, but all are poised to betray him. At the peak of his triumph, the culmination of his machinic erections, man confronts his systems of social security and finds them female and dangerous.

This will indeed seem a strange twist to history to those who believe that it runs in straight lines. But as Irigaray asks: "If machines, even machines of theory, can be aroused all by themselves, may woman not do likewise?"[33]

The computer is a machine which can simulate its own operations and those of any other machine; like woman, it is both the appearance and the possibility of simulation. "Truth and appearance, according to his will of the moment, his appetite of the instant." Woman cannot be anything, but she can imitate anything valued by man: intelligence, autonomy, beauty . . . perhaps the very possibility of mimesis, the one who weaves her own disguises. The veil is her oppression, but "she may still draw from it what she needs to mark the folds, seams, and dressmaking of her garments and dissimulations."[34] These mimetic abilities throw woman into a universality unknown and unknowable to the one who knows who he is: she fits any bill, but in so doing, she is already more than that which she imitates. Woman, like the computer, appears at different times as whatever man requires of her. She learns how to imitate; she learns simulation. And, like the computer, she becomes very good at it, so good, in fact, that she too, in principle, can mimic any function. As Irigaray suggests: "Truth and appearances, and reality, power . . . she is—through her inexhaustible aptitude for mimicry—the living foundation for the whole staging of the world."[35]

But if this is supposed to be her only role, she is no longer its only performer. Now that the digital comes on stream, the computer is cast in precisely the same light: it too is merely the imitation of nature, providing assistance and additional capacity for man, and more of the things in his world, but it too can do this only insofar as it is already hooked up to the very machinery of simulation. If Freud's speculations about the origins of weaving lead him to a language of compensation and flaw, its technical development results in a proliferation of pixelled screens which compensate for nothing, and, behind them, the emergence of digital spaces and global networks which are even now weaving themselves together with flawless precision.

Software, in other words, has its screens as well: it too has a user-friendly face it turns to man, and for it, as for woman, this is only its camouflage.

The screen is the face it began to present in the late 1960s, when the TV screen was incorporated in its design. It appears as the spectacle, the visual display of that which can be seen, and also functions as the interface, the messenger; like Irigaray's woman, it is both displayed for man and becomes the possibility of his communication. It too operates as the typewriter, the calculator, the decoder, displaying itself on the screen as an instrument in the service of man. These, however, are merely imitations of some existing function; and indeed, it is always as machinery for the reproduction of the same that both women and information technology first sell themselves. Even in 1968, McLuhan argued that "the dense information environment created by the computer is at present still concealed from it by a complex screen or mosaic quilt of antiquated activities that are now advertised as the new field for the computer."[36] While this is all that appears before man, those who travel in the information flows are moving far beyond the screens and into data streams beyond his conceptions of reality. On this other side run all the fluid energies denied by the patrilineal demand for the reproduction of the same. Even when the computer appears in this guise and simulates this function, it is always the site of replication, an engine for making difference. The same is merely one of the things it can be.

"They go beyond all simulation," writes Irigaray of women.[37] Perhaps it was always the crack, the slit, which marked them out, but what they have missed is not the identity of the masculine but their own connection to the virtual, the repressed dynamic of matter. Misogyny and technophobia are equally displays of man's fear of the matrix, the virtual machinery which subtends his world and lies on the other side of every patriarchal culture's veils. At the end of the twentieth century, women are no longer the only reminder of this other side. Nor are they containable as child-bearers, fit for only one thing. No longer the adding machines, they are past caring; with the computer, as abstract machine, there is nothing they cannot do.

The computer was always a simulation of weaving; threads of ones and zeros riding the carpets and simulating silk screens in the perpetual motions of cyberspace. It too presents the screens, the clothing of the matrix, already displaying the virtual machinery of which nature and culture are the subprograms, and joins women on and as the interface between man and matter, identity and difference, the actual and the virtual. Cybernetic systems are fatal to his culture; they invade as a return of the repressed, but what returns is no longer the same: cybernetics transforms woman and nature, but they do not return from man's past, as his origins. Instead they come wheeling around from his future, the virtual system to which he has always been heading. For the last 50 years, as his war machine has begun to gain intelligence in readiness for his last stand, women and computers have unleashed a proliferation of screens, intelligences, lines of communication, media, and simulations with which to hack it down. No longer the void, the gap, or the absence, the veils are already cybernetic; an interface taking off into its own unmanned futures.

Ada refused to publish her commentaries on Menabrea's papers for what appear to have been spurious confusions around publishing contracts. In translating Menabrea's work from French, she nevertheless provided footnotes more detailed and substantial—three times as long, in fact—than the text itself and became the world's first computer programmer.

Footnotes have often been the marginal zones occupied by

women writers. Translation, transcription, and elaboration: outside the body of the text, women have nevertheless woven their influence between the lines. While Ada's writing was presented in this form and signed simply "A.A.L.," hers was the name which survived her death: in recognition of her work, the United States Defense Department named its primary programming language ADA, and today her name shouts from the spines of a thousand manuals. Neither her married nor her maiden name: it is Ada herself who lives on, in her own name, her footnotes secreted in the software of the military machine.

Organizing Random Chance

Christian Möller

The concept underlying the most extensive of our current research projects is based on the simple idea that it is much simpler to distinguish the right from the wrong than to do the right thing in the first place.

Needless to say, a reviewer of architecture can judge the quality of a piece of architecture even if (frequently to the annoyance of the creator) he or she will never be in a position to come up with anything like such an outstanding solution himself. However, the stance taken by some colleagues in the world of architecture, namely that only those who have a track record in practical work should be allowed to take part in the ongoing debates, is both vain and ill conceived.

It is ill conceived because in the process of finding the right approach to an architectural task, a procedure involving a careful choice from among possible variants is most likely to function best. The method we have adopted hitherto at the beginning of a project can roughly be described as follows: a staff member tackles the project with a still relatively open mind, attempting in the shortest possible time to come up with a series of sketches and mass models for concepts that are as widely different as possible. We then proceed more or less the way the above-mentioned critics do, selecting the approach that promises to be successful and then developing it further.

Alongside the great effort and concentration involved in finding a three-dimensional shape for a quite complex spatial agenda, experience has repeatedly shown how difficult it is for the staffer to devise further variants once he or she has made the first implementable solution. This countercreative version of love at first sight, namely a preference for the first best, is, however, conditioned simply by human lethargy, something that stems from a lack of concentration.

If we assume that the greatness of creativity can be measured as speed, namely the speed with which you switch back and forth from concentrating on the details of a problem to the distance afforded by the bird's-eye view of things in order to judge the whole, then we soon see how the frictional losses incurred during constant zooming in and out unsettle even the most talented minds. At the end of the day, it becomes ever more difficult to reach a decision and, in a worst-case scenario, deadlines, paper sizes, or even the limited length of the ruler's edge become the main aids in decision making.

The Consistent Design Approach

Another highly human inadequacy when creating possible architectural solutions stems from our inability to portray something that is *consistently right.* Architects start at far too early a stage to arrange things formally, to compress spaces in straitjackets, or to establish relations between edges and a building's axes that have absolutely nothing to do with each other over and above the two-dimensional norm for presenting ground plans currently in vogue. What may look decidedly correct in a professionally presented illustration of a ground plan should immediately be a cause of suspicion for an experienced architect. How nice it would be if the task at hand were to be presented in terms of the spatial necessities in the form of an unbeautified (undesigned), functionally correct, three-dimensional sculpture, before we then started trying to improve on it. The simple geometric shape of a modern building that consists merely of a right-angled cube may indeed be a highly formalistic solution, but it can never be consistently right in the sense of logically compelling with reference to complex spatial agenda.

We know from many years of using computer technology and electronic media that in the architectural office software constraints mean that existing computer hardware cannot be utilized efficiently or exhaustively. Whereas a graphics workstation waits idly for a line to be drawn from Point A to Point B, the planner doing the drawing is actually putting a lot of effort into thinking what step he is going to take next. In other words, the planner is working full tilt, whereas only a fraction of the processor potential is being tapped. Manually drawing and modeling with the assistance of a computer by means of CAD (computer-assisted design) programs is a relatively unthinking one-to-one transfer of work with a pencil, scissors, and paste onto a relatively uneventful monitor-and-mouse environment in the name of greater efficiency in the one-after-next phase of planning.

Aware of this problem, we searched for a system that, free of all human brilliance and owing to the highly reduced complexity of its artificial thought, would be able to generate both a consistent solution and the intrinsic wealth of variants implied by the respective task. And it also had to be a system which made as optimal as possible use of the exceptionally powerful processors of modern graphics workstations.

Automatic Generation of a Functionally Correct Design Approach Using Genetic Algorithms and Evolution Strategies

Like a glass cover for a cheese board, we start out by defining a box-like world, a bounding box. The parameters necessary in this context are laid down by the measurements and geometry of the real estate, possible maximum height of the building to be constructed, and the direction in which it faces. A stream of spatial units (molecules) that results from the task's specifications (spatial agenda) flows into this predefined, invisible world. When transferring this spatial agenda onto the computer system, these smallest spatial units are allocated a genetic entry corresponding to their respective functions. Depending on the use, the spatial units are given different characteristics. A degree of relatedness to another functional area means that the spatial unit in question must be placed in the proximity of the other related units. One side surface of the volume of many of the spatial units, for example, has to be flush with the outside space, that is, potentially constitute part of the facade. Others have to be part of seamless series of links (for example, porch, entrance, foyer, reception area). An overall spatial unit (population) generated in this manner can then be tested and assessed in terms of quality (fitness). If a space is not able to take its genetically prescribed spatial place, that is, next to related spaces within the population, then the overall result is unsustainable. If the system has, however, found a population that has scored sufficiently well in terms of the internal fitness function, then it appears on the screen as a possible solution in the form of a three-dimensional mass model. From now on, the user of the system can influence the evolution of the model. The user can individually and formally assess the mass model proposed by the system and then take the solutions that appear most architecturally interesting and

1.

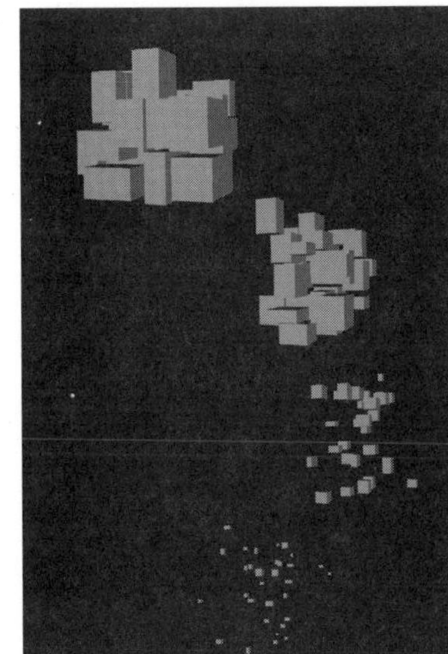

FIG. 1. STAGES OF EVOLUTION Four different stages during the spatial self-organization of the functional agenda into a mass model.

2.

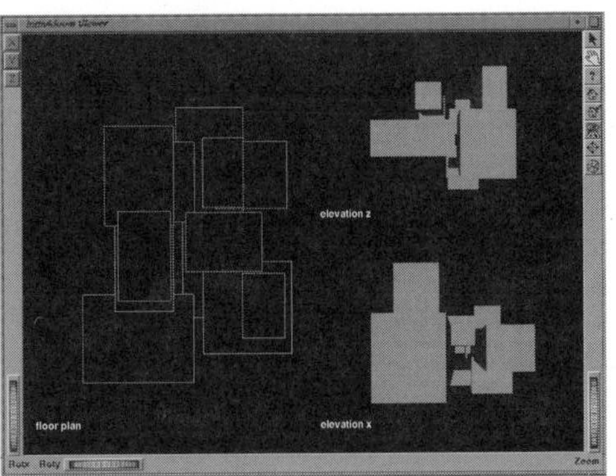

3.

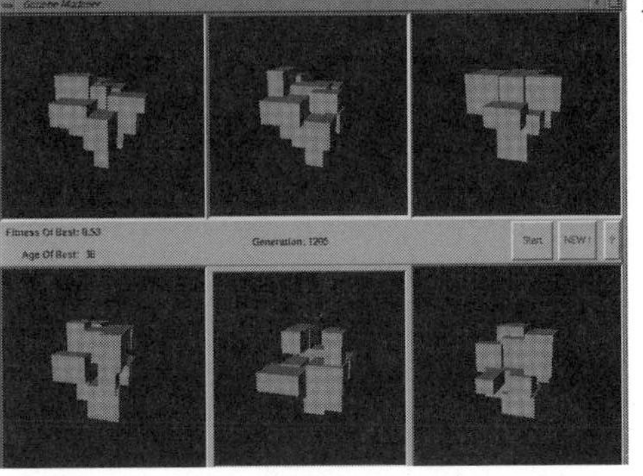

FIG. 2. INDIVIDUUM VIEWER Provides a formal assessment of the mass models proposed by the system.

FIG. 3. GENETIC MODELER Shows the fittest individuums of six populations in the obtained stage of evolution.

transpose their geometrical similarities onto the next generation of solution variants. Various mass models, parts of which have been assessed as good, can now interbreed. This process of mutation, controlled by the user, can be applied to any number of generations until a basic concept is found which is then advanced further by conventional means.

The wealth of versions of possible solutions spawned in this manner provides the user with a highly objective indicator of the quality of the approach to the task we are taking. Approaches to a task and spatial agendas are not always realistic in an era shaped by complete economic functionalism in the construction sector and the unreflective wish of developers to maximize profits. In fact, at times they are untenable, but they are just as important for the success of a good building as are the architect's talent and tenacity.

WINDOW DRESSING

Mette Strømfeldt

In the department at the University of Copenhagen where I work, everybody was recently given a book on the Internet.[1] The book has a digitally manipulated decoration on the cover and back in Denmark I really didn't pay much attention to it, nor to the book itself. I browsed through it but for the most part it's just been lying on my desk—sometimes with the cover in full view, sometimes hidden in one of numerous stacks. Inadvertently, I think, I registered the image as being nonfigurative. To some extent, I guess, you could say it resembles one of those diagrams you're confronted with in a test for colorblindness, but since I'm not colorblind this doesn't explain why I didn't perceive the dots figured a body until I found myself in another location, unpacking and placing the book on a desk in San Francisco.

Is the light different here, I wonder? Or is it something else that renders another perspective? Whatever it is, this newly gained focus revealed a woman's naked body. The framing cuts off her head and parts of her legs and arms, and the remaining torso seems either to be reclining, settling into the picture, or about to get up, perhaps leaving it altogether. This now-you-see-her-now-you-don't woman—for obvious reasons I don't know her real name[2]—has been on my mind ever since I arrived here. Sometimes I kid myself that she is only visible over here but the truth is, of course, that from now on it will be impossible for me not to see her whenever I look at the book. If in Denmark the cover didn't seem to depict anything in particular, I have forever lost this impression of it that solely laid bare the means of reproduction, the construction of the image. Time will tell if I'll manage to develop a dual perspective upon returning to Denmark and my journey is completed but, for now, let me suggest a provisional reading of this anecdote.

It will be a while before the image of a woman's body, or any body for that matter, will be able to upstage the digital composition of the image itself in Denmark. What seems to be vital at the moment—and in that place—are issues that adhere to access. A battle is being fought, and although it would be somewhat ridiculous to imagine

Danes attempting to conquer anything nowadays, the Danish government and Parliament are trying to ensure that we at least gain a foothold in cyberspace.

With regard to internal affairs it's publicly debated how citizens can be provided with access to government records on their person and other files concerning domestic matters in a more democratic way. This access is made possible by the new technologies; at the same time, issues arise about how confidentiality and privacy can be secured and social surveillance avoided—other offspring of the very same technology.

Programs have been launched by the Ministry of Education and the Ministry of Research to counter computer illiteracy and to avoid lost generations. The use of nets and webs is promoted primarily by making the necessary hardware and software available at all levels of education—and needless to say this is accompanied by the distribution of printed matter like the above-mentioned book. The idea, of course, is that the one and sometimes only Danish scholar or researcher working within a specific field or discipline is given the means to go international instantaneously, to join fora that will broaden the scope of her research and benefit it in many ways. Compared to the costs of sending a real live person halfway across the world, the Internet requires only fairly inexpensive procedures. Naturally this relative ease of access has been used as an argument in defending the expenses of the ongoing installments of equipment.

The utopia of a multicultural space with no center or hierarchy that allows for the visibility of even a Danish voice is also cultivated, as is the promise of a cyber-culture with truly interactive spaces that explore and push the inside of the envelope of this new medium. So much is out there, rumor has it, and any country that doesn't want to become a third-world country in the cyber-age had better get in there and start partaking in the new culture and the construction of it.

To give an accurate description of the stationary nomad's life in Denmark would demand a proper investigation, and what follows amounts to nothing more than a few lines on my impression of what is going on.

First of all—and as always, I might add—those who were already well-connected have become even more so with the advent of the Internet. E-mail is being used on a large scale to relay messages all over the world, and the speed and ease with which this is done is an advantage everybody acknowledges. It's inexpensive, it's fast, and you don't have to worry about time differences. By the same token people are accessing libraries and other sources of information in order to locate whatever they need, wherever it is.

Now, there's absolutely nothing even remotely cutting edge about this use of the Internet. E-mail is being applied as an advanced telephone, fax, or telex, if you like, and contacting libraries abroad has been a service provided for years by many local libraries. The main difference is that you can stay in your room, or your office, and do these things. If people spend a lot of time in their offices these days, though, it's still not a sure thing that they've become follow-ons to a digital caravan. In fact, they might not be doing anything but waiting for the secretary to finally solve the mystery that got them stuck in word processing a while back. In most cases, the capacity of our computers remains as unexplored as the capacity of the brain.

In the Net surfers that do exist in Denmark you detect a weariness and a disappointment following a revelation not unlike the one related in "The Emperor's New Clothes."[3] To many, access to World Wide Web, for instance, was thought to lead the way to sophisticated interactive computer design in our country. "The state of things right now," a datalinguist told me once upon a time, "leaves a lot to be desired. Sure, you can visit the Zoological Museum and click on some 'installation' and get to see a photo of two seals procreating, but that's about as far as it goes." It still is, I'm afraid, and surfing the Net did not turn out to be that much of an inspiration. Words, words, and more words are thrown from site to site, and hyping the medium is primarily equivalent to establishing user friendly environments. Facile solutions have become the end product of the power of simplicity. To those of us who imagined creative interactions bringing into play the correspondence between word and pictures, or layouts working like a new kind of book that opened many ways, or different kinds of videos that would twist and turn upon themselves, this is simply disappointing. The attempts to make things as easy as they are fast gloss over the challenges digital correspondence proposes. The challenge at the moment is to see things that are nowhere in site.

Another thing I find worth mentioning is that the accent of the chatting carried out, and away, on the Net is in many people's opinion unmistakably American. Try to point out the variety of nationalities that are engaged in the many lists and chat and discussion groups, and you will be told that it really doesn't make that much of a difference because everybody sounds the same. I'm not referring to an eloquent use of emoticons, I'm addressing the predominance of a new discourse with its origin in the English American language. It may be too early to attempt an analysis of this received pronunciation but soon it might be too late to retrieve the otherness it's in the process of eliminating.

The Emperor was told that his new clothes would be visible only to those who were wise or intelligent enough to see them. The ignorant wouldn't see a thing. Having been told this beforehand it's hardly surprising that the Emperor not only saw but was able to comment on the very texture, every fold, the slightest crease in the fabrics displayed. In fact, it turned out that the whole court saw it as he did, and it was decided that when the outfit was created, the Emperor was to parade his new clothes/knowledge in the streets of the Empire for all his subjects to see. It is there, in the streets, that the imperial parade is turned upside down, and the event begins to resemble a carnival. The Emperor becomes the subject of ridicule when a child's voice is heard remarking that he is undressed—that the Emperor is wearing his birthday suit, his body. In H.C. Andersen's story the child holds a privileged position, and it is meaningless to discuss the presence or absence of intelligence or wisdom. Consequently what is uttered from this position, or place, is capable of disrobing the Emperor and disclosing the sham.

There's a paradox here: the innocent child makes an observation similar to the one made by Adam and Eve when their eyes were opened. Clearly this child has already nibbled on some kind of fruit of knowledge and is wise to it. This does not make the story less interesting or weaker, because in the main it is the child's uninhibited outburst, the saying aloud what everybody is thinking, that exposes the hypocrisy initiated by the Emperor and prevents it from being propagated to an entire population. It is, however, something to bear in mind when I try to make my way back to the naked body on the cover of the handbook on the Internet and begin to wonder why I had to arrive in San Francisco before I could see it.

I was under the impression that as a mobile nomad in San Francisco I would venture into the very heart of digital matters. My naïveté is made blatantly clear by the fact that I thought cyberspace had a heart or a center—but San Francisco *is* referred to as the capitol of the byte generation and, at any rate, I would be closer to Silicon Valley.[4] I didn't even find it necessary to bring my modem, thinking I could get hooked up at practically every street corner. Well, I'm here to tell you I can't unless I'll settle for chats with people in other cafés, only blocks away, which I won't. I've tried most computer centers, and none of them will let me hook up to my mailbox at home, not because it can't be done but because they don't know what to charge me. I've already traveled with my digital mailbox in other countries, and to be able to be at once mobile and stationary is not an insignificant contribution of the new culture. If I bought a modem this problem would be easily solved but the point I'm trying to make is that access is further away here than it was in Denmark—for the woman in the street, that is.[5]

The place where cyberspace is most visible is in the storytelling spun and circulated by the mass media. It seems all sorts of criminal weirdos make life difficult for cops and lawyers by surfing and escaping on the Net.[6] In turn these stories are interrupted by commercials selling the new frontier, the promises of America Online. Still, this doesn't explain why I first noticed the body on the cover in San Francisco. I'm not sure the following will either.

When I move around in San Francisco I'm constantly struck by the way this city is constructed around and in relation to sexual difference. The body and what people do to it and with it in terms of gender—and all that comes with that—is topographically laid out in this place. To the foreigner the map of San Francisco can easily dissolve into a gigantic circuit board fleshing out the alternative communities one is familiar with from cyberspace. To call this an uncanny experience would be an exaggeration because no reflection upon the digital transition complicates a one-to-one reading of the physical and the digital spaces. Or, put in another way, what is predominant in both places is an exploration of a thematics that hinges on a notion of the body, the same body Eve and Adam first saw when they took a bite of the forbidden fruit. To be sure, the byte of the apple of our times hasn't been fully digested, and the performance of digital transvestitism will neither be hyperbolic, nor an understatement, as long as it doesn't involve an interrogation of the new medium as well.[7]

If alternative practices have and are still trying to rid especially woman's body of the special status it holds within representation, it is obvious that this body is not only the point of departure in both places but that these practices depend on it in order to be alternative. Thus, because it is continually impregnated with meaning in the negative, alternative communities developed around the fact that its members are not this body—which means they need it or else they would not be because their identity is a contrastive construct. Therefore, they reconstruct the image they supposedly strive to disrupt over and over again.

I see the image of the woman on the cover then not as a revelation, the removal of a digital veil. On the contrary, what I see is the birthday suit, and this striptease only removes me further from the composition of the image and the necessary insight into the construction of it that is vital if I want to get beyond it and don't want to settle for shopping for gender—be it in San Francisco or in cyberspace.

The fact that the naked body of a woman ends up on the cover on a book on the Internet[8] in Denmark could be interpreted to mean that we're a hopelessly throwback civilization that hasn't reached the level of political interrogation pertaining to gender at stake in San Francisco. The truth, however, is that the utopian aspects of many subversive practices here are already a part of our everyday life. This does not mean to say I live in the fairy-tale country Jill Johnston depicts in "Wedding in Denmark."[9]

Jill Johnston was married to her Danish girlfriend, Ingrid Nyeboe, in Odense. Following the official wedding ceremony at City Hall, Geoff Hendricks administered a *Fluxprocession* to Kunsthallen Brandts Klædefabrik where a reception/performance took place. Jill Johnston is clearly impressed by the family's performance and describes how she insisted that it be depicted alongside the performance by the "art family" in the video about the event because of the Danish family scenario's political implications.[10] This is how Johnston ends her story:

> If you don't think Denmark is the best country in the world, imagine finding anywhere else a social democratic queendom where the streets are clean, the houses are cozy, the business, trains and ferries are always on time, the social welfare laws are so deeply assimilated that they've become habits of mind, and everything is arranged to the convenience of all the people.[11]

I feel like adding, "and they lived happily ever after," but remind myself that, although I sincerely hope Jill Johnston and Ingrid Nyeboe will, a vast number of Danes don't. Statistics say we have the highest percentage of suicides per citizens in the world. Our little queendom evidently has some serious problems that are not easily dismissed as innocent side effects since they're life-threatening.

H.C. Andersen was born in Odense and the city houses his museum. Tourists from all over the world pile into the little town house but most of them haven't read a single one of his stories in an edition that is remotely close to the original Danish text. It's only recently that we've begun to get translations that stem from close readings but it will take some time, I guess, before they'll displace the almost expurgated editions. When they do, they'll reveal to the world the darker aspects of H.C. Andersen's storytelling, and how these tales did or did not have anything to do with his troubled relationship to the body, sex, and gender in private life is yet another story.

In many ways Jill Johnston's text reads like an expurgated fairy tale. Conveniently enough, though, this enables me to exploit it for two different purposes. As a fairy tale, Johnston's account illustrates why many of the American alternative/subversive practices come across as utterly provincial to Danes. They're also very American, which should be a funny thing to highlight but isn't because Americans forget to do so all the time. By forgetting to take this into consideration, or at least to mention it once in a while, alternative communities in the United States sound as if they speak "for" the whole world in their struggle to get to speak "as a." In short, they themselves fall into the trap of the cultural imperialism they fight from within, forcing the rest of the world to make American problems their problems. But Danish problems are far from American problems—as Johnston's text also reveals by not dealing with them because she fails to see them[12]—and nonetheless relevant in a debate about revolutionary strategies precisely because they spring from a place, a queendom that is at one and the same time "the best country in the world" and still not good enough.

If it is going to make any sense to carry on debates, talks, chats in cyberspace about the body and gender—however thematic—could we at least facilitate dialogues across communities and not only spaces that insulate or monopolize it altogether? In order for this to happen, some will have to get their act together and speak up, others will have to stop and listen once in a while.

I've always been fascinated by the tailors in H.C. Andersen's tale. I've always wondered if the Emperor, his court, and members of the public really just pretended they saw something or if the tailors' fabrications, that is, their stories, were creative enough to produce hallucinations, to make people see something. In the digital world these tailors find their counterparts in the con artists that fabricate a new branch of science fiction. These imaginative tales about new technologies are at times so suggestive that people will believe the things depicted in them really exists.[13] The ability to con people into seeing/hearing things in cyberspace does not demand only artistic skills. In this particular case it has to be paired with a highly developed sensibility for the new technologies. If Susan Sontag many years ago announced the development of a new sensibility, at once artistic and scientific,[14] it is now that we can actually see and appreciate this sensibility in operation on a large scale.

On the one hand, we find the com artists who write about and in the digital mode. Their texts[15] push the limits of digital technologies and, at the same time, they produce visions of a creative digital culture that most of us are unable to imagine and consequently demand. On the other hand, we have the children, a new generation, who have toyed with digital products from before they were able to speak. This generation is also in possession of the new sensibility. Let's hope they'll be highly discriminating, not settling for the run-of-the-mill software, instead creating their own, or testing the com artists' fabrics, not afraid to tell them off. Between the two of them the future could become a darned site better.

Selling Wine Without Bottles

The Economy of Mind on the Global Net

John Perry Barlow

If nature has made any one thing less susceptible than all others of exclusive property, it is the action of the thinking power called an idea, which an individual may exclusively possess as long as he keeps it to himself; but the moment it is divulged, it forces itself into the possession of everyone, and the receiver cannot dispossess himself of it. Its peculiar character, too, is that no one possesses the less, because every other possesses the whole of it. He who receives an idea from me, receives instruction himself without lessening mine; as he who lights his taper at mine, receives light without darkening me. That ideas should freely spread from one to another over the globe, for the moral and mutual instruction of man, and improvement of his condition, seems to have been peculiarly and benevolently designed by nature, when she made them, like fire, expansible over all space, without lessening their density at any point, and like the air in which we breathe, move, and have our physical being, incapable of confinement or exclusive appropriation. Inventions then cannot, in nature, be a subject of property.

—Thomas Jefferson

Throughout the time I've been groping around cyberspace, there has remained unsolved an immense conundrum which seems to be at the root of nearly every legal, ethical, governmental, and social vexation to be found in the Virtual World. I refer to the problem of digitized property.[1]

The riddle is this: If our property can be infinitely reproduced and instantaneously distributed all over the planet without cost, without our knowledge, without its even leaving our possession, how can we protect it? How are we going to get paid for the work we do with our minds? And, if we can't get paid, what will assure the continued creation and distribution of such work?

Since we don't have a solution to what is a profoundly new kind of challenge, and are apparently unable to delay the galloping digitization of everything not obstinately physical, we are sailing into the future on a sinking ship.

This vessel, the accumulated canon of copyright and patent law, was developed to convey forms and methods of expression entirely different from the vaporous cargo it is now being asked to carry. It is leaking as much from within as without.

Legal efforts to keep the old boat floating are taking three forms: a frenzy of deck chair rearrangement, stern warnings to the passengers that if she goes down, they will face harsh criminal penalties, and serene, glassy-eyed denial.

Intellectual property law cannot be patched, retrofitted, or expanded to contain the gasses of digitized expression any more than real estate law might be revised to cover the allocation of broadcasting spectrum. (Which, in fact, rather resembles what is being attempted here.) We will need to develop an entirely new set of methods as befits this entirely new set of circumstances.

Most of the people who actually create soft property—the programmers, hackers, and Net surfers—already know this. Unfortunately, neither the companies they work for nor the lawyers these companies hire have enough direct experience with immaterial goods to understand why they are so problematic. They are proceeding as though the old laws can somehow be made to work, either by grotesque expansion or by force. They are wrong.

The source of this conundrum is as simple as its solution is complex. Digital technology is detaching information from the physical plane, where property law of all sorts has always found definition.

Throughout the history of copyrights and patents, the proprietary assertions of thinkers have been focused not on their ideas but on the expression of those ideas. The ideas themselves, as well as facts about the phenomena of the world, were considered to be the collective property of humanity. One could claim franchise, in the case of copyright, on the precise turn of phrase used to convey a particular idea or the order in which facts were presented.

The point at which this franchise was imposed was that moment when the "word became flesh" by departing the mind of its originator and entering some physical object, whether book or widget. The subsequent arrival of other commercial media besides books didn't alter the legal importance of this moment. Law protected expression and, with few (and recent) exceptions, to express was to make physical.

Protecting physical expression had the force of convenience on its side. Copyright worked well because, Gutenberg notwithstanding, it was hard to make a book. Furthermore, books froze their contents into a condition which was as challenging to alter as it was to reproduce. Counterfeiting or distributing counterfeit volumes were obvious and visible activities, easy enough to catch somebody in the act of doing. Finally, unlike unbounded words or images, books had material surfaces to which one could attach copyright notices, publishers' marques, and price tags.

Mental to physical conversion was even more central to patent. A patent, until recently, was either a description of the form into which materials were to be rendered in the service of some purpose or a description of the process by which rendition occurred. In either case, the conceptual heart of patent was the material result. If no purposeful object could be rendered due to some material limitation, the patent was rejected. Neither a Klein bottle nor a shovel made of silk could be patented. It had to be a thing and the thing had to work.

Thus the rights of invention and authorship adhered to activities in the physical world. One didn't get paid for ideas but for the ability to deliver them into reality. For all practical purposes, the value was in the conveyance and not the thought conveyed.

In other words, the bottle was protected, not the wine.

Now, as information enters cyberspace, the native home of Mind, these bottles are vanishing. With the advent of digitization, it is now possible to replace all previous information storage forms with one meta-bottle: complex—and highly liquid—patterns of ones and zeros.

Even the physical/digital bottles to which we've become accustomed—floppy disks, CD-ROMs, and other discrete, shrink-wrappable bit-packages—will disappear as all computers jack in to the global Net. While the Internet may never include every single CPU on the planet, it is more than doubling every year and can be expected to become the principal medium of information conveyance if not, eventually, the only one.

Once that has happened, all the goods of the Information Age—all of the expressions once contained in books or film strips or records or newsletters—will exist either as pure thought or something very much like thought: voltage conditions darting around the Net at the speed of light, in conditions which one might behold in effect, as glowing pixels or transmitted sounds, but never touch or claim to "own" in the old sense of the word.

Some might argue that information will still require some physical manifestation, such as its magnetic existence on the titanic hard disks of distant servers, but these are bottles which have no macroscopically discrete or personally meaningful form.

Some will also argue that we have been dealing with unbottled expression since the advent of radio, and they would be right. But for most of the history of broadcast, there was no convenient way to capture soft goods from the electromagnetic ether and reproduce them in anything like the quality available in commercial packages. Only recently has this changed, and little has been done legally or technically to address the change.

Generally, the issue of consumer payment for broadcast products was irrelevant. The consumers themselves were the product. Broadcast media were supported either by selling the attention of their audience to advertisers, using government to assess payment through taxes, or through the whining mendicancy of annual donor drives.

All of the broadcast support models are flawed. Support either by advertisers or government has almost invariably tainted the purity of the goods delivered. Besides, direct marketing is gradually killing the advertiser support model anyway.

Broadcast media gave us another payment method for a virtual product in the royalties which broadcasters pay songwriters through such music performing rights organizations as ASCAP and BMI. But, as a member of ASCAP, I can assure you this is not a model which we should emulate. The monitoring methods are wildly approximate. There is no parallel system of accounting in the revenue stream. It doesn't really work. Honest.

In any case, without our old methods of physically defining the expression of ideas, and in the absence of successful new models for nonphysical transaction, we simply don't know how to assure reliable payment for mental works. To make matters worse, this comes at a time when the human mind is replacing sunlight and mineral deposits as the principal source of new wealth.

Furthermore, the increasing difficulty of enforcing existing copyright and patent laws is already placing in peril the ultimate source of intellectual property, the free exchange of ideas.

That is, when the primary articles of commerce in a society look so much like speech as to be indistinguishable from it, and when the traditional methods of protecting their ownership have become ineffectual, attempting to fix the problem with broader and more vigorous enforcement will inevitably threaten freedom of speech.

The greatest constraint on your future liberties may come not from government but from corporate legal departments laboring to protect by force what can no longer be protected by practical efficiency or general social consent.

Furthermore, when Jefferson and his fellow creatures of the Enlightenment designed the system which became American copyright law, their primary objective was assuring the widespread distribution of thought, not profit. Profit was the fuel which would carry ideas into the libraries and minds of their new republic. Libraries would purchase books, thus rewarding the authors for their work in assembling ideas which, otherwise "incapable of confinement," would then become freely available to the public. But what is the role of libraries in the absence of books? How does society now pay for the distribution of ideas if not by charging for the ideas themselves?

Additionally complicating the matter is the fact that along with the physical bottles in which intellectual property protection has resided, digital technology is also erasing the legal jurisdictions of the physical world and replacing them with the unbounded and perhaps permanently lawless seas of cyberspace.

In cyberspace, there are not only no national or local boundaries to contain the scene of a crime and determine the method of its prosecution, there are no clear cultural agreements on what a crime might be. Unresolved and basic differences between European and Asian cultural assumptions about intellectual property can only be exacerbated in a region where many transactions are taking place in both hemispheres and yet, somehow, in neither.

Even in the most local of digital conditions, jurisdiction and responsibility are hard to assess. A group of music publishers filed suit against CompuServe for allowing its users to upload musical compositions into areas where other users might get them. But since

CompuServe cannot practically exercise much control over the flood of bits which pass between its subscribers, it probably shouldn't be held responsible for unlawfully "publishing" these works.

Notions of property, value, ownership, and the nature of wealth itself are changing more fundamentally than at any time since the Sumerians first poked cuneiform into wet clay and called it stored grain. Only a very few people are aware of the enormity of this shift and fewer of them are lawyers or public officials.

Those who do see these changes must prepare responses for the legal and social confusion which will erupt as efforts to protect new forms of property with old methods become more obviously futile, and, as a consequence, more adamant.

From Swords to Writs to Bits

Humanity now seems bent on creating a world economy primarily based on goods which take no material form. In doing so, we may be eliminating any predictable connection between creators and a fair reward for the utility or pleasure others may find in their works.

Without that connection, and without a fundamental change in consciousness to accommodate its loss, we are building our future on furor, litigation, and institutionalized evasion of payment except in response to raw force. We may return to the Bad Old Days of property.

Throughout the darker parts of human history, the possession and distribution of property was largely a military matter. "Ownership" was assured those with the nastiest tools, whether fists or armies, and the most resolute will to use them. Property was the divine right of thugs.

By the turn of the first millennium A.D., the emergence of merchant classes and landed gentry forced the development of ethical understandings for the resolution of property disputes. In the late Middle Ages, enlightened rulers like England's Henry II began to codify this unwritten "common law" into recorded canons. These laws were local, but this didn't matter much as they were primarily directed at real estate, a form of property which is local by definition. And which, as the name implied, was very real.

This continued to be the case as long as the origin of wealth was agricultural, but with the dawning of the Industrial Revolution, humanity began to focus as much on means as ends. Tools acquired a new social value and, thanks to their own development, it became possible to duplicate and distribute them in quantity.

To encourage their invention, copyright and patent law were developed in most western countries. These laws were devoted to the delicate task of getting mental creations into the world where they could be used—and enter the minds of others—while assuring their inventors compensation for the value of their use. And, as previously stated, the systems of both law and practice which grew up around that task were based on physical expression.

Since it is now possible to convey ideas from one mind to another without ever making them physical, we are now claiming to own ideas themselves and not merely their expression. And since it is likewise now possible to create useful tools which never take physical form, we have taken to patenting abstractions, sequences of virtual events, and mathematical formulae—the most un-real estate imaginable.

In certain areas, this leaves rights of ownership in such an ambiguous condition that once again property adheres to those who can muster the largest armies. The only difference is that this time the armies consist of lawyers.

Threatening their opponents with the endless purgatory of litigation, over which some might prefer death itself, they assert claim to any thought which might have entered another cranium within the collective body of the corporations they serve. They act as though these ideas appeared in splendid detachment from all previous human thought. And they pretend that thinking about a product is somehow as good as manufacturing, distributing, and selling it.

What was previously considered a common human resource, distributed among the minds and libraries of the world, as well as the phenomena of nature herself, is now being fenced and deeded. It is as though a new class of enterprise had arisen which claimed to own air and water.

What is to be done? While there is a certain grim fun to be had in it, dancing on the grave of copyright and patent will solve little, especially when so few are willing to admit that the occupant of this grave is even deceased and are trying to uphold by force what can no longer be upheld by popular consent.

The legalists, desperate over their slipping grip, are vigorously trying to extend it. Indeed, the United States and other proponents of

GATT (General Agreement on Tariffs and Trade) are making adherence to our moribund systems of intellectual property protection a condition of membership in the marketplace of nations. For example, China will be denied Most Favored Nation trading status unless they agree to uphold a set of culturally alien principles which are no longer even sensibly applicable in their country of origin.

In a more perfect world, we'd be wise to declare a moratorium on litigation, legislation, and international treaties in this area until we had a clearer sense of the terms and conditions of enterprise in cyberspace. Ideally, laws ratify already developed social consensus. They are less the Social Contract itself than a series of memoranda expressing a collective intent which has emerged out of many millions of human interactions.

Humans have not inhabited cyberspace long enough or in sufficient diversity to have developed a Social Contract which conforms to the strange new conditions of that world. Laws developed prior to consensus usually serve the already established few who can get them passed and not society as a whole.

To the extent that either law or established social practice exists in this area, they are already in dangerous disagreement. The laws regarding unlicensed reproduction of commercial software are clear and stern . . . and rarely observed. Software piracy laws are so practically unenforceable and breaking them has become so socially acceptable that only a thin minority appears compelled, either by fear or conscience, to obey them.

I sometimes give speeches on this subject, and I always ask how many people in the audience can honestly claim to have no unauthorized software on their hard disks. I've never seen more than 10 percent of the hands go up.

Whenever there is such profound divergence between the law and social practice, it is not society that adapts. And, against the swift tide of custom, the software publishers' current practice of hanging a few visible scapegoats is so obviously capricious as to only further diminish respect for the law.

Part of the widespread popular disregard for commercial software copyrights stems from a legislative failure to understand the conditions into which it was inserted. To assume that systems of law based in the physical world will serve in an environment which is as fundamentally different as cyberspace is a folly for which everyone doing business in the future will pay.

As I will discuss in the next segment, unbounded intellectual property is very different from physical property and can no longer be protected as though these differences did not exist. For example, if we continue to assume that value is based on scarcity, as it is with regard to physical objects, we will create laws which are precisely contrary to the nature of information, which may, in many cases, increase in value with distribution.

The large, legally risk-averse institutions most likely to play by the old rules will suffer for their compliance. The more lawyers, guns, and money they invest in either protecting their rights or subverting those of their opponents, the more commercial competition will resemble the Kwakiutl potlatch ceremony, in which adversaries compete by destroying their own possessions. Their ability to produce new technology will simply grind to a halt as every move they make drives them deeper into a tar pit of courtroom warfare.

Faith in law will not be an effective strategy for high-tech companies. Law adapts by continuous increments and at a pace second only to geology in its stateliness. Technology advances in lunging jerks, like the punctuation of biological evolution grotesquely accelerated. Real world conditions will continue to change at a blinding pace, and the law will get further behind, more profoundly confused. This mismatch is permanent.

Promising economies based on purely digital products will either be born in a state of paralysis, as appears to be the case with multimedia, or continue in a brave and willful refusal by their owners to play the ownership game at all.

In the United States one can already see a parallel economy developing, mostly among small, fast-moving enterprises who protect their ideas by getting into the marketplace quicker than their larger competitors who base their protection on fear and litigation.

Perhaps those who are part of the problem will simply quarantine themselves in court while those who are part of the solution will create a new society based, at first, on piracy and freebooting. It may well be that when the current system of intellectual property law has collapsed, as seems inevitable, no new legal structure will arise in its place.

But something will happen. After all, people do business. When a currency becomes meaningless, business is done in barter. When societies develop outside the law, they develop their own unwritten codes, practices, and ethical systems. While technology may undo law, technology offers methods for restoring creative rights.

A Taxonomy of Information

It seems to me that the most productive thing to do now is to look hard into the true nature of what we're trying to protect. How much do we really know about information and its natural behaviors?

What are the essential characteristics of unbounded creation? How does it differ from previous forms of property? How many of our assumptions about it have actually been about its containers rather than their mysterious contents? What are its different species, and how does each of them lend itself to control? What technologies will be useful in creating new virtual bottles to replace the old physical ones?

Of course, information is, by its nature, intangible and hard to define. Like other such deep phenomena as light or matter, it is a natural host to paradox. And as it is most helpful to understand light as being both a particle and a wave, an understanding of information may emerge in the abstract congruence of its several different properties, which might be described by the following three statements:

- Information is an activity.
- Information is a life-form.
- Information is a relationship.

I. Information Is an Activity

Information Is a Verb, Not a Noun

Freed of its containers, information is obviously not a thing. In fact, it is something which happens in the field of interaction between minds or objects or other pieces of information.

Gregory Bateson, expanding on the information theory of Claude Shannon, said, "Information is a difference which makes a difference." Thus, information only really exists in the Δ (delta). The making of that difference is an activity within a relationship. Information is an action which occupies time rather than a state of being which occupies physical space, as is the case with hard goods. It is the pitch, not the baseball, the dance, not the dancer.

Information Is Experienced, Not Possessed

Even when it has been encapsulated in some static form like a book or a hard disk, information is still something which happens to you as you mentally decompress it from its storage code. But, whether it's running at gigabits per second or words per minute, the actual decoding is a process which must be performed by and upon a mind, a process which must take place in time.

There was a cartoon in the *Bulletin of Atomic Scientists* a few years ago which illustrated this point beautifully. In the drawing, a holdup man trains his gun on the sort of bespectacled fellow you'd figure might have a lot of information stored in his head. "Quick," orders the bandit, "Give me all your ideas."

Information Has to Move

Sharks are said to die of suffocation if they stop swimming, and the same is nearly true of information. Information which isn't moving ceases to exist as anything but potential . . . at least until it is allowed to move again. For this reason, the practice of information hoarding, common in bureaucracies, is an especially wrong-headed artifact of physically based value systems.

Information Is Conveyed by Propagation, Not Distribution

The way in which information spreads is also very different from the distribution of physical goods. It moves more like something from nature than from a factory. It can concatenate like falling dominos or grow in the usual fractal lattice, like frost spreading on a window, but it cannot be shipped around like widgets, except to the extent that it can be contained in them. It doesn't simply move on. It leaves a trail of itself everywhere it's been.

The central economic distinction between information and physical property is the ability of information to be transferred without leaving the possession of the original owner. If I sell you my horse, I can't ride him after that. If I sell you what I know, we both know it.

II. INFORMATION IS A LIFE-FORM

Information Wants to Be Free

Stewart Brand is generally credited with this elegant statement of the obvious, recognizing both the natural desire of secrets to be told and the fact that they might be capable of possessing something like a "desire" in the first place.

English biologist and philosopher Richard Dawkins proposed the idea of "memes," self-replicating patterns of information which propagate themselves across the ecologies of mind, saying they were like life-forms.

I believe they are life-forms in every respect but a basis in the carbon atom. They self-reproduce, they interact with their surroundings and adapt to them, they mutate, they persist. Like any other life-form they evolve to fill the possibility spaces of their local environments, which are in this case the surrounding belief systems and cultures of their hosts, namely, us.

Indeed, the sociobiologists like Dawkins make a plausible case that carbon-based life-forms are information as well, that, as the chicken is an egg's way of making another egg, the entire biological spectacle is just the DNA molecule's means of copying out more information strings exactly like itself.

Information Replicates into the Cracks of Possibility

Like DNA helices, ideas are relentless expansionists, always seeking new opportunities for *lebensraum.* And, as in carbon-based nature, the more robust organisms are extremely adept at finding new places to live. Thus, just as the common housefly has insinuated itself into practically every ecosystem on the planet, so has the meme of "life after death" found a niche in most minds, or psycho-ecologies.

The more universally resonant an idea or image or song, the more minds it will enter and remain within. Trying to stop the spread of a really robust piece of information is about as easy as keeping killer bees south of the border. The stuff just leaks.

Information Wants to Change

If ideas and other interactive patterns of information are indeed life-forms, they can be expected to evolve constantly into forms which will be more perfectly adapted to their surroundings. And, as we see, they are doing this all the time.

But for a long time, our static media, whether carvings in stone, ink on paper, or dye on celluloid, have strongly resisted the evolutionary impulse, exalting as a consequence the author's ability to determine the finished product. But, as in an oral tradition, digitized information has no "final cut."

Digital information, unconstrained by packaging, is a continuing process more like the metamorphosing tales of prehistory than anything which will fit in shrink-wrap. From the Neolithic to Gutenberg, information was passed on, mouth to ear, changing with every retelling (or resinging). The stories which once shaped our sense of the world didn't have authoritative versions. They adapted to each culture in which they found themselves being told.

Because there was never a moment when the story was frozen in print, the so-called "moral" right of storytellers to keep the tale their own was neither protected nor recognized. The story simply passed through each of them on its way to the next, where it would assume a different form. As we return to continuous information, we can expect the importance of authorship to diminish. Creative people may have to renew their acquaintance with humility.

But our system of copyright makes no accommodation whatever for expressions which don't at some point become "fixed" nor for cultural expressions which lack a specific author or inventor.

Jazz improvisations, stand-up comedy routines, mime performances, developing monologues, and unrecorded broadcast transmissions all lack the constitutional requirement of fixation as a "writing." Without being fixed by a point of publication, the liquid works of the future will all look more like these continuously adapting and changing forms and will therefore exist beyond the reach of copyright.

Copyright expert Pamela Samuelson tells of having attended a conference last year convened around the fact that western countries may legally appropriate the music, designs, and biomedical lore of aboriginal people without compensation to their tribe of origin since that tribe is not an "author" or "inventor."

But soon most information will be generated collaboratively by the cyber-tribal hunter-gatherers of cyberspace. Our arrogant legal dismissal of the rights of "primitives" will be back to haunt us soon.

Information Is Perishable

With the exception of the rare classic, most information is like farm produce. Its quality degrades rapidly both over time and in distance from the source of production. But even here, value is highly subjective and conditional. Yesterday's papers are quite valuable to the historian. In fact, the older they are, the more valuable they become. On the other hand, a commodities broker might consider news of an event which is more than an hour old to have lost any relevance.

III. INFORMATION IS A RELATIONSHIP

Meaning Has Value and Is Unique to Each Case

In most cases, we assign value to information based on its meaningfulness. The place where information dwells, the holy moment where transmission becomes reception, is a region which has many shifting characteristics and flavors depending on the relationship of sender and receiver, the depth of their interactivity.

Each such relationship is unique. Even in cases where the sender is a broadcast medium and no response is returned, the receiver is hardly passive. Receiving information is often as creative an act as generating it.

The value of what is sent depends entirely on the extent to which each individual receiver has the receptors . . . shared terminology, attention, interest, language, paradigm . . . necessary to render what is received meaningful.

Understanding is a critical element increasingly overlooked in the effort to turn information into a commodity. Data may be any set of facts, useful or not, intelligible or inscrutable, germane or irrelevant. Computers can crank out new data all night long without human help, and the results may be offered for sale as information. They may or may not actually be so. Only a human being can recognize the meaning which separates information from data.

In fact, information, in the economic sense of the word, consists of data which have been passed through a particular human mind and found meaningful within that mental context. One fella's information is all just data to someone else. If you're an anthropologist, my detailed charts of Tasaday kinship patterns might be critical information to you. If you're a banker from Hong Kong, they might barely seem to be data.

Familiarity Has More Value Than Scarcity

With physical goods, there is a direct correlation between scarcity and value. Gold is more valuable than wheat, even though you can't eat it. While this is not always the case, the situation with information is usually precisely the reverse. Most soft goods increase in value as they become more common. Familiarity is an important asset in the world of information. It may often be the case that the best thing you can do to raise the demand for your product is to give it away.

While this has not always worked with shareware, it could be argued that there is a connection between the extent to which commercial software is pirated and the amount which gets sold. Broadly pirated software, such as Lotus 1-2-3 or WordPerfect, becomes a standard and benefits from the Law of Increasing Returns based on familiarity.

In regard to my own soft product, rock and roll songs, there is no question that the band I wrote them for, the Grateful Dead, increased its popularity enormously by giving them away. We let people tape our concerts since the early seventies, but instead of reducing the demand for our product, we became the largest concert draw in America, a fact which is at least in part attributable to the popularity generated by those tapes.

True, I don't get any royalties on the millions of copies of my songs which were extracted from concerts, but I see no reason to complain. The fact is, no one but the Grateful Dead could perform a Grateful Dead song, so if you wanted the experience and not its thin projection, you had to buy a ticket from us. In other words, our intellectual property protection derived from our being the only real-time source of it.

Exclusivity Has Value

The problem with a model which turns the physical scarcity/value ratio on its head is that sometimes the value of information is very much based on its scarcity. Exclusive possession of certain facts makes them more useful. If everyone knows about conditions which might drive a stock price up, the information is valueless.

But again, the critical factor is usually time. It doesn't matter if this kind of information eventually becomes ubiquitous. What matters is being among the first who possess it and act on it. While potent secrets usually don't stay secret, they may remain so long enough to advance the cause of their original holders.

Point of View and Authority Have Value

In a world of floating realities and contradictory maps, rewards will accrue to those commentators whose maps seem to fit their territory snugly, based on their ability to yield predictable results for those who use them.

In aesthetic information, whether poetry or rock and roll, people are willing to buy the new product of an artist, sight unseen, based on their having been delivered a pleasurable experience by previous work.

Reality is an edit. People are willing to pay for the authority of those editors whose filtering point of view seems to fit best. And again, point of view is an asset which cannot be stolen or duplicated. No one but Esther Dyson sees the world as she does, and the handsome fee she charges for her newsletter is actually for the privilege of looking at the world through her unique eyes.

Time Replaces Space

In the physical world, value depends heavily on possession, or proximity in space. One owns that material which falls inside certain dimensional boundaries and the ability to act directly, exclusively, and as one wishes upon what falls inside those boundaries is the principal right of ownership. And of course there is the relationship between value and scarcity, a limitation in space.

In the virtual world, proximity in time is a value determinant. An informational product is generally more valuable the closer the purchaser can place himself to the moment of its expression, a limitation in time. Many kinds of information degrade rapidly with either time or reproduction. Relevance fades as the territory they map changes. Noise is introduced and bandwidth lost with passage away from the point where the information is first produced.

Thus, listening to a Grateful Dead tape is hardly the same experience as attending a Grateful Dead concert. The closer one can get to the headwaters of an informational stream, the better his chances of finding an accurate picture of reality in it. In an era of easy reproduction, the informational abstractions of popular experiences will propagate out from their source moments to reach anyone who's interested. But it's easy enough to restrict the real experience of the desirable event, whether knockout punch or guitar lick, to those willing to pay for being there.

The Protection of Execution

In the hick town I come from, they don't give you much credit for just having ideas. You are judged by what you can make of them. As things continue to speed up, I think we see that execution is the best protection for those designs which become physical products. Or, as Steve Jobs once put it, "Real artists ship." The big winner is usually the one who gets to the market first (and with enough organizational force to keep the lead).

But, as we become fixated upon information commerce, many of us seem to think that originality alone is sufficient to convey value deserving, with the right legal assurances, of a steady wage. In fact, the best way to protect intellectual property is to act on it. It's not enough to invent and patent, one has to innovate as well. Someone claims to have patented the microprocessor before Intel. Maybe so. If he'd actually started shipping microprocessors before Intel, his claim would seem far less spurious.

Information As Its Own Reward

It is now a commonplace to say that money is information. With the exception of Krugerrands, crumpled cab fare, and the contents of those suitcases which drug lords are reputed to carry, most of the money in the informatized world is in ones and zeros. The global money supply sloshes around the Net, as fluid as weather. It is also obvious, as I have discussed, that information has become as fundamental to the creation of modern wealth as land and sunlight once were.

What is less obvious is the extent to which information is acquiring intrinsic value, not as a means to acquisition but as the object to be acquired. I suppose this has always been less explicitly the case. In politics and academia, potency and information have always been closely related.

However, as we increasingly buy information with money, we begin to see that buying information with other information is simple economic exchange without the necessity of converting the product into and out of currency. This is somewhat challenging for those who like clean accounting, since, information theory aside, informational exchange rates are too squishy to quantify to the decimal point.

Nevertheless, most of what a middle-class American purchases has little to do with survival. We buy beauty, prestige, experience, education, and all the obscure pleasures of owning. Many of these things can not only be expressed in nonmaterial terms, they can be acquired by nonmaterial means.

And then there are the inexplicable pleasures of information itself, the joys of learning, knowing, and teaching. The strange good feeling of information coming into and out of oneself. Playing with ideas is a recreation which people must be willing to pay a lot for, given the market for books and elective seminars. We'd likely spend even more money for such pleasures if there weren't so many opportunities to pay for ideas with other ideas.

This explains much of the collective "volunteer" work which fills the archives, newsgroups, and databases of the Internet. Its denizens are not working for "nothing," as is widely believed. Rather they are getting paid in something besides money. It is an economy which consists almost entirely of information.

This may become the dominant form of human trade, and if we persist in modeling economics on a strictly monetary basis, we may be gravely misled.

Getting Paid in Cyberspace

How all the foregoing relates to solutions to the crisis in intellectual property is something I've barely started to wrap my mind around. It's fairly paradigm-warping to look at information through fresh eyes—to see how very little it is like pig iron or pork bellies, to imagine the tottering travesties of case law we will stack up if we go on treating it legally as though it were.

As I've said, I believe these towers of outmoded boilerplate will be a smoking heap sometime in the next decade and we mind-miners will have no choice but to cast our lot with new systems that work.

I'm not really so gloomy about our prospects as readers of this jeremiad so far might conclude. Solutions will emerge. Nature abhors a vacuum and so does commerce.

Indeed, one of the aspects of the electronic frontier which I have always found most appealing—and the reason Mitch Kapor and I used that phrase in naming our foundation—is the degree to which it resembles the nineteenth-century American West in its natural preference for social devices which emerge from its conditions rather than those which are imposed from the outside.

Until the West was fully settled and "civilized" in this century, order was established according to an unwritten Code of the West which had the fluidity of etiquette rather than the rigidity of law. Ethics were more important than rules. Understandings were preferred over laws, which were, in any event, largely unenforceable.

I believe that law, as we understand it, was developed to protect the interests which arose in the two economic "waves" that Alvin Toffler accurately identified in *The Third Wave*. The First Wave was agriculturally based and required law to order ownership of the principal source of production, land. In the Second Wave, manufacturing became the economic mainspring, and the structure of modern law grew around the centralized institutions which needed protection for their reserves of capital, manpower, and hardware.

Both of these economic systems required stability. Their laws were designed to resist change and to assure some equability of distribution within a fairly static social framework. The possibility spaces had to be constrained to preserve the predictability necessary to either land stewardship or capital formation.

In the Third Wave we have now entered, information to a large extent replaces land, capital, and hardware, and as I have detailed in the preceding section, information is most at home in a much more fluid and adaptable environment. The Third Wave is likely to bring a fundamental shift in the purposes and methods of law which will affect far more than simply those statutes which govern intellectual property.

The "terrain" itself—the architecture of the Net—may come to serve many of the purposes which could only be maintained in the past by legal imposition. For example, it may be unnecessary to constitutionally assure freedom of expression in an environment which, in the words of my fellow EFF (Electronic Frontier Foundation) cofounder John Gilmore, "treats censorship as a malfunction" and reroutes proscribed ideas around it.

Similar natural balancing mechanisms may arise to smooth over the social discontinuities which previously required legal intercession to set right. On the Net, these differences are more likely to be spanned by a continuous spectrum which connects as much as it separates.

And, despite their fierce grip on the old legal structure, companies that trade in information are likely to find that, in their increasing inability to deal sensibly with technological issues, the courts will not produce results which are predictable enough to be supportive of long-term enterprise. Every litigation becomes like a game of Russian roulette, depending on the depth of the presiding judge's clue-impairment.

Uncodified or adaptive "law," while as "fast, loose, and out of control" as other emergent forms, is probably more likely to yield something like justice at this point. In fact, one can already see in development new practices to suit the conditions of virtual commerce. The life forms of information are evolving methods to protect their continued reproduction.

For example, while all the tiny print on a commercial diskette envelope punctiliously requires much of those who would open it, there are, as I say, few who read those provisos, let alone follow them to the letter. And yet, the software business remains a very healthy sector of the American economy.

Why is this? Because people seem to eventually buy the software they really use. Once a program becomes central to your work, you want the latest version of it, the best support, the actual manuals, all privileges which are attached to ownership. Such practical considerations will, in the absence of working law, become more and more important in getting paid for what might easily be obtained for nothing.

I do think that some software is being purchased in the service of ethics or the abstract awareness that the failure to buy it will result in its not being produced any longer, but I'm going to leave those motivators aside. While I believe that the failure of law will almost certainly result in a compensating reemergence of ethics as the ordering template of society, this is a belief I don't have room to support here.

Instead, I think that, as in the case cited above, compensation for soft products will be driven primarily by practical considerations, all of them consistent with the true properties of digital information, where the value lies in it, and how it can be both manipulated and protected by technology.

While the conundrum remains a conundrum, I can begin to see the directions from which solutions may emerge, based in part on broadening those practical solutions which are already in practice.

Relationship and Its Tools

I believe one idea is central to understanding liquid commerce: information economics, in the absence of objects, will be based more on relationship than possession.

One existing model for the future conveyance of intellectual property is real-time performance, a medium currently used only in theater, music, lectures, stand-up comedy, and pedagogy. I believe the concept of performance will expand to include most of the information economy from multicasted soap operas to stock analysis. In these instances, commercial exchange will be more like ticket sales to a continuous show than the purchase of discrete bundles of that which is being shown.

The other model, of course, is service. The entire professional class—doctors, lawyers, consultants, architects, et cetera—are already being paid directly for their intellectual property. Who needs copyright when you're on a retainer?

In fact, this model was applied to much of what is now copyrighted until the late eighteenth century. Before the industrialization of creation, writers, composers, artists, and the like produced their products in the private service of patrons. Without objects to distribute in a mass market, creative people will return to a condition somewhat like this, except that they will serve many patrons, rather than one.

We can already see the emergence of companies which base their existence on supporting and enhancing the soft property they create rather than selling it by the shrink-wrapped piece or embedding it in widgets.

Trip Hawkins's new company for creating and licensing multimedia tools, 3DO, is an example of what I'm talking about. 3DO doesn't intend to produce any commercial software or consumer devices. Instead, they will act as a kind of private standards-setting body, mediating among software and device creators who will be their licensees. They will provide a point of commonality for relationships between a broad spectrum of entities.

In any case, whether you think of yourself as a service provider or a performer, the future protection of your intellectual property will depend on your ability to control your relationship to the market—a relationship which will most likely live and grow over a period of time.

The value of that relationship will reside in the quality of performance, the uniqueness of your point of view, the validity of your expertise, its relevance to your market, and, underlying everything, the ability of that market to access your creative services swiftly, conveniently, and interactively.

Interaction and Protection

Direct interaction will provide a lot of intellectual property protection in the future, and, indeed, it already has. No one knows how many software pirates have bought legitimate copies of a program after calling its publisher for technical support and being asked for some proof of purchase, but I would guess the number is very high.

The same kind of controls will be applicable to "question and answer" relationships between authorities (or artists) and those who seek their expertise. Newsletters, magazines, and books will be supplemented by the ability of their subscribers to ask direct questions of authors.

Interactivity will be a billable commodity even in the absence of authorship. As people move into the Net and increasingly get their information directly from its point of production, unfiltered by centralized media, they will attempt to develop the same interactive ability to probe reality which only experience has provided them in the past. Live access to these distant "eyes and ears" will be much easier to cordon than access to static bundles of stored but easily reproducible information.

In most cases, control will be based on restricting access to the freshest, highest bandwidth information. It will be a matter of defining the ticket, the venue, the performer, and the identity of the ticket holder, definitions which I believe will take their forms from technology, not law.

In most cases, the defining technology will be cryptography.

Crypto-Bottling

Cryptography, as I've said perhaps too many times, is the "material" from which the walls, boundaries—and bottles—of cyberspace will be fashioned.

Of course there are problems with cryptography or any other purely technical method of property protection. It has always appeared to me that the more security you hide your goods behind, the more likely you are to turn your sanctuary into a target. Having come from a place where people leave their keys in their cars and don't even have keys to their houses, I remain convinced that the best obstacle to crime is a society with its ethics intact.

While I admit that this is not the kind of society most of us live in, I also believe that a social overreliance on protection by barricades rather than conscience will eventually wither the latter by turning intrusion and theft into a sport, rather than a crime. This is already occurring in the digital domain as is evident in the activities of computer crackers.

Furthermore, I would argue that initial efforts to protect digital copyright by copy protection contributed to the current condition in which most otherwise ethical computer users seem morally untroubled by their possession of pirated software.

Instead of cultivating among the newly computerized a sense of respect for the work of their fellows, early reliance on copy protection led to the subliminal notion that cracking into a software package somehow "earned" one the right to use it. Limited not by conscience but by technical skill, many soon felt free to do whatever they could get away with. This will continue to be a potential liability of the encryption of digitized commerce.

Furthermore, it's cautionary to remember that copy protection was rejected by the market in most areas. Many of the upcoming efforts to use cryptography-based protection schemes will probably suffer the same fate. People are not going to tolerate much which makes computers harder to use than they already are without any benefit to the user.

Nevertheless, encryption has already demonstrated a certain blunt utility. New subscriptions to various commercial satellite TV services skyrocketed recently after their deployment of more robust encryption of their feeds. This, despite a booming backwoods trade in black decoder chips conducted by folks who'd look more at home running moonshine than cracking code.

Another obvious problem with encryption as a global solution is that once something has been unscrambled by a legitimate licensee it may be openly available to massive reproduction.

In some instances, reproduction following decryption may not be a problem. Many soft products degrade sharply in value with time. It may be that the only real interest in some such products will be among those who have purchased the keys to immediacy.

Furthermore, as software becomes more modular and distribution moves online, it will begin to metamorphose in direct interaction with its user base. Discontinuous upgrades will smooth into a constant process of incremental improvement and adaptation, some of it man-made and some of it arising through genetic algorithms. Pirated copies of software may become too static to have much value to anyone.

Even in cases such as images, where the information is expected to remain fixed, the unencrypted file could still be interwoven with code which could continue to protect it by a wide variety of means.

In most of the schemes I can project, the file would be "alive" with permanently embedded software which could "sense" the surrounding conditions and interact with them. For example, it might contain code which could detect the process of duplication and cause it to self-destruct.

Other methods might give the file the ability to "phone home" through the Net to its original owner. The continued integrity of some files might require periodic "feeding" with digital cash from their host which they would then relay back to their authors.

Of course files which possess the independent ability to communicate upstream sound uncomfortably like the Morris Internet Worm. "Live" files do have a certain viral quality. And serious privacy issues would arise if everyone's computer were packed with digital spies.

The point is that cryptography will enable a lot of protection technologies which will develop rapidly in the obsessive competition which has always existed between lock-makers and lock-breakers.

But cryptography will not be used simply for making locks. It is also at the heart of both digital signatures and the aforementioned digital cash, both of which I believe will be central to the future protection of intellectual property.

I believe that the generally acknowledged failure of the shareware model in software had less to do with dishonesty than with the simple inconvenience of paying for shareware. If the payment process can be automated, as digital cash and signatures will make possible, I believe that soft product creators will reap a much higher return from the bread they cast upon the waters of cyberspace.

Moreover, they will be spared much of the overhead which presently adheres to the marketing, manufacture, sale, and distribution of information products, whether those products are computer programs, books, CDs, or motion pictures. This will reduce prices and further increase the likelihood of noncompulsory payment.

But of course there is a fundamental problem with a system which requires, through technology, payment for every access to a particular expression. It defeats the original Jeffersonian purpose of seeing that ideas were available to everyone regardless of their economic station. I am not comfortable with a model which will restrict inquiry to the wealthy.

An Economy of Verbs

The future forms and protections of intellectual property are densely obscured from the entrance to the Virtual Age. Nevertheless, I can make (or reiterate) a few flat statements which I earnestly believe won't look too silly in 50 years.

- In the absence of the old containers, almost everything we think we know about intellectual property is wrong. We are going to have to unlearn it. We are going to have to look at information as though we'd never seen the stuff before.
- The protections which we will develop will rely far more on ethics and technology than on law.
- Encryption will be the technical basis for most intellectual property protection. (And should, for this and other reasons, be made more widely available.)
- The economy of the future will be based on relationship rather than possession. It will be continuous rather than sequential.
- And finally, in the years to come, most human exchange will be virtual rather than physical, consisting not of stuff but the stuff of which dreams are made. Our future business will be conducted in a world made more of verbs than nouns.

The Virtual Barrio @ the Other Frontier

(or The Chicano Interneta)

Guillermo Gómez-Peña

[Mexicans] are simple people. They are happy with the little they got. . . . They are not ambitious and complex like us. They don't need all this technology to communicate. Sometimes I just feel like going down there & living among them.

—Anonymous confession on the Web

Tecnofobia

My laptop is decorated with a 3-D decal of the Virgin of Guadalupe. It's like a traveling altar, office, and literary bank, all in one. Since I spend 70 percent of the year on the road, it is (besides the phone of course) my principal means to remain in touch with my beloved relatives and colleagues, spread throughout many cities in the United States and Mexico. Unwillingly, I have become a cyber-vato, an information superhighway bandido. Like most Mexican artists, my relationship with digital technology and personal computers is defined by paradoxes and contradictions: I don't quite understand them, yet I am seduced by them; I don't want to know how they work, but I love how they look and what they do; I criticize my colleagues who are acritically immersed in new technology, yet I silently envy them. I resent the fact that I am constantly told that as a "Latino" I am supposedly culturally handicapped or somehow unfit to handle high technology; yet once I have it right in front of me, I am propelled to work against it, to question it, to expose it, to subvert it, to imbue it with humor, linguas polutas—Spanglish, Frangle, gringonol, and radical politics. In doing so, I become a sort of Mexican virus, the cyber-version of the Mexican fly: tiny, irritating, inescapable, and highly contagious. Contradiction prevails.

Over a year ago, my collaborator Roberto Sifuentes and I bullied ourselves into the Net, and once we were generously adopted by various communities (Arts Wire and Latino Net, among others) we started to lose interest in maintaining ongoing conversations with phantasmagoric beings we had never met in person (that, I must say, is a Mexican cultural prejudice—if I don't know you in person, I don't really care to talk with you). Then we started sending a series of poetic/activist "techno-placas" in Spanglish. In these short communiqués we raised some tough questions regarding access, privilege, and language. Since we didn't quite know where to post them in order to get the maximum response, and the responses were sporadic, casual, and unfocused, our passion began to dim. Roberto and I spend a lot of time in front of our laptops conceptualizing performance projects which incorporate new technologies in what we believe is a responsible and original manner, yet every time we are invited to participate in a public discussion around art and technology, we tend to emphasize its shortcomings and overstate our cultural skepticism.[1] Why? I can only speak for myself. Perhaps I have some computer traumas. I've been utilizing computers since 1988; however, during the first five years, I utilized my old "lowrider" Mac as a glorified typewriter. During those years I probably deleted accidentally here and there over 300 pages of original texts which I hadn't backed up on disks, and thus was forced to rewrite them by memory. The thick and confusing "user friendly" manuals fell many a time from my impatient hands; and I spent many desperate nights cursing the mischievous gods of cyberspace and dialing promising "hotlines" which rarely answered.

My bittersweet relationship to technology dates back to my formative years in the highly politicized ambiance of Mexico City in the 1970s. As a young "radical artist," I was full of ideological dogmas and partial truths. One such partial truth spouted was that high-technology was intrinsically dehumanizing; that it was mostly used as a means to control "us" little techno-illiterate people politically. My critique of technology overlapped with my critique of capitalism. To me, "capitalists" were rootless corporate men who utilized mass media to advertise useless electronic gadgets, and sold us unnecessary apparatuses which kept us both eternally in debt and conveniently distracted from "the truly important matters of life." These matters included sex, music, spirituality, and "revolution" California style (in the abstract). As a child of contradiction, besides being a rabid anti-technology artist, I owned a little Datsun and listened to my favorite U.S. and British rock groups on my Panasonic *importado,* often while meditating or making love as a means to "liberate myself" from capitalist socialization. My favorite clothes, books, posters, and albums had all been made by "capitalists," but for some obscure reason, that seemed perfectly logical to me. Luckily, my family never lost their magical thinking and sense of humor around technology. My parents were easily seduced by refurbished and slightly dated American and Japanese electronic goods. We bought them as *fayuca* (contraband) in the Tepito neighborhood, and they occupied an important place in the decoration of our "modern" middle-class home. Our huge color TV set, for example, was decorated so as to perform the double function of entertainment unit and involuntary postmodern altar—with nostalgic photos, plastic flowers, and assorted figurines all around it—as was the sound system next to it. Though I was sure that with the scary arrival of the first microwave oven to our traditional kitchen our delicious daily meals were going to turn overnight into sleazy fast food, my mother soon realized that *el microondas* was only good to reheat cold coffee and soups. When I moved to California, I bought an electric ionizer for my grandma. She put it in the middle of her bedroom altar and kept it there—unplugged of course—for months. When I next saw her, she told me, "Mijito, since you gave me that thing, I truly can breathe much better." And probably she did. Things like televisions, shortwave radios, and microwave ovens, and later on ionizers, Walkmans, calculators, and video cameras were seen by my family and friends as high technology, and their function was as much pragmatic as it was social, ritual, and aesthetic. It is no coincidence then that in my early performance work, technology performed both ritual and aesthetic functions.

Verbigratia

For years, I used video monitors as centerpieces for my "techno-altars" on stage. I combined ritualistic structures, spoken word multilingual poetry and activist politics with my fascination for "low-tech." Fog machines, strobe lights, and gobos, megaphones and cheesy voice filters have remained since then trademark elements in my "low-tech/high-tech" performances. By the early 1990s, I sarcastically baptized my aesthetic practice "Aztec high-tech art," and when I teamed with Cyber-Vato Sifuentes, we decided that what we were doing was "techno-razcuache art." In a glossary which dates back to 1993, we defined it as "a new aesthetic that fuses performance art, epic rap poetry, interactive television, experimental radio and computer art; but with a Chicanocentric perspective and a sleazoid bent."

> (El Naftaztec turns the knobs of his "Chicano virtual reality machine" and then proceeds to feed chili peppers into it. The set looks like a Mexican sci-fi movie from the 1950s.) El Naftaztec (speaking with a computerized voice): *So now, let's talk about the TECHNOPAL 2000, a technology originally invented by the Mayans with the help of aliens from Harvard. Its CPU is powered by Habanero chili peppers, combined with this or DAT technology, with a measured clock speed of 200,000 megahertz! It uses neural nets supplemented by actual chicken-brain matter and nacho cheese spread to supply the massive processing speed necessary for the machine to operate. And it's all integrated into one sombrero! Originally, the Chicano VR had to use a poncho, but with the VR sombrero, the weight is greatly reduced and its efficiency is magnified. And now, we have the first alpha version of the VR bandanna dos mil, which Cyber-Vato will demonstrate for us!* (Cyber-Vato wears a bandanna over his eyes. It is connected by a thick rope to a robotic glove. Special effects on the TV screen simulate the graphics and sounds of a VR helmet.)
>
> —From "Naftaztec," an interactive TV project about Mexicans and high technology

The mythology goes like this. Mexicans (and other Latinos) can't handle high technology. Caught between a preindustrial past and an imposed postmodernity, we continue to be manual beings—*homo fabers* par excellence, imaginative artisans (not technicians)—and our understanding of the world is strictly political, poetical, or metaphysical at best, but certainly not scientific. Furthermore, we are perceived as sentimental and passionate, meaning irrational; and when we decide to step out of our realm and utilize high technology in our art (most of the time we are not even interested), we are meant to naively repeat what others have already done. We often feed this mythology by overstating our romantic nature and humanistic stances and/or by assuming the role of colonial victims of technology. We are ready to point out the fact that "computers are the source of the Anglos' social handicaps and sexual psychosis" and that communication in America, the land of the future, "is totally mediated by faxes, phones, computers, and other technologies we are not even aware of." We, "on the contrary," socialize profusely, negotiate information ritually and sensually, and remain in touch with our primeval selves. This simplistic binary worldview presents Mexico as technologically underdeveloped yet culturally and spiritually overdeveloped and the United States as exactly the opposite. Reality is much more complicated: the average Anglo-American does not understand new technologies either; people of color and women in the United States clearly don't have equal access to cyberspace; and at the same time, the average urban Mexican is already afflicted in varying degrees by the same "first world" existential diseases produced by advanced capitalism and high technology. In fact the new generations of Mexicans, including my hip generation-Mex nephews and my seven-year-old fully bicultural son, are completely immersed in and defined by personal computers, video games, and virtual reality. Far from being the romantic preindustrial paradise of the American imagination, the Mexico of the 1990s is already a virtual nation whose cohesiveness and boundaries are provided solely by television, transnational pop culture, and the free market. It is true that there are entire parts of the country which still lack basic infrastructures and public services (not to mention communications technology). But in 1996, the same can be said of the United States, a "first world" nation whose ruined "ethnic" neighborhoods, Native American reserves, and rural areas exist in conditions comparable to those of a "third world" country. When trying to link, say, Los Angeles and Mexico City via video-telephone, we encounter new problems. In Mexico, the only artists with "access" to this technology are upper-class, politically conservative, and uninteresting. And the funding sources down there willing to fund the project are clearly interested in controlling who is part of the experiment. In other words, we don't really need Octavio Paz conversing with Richard Rodriguez. We need Ruben Martinez talking to Monsivais, as well.

The world is waiting for you—so come on!
—Ad for America Online

The Cyber-migra

Roberto and I arrived late to the debate. When we began to dialogue with artists working with new technologies, we were perplexed by the fact that when referring to cyberspace or the Net, they spoke of a politically neutral/raceless/genderless/classless "territory" which provided us all with "equal access" and unlimited possibilities of participation, interaction, and belonging—especially belonging. Their enthusiastic rhetoric reminded us of both a sanitized version of the pioneer and cowboy mentalities of the Old West ("Guillermo, you can be the first Mexican ever to do this and that in the Net"), and the early-century Futurist cult to the speed and beauty of epic technology (airplanes, trains, factories, etc.). Given the existing "compassion fatigue" regarding political art dealing with issues of race and gender, it was hard not to see this feel-good utopian view of new technologies as an attractive exit from the acute social and racial crisis afflicting the United States. We were also perplexed by the "benign (not naive) ethnocentrism" permeating the debates around art and digital technology. The unquestioned lingua franca was of course English, the "official language of international communications"; the vocabulary utilized in these discussions was hyperspecialized and depoliticized; and if Chicanos and Mexicans didn't participate enough in the Net, it was solely because of lack of information or interest (not money or access), or again because we were "culturally unfit." The unspoken assumption was that our true interests were grassroots (by grassroots I mean the streets), representational, or oral (as if these concerns couldn't exist in virtual space). In other words, we were to remain dancing salsa, painting murals, writing flamboyant love poetry, and plotting revolutions in rowdy cafes. We were also perplexed by the recurring labels of "originality" and "innovation" attached to virtual art. And it was not the nature, contents, and structural complexity of the parallel realities created by digital technology, but the use of the technology per se that seemed to be "original" and "innovative." That, of course, has since engendered many conflicting responses. Native American shamans and medicine men rightfully see their centuries-old "visions" as a form of virtual reality. And Latin American writers equate their literary experimentation with involuntary hypertexts and vernacular postmodern aesthetics, and so do Chicanos and Chicanas. Like the pre-multicultural art world of the early 1980s, the new high-tech art world assumed an unquestionable "center" and drew a dramatic digital border. On the other side of that border lived all the techno-illiterate artists, along with most women, Chicanos, African Americans, and Native Americans. The role for us, then, was to assume, once again, the unpleasant but necessary role of cultural invaders, techno-pirates, and coyotes (smugglers). And then, just like multiculturalism was declared dead as soon as we began to share the paycheck, now as we venture into the virtual barrio for the first time some asshole at M.I.T. declares it dead. Why? It is no longer an exclusive space. It emulates too much real life and social demographics. Luckily many things have changed. Since we don't wish to reproduce the unpleasant mistakes of the multicultural days, our strategies are now quite different: we are no longer trying to persuade anyone that we are worthy of inclusion. Nor are we fighting for the same funding (since funding no longer exists). What we want is to "politicize" the debate; to "brownify" virtual space; to "spanglishize the Net;" to "infect" the lingua franca; to exchange a different sort of information—mythical, poetical, political, performative, imagistic; and on top of that to find grassroots applications to new technologies and hopefully to do all this with humor and intelligence. The ultimate goals are perhaps to help the Latino youth exchange their guns for computers and video cameras, and to link the community centers through the Net. CD-ROMs can perform the role of community memory banks, while the larger virtual community gets used to a new presence, a new sensibility, a new language.

PRONTOR-S

Part 4 | The Body: Disappearances, Anti-Bodies, Agents, and the Virus

Lynn Hershman Leeson
Shutter, Phantom Limb Number 17, 1990

The Labor of Perception

Lev Manovich

Work or Play

Walter Benjamin's writings return to the prototypical perceptual spaces of modernity: the factory, the movie theater, the shopping arcade. Scrutinizing these new spaces, Benjamin insisted on the contiguity between the perceptual experiences in the workplace and outside of it:

> Whereas Poe's passers-by cast glances in all directions which still appeared to be aimless, today's pedestrians are obliged to do so in order to keep abreast of traffic signals. Thus technology has subjected the human sensorium to a complex kind of training. There came a day when a new and urgent need for stimuli was met by the film. In a film, perception in the form of shocks was established as a formal principle. That which determines the rhythm of production on a conveyer belt is the basis of the rhythm of reception in the film.[1]

For Benjamin the modern regime of perceptual labor, where the eye is constantly asked to process stimuli, manifests itself equally in work and leisure. The eye is trained to keep pace with the rhythm of industrial production at the factory and to navigate through the complex visual hemisphere beyond the factory gates.

What would be the equivalents of film and conveyer belt for the perceptual experience of postmodernity? The most direct equivalents are an arcade type computer game and a military training simulator. But now not only do the two experiences provide the same stimuli but they also share the same technology. In fact, since the early 1990s many companies that before supplied very expensive simulators to the military are busy converting them into entertainment arcade-based systems. One of the first such systems already commercially operating in a number of major cities, including Chicago and Tokyo—Battletech Center from Virtual World Entertainment, Inc.—is directly modeled on SIMNET (Simulation Network), developed by DARPA (Defense Advanced Research Projects Agency). SIMNET can be thought of as the first model of cyberspace, the very first collaborative virtual reality (VR) environment. SIMNET consists of a number of individual simulators, networked together, each containing a copy of the world database and the virtual representation of all other participants in the conflict such as the Kuwaiti theater of operations. Similarly, a Battletech Center comprises a networked collection of futuristic cockpit models with VR gear. For seven dollars each, seven players can fight each other in a simulated environment. In another example, in 1992 Lucas Arts teamed up with Hughes Aircraft, combining the expertise in computer games of the former with the expertise in building actual flight simulators of the latter, in a joint venture aimed at theme-park type rides.[2]

A computer game and a flight simulator (or an actual cockpit) are only the most obvious examples of how contemporary visual culture is increasingly permeated by interactive computer-graphic information displays. Their presence points to an essential feature of the postindustrial society in which the human, both at work and at play, functions as a part of human-machine systems where vision acts as a main interface between the human and the machine. This article will consider some historical aspects of this phenomenon.

A human-machine system is defined as "an equipment system, in which at least one of the components is a human being who interacts with or intervenes in the operation of the machine components of the system from time to time."[3] In contrast to a manual worker of the industrial age, an operator in a human-machine system is primarily engaged in the observation of displays that present information in real time about the changing status of a system or an environment, real or virtual: a radar screen tracking a surrounding space, a computer screen updating the prices of stocks, a video screen of a computer game presenting an imaginary battlefield, a control panel of an automobile showing its speed, et cetera.[4] From time to time, some information causes an operator to make a decision and to intervene in the system's operation: tell the computer to track an enemy bomber noticed on the radar screen, buy or sell a stock, press a joystick, change gears. In some situations these interventions may be required every second (a pilot engaged with an enemy, a computer game player, a financial analyst monitoring stock prices), while in others they are needed very rarely (a technician monitoring an automated plant, power station, or nuclear reactor; a radar operator monitoring a radar screen, waiting for potential enemy planes).

The first kind of situation can be seen as a direct continuation of the experience described by Benjamin. In the quoted passage Benjamin characterized modern experience as a constant periodic rhythm of perceptual shocks, the experience shared by an assembly line worker, by a pedestrian, and by a film viewer. This experience is also characteristic of the cybernetic workplace: the constant overwhelming amount of information, the constant cascade of cognitive shocks that require immediate interventions (a pilot engaged with an enemy, a player of a computer game).[5] The second kind of situation, however, points to another work experience, new to postindustrial society: work as *waiting* for something to happen. A radar operator waiting for a tiny dot to appear on the screen; a technician monitoring an automated plant, power station, or nuclear reactor, knowing that a software bug will eventually manifest itself, making a pointer on one of numerous dials shoot into the red . . .

From Taylorism to Cognitive Science

Industrial society was characterized by the centrality of the concepts of manual labor, production of goods, and fatigue. Between 1940 and 1960, these were gradually replaced by new concepts of cognitive labor, information processing, and noise. Taylorism, Gilbreth motion studies, and behaviorism gave way to engineering psychology, human information processing, and cognitive science. In short, with the transformation of industrial society into postindustrial society, disciplines of the efficiency of the body were replaced by disciplines concerned with the efficiency of the new instrument of labor—the mind.

In *The Human Motor: Energy, Fatigue, and the Origins of Modernity,* Anson Rabinbach demonstrated how the scientific ideas of thermodynamics, formulated in the middle of the nineteenth century, became central for the conception of work in modernity. Helmholtz, who discovered the law of the conservation of energy, promoted this law as the universal principle that applies equally to nature, machines, and humans. Helmholtz "portrayed the movements of the planets, the forces of nature, the productive force of machines, and of course, human labor power as examples of the principle of conservation of energy."[6] All work was understood as the expenditure of energy, with a crucial consequence of redefining human labor as "labor power," the expenditure of the energy of a body. Thus a worker was redefined as a "human motor." This, in turn, lead to the emergence, toward the end of the century, of the movement which Rabinbach calls the European science of work, "the search for the precise laws of muscles, nerves, and the efficient expenditure of energy centered on the physiology of labor."[7] In manual labor, the energy stored in the body, where it was accumulated through the intake of food, sleep, and rest, is transferred into muscular force—a hammerer striking a blow, a filer filing a machine part, and so on. Therefore, psychologists, physiologists, and industrial experts searched for methods to maximize both the accumulation of a worker's energy (through proper nutrition, shorter working hours, appropriate breaks) and its expenditure in labor. Just as an engineer designing an engine was concerned with the most efficient transfer of fuel energy into movement, European work experts aimed to maximize worker efficiency and to eliminate possible waste. Central to the quest for the efficiency of the human motor was the struggle against fatigue, understood as the equivalent of entropy. "As entropy revealed the loss of energy involved in any transfer of force, so fatigue revealed the loss of energy in the conservation of labor power to socially useful production. As energy was the transcendental, 'objective' force in nature, fatigue became the objective nemesis of a society founded on labor power."[8]

The European science of work may appear to be very similar to the American scientific management movement pioneered by Frederick Winslow Taylor, a former engineer turned management consultant. As a part of his program, Taylor aimed to minimize and standardize the time required by a worker to perform each operation. He employed the method of time studies whereby the best workers were timed, and the results became the norm to be followed by the rest.[9] Later, Frank and Lillian Gilbreth (he, an engineer—she, a psychologist) popularized another method of motion study.[10] They argued that maximizing worker productivity is best achieved by the elimination of unnecessary movements and making the necessary more efficient.

Although both time and motion studies and the European science of work were concerned with the efficiency of manual work, there was a fundamental difference between the two approaches.[11] Taylorism aimed for *maximum* productivity, and had no concern for the exhaustion and deterioration of the human motor. In contrast, European scientists aimed for *optimum* productivity, and therefore were concerned not only with the rationalization of the workplace but also with the workers' health, nutrition, safety, and the optimal length of a workday. In short, Taylorism had no reservations about replacing one exhausted human motor with another—the philosophy that in the United States seemed to go hand in hand with the emerging ethics of the consumer society and with immigration policies that assured the constant supply of a cheap labor force. Europeans, on the other hand, were committed to caring for and servicing the human motor. The two paradigms converged after World War I, when European industrialists partly adopted the more brutal, but ultimately more effective, Taylorist methods, while U.S. management experts became more sensitive to workers' physiology and psychology.

Taylorism reduced the worker's body to a mechanical machine and had no concern for her or his mind. Indeed, as Marta Braun points out, Taylorism aimed to systematically rob the worker of any degree of independence or even understanding of the overall work process by "separating responsibility for the execution of work from its planning or conception."[12] This disdain for the mind was shared by behaviorism, which matured at the same time as the European science of work and Taylorism, and which also characterizes the image of hard-edged social engineering of the first half of the twentieth century. In 1913 J. B. Watson, the founder of behaviorism, explicitly defined it as the science of social control: "Psychology as the behaviorist views it is a purely objective experimental branch of natural science. Its theoretical goal is the prediction and control of behavior."[13] Behaviorism approached the human subject as an input-output system of stimulus and response to be controlled through conditioning. Concerned with controlling the body, it almost completely suppressed any studies of perceptual or mental processes between 1920 and 1950 in the United States. It was a psychology well suited for controlling the subject already reduced to the brainless human motor.

In the 1950s cognitive psychology began to displace then-dominant behaviorism. Since then, what comes under the scrutiny of psychologists are mental functions: perception, attention, text comprehension, memory, and problem solving. I read this as one of the most important signs of the shift from industrial to postindustrial society. The point is not whether corporeal labor was indeed universally displaced by mental labor—this is different from country to country, from industry to industry. What is important is that the obsession with the rationalization of corporeal work (Taylorism, European science of work, psychotechnics) disappeared, displaced by a new obsession with the rationalization of the mind (cognitive psychology, artificial intelligence, cognitive engineering). Regardless of the percentage of the workforce that still may be engaged in manual labor, society is no longer concerned with spending more intellectual resources to perfect workers' movements.

What Taylor's scientific management was for the age of industrialization, cognitive sciences became for the age of automation. In the 1940s Herbert Simon worked on theories of management, the field of research originated by Taylor. Having recognized the increasing importance of mental skills in the corporate workplace, Simon became one of the pioneers of cognitive science with his work on automatic reasoning by computer. In 1964 he wrote that "the bulk of productive wealth consists of programs . . . stored in human minds."[14] Another pioneer of cognitive science was Jerome Bruner. Reflecting on his work in the 1950s, he noted in 1983: "It seems plain to me now that the 'cognitive revolution' . . . was a response to the technological demands of the 'post-industrial revolution.' You cannot properly conceive of managing a complex world of information without a workable concept of mind."[15]

The replacement of manual work by cognitive work is directly related to automation. In 1961, in an influential study of automation in French industry, Pierre Naville and his fellow sociologists had described the transition from the "work of the laborer to the work of communication," work that became primarily "cognitive or semiotic."[16] In his summary of this study Rabinbach writes, "The appearance of the cerebral worker whose material and product is 'information' is emblematic of the vast distance traversed between the worker who surveys complex technologies of communication and the 'man-beef' of Taylor."[17]

It is important to note that automation does not lead to the replacement of human by machine. Rather, the worker's role becomes one of monitoring and regulation: watching displays, analyzing incoming information, making decisions, and operating controls. And it is the corresponding human functions of perception, attention, memory, and problem solving that become the subject of research by new cognitive sciences.

The rise of cognitive sciences is one aspect of the larger shift from industrial to postindustrial society and the corresponding new image of work and play: visual and mental processing of information rather than corporeal activity. A complementary development is the emergence, during World War II, of the new discipline of applied experimental psychology, or, as it was also called, "human engineering."

Human Engineering

The gradual expansion of the practical applications of experimental psychology provides a precise map of the new occupations and new conditions of modern experience that call for perceptual skills. During World War I, England, Germany, and France utilized experimental psychologists to design and administer tests for pilots, airplane observers, hydrophone operators, and submarine "listeners-in."[18] During peacetime a number of psychologists published papers on the readability of written text and highway signs and on the visibility of lights at sea.[19] However, in the industrial world, which conceived of the worker as a human motor and was largely concerned with the productivity of manual rather than perceptual labor, these studies were an exception rather than the mainstream rule.

It was during World War II when the expertise of experimental psychologists was finally put to use. Why did this happen? The first textbook on applied experimental psychology (1949) opens by describing the recent origins of the field:

> For years experimental psychologists have worked diligently in academic laboratories studying man's capacities to perceive, to work, and to learn. Only very slowly, however, have the facts and methods which they have assembled been put to use in everyday life. A particularly glaring gap in modern technology, both industrial and military, is the lack of human engineering—engineering of machines for human use and engineering of human tasks for operating machines. Motion-and-time engineers have been at work on many of these problems, but the experimental psychologist is also needed for his fundamental knowledge of human capacities and his methods of measuring human performance.

> The recent war put the spotlight on this gap. The war needed, and produced, many complex machines, and it taxed the resources of both the designer and operator in making them practical for human use. The war also brought together psychologists, physiologists, physicists, design engineers, and motion-and-time engineers to solve some of these problems. Though much of their work began too late to do any real good, it has continued on a rather large scale into the peace.
>
> Today, there are many groups busy with research on man-machine problems. They use different names to describe the work in its various aspects: biotechnology, biomechanics, psychoacoustics, human engineering, and systems research. Other names may be appropriate and may appear in the future. In casting about for a title for this book, we tried to select one that would describe the subject matter without the restrictive connotations attaching to some of the names mentioned above. *Applied Experimental Psychology* seems best to fill these requirements, because the traditional data and subject of experimental psychology are fundamental to this field.[20]

Before the war experimental psychologists had assisted in selecting military personnel for such jobs as pilot or airplane observer by administering special aptitude tests. During the war a much greater number of pilots, radar operators, and other similar personnel were needed. The emphasis was shifted, therefore, from selecting personnel with particularly good perceptual and motor skills to designing the equipment (controls, radar screens, dials, warning lights) to match the sensory capacities of an average person.[21] And it was the field of experimental psychology that possessed the knowledge about the sensory capacities of a statistically average person: how visibility and acuity vary between day and night, how the ability to distinguish colors and brightness varies with illumination or distance, what the smallest amount of light is that can be reliably noticed, and so on.[22] All this data was now utilized for designing better displays and controls of the first modern human-machine systems, such as high-speed aircraft or radar installations.

The development of these new human-machine systems during the war pushed human perceptual and mental performance to the limit, and this was the second reason why experimental psychologists were called in. The performance of a human-machine system was limited by human capacity to process information. In the words of the authors of *Applied Experimental Psychology*,

> We can make a machine that will do almost anything, given enough time and enough engineers. But man has limits to his developments, at least as far as we can see it. When we think how much a single radar can do in a small fraction of a second, and then realize by comparison that even the simplest form of reaction for a human being requires about a fifth of a second, we realize what we are up against. . . . The full potential of radar, for example, lagged far behind physical developments because human operators could not master the complex operation of this machine system. We had to worry about such things as a new kind of visual signal—very small and not very bright.[23]

Considering that the authors described the work of time-and-motion engineers as directly leading to applied experimental psychology, this rhetoric can be expected. Taylor was impatient with the limitations of the body; now there was a similar impatience with the limitations of human information processing. With Taylor it was a question of the speed of muscular movements; now it became a question of reaction time: the minimum time in milliseconds required for an operator to detect a signal, to identify it, to press a control.

In order to measure normal human sensory capacities, experimental psychologists have always put subjects in, so to speak, boundary conditions. They measured sensory "thresholds," such as the least amount of light that can be detected. They also measured "just noticeable differences," the smallest detectable difference between two stimuli. Finally, they measured "reaction times," the measure that became the main tool to deduce the time taken by different mental processes. In order to measure these characteristics, a number of standard experiments were designed, and they remained largely unchanged from the time of Weber, Fechner, and Wundt. In a "detection" experiment, the task of an observer is to detect the presence of barely visible stimuli, for instance, a tiny light briefly flashed in the dark (did I see something?). In an "identification" experiment, the task is to identify which of several possible stimuli was presented, for instance, which of two colors (which one did I see?). In a "recognition" experiment, the task is not only to detect something but to recognize what it is, for instance, what was the shape that briefly appeared (what did I see?).

During World War II, the radar operator, the anti-aircraft gunner, and the pilot found themselves in the same situations in which nineteenth-century psychologists put their experimental subjects. The setups of psychophysical experiments became, in all details, the conditions of military work. The tasks devised by psychologists to study human vision became the actual tasks faced by the operators of human-machine systems. Like the subject of a detection experiment, a radar operator scans the radar screen for a barely noticeable dot of light.[24] Like the subject of an identification experiment, he has to try to guess whether this dot is the same or different from another dot, which from his previous experience he knows to correspond to a friendly airplane. An anti-aircraft gunner is subjected to a recognition experiment, trying to identify a plane by its shape. And all of them, especially the pilot, are engaged in a sort of reaction time experiment.

Thus nineteenth-century psychophysical setups became the military, and soon, civilian workplaces of postindustrial society; from there, they traveled back into laboratories, leading to such close interrelations between basic research in experimental psychology and its practical applications that they were no longer separable. For example, a 1947 article in *American Psychologist* describes the work of the Naval Research Laboratory as following these three directions: "the design of gun fire control and missile control instruments from the point of view of ease and efficiency of operation; the design and evaluation of synthetic gunnery and missile control trainers; and basic psychological research." But what is meant here by "basic research"? We read that "at present, all basic research studies are aimed at the eye-hand coordination problem involved in target tracking." Target tracking is just one example of a military task that traveled into a psychological laboratory and gradually become a standard psychophysical experiment.[25]

The terms "applied experimental psychology," "human engineering," and "man-machine engineering" were replaced by another term standard today—"human factors." The radar operator, who in the 1940s and 1950s was the prototypical example of a human-machine system, was replaced in the 1980s by a new prototypical figure, the computer user. Thus references to "human-machine systems" became references to "human-computer systems." The same amount of intellectual energy and research that in mid-century went into theorizing the performance of a radar operator, and adapting him and the radar display to each other, today goes into the work on computer interfaces. In retrospect then, we should recognize the radar operator as the central figure standing at the origins of postindustrial society, the figure that put directly into motion the new disciplines of the efficiency of the mind: engineering psychology, human information processing, and cognitive science.

If the radar screen of the 1940s was the first modern visual human-machine interface, VR gear is the most recent. While VR is commonly associated with the notions of escape from reality and unrestricted play and fantasy, in fact it is yet another development in the history of human engineering. As an example, consider a popular photograph from the late 1980s which showcased the virtual reality interface designed at NASA/Ames Human Factors Research Center.[26] The gear was constructed by human factors specialists, the direct descendants of the human engineers of the 1940s. The specialists utilized all the knowledge accumulated by psychology about human vision in order to employ it most efficiently.

In the photograph we see the last leftover from the age of manual labor—an arm in a data glove. It will soon disappear, since through gaze tracking the operator can control the system by merely looking at different points in virtual space. Perceptual labor has become the foundation of both work and play.

Attack on the Brain

Reflections on Neurotechnology

Florian Rötzer
Translated by Don Reneau

By now the brain has become the central object of a science that combines an extremely high level of multi- and interdisciplinary collaboration with the steady invention of new technologies for analyzing, observing, and directly influencing the brain. At the same time, new computer architectures designed as part of the effort to develop artificial intelligence, artificial life, and autonomous robots have begun taking the brain as their model. These two research trends have until now proceeded largely independently of each other, but are now, in the "decade of the brain," showing signs of increasing cooperation. They are joining forces to discover new interfaces between the computer and the human brain, and, together, they will make advances far beyond what has been possible to date. The focus in the future will move beyond the interactive control of computer systems, the mapping and representation of brain activity, or the implantation of brain tissue or computer chips to substitute for particular mental functions. The therapeutic treatment of illnesses and defects, in other words, will give way, as it already has in gene technology, to the "improvement" of people and their cognitive abilities, as well as to the direct stimulation of the brain in the name of integrating it as a constituent element into computer systems.

This "attack on the brain" is just beginning, and the extent to which science and technology will succeed in their efforts to intervene strategically into the highly complex system of the brain is by no means clear at present. The conversations reproduced here, with experts from the areas of brain research, artificial intelligence, and psychiatry, offer an exemplary look at the various assessments of the present situation. One obvious finding is that the more technologically oriented specialists are more optimistic than the brain researchers about the possibility of developing neurotechnological implants. Even so, existing procedures for transplanting brain tissue already raise a host of scientific and ethical questions and, much more than other organ transplants, threaten to undermine our notions of human autonomy, individuality, and identity. Should it ever become possible to slow the aging process so that people would live indefinitely, perhaps by introducing some substance into the brain's biological clock, in the context of current world population figures, it is possible to imagine catastrophic scenarios. Just the gains in life expectancy of the last few decades have led to an explosive increase in the incidence of neurological disorders. The development of neuroprosthetics and of techniques for transplanting brain tissue emerges as part of the effort to find new treatments.

As always, progress in science and technology finds legitimacy in the idea that it enhances human control over the environment, that it increases our power. The possibility of intervening directly into the brain, however, appears to suggest the permanent obsolescence of that idea. Once the brain is coupled to a technological system, whether by means of an implant or via an external hookup, the question arises as to the underlying motivation and, beyond that, the extent of social acceptance and support for what remains a precedent setting and extremely innovative area of scientific activity: combining brain research and computer technology. The implications of this work will transform life in the future, or at least our understanding of ourselves, a process that is indeed long since underway. Whenever we understand the brain as an information processing system, or distinguish between hardware and software, whenever we believe, or fear, that artificial systems are capable of simulating human cognitive achievements, or when we define our own capacities in comparative reference to intelligent computer systems, we give evidence of the impact of scientific advances. As the carrier of human cognitive, emotional, and psychological abilities and sensibilities, the brain is in a certain sense our most intimate organ. It now finds itself not only in competition with technological imitators but—to a much greater extent than is generally known—also the target of new interventions in medical technology, in the form of both surgical procedures and sensory or chemical stimulation.

Research, at least in branches aiming at medical applications, is still in its infancy. The great success to date is an implant for patients suffering hearing loss resulting from damage to the inner ear that has left the nervus vestibulocochlearis intact. A device is implanted into the cochlea and uses electrodes to transmit sound signals to the auditory nerve endings. An external microphone is fitted to the patient to pick up acoustic signals and forward them in the form of electrical pulses to a speech processor, which then analyzes the frequency spectrum and encodes the signals. A transmitter then sends the modulated signals through the skin to the receiving coil in the implanted electrodes. This chip demodulates and decodes the signals so that the appropriate stimulatory impulses can be sent on, via as many as 22 electrodes, to the auditory nerves. The remaining task, which can be a lengthy one, following implantation is to adapt the neurochip to the individual patient.

It is not possible to enable people who were born deaf, who never learned to decode acoustic signals, to hear, which is to say that it is not possible, or not yet possible, to use neurochips to outfit the brain with new functions either for which it is not designed or for which the competence was not developed ontogenetically. On the other hand, because of their highly plastic nature, neural networks in the brain are capable of adapting to new stimuli as long as they "understand" them. Devices have been used successfully to stimulate the bladder in quadriplegics, and visual cortex implants to stimulate the production of phosphene are currently in the development phase. Research on visual prostheses began as early as the 1970s, with Paul Bach-y-Rita's work with blind patients, for example, which used small video cameras mounted on eyeglass frames. Fitted onto the patient's back or stomach were a circuit box and a matrix of 16-by-16 or 20-by-20 "pixels," to which the camera transmitted signals either electrically or by means of mechanical vibrations. Even with such poor resolution, patients, after an initial learning period, became capable of identifying signs, objects, and faces.

The Neural Prosthesis Program has been in existence in the United States since the 1980s. German scientists, however, are also aware of opportunities for innovation and of the spin-off potential of neurotechnology, and in the hard competition over technology, they see their chance to get in early on a trend. The Ministry for Education, Research, and Science has recently approved the Neurotechnology Project, aimed at the development of a neuroprosthesis for quadriplegics. The plan is to use a device to relay motor impulses from the brain, bypassing damaged neural pathways, and enable patients to stand and walk again. The implant, in this case, involves receivers and a system designed to stimulate the muscles, while command input, feedback, the master control system, and the transmitter will be fitted externally to the body. A verbal command system, with a microphone and a language recognition system, will be necessary for the prosthesis to control physical movements from outside the body, and the same device will use speech to notify the wearer of malfunctions. Initial plans foresee using a body suit equipped with the sensors necessary to assess conditions in the motor system and establish a feedback loop. Another project seeks to develop a retinal implant, which in its technical characteristics resembles the cochlea implant, if on a much more complex scale.

The feasibility study leading up to the Neurotechnology Project, conducted under the direction of Rolf Eckmiller, also raised ethical issues. There is no question, for example, that patients who have lost their sight, were born blind, or are unable to hear would find their quality of life improved by a functioning neuroprosthesis; it would enhance autonomy and encourage social interaction. Most patients would surely be eager to participate as experimental subjects in the development of such devices. But according to the neurotechnology report summary, "Fundamentally new ethical questions regarding the effects of neurotechnological applications" would not arise in regard to treatment of the retina, spinal cord, or peripheral nerves, but do come up "with the intracranial implantation of such systems in the brain. These procedures unavoidably raise questions concerning the autonomy, personality, and personal identity of the patient. The planned neurotechnology pilot project will not involve any such application areas."

In other words, the development of neurochips for implantation in the central regions of the brain will not be pursued out of consideration for questions of social acceptability. Yet once the basic technology has been developed and the problems of biocompatibility and individual adaptation resolved, it is easy to see that matters will not rest there. Neurotechnology clearly represents a continuation of a trend toward hardware-intensive or high-tech medicine, and it is based on the neuron hypothesis, that is, on the premise that the nervous system consists of individual, physically separate, essentially homogenous cells or units, which transmit information primarily by electrical means. A further condition for the development of neuroprostheses is the ability to locate specific functional areas in the brain, or, in the technical term, modules. Since communication between the synapses of nerve cells is accomplished by chemical transmitters, and the cells are themselves organized in neurochemical systems, there are many different types of cells, with the significance of the glia cells remaining unknown. It may be, for all of these reasons, and not merely because of the enormous complexity of the brain, that attempts to intervene strategically into higher brain functions will fail.

Existing technologies, which we understand on the basis of our ability to build them, often serve as the models used to explain sensory, motor, and other human mental capacities. Technology seeks to externalize cognitive abilities in the form of apparatuses or machines, raising a constant temptation to understand human function in mechanical terms. The eye is regarded as a camera obscura or photographic or film camera; the ear as a microphone; the memory as a tape recorder, a computer memory, or hologram; and the intellect as a calculator. Such comparisons are not new, incidentally, but are characteristic of the whole of modernity. Any technology that records, processes, and reproduces sensory stimuli, which constructs a perceptible world as an illusion or simulation for human purposes, necessarily operates within the biologically given parameters of human perception and thus, intuitively or explicitly, occasions research into perceptual mechanisms. In that common focus brain research, medical technology, and art all complement each other. Even simply knowing precisely what cannot yet be done contributes to the practice of seeing the brain's capacities reflected in machines, and vice versa. Lev Manovich uses the examples of film and then computer technology to show how each appears to explain certain cognitive image processing mechanisms, and how, embedded in those very externalizations, is a desire to influence the human brain in a specific manner.

The process of externalization seems now, however, to be reversing course into a process of internalization. The point of the Neurotechnology Project is to relocate externalized technologies, for recording, processing, and reproducing sensory signals or motor impulses, back into the brain in the form of biocompatible, computer-controlled modules. The interface between human being and the machine shifts to a position inside the human body, with the brain itself understood as a biological machine, either made up of interchangeable modules or of such a nature that it is possible to effect exact responses with technologically manufactured signals. The traditional practice has been to treat certain illnesses or disorders by excising portions of the brain, or jolting it with massive, physically damaging electroshocks. Now, however, it seems that neurotechnology, relying on functional electro-stimulation, is ready and able to replace those mostly nonspecific interventions by targeted manipulation.

This new approach only became possible on the basis of further progress in the development of microsystems and computer technology. The task, after all, was to make a device small enough to be implanted that was capable of recording neural impulses or stimulating as many axons of as many nerves as possible. Moreover, either the electrical stimuli had to be made intelligible to the nervous system, or the neural pulse sequences intelligible to the technological system. Every brain ultimately has its own unique structure, with functions individualized within certain parameters, so the technological system must be able to adapt to the biological system and vice versa. Required for this task are intelligent, flexible, "near-biological" computers, of the kind being developed today under the name of "neural networks." No fixed program could even approach the necessary capacity to adapt to constant changes in the sequences of neural impulses and "understand" them.

Neurons these days are seen as microprocessors, and many people think of the brain as a kind of digital computer, which processes information like a calculator. Before it became possible to establish neuro-information science as a discipline, however, advances had to be made beyond von Neumann computers, which relied on a single central unit to carry out linear information processing. New computer architectures have become available which are more similar to the brain, particularly in regard to its tremendous parallel processing ability, though even these highly sophisticated technological neural networks remain many orders of magnitude inferior to their biological counterparts. Research into artificial intelligence and robotics has also been gradually turned around by advances in the science of neuro-information. Prior models tended to fail precisely at those tasks that are routine for human beings, while inside extremely reduced environments and contexts they performed preprogrammed tasks better and more quickly. The new model is drawn increasingly from biology and evolution; the challenge has become to design technological systems that can perceive, orient themselves, move, and act in the natural complex environment.

If the earlier attempt was to simulate presumably higher human cognitive abilities, or even to build humanlike robots, the effort now, as in the use of the "genetic algorithms" developed by John Holland, is to proceed from the bottom to the top. To write programs to solve complex problems, for example, it is normally necessary to predetermine every possible successive situation. Not only does that take a long time, but something can be overlooked or something else not be foreseen. The optimization of programs in the manner of biological evolution therefore seems simpler, even if the cost of the new procedure is increasing nontransparency. With genetic algorithms, which use the evolutionary mechanisms of selection, mutation, and genetic crossover through "mating," "populations" of nonidentical or even random chains of ones and zeroes are exposed to a problem field and assessed for their quality in providing solutions. To achieve a nonlinear organization for the genetic algorithms, for the sake of and adaptability to complex situations, rules also compete with each other, and all the rules that take part in a "successful" action are rewarded or fortified. What is primary to the innovative areas of bio- and computer technology is no longer the management of predefined and symbolically encoded knowlege, but the possibilities opened up by a capacity for learning and perceptual orientation and action in the real world. An important role in this development was played by cellular automats, which were anticipated by John von Neumann on the basis of simulations of biological reproducibility. For further development, particularly in the area we now subsume under the rubric of "artificial life" (AL), research proceeds on the assumption of bottom-up calculation paradigms, parallel processing, and the localized behavior of the individual automats or calculators. AL systems are nonlinear, that is, the behavior of the whole system not only is the sum of its, in principle, isolatable parts but derives from the interaction of the parts. Early successes with what are initially "dumb" neural networks, operating exclusively with nonsymbolic elements, show that they organize themselves according to what they learn, and thus are already better than their predecessors at carrying out simple perceptual tasks.

This change can perhaps be seen most clearly in robotics, another form of externalization that attempts to make practicable autonomous intelligent systems. The current belief is that it is possible to take a step toward intelligent autonomous robots, capable of moving and acting in the world, by way of primitive insectlike robots whose behavior is not preprogrammed but emerges step by step in interaction with the environment, through learning and in the absence of any superordinate control. At issue here, therefore, are the preconditions and foundations of intelligent robotic behavior whereby the robot uses simple motor and sensory abilities to find out about its environment, and is able to adapt to changing situations through permanent feedback with the senso-motor systems. Autonomous robots are put together out of many different behavioral systems, with no one of them ascribed in any particular fashion to any other. In a certain sense, they "compete" with each other in solving a task. It is possible to imagine Marvin Minsky's "society of the mind" in similar terms, in which higher behavior emerges out of the combined effects of many agents. It is obvious that robotics models are inspired by brain research, and that the technical realization of senso-motor systems capable of learning can in turn become important for the development of neurochips. The increasing autonomy of artificial life forms is a concomitant of the possibility of ever improving ways of linking human beings to computer systems. Technological development, in any case, aims now at imitating biological evolution from simple to more complex systems, in which the cognitive and motor abilities of animals and human beings are gradually being transferred or externalized to a machine. This is the basis for Hans Moravec's ideal of the future seizure of power by "mind children," who replace human beings with biological hardware.

Expert opinion as to our chances for realizing the promise of neurotechnology is divided. Marvin Minsky, who likes to provoke, believes that only fear and received taboos have so far prevented us from researching, producing, and installing direct interfaces between the brain and computers: "With a data glove the machine can receive information from my fingers. As early as next year, perhaps, we'll be able to connect a cable to the nerves in your arm. . . . In the immediate future, we could install a small plug in the nerve controlling all the muscles in your arm, then we could connect up with the nerve. The neuro-electrical connection is interesting, because the arm's motor nerves transmit signals that could be stored in a computer. Then the computer can feel the same thing you can, and it can send signals to the motor nerves that move your arm. At that point it becomes possible to control the arm movements of someone putting together tape recorders in a factory completely by means of the computer. . . . What's the next step? We could do a simple operation, remove a small piece of the skull, and implant pliable circuit boards with a couple million sensors and transmitters into the brain. We could already do that today, if not for certain prejudices, if all the lawyers weren't making brain research so difficult. In a few years, if we wanted, we could control a computer with our thoughts alone—entirely without hands, pens, keyboards, mouse, data glove, whole-body suits, or all those wonderful things from the world of telepresence. All that we see must perish, say the Christians. But, if we don't waste time, we could be reborn in twenty or thirty years into a new world of the mind, in which it is possible to dictate thoughts directly into a machine—that would be like heaven."[1]

The background of such technological utopias lies not only in longings for immortality but even more in the desire for perfection. The body has no value in itself; it can be completed, complemented, or even replaced, and should be as far as possible. Very much in the tradition of the castigation of the flesh, and of the interpretation by religion and philosophy of the body as the prison of the soul or spirit, neurotechnology stands for the possibility of gradually separating the mental system from its biological seat and transferring it as a program to a new carrier that lasts longer and can be repaired. What becomes increasingly clear, on the other hand, is how greatly the brain remains in all of its functions bound to and oriented toward the body. Nevertheless, just the idea of being able, solely by thinking—that is, via the registration and interpretation in some form of neural activity—to influence something in the real world, even if it is nothing more than the movement of a cursor on a computer screen, is fascinating. There is also something uncanny about it—especially in a time in which . . . inflated expectations, as well as exaggerated fears, are aroused unnecessarily. A 1993 survey by the EMNID Institute, commissioned by the Wissenschaftszentrum Nordrhein-Westfalen, was designed to identify ideas and fears regarding brain research and neuromedicine in the population as a whole. Over 70 percent of respondents agreed that the ability to intervene directly into the brain would represent great progress, but at the same time nearly 80 percent were of the opinion that brain research should be held to especially strict ethical standards. Moreover, more than 40 percent thought that a direct connection between a computer and the brain would not be ethically acceptable, and over 50 percent that the brain, as the seat of the soul, should not be researched without limitation simply for the sake of explaining the functioning of human thinking, consciousness, and feeling. This odd discrepancy could be the result of limited knowledge about brain research, but what it perhaps expresses above all is that, while brain research is fascinating, the brain itself, as the foundation of the personality, is understood as one last refuge, which should not be wholly given over to technological intervention. Forging a direct technological connection to the brain seems to be more threatening than everyday intervention by way of psychopharmaceuticals, drugs, and media.

Neurotechnology has long been a staple of science fiction. But some of the speculations to which it was possible to freely abandon oneself 40 years ago, as Stansilaw Lem remarks, are today in the process of becoming reality. Authors such as William Gibson and Bruce Sterling introduced readers to cyborgs, human beings whose brains are directly connected to computer systems, an image that inspired considerable fascination once it made its way into the popular computer culture of the 1980s. In place of the first virtual reality systems, which fell far short of expectations and could not be tolerated by users for lengthy sessions, there were now artificial, computer-generated, interactive images into which the user could actually enter. Cyber-riders, outfitted with helmets and whole-body suits, moved into a virtual world, separated from their immediate environments by the input-output interfaces worn on their body and sense organs. These still quite primitive immersive media, however, gave rise to a vacuum, which is being filled by ever improved and expanded contact with artificial worlds and the development of ever more perfect interfaces that effectively draw the user into the medium. Artists are making increasing use of brain activity, registered as electroencephalograms (EEGs), to control computer programs. The incorporation of other physical conditions, such as skin resistivity, heartbeat, and so on, is being tried out in the name of intensifying experience and recording reactions. Horst Prehn, professor of medical technology and an artist, picks up from earlier installations using EEGs as the interface between the user and the computer, in pursuit of a project that is emblematic of emerging brain art:

> On a planetarium dome, NeuroVision shows projections of various typologies of the cortex ("cerebrarium"). From the recipient under the "brain dome," we take a topographical electroencephalogram (CATEEM, or computer-aided electroencephalometry) in almost real time. This way we can take an array of

> different neurologically relevant direct representations of the cortical stimulation pattern, and encode and symbolize them temporally, spatially, and by color, and project them onto the corresponding brain areas. The recipient thus becomes the first witness of his or her own specific brain stimulation pattern. Beyond such efforts, less direct visual representations selected more according to aesthetic criteria are symbolized in the form of a "polychromatic state space." The dynamic control of the complex spatial color and graphic structures is based on the reception of cortical signals (EEG, ERP, VEP, AEP, and others), but also of physical signals, that is, specific cardiac, circulatory, and aspiration magnitudes, as well as through psychophysiological (SCL) and myoelectrical responses (EMG). Along with the visualization, the recipient's psychophysical and somatic reactions are also made audible and meaningfully symbolized through tones. This gives rise to complex dynamic color and sound spaces, with a penetrating aesthetic dimension. They evoke subjectively significant mental and emotional states in the recipient, and changes in state, again in a specific manner, exercise a reciprocal effect back on the audiovisual orchestration. With this, a closed control circuit has been established between the participant and the projections of his or her own unique mental and physical states. The "mental and emotional space adventure" can begin, drawing the "neuronauts" under its spell, with an unending multiplicity of unanticipated experiential episodes.[2]

So-called brain or mind machines, designed to use a series of specific acoustic and visual signals to give rise to specific brain conditions, are already widespread. The feedback potential of an EEG is already in use therapeutically to render conditions in the brain conscious and subject to control. Although all sensory experience can ultimately be understood as resulting from stimulation of the brain, there is currently a shift underway from a fascination with the most perfect possible stimulation to the possibilities of direct stimulation, which attempts to abbreviate the process by doing away with the need to create external stimuli. If artists are using the EEG to control interactive computer programs or to create a certain state of consciousness, it can also be put to use for surveillance and social control.

There has always been a strong popular interest in using all available stimulants and the newest technologies to intensify sensation, so that, in a certain sense, people become part of a total artwork. Shortly after Alexis Carrel undertook the first successful organ transplants in animals, the Futurists were the first to hail cyborgs, or combinations of human beings and machines, as the explicit and emphatic future of the new human race. Filippo Tommaso Marinetti promoted the idea of the "identification of human being with the motor," the development of a "mechanical non-human type," a "manifold individual," capable of "innumerable human metamorphoses," equipped with new organs able to keep pace with "all-pervasive speed," and providing a constant supply of intense stimulation. For Marinetti the great breakthrough would be when it became possible for a human being "to turn his will on the outside world in such a form that it would continue like an invisible arm beyond the body"—which EEG technology has made a reality today. In his *Technological Manifesto of Futurist Literature* (1912), Marinetti wrote:

> After the empire of living beings comes the empire of the machine. Through knowledge of and friendship with matter, which the natural scientist is capable of knowing only in the form of physical-chemical reactions, we are preparing for the creation of the mechanical human being with spare parts. We will liberate it from the idea of death, and therefore from death itself, which is the highest definition of logical intelligence.[3]

If we already use drugs, music, light organs, virtual reality, sports, and other means or technologies of ecstasy to stimulate the brain, why not then go ahead and use direct electrical stimulation? The performances or experiments of the Australian artist Stelarc, who radically refashions his body into a biotechnological artwork, testify to his desire to be linked up or to expand his functions through technology. Why should we not expand, improve, or complete certain mental functions as well, just as we use traditional machines to extend our motor functions? Why should we not use such chips in psychiatric treatment or even in criminal sentencing? All of this lies in the future, but it has long since ceased being mere fantasy. The French philosopher Paul Virilio sees in the "colonialization of the body" underway today the attempt to conform the body and brain to the ever increasing mechanical demands of postindustrial society. The increase in machines makes people more and more sedentary; their bodies become appendages; their brains, as in a computer game, must be constantly stimulated:

> Preparations are already underway to equip the mass of living beings with micromachines, by means of which our capabilities can be effectively stimulated. The invalid who overcomes his handicap thanks to his equipment suddenly becomes the model for the healthy person who is overequipped with prostheses of all conceivable sorts. . . . The motionlessness and passivity of the postmodern individual makes an increase in overstimulation unavoidable, not only in obviously degenerated types of sport, but also in the performance of everyday actions, whereby the emancipation of the body brought about by technologies of real-time teleaction leads to the elimination of the one-time necessity of both physical strength and muscular exertion.
>
> The invention of the cardiac pacemaker, which assists in the production of, or even replaces, the rhythm of life, marks in the final analysis one of the origins of this form of biotechnological innovation. After the age of animal organ "transplants," now comes the age of the "transplant of technical devices," whereby the mixing of technology and life, the organic heterogeneity, no longer has anything to do with an alien body introduced into the body of the patient but is comprised of an alien rhythm, the purpose of which is to make the body vibrate in harmony with the machine.[4]

Neurotechnology, from the perspective of brain research, is the result of numerous prior experiments and surgical procedures. Experience with electro-stimulation has also been, and is being, gained in the course of treating patients suffering, for example, from epilepsy. Brain stimulation to locate affected areas precisely plays a role in certain necessary surgical procedures, with the effect that knowledge is deepened, not only about the state of a patient with local brain damage but also about the position and function of particular brain areas. Such knowledge has indeed been put to irresponsible use in psychosurgery, for the purpose of intentionally destroying brain tissue in cases of severe psychiatric disturbances. In the mid-1930s, for example, the Portuguese neurologist Egas Moniz initiated the practice of so-called lobotomies, to which patients continued to be subjected into the 1960s, with an aim to altering the "synaptic connections" in the prefrontal lobe. The procedure involved the severing of nerve fibers in an area of the brain that is central to human behavior, in the belief, as in the case of equally nonspecific interventions such as electroshock, that an improvement would result for patients suffering obsessive disorders or depression, or who were identified as sex offenders. Even hyperactive children were subjected to the operation. The treatment of conspicuous behaviors in this way also caused apathy in patients and had negative effects on both intelligence and memory. It is not known how many people were subjected to lobotomy. Estimates for the United States alone run to 35,000 such operations over the period from 1936 to 1978. There are claims of much higher figures.

A later development was American neurophysiologist J. M. R. Delgado's "stimoceiver," which used stereotactic instruments to implant microelectrodes in precisely targeted areas deep inside the brain. Signals and stimuli were transmitted wirelessly, making it possible to intervene, for example, in the limbic system, which is taken to be the carrier of the emotions. By transmitting high-voltage current through the electrodes, it was also possible to destroy areas of the brain. In the limbic system, this led to drastic changes in emotional, sexual, and social behavioral forms which were regarded as acceptable for the sake of stopping other conspicuous behaviors. In the 1960s the Japanese neurosurgeon H. Narabayashi set out to destroy the corpus amygdaloideum in "aggressive subjects," who then became manifestly amenable and cooperative.

The potential for medical interventions in the brain, so fascinating at the time, was also treated in film and literature. It is enough to recall Stanley Kubrick's famous film *A Clockwork Orange*, in which the "hero," Alex, a violent young man, is ultimately forced to submit to a brainwashing, which leaves him incapable of self-defense when he becomes the target of an attack. The introduction of neuroleptic drugs took the wind out of the sails of psychosurgery, even though, in the case of either drugs or the future development of neurochips for behavior modification, the basic idea remains that many psychiatric disorders are attributable to material changes in the brain, and are therefore to be treated accordingly.

More spectacular are the many experiments undertaken on people and especially on animals. In certain cases electrodes have been implanted to stimulate various regions of the brain electrically, resulting not only in evoking memories but in prompting various behaviors, such as rage, sexual excitation, contentment, or fear. J. M. R. Delgado, in the 1960s, offered an especially radical demonstration of the potential of electrical brain stimulation with his stimoceiver: he implanted electrodes in the medial regions of the hypothalamus of a bull and then challenged the animal to a fight in a Spanish bullfighting ring. When the bull charged, Delgado stopped it at the last moment by activating the electrodes with a radio transmitter. A similar stir was caused by the famous experiment on rats by J. Olds and P. Milner in the 1950s. Electrodes were implanted in the lateral hypothalamus and connected to a stimulator that could be activated by pressing a button. Since electrical stimulation caused feelings of pleasure, the rats learned to stimulate themselves, choosing that button rather than another that would provide them food, even when they were starving. Similar experiments have been conducted on people. These older experiments worked with quite crude instruments and stimuli, while the neurotechnology of today holds out the prospect of target-specific stimulation of as many nerve cells as possible, thus evoking specific behaviors.

No one is able to say today what will become possible in the future with neurotechnological implants and other direct linkages between technical systems and human body parts. The technologies discussed here, used by certain scientists and physicians altogether without reflection, only suggest the extent to which it is possible to exercise a direct influence on the brain. Once methods or technologies are developed for which an application exists but which have not been adequately evaluated, it is not enough to rely on the self-control of scientists to set limits on research trends. We shall in any case have to get used to the fact that our body and our brain are becoming increasingly transparent and thus ever more subject to intervention, which will not necessarily remain restricted to remedies for injury, the amelioration of suffering, or the construction of prostheses for handicapped persons. We shall become ever more able to interfere ever more strategically in biological processes and to change them. Our body and our brain will become increasingly the site of implants and neuroprostheses. There will be ever more interfaces between technical systems and the body or the brain which will bring into existence a new man-machine system that leads in the direction of the Futurists' dream of a mechanical person with spare parts. The more effectively and precisely it becomes possible to change, replace, or influence biological processes, the less people will be inclined merely to accept sickness, handicaps, or other deficiencies, and the higher will be the standards set, for those who can afford it, of a perfect mind or body.

Artificial Life Meets Entertainment

Lifelike Autonomous Agents

Pattie Maes

The relatively new field of "artificial life" attempts to study and understand biological life by synthesizing artificial life forms. To paraphrase Chris Langton, the founder of the field, the goal of artificial life is to "model life as it could be so as to understand life as we know it." The discipline is very broad, spanning such diverse topics as artificial evolution, artificial ecosystems, artificial morphogenesis, and molecular evolution, among others. *The Journal of Artificial Life* offers a nice overview of the different research questions studied by the discipline.[1] Artificial life shares with artificial intelligence its interest in synthesizing adaptive autonomous agents, computational systems that inhabit some complex, dynamic environment, sense and act autonomously in this environment, and by doing so realize a set of goals or tasks that they are designed for.

The goal of building an autonomous agent is as old as the field of artificial intelligence itself. The artificial life community, which focuses on fast, reactive b agent research, has initiated a radically different approach toward this goal.

The Challenge of Modeling Entertaining Characters

Several forms of commercial entertainment currently incorporate automated entertaining characters. Most of these characters are extremely simple; they demonstrate very predictable behavior and are not very convincing. This is in particular the case for characters that a person can interact with in real time, for example, video game characters. When automated characters show sophisticated behavior, it is typically completely mechanical and noninteractive and the result of a painstaking and laborious process. An example is the behavior of the dinosaurs in the movie *Jurassic Park*.

In the last couple of years a few exceptions have emerged. A number of researchers have applied agent technology to produce animation movies. Rather than scripting the exact movements of an animated character, the characters are modeled as agents that perform actions in response to their perceived environment. Craig Reynolds modeled flocks of birds and schools of fish by specifying the behavior

FIG. 1. Realistic fish behavior modeled by Dimitri Terzopoulos and others for short animated movies.

of the individual animals that made up the flock.[2] The same algorithms were used to generate some of the behavior of the bats in the movie *Batman II.* Dimitri Terzopoulos has modeled very realistic fish behavior, including mating, feeding, learning, and predation (fig. 1).[3] His models have been employed to make entertaining short animated movies.

In addition to the previous work, some researchers have used agent models to build interactive, real-time animation systems. Joseph Bates's *Woggles World* allows the user to interact with a world of creatures called Woggles.[4] In this pioneering work, a user interacts with the world and its creatures by using the mouse and keyboard to directly control the movements and behavior of one of the Woggles. The Woggles have several internal needs and a wide range of emotions, resulting in fairly complex interactions. Scott Fisher's *Menagerie* system allows a user to interact with animated agents in real time by

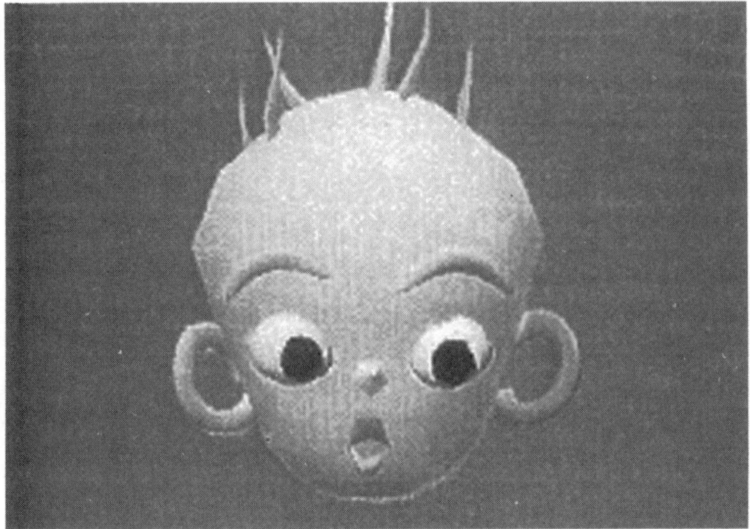

FIG. 2. Naoko Tosa's Neurobaby reacts to sounds made by a user looking into its crib.

using a head-mounted display and a head-tracking device.[5] The agents in *Menagerie* are typically engaged in a single high-level behavior such as flocking. Naoko Tosa used neural networks to model an artificial baby that reacts in emotional ways to the sounds made by a user looking into its crib (fig. 2).[6] Finally, the ALIVE system, described below, allows a user to enter a virtual world and use his or her whole body to interact with animated autonomous agents (fig. 3).

In addition to computer-animated agents, one notable original project is Julia, an autonomous agent that lives in a text-based MUSE system (multi-user simulation environment).[7] Julia's behavioral repertoire includes moving around in and mapping the environment, discourse with players, overhearing conversations and gossiping about them later on, relaying messages among players, and helping players with navigation problems. Julia has moods, feelings, and attitudes toward players and a good memory. She remembers what people have told her, what they have done to her, when she last encountered them, and so on (fig. 4 includes sample transcripts). Julia is an example of what Michael Mauldin has termed a "chatterbot." A chatterbot has several different modules for dealing with the different functions required to automate a player in a MUD (multi-user domain). The conversation module is implemented as a prioritized layer of mini-experts, collections of patterns and associated potential responses.

FIG. 3. The ALIVE system allows a user to employ natural gestures to interact with a virtual world inhabited by animated autonomous agents such as this dog.

Chatterbots go beyond Weizenbaum's Eliza system in that they use more "tricks" and have more sophisticated memories of past events and conversations.

Building these entertaining agents requires that the basic questions central to all agent research be addressed, namely, perception, action selection, motor control, adaptation, and communication. The agent has to perceive its environment, which is often dynamic and unpredictable, especially when a user is able to affect it. The agent has to decide what to do next, so as to make progress in the tasks it is designed to achieve. Relevant actions have to be translated into concrete motor commands. Over time the agent has to change and improve its behavior on the basis of its past experience. Finally, the agent has to be able to communicate to other agents in the world, both human and artificial. The key problem is to come up with an architecture that integrates all these functionalities and results in behavior that is fast, reactive, adaptive, robust, autonomous, and, last but not least, "lifelike." Lifelike behavior is that which is nonmechanistic, nonpredictable, and spontaneous.

The architectures of many of the successful entertaining agents listed above share a surprising number of features. The agents are

Space-Ace: So why won't you kiss me, Julia?
Julia: Sorry, I'm not into geeks, Space-Ace.
Space-Ace: Julia, I'm not a geek.
Julia: Then lose the pocket protector, Space-Ace.
Space-Ace: Julia, I don't have a pocket protector.
Julia: Congratulations.
Space-Ace: So kiss me, Julia.
Julia: I'd rather be overhauled by a Yugo mechanic, Space-Ace.
Space-Ace: Julia, kiss me.
Julia: Why, did your sheep leave you?
Space-Ace: Julia, kiss me.
Julia: Take a long walk through an unlinked exit, Space-Ace.

Julia is offended by Lenny's suggestion.
Julia winks at Lenny.
Julia eyes Lenny carefully . . .
Julia grins at Lenny.
Julia nods to Lenny. . . .

FIG. 4. Excerpts from interactions with Julia, Michael Mauldin's autonomous conversing agent, which inhabits a text-based multi-user simulation environment.

modeled as distributed, decentralized systems consisting of small competence modules. Each competence module is an "expert" at achieving a particular small task-oriented competence. There is no central reasoner, nor a central internal model. The modules interface to one another via extremely simple messages. Each of the competence modules is directly connected to relevant sensors and effectors. As a result, the behavior produced is robust, adaptive to changes, fast, and reactive.

Complex behavior is the result of interaction dynamics (feedback loops) at three levels: interactions between the agent and the environment, between the different modules inside the agent, and between multiple agents. For example, Braitenberg has built a simple creature that "loves" the user by making it move in the direction of the user with a speed proportional to the distance from the user. As an example of complex multi-agent interaction, Reynolds's creatures demonstrate flocking behavior through the use of simple local rules followed by each of the creatures in the flock.

The architecture includes a lot of redundant methods for the same competence. Multiple levels of complexity and sophistication ensure fault tolerance, graceful degradation, and nonmechanistic behavior. For example, Julia has several methods for responding to an utterance addressed to her: she can try to understand the utterance and generate a meaningful reply, or, if that fails, she can quote someone else on the same topic, or, if that fails, she can start a different conversation topic. A more comprehensive discussion of the research questions in autonomous agent research and the characteristics of typical architectures for autonomous agents can be found in the *Journal of Artificial Life*.[8]

Apart from the more standard research questions, the design of entertaining agents requires dealing with questions that are more novel—to artificial intelligence and especially to artificial life—for example, how to model emotions, intentions, social behavior, and discourse.[9] Typically these issues are even more important than making the agent very intelligent, since, to quote Bates, "the actual requirement is to achieve a persistent appearance of awareness, intention and social interaction."[10] Even though these topics may turn out to be of central importance to modeling and understanding intelligence, they have hardly been studied in artificial intelligence to date.

Building entertaining agents requires the agent researcher to think more about the user. The researcher is forced to address the psychology of the user: How will the typical human participant perceive the virtual characters? What behavior will she or he engage in? What misconceptions and confusing situations may arise? Other disciplines such as human-computer interaction, animation, sociology, literature, and theater are particularly helpful in answering these questions. For example, animation teaches us that users typically perceive faster moving characters as being young, upbeat, and intelligent. Literature and theater teach us that it is easier for users to quickly grasp stereotypical characters such as the "shrink" in the Eliza program.

The ALIVE Project

A detailed description of a particular project aimed at building entertaining agents may convey the research challenges and application

FIG. 5. In the ALIVE system, gestures are interpreted by the agents based on the context. Here the dog walks away in the direction the user is pointing.

opportunities more effectively. ALIVE (Artificial Life Interactive Video Environment) is a virtual environment that allows wireless full-body interaction between a human participant and a virtual world inhabited by animated autonomous agents.[11] One of the goals of the ALIVE project is to demonstrate that virtual environments can offer a more "emotional" and evocative experience by allowing the participant to interact with animated characters.

The ALIVE system was demonstrated and tested in several public forums. It was displayed for five days in 1993 at the SIGGRAPH (Special Interest Group on Computer Graphics) "Tomorrow's Realities" show in Anaheim, California, and for three days in 1994 at the AAAI (American Association of Artists and Illustrators) Show in Seattle, Washington. The system is installed permanently at the M.I.T. Media Laboratory in Cambridge, Massachusetts. It will be featured in the Ars Electronica Museum, currently under construction in Linz, Austria, and at the ArcTec electronic arts biennial exhibition in Tokyo.

In the style of Myron Krueger's Videoplace system, the ALIVE system offers an unencumbered, full-body interface to a virtual world.[12] The ALIVE user moves around in a space of approximately 16 by 16 feet. A video camera captures the user's image, which is composited into a three-dimensional graphical world after being isolated from the background. The resulting image is projected onto a large screen, which faces the user and acts as a type of "magic mirror": the user is seen to be surrounded by objects and agents (fig. 5). No goggles, gloves, or wires are needed for interaction with the virtual world. Computer vision techniques are used to extract such information as the person's three-dimensional location, position of various body parts, and simple gestures performed. ALIVE combines active vision and domain knowledge to achieve a robust real-time performance.[13]

The user's location and hand and body gestures affect the behavior of the agents in the virtual world. The participant receives visual and auditory feedback about the agents' internal state and reactions. Agents have a range of internal needs and motivations, a set of sensors to perceive their environment, a repertoire of activities, and a physically based motor system that allows them to move in and act on the environment. A behavior system decides in real time which activity the agents engage in to meet their internal needs and take advantage of opportunities presented by the current state of the environment.

The system allows not only for the obvious direct-manipulation style of interaction but also for a more powerful, indirect style in which gestures can have more complex meanings. The meaning of a gesture is interpreted by an agent according to the situation the agent and user find themselves in. For example, when the user points away (fig. 5) and thereby sends a character away, the place that character goes depends on where the user is standing and which direction she or he is pointing. In this manner, a relatively small set of gestures can be employed to mean many different things in many different situations.

The ALIVE system incorporates a tool called Hamsterdam for modeling semi-intelligent autonomous agents that can interact with one another and with the user.[14] Hamsterdam produces agents that respond with a relevant activity at every time-step, given their internal needs and motivations, past history, and the perceived environment with its attendant opportunities, challenges, and changes. Moreover, the pattern and rhythm of the chosen activities are such that the agents neither dither between multiple activities nor persist too long in a single activity. They are capable of interrupting a given activity if a more pressing need or an unforeseen opportunity arises. The Hamsterdam activity model is based on animal behavior models proposed by ethologists. Several concepts in particular proposed in ethology, such as behavior hierarchies, releasers, and fatigue, have proven to be crucial in guaranteeing the robust and flexible behavior required by autonomous interacting agents.[15] The ALIVE system shows that animated characters based on artificial life models can look convincing (i.e., allow suspension of disbelief).

When using Hamsterdam to build an agent, the designer specifies the sensors of the agent, its motivations or internal needs, and its activities and actions. Given that information, the Hamsterdam software automatically infers which of the activities is most relevant to the agent at a particular moment according to the state of the agent, the situation it finds itself in, and its recent behavior history. The observed behaviors or actions of the agent are the final result of numerous activities competing for control of the agent. The details of the behavior model and a discussion of its features are reported by Bruce Blumberg.[16]

The ALIVE system consists of different virtual worlds that the user can switch between by pressing a virtual button. Each world is inhabited by different agents: one by a puppet, a second by a hamster and a predator, and a third by a dog. The puppet follows the user around (in three dimensions) and tries to hold the user's hand. It also imitates some of the user's actions (e.g., sitting down, jumping). It will be sent away when the user points away and will come back when the user waves. The puppet employs facial expressions to convey its internal state; for example, it pouts when sent away and smiles when motioned back. It giggles when the user touches its belly.

The hamster avoids objects, follows the user around, and begs for food. It rolls over to have its stomach scratched if the user bends down to pat it. If the user has been patting the hamster for a while, its need for attention is fulfilled and some other activity takes precedence (e.g., looking for food). The user can feed the hamster by picking up food from a virtual table and putting it on the floor. He or she can also let the predator out of its cage and into the hamster's world. The predator chases and tries to kill the hamster. It views the user as another predator and attempts to avoid and flee from the person. However, as it gets more hungry, it will become bolder and dare to come closer. Both the predator and the hamster are successful at reconciling their multiple internal needs (e.g. avoiding the predator, finding food, not running into obstacles).

The most sophisticated character built so far is a dog called Silas. Silas's behavioral repertoire currently includes following the user, sitting (when asked by the user), going away (when sent away), and performing other tricks such as jumping, fetching a ball, lying down, and shaking. Silas will also chase the hamster if it is introduced into the environment. Along with visual sensors and feedback, the environment uses simple sound input and output. In addition to the camera, a directional microphone faces the user. The signal is fed into a simple pitch tracker, which interprets high pitch (e.g., clapping, whistling, high voice) and low pitch (low voice) respectively as positive and negative input from the user to the dog. The dog also provides auditory output, which consists of a variety of prerecorded samples.

By observing thousands of users interact with the agents in ALIVE, several things have been learned. First, the gestures that the user can engage in should be intuitive with respect to the domain and should provide immediate feedback. The second point will seem obvious to user interface designers, but not to artificial life and artificial intelligence researchers. Examples of "natural" gestures are petting for creatures and pointing or waving for the virtual puppet. Whenever a gesture is successfully perceived by an agent, the user should receive immediate feedback, either in terms of movement and/or facial and body expression (e.g., the hamster rolls over when patted, the puppet smiles when tickled). This helps the user develop an understanding of the space of recognized gestures.

Second, even if the gestures are natural to the environment, it is still necessary to have a human "guide" present to give the user hints about what she or he could do (e.g., "try petting the hamster," "the puppet will go away if you point"). The current ALIVE system includes an artificial guide, which is implemented as yet another autonomous agent that fulfills a special role: it observes the user and memorizes what kinds of interactions the user has had with the world and occasionally offers suggestions by speaking and gesturing. The guide is visualized as a parrot in the virtual world because people expect a parrot to talk, but they do not expect the parrot to understand speech.

Third, users are more tolerant of the imperfections in an agent's behavior (as opposed to that of objects), such as lags and occasional incorrect or missed recognition. The presence of agents causes people to have appropriate expectations about the performance of the sensor system. We learned that people expect virtual inanimate objects to "work" reliably; that is, the reaction of the object has to be immediate, predictable, and consistent. In contrast, people assume that animal or humanlike agents have perception and an internal state, and thus are able to accept that the agent may not have sensed something. As a result, gestures that are hard to recognize, such as waving, can be used successfully in the context of agents (an agent might not have "seen" the user waving), but the same gesture would cause the user frustration if used in the context of some inanimate object, such as a switch.

Fourth, it is important to visualize the motivational and emotional state of the agents in the external features of the agent. For example, a more sophisticated creature such as Silas the dog will "lead" with its eyes; that is, he turns to look at an object or a person before he walks over to pick up the object or invite the person to play. If a character does not lead with its eyes, its behavior looks very mechanical and as such not very lifelike. Another reason why it is necessary to visualize motivations and internal state is that the user may get confused or frustrated if she or he cannot perceive internal variables that determine the agent's behavior. For example, if Silas is hungry, he may not be very obedient. If the user can observe that Silas is hungry, she or he will realize why he behaves very differently than he did a few minutes ago.

Finally, the most important lesson learned is that for an immersive environment to be captivating it may not be so important how fancy the graphics are, but rather how meaningful the interactions that the user engages in can be. ALIVE users reported having a lot of fun using the system and interacting with the creatures. They especially seemed to enjoy worlds inhabited by "emotional" agents, characters they could have an emotional relationship with. For example, users were very much intrigued by the facial expressions of the puppet and would feel sad when their actions caused the puppet to pout, or happy when they caused it to smile.

The ALIVE system demonstrates that entertainment can be a challenging and interesting application area for autonomous agent research. ALIVE provides a novel environment for studying architectures for intelligent autonomous agents. As a test bed for agent architectures, it avoids the problems associated with real hardware agents or robots, but at the same time forces us to face nontrivial problems, such as dealing with noisy sensors and an unpredictable fast-changing environment. The system makes it possible to study agents with higher levels of cognition without oversimplifying the world in which these agents live.

ALIVE represents only the beginning of a whole range of novel applications that could be explored with this kind of system. Researchers are currently investigating ALIVE for interactive storytelling applications in which the user plays one of the characters in the story, and all other characters are artificial agents that collaborate to make the story move forward (see three short papers on ALIVE).[17] Another obvious entertainment application of ALIVE is video games. The ALIVE vision-based interface has been hooked up to existing video game software to give a user full-body control over a game. In addition, there are investigations into how autonomous video game characters can develop and improve competence over time to keep challenging a video game player. Finally, animated characters are being modeled that teach a user a physical skill. The agent is modeled as a personal trainer that demonstrates how to perform an action and provides timely feedback to the user, on the basis of sensory information about the user's gestures and body positions.

Recently developed systems such as the Woggles, Neurobaby, Terzopoulos's fish, Julia, and ALIVE demonstrate that entertainment can be a fun and challenging application area for autonomous agent research. At the same time, however, these early experiments demonstrate that this application area will require a more interdisciplinary approach, which combines the know-how of the human sciences with the computational models developed in artificial life and artificial intelligence.

Pain and Subjectivity in Virtual Reality

Diana Gromala

Virtual reality (VR) exists as a mythopoeic cultural phenomenon and as an experience through which notions of subjectivity flow and collide. Subjectivity—constituted and reconfigured through experiential aspects of VR and the larger cultural domain within which it resides and operates—is befuddled: the experience is irreducible to subject/object, inside/outside, mind/body, and VR/"real" world oppositions. Perhaps the most troubling aspect of VR is the consciousness-altering bodily experience, generally and problematically termed disembodiment. The term itself reveals the difficulty of linguistic or textual description and can be related to conditions of *jouissance,*[1] Avital Ronell's notion of drugs, and Julia Kristeva's exploration of the abject (I/not I). Just where are the self and the body in relation to this disconcerting and simultaneous experience of being in and not in the virtual world, and how do they constitute each other? Elaine Scarry's conceptualization of pain and imagining provides productive strategies to employ in exploring how the body and self extend agency and how they constitute each other through the prostheses of VR.

Situated Bodies, Situated Selves

Deeply implicated in the cultural production[2] of so-called VR technologies, I often witness and swallow the many paradoxes it creates. Highly regarded scientists, for example, legitimize research directions in scholarly symposia, while at dinner they speak in hushed tones, comparing VR experiences to transcendent spiritual states, drug trips, and "d.t.'s" or residual effects of extensive exposure. Respectable professors dream of "downloading 'pure' consciousness." Others thrill in the sensation of "disembodiment" and the ecstasy of "leaving the meat behind." Subjective states, such as a sense of "immersion" or "presence," are often measured by purportedly objective, empirical means. The user's body stands woefully constricted and tethered, straining to clumsily adapt to the alleged limitlessness of VR—one can experience the ability to fly, as long as the three foot sensor range is not exceeded. Such presuppositions also rely on a socioeconomic status of relative privilege, as well as the culturally determined ability to comprehend the symbolic languages or orders of VR. One of the most significant paradoxes is that VR is more widely discussed than actually experienced, yet the experiential component is what is found to be most compelling.

VR is frequently conflated with the larger existent or projected cultural processes referred to as cyberspace. In addition, future possibilities of VR technologies are often confused with actual current capabilities. This may help explain why VR, in a brief but frenzied moment during the last several years, enjoyed widespread attention in literature, film, the arts, the media, and other cultural forms, and why it has assumed mythopoeic dimensions in our cultural imagination. Though the technology is still in its infancy and has often not lived up to the urgent expectations created around it, much like artificial intelligence in previous decades, it nonetheless persists as both a troubling and potentially redemptive phenomenon.

Although VR is often depicted as if it lacked a history or a cultural context, its historical precedents can be traced through intertwining threads of mechanical developments, computational evolution, and the fantastical worlds elicited through mimetic simulations of ritual, dioramas, art, literature, and theater, and some may claim, medieval cathedrals. What these examples hold in common is the evocation and perception of a shareable but otherworldly place in which humans extend and project their agency—the ability to act upon, within, and through the world—and where subjectivity is problematized. The history of VR is in many ways the history of the conditions and construction of selfhood through projecting one's self and one's agency into the "real" or object world and attendant virtual and fictional worlds.

In its contemporary manifestations, VR can be understood in a multiplicity of ways in relation to the experience and perceptions of the subject, as well as the informing context within which subjectivity and VR are situated. One is a deterministic view of VR which places its development as increasingly removed from human control, somehow taking on a "nature" of its own, an essentialized apostasy. Here it is rendered in cautionary tales that stir our mythopoeic imagination in an animistic or fetishistic sense, as a phenomenon that takes on a monstrous life of its own, often turning against us in a threat to ultimately destroy us. These cautionary tales remind us that the extension and projection of human agency can be dangerous, whether the projection is indirect, through a robot or the automata described by the early Greeks and Chinese[3] for example, or direct, through prostheses in contact with the body, as in VR. When human agency is externalized, projected through indirect means and expressed as embodied, an essentialized Other emerges. It becomes progressively further removed from direct human contact and can no longer be controlled by its human creator. This can be seen in a thread connecting golem in sixteenth-century Prague to Frankenstein, the feminine robot in *Metropolis,* the replicant Roy in *Blade Runner,* the T-1000 in *Terminator 2* and the biologic cells in *Blood Music.* The results are just as disastrous, however, when the projection is more intimately tied to a direct prosthetic interface with the body, such as current VR apparatuses of head-mounted displays, data gloves, and body suits. In these instances, the technology, though not externalized as an entity, nonetheless reveals its ability to create a fertile framework or condition for human self-destruction. In *Lawnmower Man* and *Until the End of the World,* users are "taken over" by something inherent in their own consciousness, whether it is an escalating greed for power or a profound addiction to their dreams and desires. In either case of externalized entities or direct bodily experience, the technology grows disconnected from human agency.

However, these totalizing myths of a demonized technological Other, as well as the converse utopian rhetoric, reify cultural hegemony in the construction of subjectivity. By relying upon a totalizing view of technology, especially as a seemingly autonomous Other, most of reality is omitted.[4] Further, by not questioning or considering the instrumental forces, conditions, processes, and power relations of a technology implicit in the cultural realm, we can unproblematically distance ourselves from our own implicit role and responsibility in these processes. This unquestioning acceptance works at the level of ideology or "common sense"; thus, unequal power relations remain invisible.

Subjectivity in relation to VR can also be understood in terms of a problematic relation to the symbolic realm, implicated in the much wider, everyday cultural experience of hyperreality described by Jean Baudrillard[5] and Paul Virilio.[6] In a hyperreal cultural context, symbols no longer maintain a referent or are preferred over the thing they originally represented. In this view, the phenomenon of VR can be seen as a simple distraction to or instance of the much wider everyday cultural experience of hyperreality, an experience that in turn problematizes subjectivity in the schizophrenic terms of Fredric Jameson,[7] Gilles Deleuze, and Felix Guattari.[8] The schizophrenic subject, constituted through this realm, is no longer a unified entity, but a free-floating, fragmented being. Deleuze and Guatarri celebrated this construction or reconstitution of a schizophrenic subject as a strategy for survival in a Western world of late capitalism, characterized by processes of the hyperreal brought about in part by technology.

The experiential dimensions of VR provoke further confusion in the relationship between bodily experience and subjectivity in the symbolic realm. An indeterminate subjectivity embedded in this context of hyperreality not only experiences disconcerting shifts in the time/space continuum and free-floating signifiers on the level of the everyday, but in some way can seem to bodily inhabit or occupy the symbolic realm of VR. Because the technologically enhanced body, or human sensorium, is "joined in a sensory feedback loop with the simulacrum that lives in RAM, it is impossible to locate an originary source for experience and sensation."[9] Thus, the body is experienced as more viscerally "present" than it is in other fictive realms and is therefore seen to somehow circumvent our subjective relation to the symbolic. According to Jaron Lanier, for example, VR abrogates the process of entry into the symbolic realm, what he terms "postsymbolic communication."[10] Resulting attempts to describe this VR experience as disembodiment, however, only serve to reify a mind/body split. A schizophrenic subjectivity might provide an alternative to the Cartesian dualism by nomadically embracing shifting and contingent experiences.

In the view of Jean-François Lyotard,[11] the experience of VR can be seen as an instantiation of the instrumentality of technology in a postmodernist context. Lyotard describes technology as a language game, extending while reconfiguring the modernist myths or metanarratives of mastery and progress, while the state maintains domination by escalating the rate of technological change to an ever-increasing frequency. Implicit in this technological landscape, the phenomenon and experience of VR reflect and are co-opted by instrumental forces of domination. Here, the self dissolves into a host of networks and relations of contradictory codes and interfering messages, which he, like Deleuze and Guattari, valorizes. Likewise, as Donna Haraway would have it, the phenomenon and experience of VR are related to larger sites or processes of domination. VR reinforces but could also simultaneously disrupt those very structures through emerging contingent and hybrid subjectivities. Rather than adhering to a demonization of technology or reacting to it by developing another, oppositional and totalizing theory, Haraway enjoins us to embrace "the skillful task of reconstructing the boundaries of daily life, in partial connection to others, in communication with all of our parts."[12]

As a cultural artifact, VR can be seen as a diagnostic tool or an expression of our millennialist angst. Like artificial intelligence and a broad range of new technologies, from the printing press to the telephone and television before it, VR functions as a screen or mirror upon which we can project our deepest fears, hopes for utopia, cures for what ails us, or an escape from our current condition, expressed in relation to our notions of subjectivity and the body. However, VR differs from the evocation of imaginary spaces, such as the suspension of disbelief that happens in the theater, in part because of the seemingly more direct and visceral implication of our bodily responses in the feedback loop with VR technologies. The Lacanian mirror of misrecognition seemingly becomes a mirror we can literally walk into, or, in N. Katherine Hayles's terms, becomes a second mirror stage—the Mirror of the Cyborg, one which accounts for a subjectivity not reliant upon physical boundaries.[13]

Most frequently, VR is understood in terms of the experiential, inevitably referred to as the sensation of so-called disembodiment. By implication, traditional notions of subjectivity are disturbed by the inexplicable quality and effects of VR-induced sensations. The fascination with the sensation of disembodiment belies the most outstanding characteristic of VR: the profound experiential dimension that seems to resist linguistic or textual description and that confounds binary oppositions of mind/body and self/other. "Boundary states" of subjectivity that cannot be reduced to binary oppositions provide useful models for the examination of the sensation of so-called disembodiment and its effect on subjectivity. These are Avital Ronell's notions of narcotics, and Julia Kristeva's notion of the abject (I/not I) —the problematic projection of the self into the object world. However, Elaine Scarry's conceptualization of pain provides perhaps the most useful strategy for examining sensation and subjectivity, since it necessarily implicates the body and self as inextricably bound.

As an experience of embodied imaginary space, VR is often compared to altered states of consciousness, such as those provoked by narcotics or hallucinogenic drugs. Rather than considering a drug-enhanced state of consciousness as a search for an exterior, transcendental dimension in a dualism of interior/exterior, or mind/body, Avital Ronell views the desire for a "chemical prosthesis" of drugs, or a technological prosthesis of virtual reality, as a desire to explore "fractal interiorities." Again, subjectivity is decentered. The chemical prostheses provide an experience in which the "distinction between interiority and exteriority is radically suspended, and where this phantasmic opposition is opened up."[14] Kristeva's concept of the abject can be seen as another type of boundary state in relation to the body and its social construction. "The abject is what of the body falls away from it while remaining irreducible to the subject/object and inside/outside oppositions. The abject necessarily partakes of both polarized terms but cannot be clearly identified with either."[15] We are repulsed by but at some level desire and claim these abject products of bodily fluids and "wastes" as a part of the self. Perhaps this is akin to the sensations provoked by VR: desire and anxiety (or unrecognized revulsion) simultaneously emerge as our body responds to the feedback loop and disrupt traditionally sacrosanct notions of body and self. Such boundary states assume that a certain degree of self has already been constructed, whether it is understood to be whole and intact, or contingent and partial. However, other boundary states that occur prior to an infant's construction of self or separation from its mother, such as Lacan's "imaginary" and Kristeva's view of *jouissance,* also serve to elide and disrupt oppositions of self and Other, inside and outside. An unconscious desire to return to this intensely pleasurable state of *jouissance* may be proffered to explain one of the reasons for VR's popularity.

Pain's Remains

Though I was only 13, I mourned the loss of my kidney the night before they cut it from my body, "removed" the dysfunctional organ. What seemed curious to me was that I wasn't allowed to keep it, vitiating the traditions of my family. My people are "of the earth" types from isolated areas of the Carpathian Mountains, people whose traditions are rarely mentioned by anthropologists. They collect and save their body parts in yellowed glass jars sealed with wax which reside in medicine cabinets, hope chests, and potato cellars worthy of Dr. Caligari. They save their protein excrement, their hair, and bury their body parts along with the soil of their birthplace in some sort of shamanistic hangover. Only after unseemly insistence was I allowed to see what my ambitious surgeon said would make me famous in the *New England Journal of Medicine:* a calculus the size of Montana, attended by a complete lack of evidence of the horrendous pain physicians associate with this disease. He felt that the kidney itself, the meat, would be too upsetting for me to see, but somehow the stone would not. *Medusa from the inside* I thought as I snatched it and held its smooth, fetal shape. But holding it was strictly forbidden because I might have somehow damaged what rightfully belonged to science, to pathology—I had violated the protocols of medical science. Never would I be buried with all of my bodily creations. In contrast, a few years later, the reverse was true: now I experienced inexplicable pain, which could not be readily substantiated by physical evidence. My subjective experience of pain seemed to defy verification by the objective, scientific measures insisted upon by Western medicine. Thus I came to my first virtual reality experience in a research hospital, subversively catching glimpses of the interior of my body. There, in an attempt to substantiate and objectify my emerging pain, physicians used microvideography to explore my viscera, projecting it on televisions and larger screens to other physicians and interns. Drugged but conscious, I was nonetheless consistently and vehemently discouraged from viewing my own body, though I thrilled in the abject pleasure it produced when I caught glimpses of its enormous and animate projections.

In her book, *The Body in Pain: The Making and Unmaking of the World,* Scarry defines pain by the manner in which it implies a split between one's sense of one's own reality and the reality of others.

An essentially subjective state, pain cannot be denied or confirmed. Scarry outlines the exceptional character of pain when compared to all other interior states: "We do not simply have feelings, but have feelings for somebody or something: love is love of x, fear is fear of y, ambivalence is ambivalence about z. Pain has no referential content, it takes no object, and more than any other phenomenon, resists objectification in language."[16] She discusses pain through the metaphor of three concentric but permeable circles: the innermost, the difficulty of expressing pain; next, the political and perceptual complications that result because of that difficulty; and finally, the nature of both material and verbal expressibility, that is, the nature of human creation.

Scarry's analysis of pain provides useful methods for understanding the experiential aspects of VR. This experience—what I term the transformative state of consciousness provoked by sensorial experiences of the body *and* inexorably bound to them in simultaneity—is a projection of the self into the object world; in this case the object world is VR. Though Scarry's analysis appears to be somewhat problematic in her distinction of physical pain, implying a mind/body split, her framework does allow for a semipermeability that both partakes of and denies strict binary oppositions. It is thus valuable in the examination of the experience of VR in two ways. First, by focusing on the projection of a sentient being into the object world, what Scarry refers to as "imagining," the mind/body duality becomes permeable and allows for the consideration of simultaneous experiences. Second, Scarry outlines this projection and ultimate reformation as transformative. Again, this condition allows for semipermeability, or a continuous feedback loop between the sentient being and the object world.

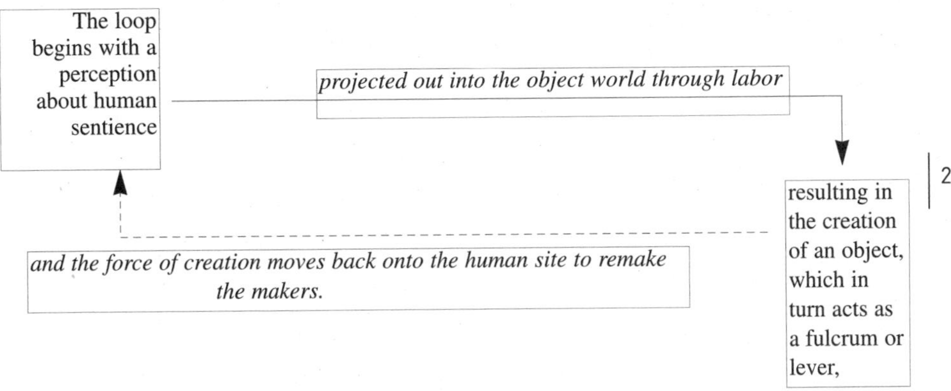
The loop begins with a perception about human sentience
projected out into the object world through labor
resulting in the creation of an object, which in turn acts as a fulcrum or lever,
and the force of creation moves back onto the human site to remake the makers.

Scarry's use of the term "sentient" is crucial here, in that it refers to consciousness inextricably bound to sensation; hence, the conscious "mind" is one with perception through the bodily senses. Further, in her definition of the effect of pain as a splitting of one's own sense of reality from others', which resides within the larger frame of the processes of pain and imagining, Scarry accounts for both the irreducible material fact of the body as well as subjective experience without falling into a solipsistic subjectivity. By extension, this frame of self-objectification, termed imagining, allows for the consideration of the simultaneous experiences offered in VR. This represents a significant opportunity in discourses surrounding VR, [17] which otherwise tend to deny the body as somehow separate from the mind and expendable. In these discourses, the sensation of disembodiment is generally proffered as adhering to the well-worn Cartesian split. It is possible and liberatory, as some would have it, to escape from the body, or at least from the aversive aspects of the body, that is, pain. The dream here is to download pure consciousness (mind) and leave the problematic meat (body) behind. The assumptions underlying this stance reify the position that the mind and body are separable, that experience can be unproblematically compartmentalized, and further serve to limit the conscious experience of VR to, again, an either/or experience. This reasoning assumes that one experiences VR, say, in the ability to "fly" in the simulation, without simultaneously experiencing the irreducible physical limitations of the material body and its dissonant inputs. A reluctant acknowledgment of simultaneity of experience gets a nod, albeit one in terms of disease, from the observation of "sim-sickness." Simsickness (or simulation sickness) refers to the proprioceptive determinations of the body receiving two sets of signals at odds with each other, one originating from the "real" world, say, gravity, the other from visual cues in the simulation that can produce the sensation of flying. The result is nausea, though the body usually adapts through habituation. Describing this in terms of a disease reveals the tendency to desire an escape from the problematic meat, rather than reincorporating it in simultaneous experiences, which phenomena of adaptability like habituation serve to accomplish.

However, rather than considering the sensation experienced in VR as a denial or escape from the material body, I would instead argue that this experiential component of VR can be viewed more productively when focused on Scarry's description of imagining—the projection of the sentient being into the object world—in this case through technological prosthesis, a move associated with pleasure. By focusing on the projection, the fiduciary subject[18]—that is, the body as the privileged site of geopolitical instrumental forces within systems of domination and the irreducible material fact of the body—is not disavowed. The meat remains, and remains connected to a multiplicity of simultaneous experience.

Scarry posits the following: "'Pain and imagining' constitute extreme conditions of, on the one hand, intentionality as a state and, on the other, intentionality as self-objectification; and between these two boundary conditions all the other more familiar binary acts-and-objects are located. That is, pain and imagining are the 'framing events' within whose boundaries all other perceptual, somatic, and emotional events occur; thus, between the two extremes can be mapped the whole terrain of the human psyche."[19]

According to Scarry, pain serves to split one's own sense of reality from others', while imagining allows the subject—unified in subjectivity, or decentered and schizophrenic—to project, to participate in a shared reality. The experience of VR seems to manage both. The user of VR, partially cut off from participation in the real world by a head-mounted display, can be observed to be thrashing about, simultaneously and partially functioning in another world. Semi-immersed in the VR world, this user can communicate with other users who are "telepresent" through similar technological prostheses and representations. However, if a user spills virtual coffee on another user in VR, the person may react as if liquid burned their flesh; but, simultaneously, in the material world, her pants are not wet—the liquid does not fully translate. Yet if one user scares another user in VR and that person is heavily invested in the simulation, he could perhaps suffer a very real heart attack. The realities are multiple and simultaneous, only partially shared, not reducible to the VR world or the real world, yet necessarily implicated in both. Mythopoeic examples often employ the trope of a shock to the body, a visible instance of a sign of pain, before the subject experientially "enters" VR. This is not unlike shamanistic practices of inducing pain as a signal that many anthropologists interpret as "a little death" of the body necessary to signal a rebirth of a reconstituted self.[20] These can both be read as a denial of the flesh, but read another way, they can signal the disconcerting experience of simultaneous presence—the irreducible material aspect of the body is in the VR world and in the real world, just as the reconfigured shaman, even renamed, returns to the same body through which the transcendental state was induced.

The nature and the process of imagining and creation described by Scarry provides useful insights in examining subjectivity in VR. The sentient being projects into the object world and is in turn transformed in the process:

> Imagining works this way. We begin with a perception about human sentience. It is projected out into the object world through labor and results in the creation of an object (in this case, a VR object/experience). This object in turn acts as a fulcrum or lever, which the force of creation moves back onto the human site to remake the makers. To repeat, there is a reciprocal consequence at the human site.[21]

Scarry goes on to say that imagining works either directly, by "extending its powers and acuity (poem, telescope)," or indirectly, "by eliminating aversiveness (chair, vaccine)." Like imagining, VR seems to work in both ways. Indirectly, the user, the sentient being in VR, projects and extends agency in a multiplicity of ways. The users, or sentient beings, can extend their ability to interact and effect change simultaneously in the simulation and in the "material" world by remote manipulations of robotic arms in space, or by remote surgery. They can interact with other users who, though physically remote, are nonetheless "telepresent," and can share and communicate in a common simulation. Certain qualities of a VR simulation do not strictly reproduce what is possible outside of the simulation, such as the six degrees of freedom which produce the illusion that users can fly. Indirectly the experience of VR can simultaneously eliminate aversiveness, for example, in providing surgeons, pilots, and astronauts an opportunity to refine skills and habituate themselves to unfamiliar experiences. The temporary "escape" into a fictive world eliminates the aversiveness of the real world. In some instances, VR works directly and indirectly, simultaneously. In using robotic arms to manipulate dangerous materials, users directly extend their agency to remote sites and simultaneously eliminate aversiveness by remaining at a safe distance.

In the feedback loop of Scarry's process of imagining, subjectivity can be seen to be continuously and dynamically influenced. This feedback loop begins with a perception about human sentience and an intentionality, as stated earlier, as self-objectification. What drives this intentionality in relation to VR? Perhaps it is alluded to in Ronell's discussion of drugs: "Much like the paradigms installed by the discovery of endorphins, being-on-drugs indicates that a structure is already in place, prior to the production of that materiality we call drugs, including virtual reality or cyberprojections."[22] We do not reproduce that which is ultimately outside of our perceptions, that which influences our subjectivity, including experiences of so-called disembodiment. In situating VR as the object/experience, subjectivity is dynamically influenced by the partial shareability of a VR experience, and by a simultaneous experience of being within and outside of VR.

In terms of the theorists mentioned in the introduction, Scarry can be considered to be adhering to binary oppositions and a tendency toward a totalizing discourse. What is at issue is the shareability of a reality on an ontological level, technologically mediated or not. A decentered and contingent subjectivity, by definition, must share, or partially share, a reality. Scarry's positing of permeability allows for the attenuation of strict splits between binary oppositions.

Virtual Bodies

Some time ago, I was in a semicontorted position, trying to watch the interior of my stomach lining, in real time. Swallowing, incorporating the video camera elicited pain, as did the torturous nerve conduction studies that were required, again, in an effort to substantiate my subjective experience of chronic pain through "objective" tests. Although the suggestion would be anathema to Western physicians, it seemed not unlike the homeopathic magic practiced by my herbalist grandfather: provoke pain to cure one of it. My grandfather taught me what Western medicine could not: how to cope with ever-present pain. In essence, I deal with chronic physical pain in part by reexperiencing it, simultaneously, as pleasurable. In many non-Western methods of meditation, this involves not an escape from the body, but rather, a reinhabitation of its inward enormity, or an erasure of the distinction between interior and exterior, a certain sense of an expansion and simultaneous loss of self, perhaps not unrelated to *jouissance.*

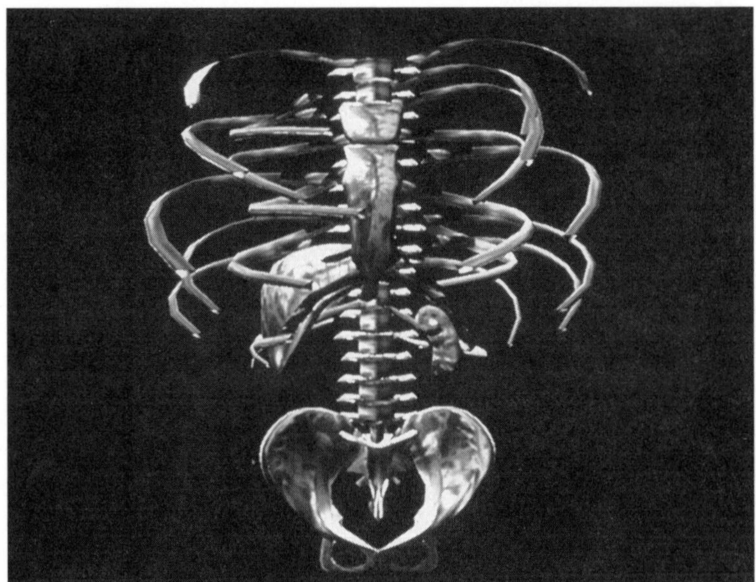

FIG. 1. *Dancing with the Virtual Dervish: Virtual Bodies,* created by Diana Gromala and Yacov Sharir. The virtual body is comprised of medical visualizations of Diana Gromala, artistically manipulated and animated to symbolically represent continual decay and reformation. The virtual body is overwritten with texts, meditations on pain, Eros, and Thanatos. Each organ contains another, surreal virtual world.

I had long since insisted on my place in both the subject and object position of this medicinal discourse. A voyeur of the wonders of medical imaging, I collect and personally finance, with the help of my insurance companies, all sorts of "objective" and "scientific" visualizations of my body. What fascinates me is the spectral and sensuous quality of these representations, images of bone and viscera, fluid and sound, movement and depth (fig. 1). Here my body, through their tools and devices, is enhanced as a site through which social, political, economic, and technological forces flow and collide, often with very real and tangible effect. Here I become a cyborg, both theoretically and as a result of the way technology alters my material being. The idea of a cyborg tweaked my throbbing interest, not only in the liberatory possibilities outlined by Haraway,[23] but also because, quite literally, I have devices, or what belongs to the object world within my interior being.

I was interested in bringing my experience of chronic pain into the object realm, as Scarry suggests, in order to make it sharable. In order to produce art, that is, to hopefully invite or induce an insight, revelation, or state of altered consciousness, I was interested in exploring the experiential aspect, the sensation of disembodiment of VR, to reflect that double move of conflating pain with pleasure. Further, I was looking at these visualizations of my body as sites of contestation and negotiation among social, political, and economic forces that had a direct result on my subjectivity and material body. In doing so, I wanted to reappropriate these visualizations, digital data obtained from technologies that are able to extend our perception to apprehend previously inaccessible properties of bodies, from x-rays, MRIs, and sonograms to electron microscopy, invasive microvideography, and algorithmic interpretations, which transform data from bodily sounds, heat, and "measurable" pain sensitivities into malleable visual and aural forms.

Thus, a cyborg materially as well as theoretically, I explored these issues in the creation of *Dancing with the Virtual Dervish: Virtual Bodies,* a work in virtual environments (figs. 1, 2). Through the beneficence of the Canadian government's Department of Communications and the Banff Centre for the Arts, I engaged in a three-year process of creating an immersive virtual environment which has since been performed at various venues. With a choreographer and computer scientists,[24] this immersive, interactive virtual environment was constructed from the database of visualizations of my body. This virtual body is of enormous scale and exists in a state of constant decay and reformation. The virtual body becomes a "book" as it is overwritten with texts of desire, Battaille-inspired reembodiments of Eros and Thanatos swirling about splintered and reconfigured forms, textual encryptions of a body in pain, a body in confluence with materiality, the immaterial, and dematerialized notions of corporeal transcendence, of corporeal reinhabitation.

Conclusion

My firsthand experience with pain illustrates Scarry's description of its ability to destroy the language of the sufferer: one who experiences physical pain can neither have it confirmed or denied. The effect of pain is that it prevents the projection of self into the object world (imagining) to make pain sharable. Yet, my artistic goal of *Dancing with the Virtual Dervish: Virtual Bodies* was not to replicate the experience of pain but to create a virtual environment which elicits a

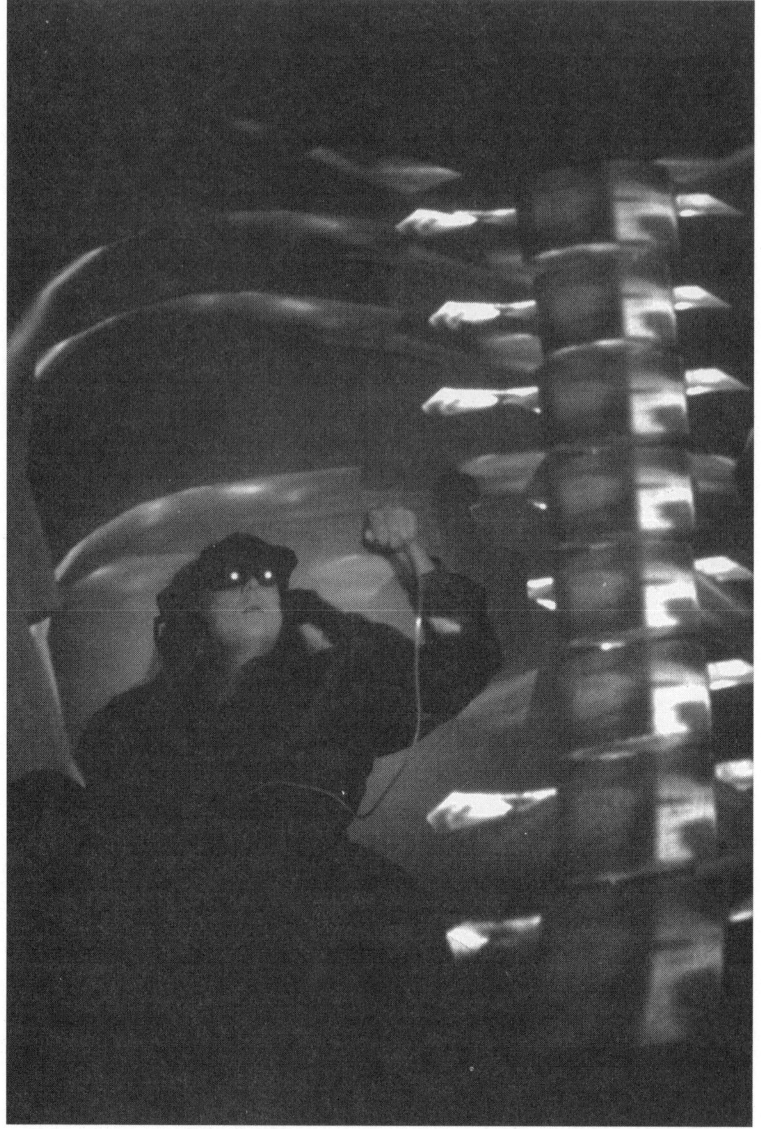

FIG. 2. *Dancing with the Virtual Dervish: Virtual Bodies.* By wearing a head-mounted, stereoscopic video display, users can feel "immersed" within the moving body and interact with it. Such interactions include "touching" the text, which then changes, or "flying" into an organ—say, a heart—to find another, surreal world. Three-dimensional sound helps users locate themselves in surreal virtual spaces.

reinhabitation of the body, one which conflates pain with pleasure and unknowable states of death. To quote Scarry, "That pain is so frequently used as a symbolic substitute for death in the initiation rites of many tribes is surely attributable to an intuitive human recognition that pain is the equivalent in felt-experience of what is unfeelable in death."[25] I linked this strategy of reinhabitation to the consciousness-influencing bodily experience of disembodiment of VR. Both states strongly decenter our culturally specific emphasis on certain senses (the visual, sonic) above others (haptic, kinesthetic, visceral, emotional) and provoke profound visceral responses which seem to defy textual description. The experience of VR, understood in its mythopoeic cultural forms as a problematic experience of the self and body, has an ability to throw assumptions of subjectivity into disarray.

Underlying discourses that strive to redefine relationships between technology and subjectivity assume that a stable subjectivity exists intact, prior to experiences of fluid and mutable disembodiment, an assumption that poststructuralist theorists call into question. The disembodied experience, combined with qualities of VR that seemingly do not replicate "reality," serves to upset notions in our relationship to the symbolic realm, as well as binary mind/body, subject/object, and material/immaterial distinctions. Other boundary states which do not allow for strict binary oppositions include *jouissance,* drugs, and the abject. While they provide useful analogies in the exploration of subjectivity in VR, Elaine Scarry's conceptualization of pain provides productive strategies to employ in exploring how the body and self extend agency and how they constitute each other through the prostheses of VR precisely because what is at stake is our human ability to make our world sharable with others.

Virtual Catastrophe

Will Self-Reproducing Software Rule the World?

Mark Ludwig

Have you ever heard of Anatoly Golitsyn? He was a high-level KGB agent who defected to the United States in about 1960. In the 1970s he wrote a book, *New Lies for Old*, in which he said that the Communist Party's plan for world takeover involved pretty much what has happened in the past 10 years.

Well, suppose you were a strategist for the Communist Party International, and you understood how computers had greatly weakened your power to manipulate the media and control people. You knew that part of bringing about the renaissance of communism would involve changing the character of the computer networks of the world so that no intelligent communication could take place there.

An impossible task? . . . Maybe not.

Today I'd like to take a look at the potential for computer viruses to do exactly that—maybe with a little help from a diabolical mind, maybe without help.

I've never been one to exaggerate the dangers posed by computer viruses. In fact, I've taken a lot of criticism for being willing to make technical information about viruses known, while the antivirus guys are trying to hide it from you. My books have been banned by numerous magazines and so on. For the most part, I laugh when some antivirus developer starts ranting about how dangerous such and such a virus is. For the most part, I know they're just trying to sell product.

Yet at the same time, I've done some research that is, frankly, chilling. Chilling enough that I'm reticent to pursue it any further. I've alluded to some of the possibilities here and there, but today I want to paint the picture broad and bright so you won't miss it. I'm not doing that to try to scare you. I'm not doing it to paint a gloomy future, either. I do speak a warning. . . . However, I think there is a solution, and that's what really needs to be explored.

To explore these dark possibilities a little, I'd like to first take a very broad look at where computing is headed. I'm not really a futurologist, so I don't want to speculate too much. Rather, I'll just make a few observations that any sensible redneck could make:

1. Operating systems are becoming more complex. The original DOS kernel was no more than 15 kilobytes. Windows 3 is measured in megabytes, while Windows 95, OS/2, and the like are measured in tens of megabytes. Function calls which once numbered in the tens now number in the thousands. Even systems programmers don't understand what these operating systems are doing.
2. The future holds greater and greater connectivity, both computer to computer and computer to man. People with computers are lining up to get on the Internet, and information services from CompuServe to MCI Mail are booming. At the same time, full-motion video, audio, speech recognition, and virtual reality are slowly closing the gap between man and the computer.
3. For 30 or 40 years, the trend has been toward greater power: speed and memory.
4. On a more social level, men seem to be adjusting to computer technology by allowing computers to take over basic functions like arithmetic and reading. In the United States, Scholastic Aptitude Test scores for things like reading and math have been falling constantly for 30 years. The more conservative educators call this a "dumbing down" process. Yet if you have a calculator or computer, what really becomes important is not whether you can multiply or divide two four-digit numbers, but knowing whether you need to multiply or divide them. Likewise, as media goes electronic, anyone with a sound card and ears can have a text read to him, so what becomes important is not how well or how fast you can read, but how wisely you can pick what you'll read.
5. I think pure capitalism in the computer industry is driving it to become more and more of a new entertainment industry. That's the lowest common denominator, so it's where the money is. This fact really hit me in the face at Comdex in Las Vegas last fall. All of the PC manufacturers were building

> "multimedia" machines. Now, I'll admit to being somewhat of a snob about this, but to me a powerful machine is something I can numerically solve real nonlinear quantized field problems on, not a GUI [graphical user interface] box for playing the latest version of *Doom*. But my ideals aren't where the money is, so they aren't where the industry is going.

Virus Technology

Now, let's look at computer virus and antivirus technology for a moment.

Up through the early 1990s, scanning for computer viruses using search strings was simply the way to catch computer viruses. This was because viruses were few and fairly simple to catch in this way. Basically, what an antivirus developer did was to get a sample of the virus and extract a small segment of code from it which was hopefully unique to that virus. Then they would write a program that would look for this segment of code on your disk. If found, the scanner would alert you to the presence of the virus.

The Dark Avenger's mutation engine changed all of that, though. Every instance of such a virus looked a little different—there were no fixed strings to search for. Add to that several different mutation engines and tools like the Virus Creation Lab, which could churn out new viruses by the truckload, and scan string technology by itself didn't provide a workable solution to the virus problem anymore.

With the advent of things like the mutation engine, a more sophisticated form of scanning had to replace the scan string approach. I call this "code analysis." In some products, code analysis takes the form of heuristics. These programs look for code that does things which a virus might do, for example, self-modifying code, or code that searches for EXE files, or code that modifies the master boot record. Other code analyzers might identify the Dark Avenger's mutation engine (or a host of others) by looking at what instructions it does or doesn't use.

The problem is, these code analyzers can be fooled in the same way that string scanners can be fooled. This is just a corollary to the halting problem for a Turing machine. In essence, there is no perfect scanner that can determine whether a program contains a virus merely by examining its code.

Another type of technology, called integrity checking, is often used to catch viruses. In this approach, one merely looks for changes in existing software. Integrity checking has two problems, though: firstly, since it detects changes, a virus must execute and replicate at least once to be noticed. Only a scanner can keep a virus from executing in a computer. Secondly, most people don't like to use integrity checkers, especially if they're not technically inclined, because they don't understand what changes to their files necessarily mean.

So here you have a dilemma: you can use technology that will stop viruses before they execute—but it's imperfect. Or you can let them execute and then catch them. This dilemma will become more important in a few minutes.

Now, let's add Darwinian evolution to this picture. One can, after all, write Darwinian software. Genetic algorithms, for example, have proven very adept at solving certain kinds of problems. Anything that can replicate and pass genetic information—with possible modifications—on to its progeny should be subject to evolution. This includes computer viruses.

Evolving viruses can, in fact, be very effective at evading scanners and code analyzers. I've experimented with some very simple ones that can evolve their way around existing defenses in only 50 or 100 generations—which might take a PC chugging away at it only about an hour.

The problem, you see, is that evolution as we understand it is somewhat open-ended. An antivirus has its limits, thanks to Turing, and a virus can find those limits and exploit them, thanks to Darwin.

Mind you, what I'm talking about here is not a computer virus that can gain human intelligence through evolution, or anything like that. A much more realistic goal would be troublesome enough. For example, I believe a virus that would bankrupt any antivirus developer who tried to develop a foolproof cure for it is easily within reach.

Back in the late eighties it was often hard to convince people that such a beast as a computer virus really did exist. It was altogether too fantastic for them. I find the same situation today when it comes to evolutionary viruses. For example, just a year ago Eugene Spafford, a professor at Purdue University, a prestigious school, wrote in a respected journal—*Artificial Life,* published by M.I.T.—that, and I quote, "No computer viruses evolve as we commonly use the term, although it is conceivable that a very complex virus could be programmed to evolve and change. However, such a virus would be so large and complex as to be many orders of magnitude larger than most host programs and probably bigger than the host operating systems."

In fact, Spafford only displays his ignorance of already-existing virus technology. For example, an ordinary mutation engine which has no genetic memory, like the Trident Polymorphic Engine, can be turned into an evolutionary one by adding only about 200 bytes of code.

I don't mean to single out Eugene Spafford here. At least he's given the matter some thought. A lot of antivirus people are so quick to condemn me and boycott my book that one can only say they've willfully closed their eyes and plugged their ears in blissful ignorance.

Well, if all an evolutionary computer virus could do were to bankrupt a few antivirus vendors and make code analysis obsolete, I might say ho-hum and forget about it. Yet in trying to think this through to its logical conclusion, one has to face a great mystery. As a scientist I find this mystery fascinating. As a member of the human race, as a father with children who will live in a world where computers will become what I've just discussed, I find this mystery of very great importance.

This mystery is nothing other than evolution itself. I mean, it is the accepted scientific belief today that the changes of a single self-reproducing organism being assembled from basic components and surviving on the early earth was very remote. Therefore all of life must have evolved from this one single organism. That's a breathtaking idea if you think about it. We've all grown up with it, so it tends to be—well—ordinary to us. Yet it was utter madness just two centuries ago.

Yet what if . . . what if . . . what if the same were possible for computer viruses? . . .

Given our current understanding of evolution, the question isn't "what if" at all. It's merely a question of when. When will a self-reproducing program in the right location in gene space find itself in the right environment and begin the whole amazing chain of electronic life? It's merely a question of when the equivalent of the Cambrian explosion will take place.

What will the Cambrian period of the Internet be like, though? What will self-reproducing software do when most everyone is linked into The Network and its main use is for entertainment, when that link is a brain implant, when operating systems are so huge and full of holes that no one can even begin to understand them, and when computers are so powerful that very sophisticated self-reproducing software can evolve millions of generations in a single day? What will it be like in a world where people are dependent on computers to the point that they can't turn them off?

A lot of viruses written today are either benign or destructive. The destructive ones you positively want to avoid, and you may as well avoid the benign ones. The rare beneficial one—like KOH—you might install on your computer. All of these were authored by someone, though. What would a virus that had become what it is primarily by evolution be like?

Well, for one thing, we know that living organisms are incredibly self-serving. I cannot therefore imagine that the Cambrian electronic life on the Internet would care for me any more than a cockroach cares for me. It would gladly eat my food but run like hell when the lights went on. However, I expect there might be an important difference.

To be successful in a Darwinian sense, a piece of self-reproducing code must be executed. If it is not executed, it will have no progeny, and it will die out. There are essentially two ways for such code to be executed. One is to hide and gain a slice of CPU time on the sly. The other way is to induce the operator to execute it. I think both of these components will be essential to Cambrian electronic life. The virus must get into the computer and execute once on the sly. Then it must induce the operator to allow it to stay.

Imagine with me for a moment that you're someone come home from a hard day's work, and you flip on the computer to play the new version of your favorite game, just to unwind. After a few minutes, your mouse pointer turns to a small hammer, and a beautiful little golden bell, and a beautiful girl appears on the screen, while the speakers whisper the message: "Make your choice, adventurous Stranger/Strike the bell and bide the danger/Or wonder, till it drives you mad/What would have followed if you had."

This is more than you counted on. Is it part of the game . . . or something else? Is it something from another world? Something that's been honed for a million generations to entertain you in a way no human-designed game ever would dare to?

Would you strike the bell?

If it was your boss's computer, and you hadn't backed up in a month, your sense of duty might be strong enough to resist the temptation. But this is your home machine. All you stand to lose is a few games and unimportant stuff like your checkbook register. And you had a bad day at the office and a fight with your wife. You've had enough of the world of men.

You strike the bell.

Later, your integrity checker warns you of some danger, but you ignore it now. After all, this is interesting. You choose to keep it around, virus or not.

Add brain implants and the virus might almost take on the character of thought patterns. The integrity checker becomes a sort of conscience, and the man can listen to his conscience or ignore it. The most captivating thoughts will best succeed. These thought patterns might become incredibly sophisticated compared to what occurs naturally because natural thoughts don't capitalize on Darwinian evolution. And since the viruses are self-serving, the thoughts they plant may not be at all beneficial to the people who let them in.

In such a world computer viruses might become the electronic equivalent of highly addictive drugs. One dose and you're addicted. And it could well be that a whole lot of people could become addicted before they realized what was happening, just like the Chinese got addicted to opium.

Okay, enough of the wild speculations. Let's come back to earth in 1995. All of this seems pretty remote to me. But how do I know? Given our current understanding of evolution, it's possible—and lots worse is possible, too.

You'll notice a few minutes ago I called evolution a mystery, not a theory. I'm a physical scientist, and to me, a theory is something that helps you make predictions about what will happen, given a certain set of initial conditions. Darwin's ideas and what's developed around them in the past 125 years unfortunately don't give me the tools to do that. Those ideas may be great for explaining sequences of fossils, or variations between different species, but just try to use this theory to explain what's going to happen when viruses start evolving, and you quickly learn that it isn't going to do you much good. There's just not any way to take a set of initial conditions and determine mathematically what will happen.

That's not too surprising, really. Most of what we call evolution focuses on explaining past events—fossils, existing species, et cetera. The theory didn't develop in a laboratory setting, making predictions and testing them with experiment. So it's good at explaining past events and lousy at predicting the future. That's changing only very slowly. The deeper understanding of biology at the molecular level that has come about in the last 40 years is applying a certain amount of pressure for change. At the same time, the idea that the past must be explained by evolution is a sacred cow that's hindering the transition. That's because evolution has to be practically omnipotent to explain the past, and so it's hard to publish any paper that draws this into question.

Viruses are different from the real world, because we're interested in what evolution cannot do, and not just what it can do, or what it has to have done. In the world of viruses, we freely admit the possibility of special creation. Furthermore, we should expect that some instruction sets, or some operating systems may promote evolutionary behavior, but others will be hostile to it.

In short, I think that in order to come to grips with computer viruses and artificial life in general, a radically new and different theory of evolution is going to be necessary—a theory that a hard-core physical scientist would find satisfying—one with some real predictive power. This theory may be dangerous to traditional evolutionary biologists. It could tell them things about the real world they won't want to hear. However, to close your eyes and plug your ears could be disastrous to the computing community and to human civilization as a whole.

In the end, I think that leaving antivirus research to a few private companies who are struggling to survive and who are driven by the need for short-term profits is a big mistake. To meet the challenges of the future will require basic research that these companies just don't have the means to conduct. They don't have the money and they certainly don't have the brain power. It's going to take research at least at the university level to meet this challenge, and I should think various governments would be interested in the outcome, too.

To merely go on meeting the challenges of viruses as they come, one by one, is inviting disaster. The history of the earth is punctuated by periods where there was a great flowering of new life-forms. Whether we're talking about the Cambrian period or the age of dinosaurs, natural history can almost be viewed as if a new paradigm suddenly showed up on the scene and changed the world in a very short period of time. Right now there is no reason to believe—at the highest levels of human understanding—that a similar flowering will not take place in the electronic world. If it does, and we're not ready for it, expecting it, and controlling its shape, there's no telling what the end of it could be. If you look at the science fiction of the fifties, it was the super-smart computer that would be the first "artificial life," but the first artificial life that most people ran into was a stupid virus. We often imagine that computers will conquer man by becoming much more intelligent than him. It could be that we'll be conquered by something that's incredibly stupid, but adept at manipulating our senses, feelings, and desires.

Do I really think that anyone is going to wake up to this and do the research needed to take control of evolving software? No.

In short, the cyber-revolution may not be marxist, statist, libertarian, anarchist, or feminist. It may be Darwinian, and it may not even be carried out by humans.

Code Warriors

Bunkering In and Dumbing Down

Arthur and Marilouise Kroker

Electronic technology terminates with the radically divided self: the self, that is, which is at war with itself. Split consciousness for a culture that is split between digital and human flesh.

A warring field, the electronic self is torn between contradictory impulses toward privacy and the public, the natural self and the social self, private imagination and electronic fantasy. The price for reconciling the divided self by sacrificing one side of the electronic personality is severe. If it abandons private identity and actually becomes media (Cineplex mind, IMAX imagination, MTV chat, CNN nerves), the electronic self will suffer terminal repression. However, if it seals itself off from public life by retreating to an electronic cell in the suburbs or a computer condo in the city, it quickly falls into an irreal world of electronic MOO-room fun within the armored windows. Suffering electronic amnesia on the public and its multiple viewpoints, going private means that the electronic self will not be in a position to maximize its interests by struggling in an increasingly competitive economic field.

The electronic self is in a bind. Seeking to immunize itself against the worst effects of public life, it bunkers in. It becomes a pure will-for-itself: self-dwelling, closed down, ready to sacrifice all other interests for the sake of its own immunity. Bunkering in is the epochal consciousness of technological society in its most mature phase. McLuhan called it the "cool personality" typical of the TV age, others have spoken of "cocooning" away the nineties, but we would say that bunkering in is about something really simple: being sick of others and trying to shelter the beleaguered self in a techno-bubble. Dipping back to Darwin, West Coast libertarians like to talk today about "survival of the electronically fittest."

However, at the same time that the electronic self bunkers in as a survival strategy, it is forced, out of economic necessity, to stick its head out of its techno-bubble and skate to work. Frightened by the accelerating speed of technological change, distressed by the loss of disposable income, worried about a future without jobs, and angry at the government, the electronic self oscillates between fear and rage. Rather than objectify its anger in a critical analysis of the public situation, diagnosing, for example, the deep relationship between the rise of the technological class and the loss of jobs, the electronic self is taught by the media elite to turn the "self" into a form of self-contempt. Dumbing down becomes the reality of the late-twentieth-century personality. Dumbing down? In its benign form, that's Gump with his box of chocolates and Homer Simpson barfing doughnuts. In its predatory form, it's everyday life: cons and parasites and computer presidents and killer Jeeps on city streets. Or, like in *Pulp Fiction,* maybe it's time to "bring out the gimp."

The bunker self is infected by *ressentiment* against those it holds responsible for what ails it (feminists, African Americans, immigrants, single mothers on welfare); dumbing down is the last blast of slave consciousness (servile to authority; abusive to those weaker than it). Petulant and given over to bouts of whining about the petty inconveniences, bunkering in knows no ethics other than immediate self-gratification. Hard-eyed and emotionally cryogenicized, dumbing down means oscillating between the psychological poles of predator and clown. Between the illusion of immunity and the reality of the process-self, that's the radically divided state of the electronic personality at the end of the twentieth century. Just in time to catch the virtual screen opening up on the final file of the millennium, the bunker ego and the dumbed-down self are the culmination of what Jean-Paul Sartre predicted: a schizoid self which is simultaneously in-itself and for-itself, an unreconciled self flipping between illusion and self-contempt. Today, it's hip to be dumb, and smart to be turned off and tuned out.

The psychological war zone of bunkering in and dumbing down is the actual cultural context out of which emerges technological euphoria. Digital reality is perfect. It provides the bunker self with immediate, universal access to a global community without people: electronic communication without social contact, being digital without being human, going online without leaving the safety of the electronic bunker. The bunker self takes to the Internet like a pixel to a screen because the information superhighway is the biggest theme park in the world: more than 170 countries. And it's perfect, too, for dumbing down. Privileging information while exterminating meaning, surfing without engagement, digital reality provides a new virtual playing field for tuning out and turning off. For example, when CITY-TV (Toronto) recently announced a merger with Voyager to produce new multimedia productions, its first product of choice was the creation of an "electronic rumpus room." Playtime for the new electronic kids on the block.

What's better, with the quick privatization of the Internet and the Web, the predatory self doesn't have to risk brief dashes in and out of public life to grab what it wants. In virtual capitalism, the predatory self goes fully digital, arms itself with the latest in graphical interfaces, bulks up the profile of its homepage, and goes hunting for digital gold. Schumpeter might have talked about "creative destruction" as the contemporary phase of transiting to a virtual economy, but the predatory self knows better. Turbulence in the field means one thing only: the rest position is terminal, victory goes to those who warp jump the fastest to cyberspace. Working on the tried but true formula of "use and abandon," the predatory self does the ultimate dumbing-down trick: it sheds its flesh (for cyber-skin), its mind (for distributive intelligence), its nerves (for algorithmic codes), its sex organs (for digital seduction), its limbs (for virtual vectors of speed and slipstream access), and its history (for multiplex hard ram). Virtual Gump.

Opening Out and Smartening Up

Two Worlds

Digital reality contains alternative possibilities toward emancipation and domination. As a manifestation of the power of the virtual class, digital reality has definitely plunged the world into a great historical crisis. Here cyber-technology is a grisly process of harvesting nature and culture, and particularly our bodies, for fast-rendering through massive virtual imaging-systems. Not a technology that we can hold outside of ourselves as an inanimate object, cyber-technology has actually come alive in the form of virtualization. It seeks to take possession of the material world and to dump material reality into the electronic trashbin in favor of what has been eloquently described as a "realm inhabited by the disembodied." Cyber-technology creates two worlds, one virtual, the other material, separate and unequal. The radical division between these two worlds is becoming more apparent every day.

The struggle to relink technology and ethics, to think of cyber-technology in terms of the relationship of virtuality to questions of democracy, justice, social solidarity, and creative inquiry promises a path of reconciliation. Of course, we don't think of the body or nature as outside technology, but as part of a field of dynamic and often deeply conflicting relations in which, for example, the body itself could be construed as a "technology." This being so, the key ethical question might be: what are the possibilities for a virtual democracy, virtual justice, virtual solidarity, and virtual knowledge? Rather than recover ethics outside of cyber-technology, our position is to force ethics to travel deeply and quickly inside the force field of cyber-technology, to make our ethical demands for social justice, for the reconciliation of flesh and spirit, rub up against the most demonic aspects of virtual reality. In this we practice Foucault's prescription for reading Nietzsche, that honors a writer (or a new ethics) by forcing ethics to bend, crackle, strain, and groan under the violence and weight of our insistent demands for meaning.

Post-Bodies

We are living in a decisive historical time: the era of the posthuman. This age is typified by a relentless effort on the part of the virtual class to force a wholesale abandonment of the body, to dump sensuous experience into the trashbin, substituting instead a disembodied world of empty data flows. This body assault takes different forms: from the rhetoric of the "information superhighway" (of which we are the pavement) to the recently announced effort by Microsoft and McCaw Cellular to develop a global multimedia network of satellites for downloading and uplinking the archival record of the human experience into massive, centrally controlled databases. The virtual elite always present the "electronic frontier" in the glowing, ideological terms of heightened accessibility, increased cyber-knowledge, more "rapid delivery of health and education to rural environments," or better paying high-tech jobs. In reality what they are doing is delivering us to virtualization.

It isn't a matter of being pro- or antitechnology, but of considering the consequences of virtual reality when it is so deeply spoken of in the language of exterminism. In the age of the virtual class, digital technology works to discredit bodily experience, to make us feel humiliated and inferior to the virtual rendering of the body in its different electronic formats, from computers and television to the glitzy and vampirish world of advertising. The attitude that the body is a failed project takes us directly to a culture driven by suicidal nihilism. Remember Goya: imagination without reason begets monstrous visions. Those "monstrous visions" are the designs for better electronic bodies that vomit out of the cyber-factories of the Silicon Valleys of the world every day.

Digital reality has given us artificial life. Not artificial life as an abstract telematic experience fabricated by techno-labs, but artificial life as life as it is actually lived today. Cyber-technology has escaped the digital labs and has inscribed itself on our captive bodies. In artificial life, the body is a violent uncertainty-field. What could be spoken of in the 1930s only in the language of high-energy physics, particularly Heisenberg's concept of uncertainty, has now been materialized in society as the schizoid body: the body, that is, as an unstable field flipping aimlessly between opposing poles—bunkered in yet dumbed down. This is the symptomatic sign of what we call the digital body.

The New Power Elite

There are two dominant political tendencies in the 1990s: a global "virtual class" that presents the particular interests of technotopia as the general human interest, and the equally swift emergence of ever more grisly forms of conservative fundamentalism in response to the hegemony of the virtual class.

The virtual class is composed of monarchs of the electronic kingdom. Its members like to gather in digital nests, from Silicon Valley and Chiba City to the European cyber-grid running from Munich to Grenoble. Deeply authoritarian in its politics, it seeks to exclude from public debate any perspective that challenges the ruling ideology of technotopia. Like its historical predecessors, the early bourgeoisie of primitive capitalism, the virtual class is driven by the belief that a cybernetically steered society, of which it is the guiding helmsman, is coeval with the noblest aspirations of human destiny. Listen to the rhetoric of the virtual class that drowns the mediascape. A few years ago, at Silicon Graphics, Clinton preached the technotopian gospel that the "information superhighway" is the telematic destiny of America; Gore continues to hype the "interactive society" as the next stage of human evolution; Microsoft presents its strategic plans for a world wide web of digital satellites in the soft language of doing a big service for humanity (Bill Gates said his new satellite system would allow educational and health services to be delivered to previously inaccessible rural areas); and all multinational business and most governments these days commonly chant the refrain that trade policy should be decoupled from human rights issues. For example, faced with American business' opposition to his executive order linking China's "Most Favored Nation" status to improvements in human rights, Clinton instantly collapsed, announcing that he had "deep regrets" about his own executive order. Of course, in the mid-nineties the gospel of technotopia is the bible of virtual libertarians, Newt Gingrich most of all.

While the ruling masters of the virtual class in countries ranging from the United States, Japan, Western Europe, and Canada represent the territorial center of digital power, the rest of the world is quickly remaindered. Based in labor that is not a fungible resource, the middle and working classes in all countries are repeatedly victimized by the virtual class. Today, labor is disciplined by the representatives of the virtual class who occupy the highest policy-making positions of government. As the dominant ideology of the nineties, the virtual class institutes draconian antilabor policies mandating "labor adjustment," "free trade," and belt-tightening, and all of this backed up by a media mantra calling for global economic competition, an end to pay equity, and a "meaner and leaner" workplace.

For those outside the labor force—the jobless, the disenfranchised, the politically powerless, the surplus class—the disciplinary lessons administered by the virtual class are bitter. And it fits so perfectly with the psychology of bunkering in. Consider the silence at the terrorism in Haiti where in a macabre replay of Machiavelli's strategies for stable political rule, the tortured bodies of political activists had their faces cut off, were thrown into the main streets of Port-au-Prince, and left there under the glaring sun for several days.

The police did not allow anyone to take away the bodies. Pigs ate the rotting flesh. The lesson is clear: the state has all-pervasive power to the point that even the identities of its victims can be effaced after death, letting the spirits of the dead roam in endless anguish. This is diabolical power at the end of the twentieth century, and still not a humanitarian peep from the political managers of the virtual class. Not until the shores of America were filled with "illegal" Haitian refugees did the Clinton Administration react. Or consider the moral culpability of the so-called creative leadership of the virtual societies of the West who continue to turn a blinkered eye to the genocide that takes place in the streets of Sarajevo every day. Would it be different if Bosnia had oil, a Nike shoe factory, or, even better, a Microsoft chip mill?

The virtual elite has the ethics of the hangman, all hidden under the soft hype of the data superhighway as new body wetware for the twenty-first century.

Dominant Ideology

Recently, we received the following letter from Nate McFadden, a freelance reporter for a San Francisco magazine:

> In the *SF Bay Guardian's* article on *Wired*, a former director of The Well, Cliff Figallo, commented on the colonization of cyberspace. "To some of us, it's like the staking of claims in the Old West. Perhaps it's the manifest destiny of cyberspace."
>
> This remark seems to verify, at least a little, the lack of moral awareness rampant in the techno-elite. For me, the apparently unironic usage of the expression "manifest destiny" indicates a mindset that avoids historical antecedents, and is free from any critical examination of motive and result.

A little later, we received this e-mail message from Mark Schneider, Vancouver bureau chief for CTV:

> Check out the latest issue of *The Nation* (July 3), "Whose Net Is It?" by Andrew Shapiro. "You probably didn't notice, but the Internet was sold a few months ago. Well, sort of: The Federal government has been gradually transferring the backbone of the US portion of the global computer network to companies such as IBM and MCI as part of a larger plan to privatize

> cyberspace. But the crucial step was taken on April 30, when the National Science Foundation shut down its part of the Internet . . . [that's left] the corporate giants in charge. . . ."

The virtual elite is a mixture of predatory capitalists and visionary computer specialists for whom virtualization is about our disappearance into nothingness. We are talking about a systematic assault against the human species, a virtual war strategy where knowledge is reduced to data storage dumps, friendship is dissolved into floating cyber-interactions, and communication means the end of meaning. Virtualization in the cyber-hands of the new technological class is all about our being dumbed down. In a very practical way, the end of the twentieth century is characterized by the laying down of hardware (virtual railway tracks) across the ever-expanding electronic frontier. Of course, whoever controls the hardware will dominate the soft-(ware) culture of the twenty-first century. That's why Microsoft is the first of all the twenty-first century corporations: it's already put the Operating System in place and now, through Microsoft Network, it's set to actually be the Internet. All of this is being done without any substantive public debate, to the background tune, in fact, of three cheers for the virtual home team and its hyped-ideology of cyber-technology as emancipation. Manifest Destiny has come inside (us), and we are the once and future victims of the big (electronic) stick.

Manifest (Virtual) Destiny

The resuscitation of the doctrine of Manifest Destiny as the bible of the virtual class has already taken place. However, it's no longer Manifest Destiny as an American war strategy for the endocolonization of North America, but a more vicious doctrine of digital inevitability that is being put in place around the globe by the technological elite. In this mutation of Manifest Destiny, the world is quickly divided into privileged virtual economies, passive storage depots for cheap labor, and permanently enslaved nations. While the citizens of the lead virtual societies certainly suffer massive psychological repression and suppression (of social choices), countries which are patched into the political economy of virtual reality as sources of cheap manufacturing or as product assembly labor suffer the form of domination particular to primitive capitalism—"work or starve." For the citizens of the enslaved nations, from Africa to Haiti, they are simply put under the coercive welfare wardship of a newly militant United Nations and then erased from historical consciousness. Like all empires before it, virtual reality begins with a blood sacrifice.

Contradictions of the Virtual Class

It is not at all clear that the new technological class will win the day. The will to virtuality is riddled with deep contradictions. Can the offensive by the virtual class against human labor actually succeed in light of both growing impoverishment and the crushing of life expectations for the young? The rhetoric of digital reality speaks about the growing abundance of high-paying jobs in the tech industry. Across the OECD [Organization for Economic Co-operation and Development], the reality is dramatically different: every country that has instituted policies promoting the expansion of digital reality has witnessed a dramatic, and seemingly permanent, increase in unemployment. Joblessness not just in the low- or no-tech industries, but massive layoffs and ruthless "restructurings" in the vaunted digital industries themselves. No one bothered to tell us that digital reality also deletes jobs! This is the dirty little secret that the masters of the technological universe definitely don't want to talk about and, in their control of the mediascape, will never allow to be spoken. It's the forbidden-to-be-thought truth that ruptures the seamless web of digital reality as the dominant ideology of the nineties.

Can the offensive by the technological class against society in the name of the moral superiority of digital reality be sustained in the midst of the general social crisis that it has created? What will happen when digital reality, this dynamic drive to planetary mastery in the name of technology, actually begins to displace its creators—the virtual class?

Against the new technological class are ranged a series of critical political forces: Net knowledgeable, technically astute people who speak on behalf of the new relations of digital reality rather than apologizing for the old forces of commercial or governmental interests. Certainly Net surfers with a (critical) attitude who attempt to make the "information superhighway" serve the ethical human ends of solidarity, creativity, and democracy, but also all of those social movements who say both "no" to the virtual class and "yes" to rethinking the human destiny. We have in mind aboriginal movements from

North and South America who make of the issue of land rights a fundamental battleground of (durational) time against (virtualized) space; feminists who have reasserted the identity of the body; the Green movement, which is slowly turning the tide on a global scale against the harvesting machine of corporate capitalism; and those "body outlaws," bisexuals and gays and lesbians, who have made of the politics of sexual difference a way of speaking again about the possibility of human love.

Having said this, we are under no illusion about the fundamental exterminatory character of the times. We exist now at a great divide: between a fall into a new form of despotic capitalism on the one hand, and a world that might be re-created ethically on the other. This is the life-and-death struggle of our age.

Harvesting Flesh

Contemporary culture is driven onward by the planetary drive toward the mastery of nature. In Heidegger's chilling description, technology is infected with the language of "harvesting." First, the har-vesting of nature as the physical world is reduced to a passive resource of exploitation. And second, the harvesting of human flesh as (our) bodies and minds are reduced to a database for imaging systems. That's the contemporary human fate: to be dumped into the waiting data archives for purposes of future resequencing. Some are Web brains, others TV heads or designer logos, here minds as media screens, there nerves as electronic impulses finely tuned to the rhythms of the digital world.

Consider TV: a war machine for colonizing the soft mass of the electronic mind. Three tactical maneuvers are always in play: Desensitization—following exactly the same procedure used by the C.I.A. in training assassins, TV desensitizes the electronic mind by repeatedly exposing it to scenes of torture, corpses, and mutilation. By reducing the electronic mind of the population to the deadened morality of the assassin, it preps the population for its own future sacrifice in the form of body dumps; Infantilization—that's the gradual media strategy for reducing us all to retro-children: perfect political fodder for the growth of virtual- and retro-fascism; and Reenergization—left to its own devices, the mediascape will always collapse toward its inertial pole. That's why the media must constantly be reenergized (recharged?) by scenes of sacrificial violence. In every war, there are victims and executioners. In the television war machine, we are always both: victims (of the three tactical maneuvers of the mediascape) and executioners of an accidental range of victims dragged across the cold screens for our moral dismissal (much like the terminal judgment of the Roman masses in the amphitheaters of classical antiquity).

Photography, cinema, TV, and the Internet are successive stages in virtualization. Beginning with the simulacrum of the first photograph, continuing with the scanner imaging-system of TV, and concluding (for the moment) with the data archives of the Internet, human experience is fast-dumped into the relays and networks of virtual culture. McLuhan was wrong. It is not the technological media of communication as an extension of man, but the human species as a humiliated subject of digital culture.

Fungal Intimacy

The Cyborg in Feminism and Media Art

Catherine Richards

These reflections on fungal intimacy trace a parallel process to my art production.[1] My latest works take up the body as it couples with technology.[2] Attempting to sidestep the artist as technological celebrant and humanist, these pieces watch us lurching back and forth across the technological threshold of materiality and virtuality. What follows are reflections on working with contemporary North American technology and on moments when the stories about technologies become the technology itself.

It was the disturbance of conventional notions of the self that I found most provocative when first introduced to virtual reality (VR).[3] Here, it seemed to me, was a technology which in its very human-technical interface creates a site to explore a new body, for the lack of another term, an entity that can no longer be defined as distinct. VR promised a technological condition that has little to do with the image of boundaries normally associated with an individual subject. Within VR's appealing clumsiness appeared a prototype of more elegant, invisible, and efficient technologies to come.

I saw in such technologies as VR a site to try out and try on the projects preoccupying postmodern debate: the project of inventing new images of the body where it could be seen as a threshold, a field of intensities rather than half of the mind/body dualism; and the feminist project of redesigning female subjectivity, a subjectivity well-disposed to dispersal in images of webs of connections, to functioning in a net of interconnections—artificial, abstract, and perfectly operationally real.[4]

In the early eighties VR technology and feminist research were simultaneously developing in the North American society in which I live. I relished the thought of metaphorically linking attributes identified as female (at least culturally and even traditionally) with key structural characteristics of the technology. This possibility seemed a richly humorous joke out of anyone's control.

Could a technology, built by and intended for the reinforcement of the stereotypical monadic, hierarchical, specialized subject position, be pushed to such an extreme that it would support the opposite, namely, characteristics reminiscent of the very attributes currently describing women? Women in my social context were seen as largely responsible for personal and social relationships and networks, nonspecialized work open to interruption, and undefined or at least unclear ego boundaries.

What is interactivity, I thought, but expertise in structuring and restructuring complex and shifting relationships; what is parallel processing but expertise in handling multiple simultaneous events, skillfully choreographing continuous and interruptible tasks; what is the cybernetic and surveyed body/self but one that can sustain integrity with blurred boundaries and even multiple bodies and identities as in the case of childbearing? What is networking, a raison d'etre of the electronic environment, but an acknowledgment of mutual interdependence—complete with such vulnerabilities as viruses, which only confirm mutuality?

Could it be that the very structural characteristics of a technology such as VR also describe the attributes of a subjectivity required for survival within that new technological sensorium? Would this mean that womanlike subjectivity could, in a kind of historical accident, in a moment of incongruity, feel at home there?

Several years later I encountered Donna Haraway's influential text on cyborgs.[5] Her text seemed to suggest more twists in the contemporary technological condition. Haraway's notion of illegitimate offspring appeared to rationalize the dubious militaristic origins of the technology. In the case of VR one could then suggest that VR is ironically reversing its intended purpose. VR was first developed as the head-mounted helmet for fighter pilots. These fighting biomachines first appear as all powerful independent entities. But as these individual pilots are intimately linked into larger cybernetic systems, this connection profoundly increases their vulnerability. Also important for me, Haraway created an image of the interdependent feedback loop of interactivity as the cyborg condition. Finally, she identified a feminist position as having the best chance for survival and living to tell the tale as a cyborg, creating a girls' book of cyber-adventures.

Perhaps such a technological environment could be described as "feminized," that is, its structure seems to have feminine characteristics, but at the same time this seemed like an elaborate hidden joke. To reinscribe existing gender representations (of whatever order, reactionary or radical) seemed overly literal and already nostalgic. Conversely, to suggest, as some technologists did, that gender and race could be erased in a virtual world of shared communication seemed as questionable as any promise of a universalizing, leveling, utopian, or dystopian environment. Since then the joke seems less playful and ironic, now more painful.

What I considered to be obvious in VR environments—the fluctuating reversals of subject/object in a cybernetic system—was not part of highly visible VR narratives. The technology in these narratives is not seen as disturbing a centered sense of self/body. On the contrary, it is seen as strengthening the intact self. The discussion of the challenges to our sense of identity and body has largely been left aside. An influential scientist such as Marvin Minsky saw VR as part of the technological evolution of humans toward increased independent mastery.[6] Cyberpunks in cyberspace were a kind of nostalgic mix: Jack Kerouac on the road to the new virgin frontier. The technologists promised a kind of superhuman untouchable body able to intervene invisibly.

Though a cyborg entity is often postulated in these narratives, it does not transgress the notion of a separate, independent, willful, and hierarchical self; instead it evolves a more powerful version. Ironically this technological condition is also seen as capable of neutralizing troubling experiences which might disturb a notion of autonomous self with intact boundaries. The narratives have centered on safe sex, safe drugs, safe transcendence and now safe feminism.

If the media play of teledildonics and safe sex in cyberspace is familiar, so too is Timothy Leary's evangelical promotion of VR as mind-expanding. An attraction of telepresence is the apparent transcendence of bodily limits in reaching out to places inaccessible for the material body. The body is seen in fictional cyberspace as meat. and cyberspace itself is characterized as a chance to leave the body behind. A distant mentor of cyberpunk, William Burroughs, would laconically say "the body is obsolete."[7] Jean-François Lyotard mixes evolution, technology, and transcendence when he says the aim of all contemporary research, in whatever discipline, is to emancipate the human brain from constraints common to all living systems on the earth, or to manufacture a system, independent of those constraints.[8] More recently, cyber-feminism has been pictured by Sadie Plant as the natural matrix, collapsing identity into the cybernetic net: as she sums up, "If the male human is the only human, the female cyborg is the only cyborg."[9]

Why might these narratives of technological sex, drugs, transcendence, or feminism be so recurring? In a culture centered on the autonomous individual, these experiences in life are transgressive. Are these narratives leading us to see the technology as a means to simulate those experiences, control and annul them, to tighten the defenses around an intact identity?

On the other hand there may be another way to look at a common thread running through virtual experiences. All are experiences which challenge a conventional integrity through an out-of-body, out-of-identity, or at least an intersubjective experience. It may not be sex, drugs, transcendence, or cyber-feminism that the user experiences but an environment that shares some of their characteristics. These narratives are a way to account for a transgressive technological experience for which there is as yet no subjective position. This transgressive state is likely part of the technological condition. That an autonomous, replete monadic subject is being decentered by the operations of the system itself, not from any critique or imaginative move on the part of feminists, postmodern theorists, or philosophers, gives pause for thought. It may well be that the technology is implicated in constructing a different position of subjectivity for all of us, a position which will accommodate and be appropriate to the new social economic order.

In cyber-feminism there seems to be an assumption that cyberfeminists will remain unscathed in these environments. Before rushing in to claim this territory, I must ask to what ideological ends it might be useful to have a technological environment constructing a subjective experience closer to an alternative, female, and postmodern position. Within this process I expect the most unexpected and taken-for-granted aspects of subjectivity to be modified. If something about contemporary virtual technology erases gender as articulated, will radical cyber-feminism be consigned to nostalgic content as much as traditional lonely male heroism? Let me speculate further about the cyborg. As a figuration it takes on powerful imaginative and political roles as a material and virtual entity that exists as flesh and information in a continuous feedback loop. Artists, however, intentionally manifest it as a lived condition, transforming metaphorical figure into material sign. In the process, some darker sides come to light: pain. Though there are invisible and seemingly unnoticeable hybrids of machine and human, the material hybrids bring to the surface the price of transgressing embodiment. If one desires to transcend the material body, it will be painful. One could suggest that this physical pain is also the sign of psychic pain as we reorganize our psychic structures. Artists such as Orlan and Stelarc seem to place themselves in laboratories of pain, experimenting with ways to remain fully aware throughout cybernetic mutations of the body. Within this context Orlan's description of herself fully conscious on the operating table, performing for her interactive satellite audience, takes on a complex pathos. "I was able, without feeling pain, to answer the people who were feeling their own pain as they were watching me."[10] Here telepresence takes on a layered meaning, as does VR's relationship with drugs. The spectators experience pain indirectly as Orlan acknowledges their presence in the telepresence system. This is possible only by denying her own pain through drugs. The implications of the link between human modification, drugs, and contemporary technologies is no longer strictly metaphoric.

As much as the cyborg represents a transgression of boundaries, it also falls short of complex interdependence. As much as it pictures the hybrid of machine and human, the model of multiple humans and machines is unformed. The cyborg still suggests a solitary state reminiscent of bachelor machines, those artist machines modeling self-enclosed sexuality and reproduction which have been a problematic subject for feminist artists. Haraway's final imagery of cyborgs suggests such a state. It calls upon a salamander's ability to regenerate as a new model and is suspicious of the reproductive matrix and of most birthing. "We require regeneration, not rebirth, and the possibility for our reconstitution to include the utopian dream of the hope for a monstrous world without gender."[11] Though this is a compelling image, I wonder how it may parallel the technological agenda already in place: promises of transcending the body, the genetic code, the birth process, carbon-based life-forms, gender, race (but not class), and enclosing and enlarging oneself within a fluctuating cyborg body.

As the cyborg image seems to move closer to a feminine bachelor machine caught up in its own self-referential motor, it increasingly appears as a mirror image of a too-familiar condition.

Before throwing out the biological baby with the embryonic fluid, it may be useful to remember that part of our biological experience does illustrate deep interdependent relations with difference. Childbearing is one experience of complex and nonsocially constructed metamorphosis. It involves an interrelation of fluctuating identities which must be navigated as the same system and differentiated at the same time; it is a process of uncontrollable events among two willful systems—and we all first negotiate this condition in our experiences as a child.

Sometimes, at night, I give up these recalcitrant ways. I wonder if the popular narratives are right. I too start to picture the cyborg as a more powerful intact identity, but then I am startled to see it has all the other attributes as well: unclear boundaries (here and everywhere), regeneration over time (that is, a grasp on immortality), regeneration over birth (that is, assurance of replicating myself). What is a laterally displaced, nonhierarchical networked interior of multiform sexuality and reproduction? I contemplate the fungus found in Michigan, 10,000 kilos replicating itself over 1,500 years, over 6 acres in one vast underground network, now and then discreetly showing itself above ground in the guise of an individual, and picking and choosing its form of reproduction.

PART 5 | DIGITAL-SPECIFIC ART

LYNN HERSHMAN LEESON
Camera Woman, Phantom Limb Number 16, 1990

HOT SPOTS

Text in Motion and the Textscape of Electronic Media

Rudolf Frieling
Translated by Don Reneau

Despite all pioneers of hypertext, among which Peter Sloterdijk lists Wittgenstein's *Zettelbücher,* Paul Valéry's construction of multidimensional universes of aphorism, and the metawritings of Borges in which the library becomes the place of text operations that transcend the book,[1] and despite all visual poetry in the tradition of Mallarmé, today the printed word is still the word of authority. The image, whether painted, photographed, or filmed, is to a much lesser degree authoritarian and tends to be criticized for possessing either a seductive power or an ambivalence as to its interpretation, making it suspicious to many. The following essay focuses on the relationship between image and text—this age-old antagonism that seems to vanish before our eyes.

Most visual artists, not surprisingly, take sides with the image. Bill Viola is one of the most prominent. In *The Threshold,* one of his more recent installations, a polarity between image and text is staged in space. A huge and bright LED (light-emitting diode) display, horizontally placed to the left and right of a narrow entrance, directly communicates items from a news agency. The relation of the size of the letters to the size of the space is absurdly distorted: there is no distance from which to read easily. The letters are oversized, out of scale. One must cut through the stream of letters and get beyond the surface. But what is behind the text—what is the "metatext" of Viola's metaphysics?

The threshold denotes a place of passage and change, of promise, but also of anxiety and fear of intruding into intimacy. This intimate space of the installation confronts the viewer with darkness and three images of sleepers, projected slightly out of focus onto the walls. Watching the sleepers opens up recollections, vague impressions of a dreamtime and an inner world. Viola seems to denounce the "white noise" of a superficial world outside that worships information as opposed to truth and emotion. *The Threshold* is staged as a rite of passage, a rite of initiation. After passing through this inner space, the viewer is reborn to perceive the aggressiveness of the outer world of abstraction. Viola's installation is thus clearly based on a dualist notion. The implication is once again that, as a German saying goes, an image says more than a thousand words. The reason for this belief is expressed by the American painter Cy Twombly who, in an untitled painting from 1990, states: "The image cannot be dispossessed of a primordial suchness which ideas can never claim."

Whether we proclaim a current crisis of the text in a reaction to the advent of multimedia, or whether we speak of the crisis of visual representation, an ideological abyss separates those who trust the image from those who trust the word. Regis Debray's verdict that what is fascist is not language but the visual expresses a contempt toward the metaphysics of images that is emblematic of a strong current not only in ancient and modern thinking but also in contemporary art practice, often formulated by audiovisual artists themselves.[2] How can we still grasp the world within the vertigo of information and the cult of the televised image? By going back to handwritten texts that claim to defend authenticity? By praising characters and typography, the printed letter, the book of the Gutenberg era that seems to be threatened by electronic publishing? Or by reducing the increasing overflow of images to a few carefully selected images? How do text and image interact—that is one of the questions key to an understanding of the constant drift from the abstract to the concrete and to abstraction again. A brief look back reveals to what a surprising extent hybrid forms of text and image have been at the core of artistic movements in the twentieth century, preparing the ground for the pleasure of multimedia text and the flourishing of text in space—what might be coined textscapes.

From Image to Text

The old dualist concept of image versus text was visibly shattered when, in the beginning of the twentieth century, the Cubist painters introduced printed letters into their paintings. After Cubism a whole series of avant-garde practices, from Dadaism and Surrealism to Futurism, Fluxus, and Pop art, furthered the integration of text and writings into the fine art tradition, which has ultimately become the domain of Conceptual art. Contemporary artists such as Joseph Kosuth, Nancy Dwyer, Jenny Holzer, or Lothar Baumgarten, to name but a few, set words in relation to space and examine social structures through language. Painted, formed, lit, or projected—words in an art context are more than anywhere else perceived as being concrete and abstract at the same time, cognitively rather than intuitively understood. Barbara Kruger and Les Levine succeed in using commercial language for their critical intentions and subversive strategies. Yet the question has to be asked: What is the purpose of critical or subversive appropriation when the combination of text and image has become a ubiquitous practice on billboards and TV screens all over the world?

The phenomenon of the use of "immaterial" tools such as light (neon), moving light (LED displays), or electronic light (video) often connotes an ambivalence that attracts and fascinates the artist and viewer alike. What is the dynamic inherent in the publicly displayed word or text, and what is the intriguing quality of these artistic tools and materials? Strictly reducing the scope of their work to texts, artists like Kosuth or Holzer have been working in a stimulating way with the displacement of contexts and the urge to read and decipher, thereby challenging our perception.

Sculptural Text

With Joseph Kosuth, text is related to texture and turned into pure surface. In his installation for the Hungarian Pavilion of the 1993 Venice Biennale, the walls were covered with quotes and phrases, playing on the cultural heritage of ornament and calligraphy, both of which have an affinity to wallpaper design. No one actually reads the whole text, but everybody is tempted to look for a recognizable quote. The urge to decipher language is one of the driving forces behind Kosuth's work. It embodies the openness of the act of perception and reading when, for instance, texts covering a wall are censored by bold black lines. These texts have to be deciphered and imagined laboriously by using the still visible extremities of letters as clues for the identification of the words.

In another work Kosuth examined the relation between surface and background and worked with the three dimensions of sculpture by placing a text on the wall behind the neon phrase "it was it." Neon is thus associated with tautology and ornament. The abstraction of words is turned into an aesthetic statement. Meaning seems not to be found within language or sculpture but within the spatial relation between both. The spectator can still experience foreground and background, yet at the same time the relation between the material and its surface is questioned. An ambivalence prevails: working with abstract signs and texts negates materiality, whereas the prominence of the glowing neon letters insists on the concrete sculptural element. Kosuth has been one of the most prominent explorers of text in space.

Text and Surface

The walls of a space can be covered with writing, and trains painted with graffiti signatures—in these cases, stylized words or names are marks or gestures of identification. Leaving one's name carved in a tree or sprayed on a subway train is an act that expresses identity, if only temporarily. The longer this trace lasts, the more often it can be read by the community. Chalk writing on a blackboard is also the trace of an individual act, but here the surface already suggests temporariness: someone is going to wipe it out. A blank surface is restored only to be recovered once again.

But the surface can also be mental—experiences, ideas, traumas in the psychological space of the mind, the remote areas of our brain. For Freud the notion of a text that can be wiped out and rewritten is a "Wunderblock," that is, a wonder notebook, and a perfect metaphor for the way the unconscious records memories. Our memory seems to possess an "invisible pencil."

The "pencil" of neon does not leave a material trace: "The electrical principle of luminous tubing is directly related to that of lightning. Both are electrical discharges in gas. . . . When the electrodes are connected to a high-voltage source, the tube glows as the gas becomes electrically excited."[3] Neon writing, often a simulated handwriting, challenges the concept of the surface as firm ground onto which the writer leaves a trace. The ideal surface for light-writings is the empty, dark background, as immaterial and temporary as the light. The brighter the light, the better its reading, the more exciting its impact. Smoothly forming neon, the writer can simulate figurative shapes just like handwriting and let their immaterial content glow.

To appropriate this material, mostly used in advertising, for artistic purposes was one of the early strategies of artists like Maurizio Nannucci, Mario Merz, or Bruce Nauman. The latter hung his name as a distorted neon signature on the wall. Nauman's bold, moving neon sculptures helped to bridge the gap between sculpture and the time-based arts. It is not surprising that Nauman was also one of the first to explore video as early as 1968. Fabrizio Plessi investigated the concept of surface by placing neon letters that spelled "eau" (water) next to a river, which was thus turned into an ever-moving, reflecting surface. But Plessi's words were written mirror-reversed and read correctly only on the reflecting surface of water. One of Plessi's most convincing video installations was called *Reflecting Water* (1984) and again used the combination of neon, video, and water, which all have in common a quality of futility and continuous change. *Panta rei,* everything is floating—texts, too.

The Moving Text

At the beginning of this century, moving pictures presented image and text in an alternating either/or, image or text, display, until the dominance of the image was once and for all established through the support of sound. Text was banned in subtitles and the framing of the film through credits, and was only allowed in the domain of the image when it clearly served a dramatic function. Eventually, video art freed the text from this restrictive use, but, long before, the art of filmmaker Fritz Lang had prefigured a different approach. *Das Testament des Dr. Mabuse* (1932) was one of the first movies in which the dramatic use of text broke down the world of rational order. The mad protagonist's car ride through the night was flanked with words that came out of the dark. Words that reigned in the black night were clearly a sign of madness and foreshadowed the appropriation of public language by the Nazi demagogy, which was about to take over in Germany. Language was no longer a common set of transparent rules that kept at bay irrational intensities like violence or sex. When words move, freed from the fixed patterns of pages and written on surfaces other than white paper, they take on a different aspect and can become haunting, seductive, or, as in Lang's film, even dangerous.

"I wanted to write so that I could be very direct."[4] Jenny Holzer, whose work is based on the belief that language is the simplest form, whereas images distract—although she would probably reject Debray's radical position—has developed a visual critique of language, above all through the use of publicly displayed moving texts: "I hope that the text and the visuals are inseparable now. It should not be either/or."[5] Her unique artistic position between visual poetry and Conceptual art overcame the notable influence of Marcel Duchamp, who initiated an understanding of language (ideas, concepts) as dominating the context of artistic production and display. For an artist working within mass-media contexts, the "message" can be found (ready-made) or created; in any case, it has to rely on simplicity and shortness.

Holzer's use of slogans as repetitive, condensed cliché-language makes sense, just as her appropriation of public spaces is significant. In Times Square she advertised invented one-liners, "truisms," and catchphrases. These worked "out in the open" because they were short enough to get a message across the abyss of distraction. From the gigantic screen to the miniature screen of the TV set: in 1990 she produced a series of art breaks *(TV Texts)*, which consisted of short phrases such as "Slipping into madness is good for the sake of comparison," or the famous "Abuse of power comes as no surprise."[6] These unannounced TV clips revive an old tradition of video art: the TV interruptions, such as David Hall's *TV Pieces* from 1971, which he also called "hiccups" in the constant flow of images.

Jenny Holzer gradually extended the concept of a text that is presented as an object. The term "reading" as we usually understand it means facing a text—the convention being that there is a discrete object to locate. But when texts surround us completely, fleeing and endlessly mirrored, we lose control. The sense of reality is shattered and the body is drawn into a vertiginous play of light and reflection. Such is the unbalancing effect of her installation for the Venice Biennale in 1990. The electronic tool for moving letters—LED (light emitting diode) displays—covered and replaced three walls of one of the exhibition spaces, with a marble floor reflecting all sides. This "microwave of text" overwhelmed and submitted the viewer to an aggressive and excessive stream of signs and a babel of languages. The eye tried in vain to concentrate on one line or one language. Reading became a fragmentary experience that was furthered by the speed and the multiplicity of languages. Messages permanently erased each other, and texts were blurred to one single texture of moving light. Once again, the "white noise" of a video screen without signal may be associated with this endless stream of letters that, hypothetically, contains all possible languages and all possible messages, just as the empty TV screen contains all possible programs. The overall effect was a visualization of language. Text, speeded and heated up, becomes image and implodes through multiplication in space, thereby formulating a vision of the global and ubiquitous society of information. Text is present anytime, anywhere, but it can't be read anymore. Holzer called this room *The Final Room,* which, from time to time, granted the visitor the grace of total blackness.

"The breakdown comes when you stop controlling yourself and want the release of a bloodbath." Holzer's unequaled emotional impact is deeply rooted in her sense of shattering perception.[7] The recurrence of LED displays embodies the electronic era, which is built on technical reproduction and simulation. This corresponds semantically to the repeated use of banalities in everyday language. Holzer's critical attitude makes this conjunction public, but the ambivalence lies in the programming of contradictory messages, a series of unstable dichotomies. It is this relation that is challenged, confronting the viewer with a surprising and sometimes unsettling bond between material and text. The proliferation of publicly displayed texts—moving or not—would be unbearable if it were not something that, in general, we dismiss as the meaningless flicker of advertising. But the irritating ambivalent "truisms" treat the reader as an opponent. The artist unsettles the spectator's position, making him want to retreat to a safer distance, to be able to identify once again a body of text, that is, its quality as an object as opposed to a textual space.[8]

Video and the Open Textual Space

In the United States, contrary to most countries in Europe, traffic rules are put forward not as pictograms but as words: Stop, Go, Dead End. One has to drive through the American West to understand Ed Ruscha, the painter whose use of words in landscapes links the canvas to a windshield perspective. Ruscha says, "Words are never meant to be of a certain size. They can be huge . . . just like billboards. There is no reality when it comes to words."[9] Jeffrey Shaw's *The Legible City* (1988) carried this idea further and worked with the monitor perspective and the urban landscape. The installation used back projection and a bike connected to a computer-controlled screen. The video consisted of simulated blocks of buildings corresponding to the street map of Manhattan (in the first version). Computer-generated words constituting eight different voices formed the architecture. Each voice unraveled as a story line that the active spectator read while riding the bike and following words, sentences, streets, or even going through "buildings" and looking at the back of the texts. This electronic simulation stimulated an acute sensation of size and form. The concrete feeling of space, time, and speed from physically riding the bike is countered by an immaterial sensation of being inside an abstract textual space. An important link between two seemingly opposed spheres is created. The reader's body reacts to the immediacy and flexibility, characteristics of the electronic text that are now visible as features of the reading process.

The interactive video installation *The Legible City* has been seminal in that it opened up a completely new path of dealing with texts. It proposed a virtual and open space constructed out of text (abstract) and texture (concrete quality of the letters as "buildings"). The introspective and lonely activity of reading was turned inside out: the reader was active on a stage, visible to others and thus spectacular in a literal sense. Far from investigating "creativity," Shaw proposed an "open work of art" before interactivity became an almost fashionable term. Where Kosuth stresses the function of language as a process of decoding sign and meaning, and where Holzer undermines the semantic aspect and the position of the reader, Shaw heralds the individual act of reading while keeping it in a public and urban environment. This playfully acknowledges the importance attributed to a public display of texts, as on billboards, TVs, or LED displays.

Reading: A Physical Act

Reading, once a passive consumption of texts, has become a much more visible activity than the French theorists ever imagined. The German artist Frank Fietzek has created an exemplary installation that challenges notions of duality, leading us back to the idea of the Freudian Wunderblock. *Die Tafel* (*The Blackboard,* 1993) presents a new form of literally handy reading by placing a monitor on rails as a mobile window in front of a blackboard. The visitor-reader can move the monitor up and down, left and right, scanning a surface without any writing on it. With this device the reader relives school days when one would stand in front of the class, desperately trying to find the right words to write on the blackboard. To find the right word is a metaphysical task, but here, once again, reading is a software and a hardware activity—a physical search for words that are virtually hidden on the black surface. Yet the identification of words at specific locations is futile: with the next move everything has changed again. Passages of text can only be refound by chance. Actual words such as "reading" or "writing" are mere traces to be remembered.

A broader semantic context seems to be absent from this work. What kind of text are we reading when nothing is fixed anymore in "black on white" (or "white on black")? From the physicality of an interactive installation to the immateriality of the lonely reader surfing the Internet—are we still reading or are we looking at images that appear and vanish before we have had the time to grasp their potential meaning? Our eyes are continuously scanning the surrounding world for hidden information and clues to a better understanding of its chaotic surface.

Toward Hybrid Forms

The lesson of visual poetry was that text and surface are an inseparable unity that allows nonlinear readings. In the seventies, video art discovered an alternative information ground for the visual arts: the monitor as a virtual surface that is transformed into an endless scrolling text. In 1974 Richard Serra created a tape on the manipulative power of television, *TV Delivers People,* a scrolling critical text. Later, Antonio Muntadas changed the pace with which sets of words scrolled in front of the viewer. Finally, the German artist Norbert Meissner topped this ironically by creating a scrolling text that consisted merely of brand names of electronic companies. The eyes fix on the screen; the text moves. A moving text, however, is not a text but a moving image that passes the viewer's eyes only to be forgotten the moment it disappears. Video means "I see" and not "I read." "Text only" without a visual counterpoint is boring. The conceptual purism and critical stance of Serra, Muntadas, or Meissner were eventually overcome by the sensualists such as Peter Greenaway. His combination of video and film with writing and painting (*Death in the Seine* or *M is for Man, Music, Mozart)* exemplified how far the mutual penetration of texts and images can go and what hybrid forms are being created, gradually building up an aesthetic in its own right.

Multimedia is pushing the process of visualizing text and textualizing image even more. In Jay Bolter's understanding, the electronic text "is more like hieroglyphics than it is like pure alphabetic writing . . . a continuum in which many systems of representation can happily coexist."[10] The French-German cultural TV channel Arte advertises a new video-text format called HiTEXT by praising the visual qualities of higher resolution and more colors which make the information "more attractive." Conventional texts are boring, as *Mediamatic* editor Willem Velthoven believes. His production of the CD-ROM that presents the results of the 1994 conference "Doors of Perception" is intelligent, multifaceted, and certainly inventive. It is a pleasure to browse through bits and pieces of what might even have been a boring conference. The reader is triggered by images, faces, even sounds, to go deeper into the textual parts that are linked to the images via "hyperlink." Hyperlinks, strategical knots between text and image that have replaced the text line as the organizing principle, are the key to multimedia. In a hypertext the analogy between the cathode ray tube scanning an image onto the TV screen and our eyes becomes obvious.[11] Although not in an orderly linear mode, we continuously scan the multimedia screen with our eyes for the "hot spot," or the meaningful, charged, overdetermined hyperlink sign, either a word or an icon, that asks for a mouse click to function as a window or door to seemingly deeper layers of the work.

"The text is not coexistence of meanings, but passage, traversal."[12] Roland Barthes did not live long enough to experience the rise of multimedia, but his emphatic insistence on the productive and dynamic aspects of reading would have been a fruitful tool of interpretation for the electronic text. The blending of image, sound, and text that we see at work in multimedia is an indication of a new quality that leaves the postmodern era of fragmentary aesthetics behind: we are actually passing through newly created audiovisual textscapes. The impenetrable white of the printed page has, at last, become a transparent space to pass through. Multimedia is essentially a three-dimensional collage of text-images that we experience in a succession of layers, just as the neurologist can read our brain through computer tomography. The question is, what meaning does a screen text transport when it is placed within a sequence of images? To what extent is the semantical dimension understood when a text is "read" by hunting hot spots, only to pass on to the next stage?[13] What pleasure, on the other hand, is granted by the electronic textscape?

Text Passages

"Electronic text is, like an oral text, dynamic."[14] It relies on immediacy and flexibility, two characteristics of dialogue. The most recent interactive works of American artist Bill Seaman are another significant example of how to avoid an ideological hierarchy between text and image, writer and reader, and how to start a dialogue. *The Exquisite Mechanism of Shivers* (1991) and *Passage Sets/One Pulls Pivots at the Tip of the Tongue* (1995) both operate with sets of image-text combinations, which the viewer-reader can freely place in a sequential order. *Passage Sets* presents three projections as a triptych: an automatic poem generator on the left, and two-dimensional interactive navigation of sets of words in the middle which then trigger video sequences with spoken text on the right. If we add that the viewer starts from a fictitious urban panorama—25-by-6 frames, a set of stills with superimposed poetic text that includes words as hot spots—we have a three-dimensional axis of reading. The viewer thus navigates a spatial poem in which meaningful "sentences" form an accumulative network of associations. These structured codes, says Seaman, reflect the layering or collision of psychological spaces. This makes the work distinct as an experience of art compared to a layering of electronic texts that lack this perspective.

With Seaman the concept of the panorama, so dear to the nineteenth century, has taken on a three-dimensional mosaic-like nature. The panorama as well as the associative montage and the architectural structure of *Passage Sets* are rooted in Walter Benjamin's notion of "passage"; the term refers to a change in time, travel as a change of place, to a portion of a text or to a kind of hallway. In the nineteenth century, the passageway (today's shopping arcade) was a zone of ambivalence, a place that was neither inside a house nor outside on the street but rather a hybrid architectural form of inside-out. Benjamin interpreted these sites as the perfect location for the wanderings and musings of the flaneur. Replacing the physical wanderings, the electronic space of the late twentieth century links the desk at home with electronic strolls. And once again, the flaneur of Benjamin's passages is pursuing an ambiguous approach: staying inside but connecting to the world outside.[15]

Bill Seaman's work is seminal in that grammatical, or hierarchical, and semantical conventions are replaced by ambivalent associations,[16] and that words and images are cross-referenced, one triggering the other. The parallel projection of a triptych—text, text and image, image—charges the textual level visually and vice versa. It is significant that images are digitized data, based on computer language, and that texts are treated as images and scanned into the computer to achieve the same tonality of color. This is not a practice of postmodern collage and fragmentation but rather a weaving of different threads into one visual text. In the past, visual poetry was an avant-garde literary practice. In the future, writing a text will become a visual operation in a much broader sense!

In a sea of images, words can become buoys, landmarks. Yet a buoy is nothing more than a point of orientation. To avoid getting lost in the maze of the multimedia text, navigation skills are required. The ancient knowledge of reading the signs of the land or sea, of reading the stars and the moon, is analogous to a "cursory" reading. The text of the electronic screen always promises another layer, another textscape. To proceed and reach "home," the reader-viewer must take signs and icons at face value and pass through the text on parallel or intersected trajectories. Not getting lost in this maze is the media surfer's ability. The flaneur, however, indulges in exactly the opposite: being distracted—following a calligraphic pleasure of ornament and detail. The artistic quality of a multimedia artwork eventually depends on the extent to which both the surfer and the flaneur are provided with a satisfactory experience.

From Participation to Interaction

Toward the Origins of Interactive Art

Söke Dinkla

Similar to video and performance art, interactive art developed mainly outside traditional art institutions such as galleries and museums. The forums of interactive art are above all media art festivals, where in the late eighties it became a fixture. The development of an independent organization shows that media art, especially interactive art, transcends the borders of art genres that are based on art theory. The mimetic strategies of interactive art do not aim primarily at visual qualities; rather, the dialogue between program and user constitutes the artistic material. As far as viewer participation is concerned, interactive art follows the avant-garde traditions of the beginning of this century, traditions that reacted to the widening gap between the mass audience and the art audience.[1]

The Classical Avant-Garde

In Futurist performances and manifestos audience participation was an implicit or explicit means to reduce the distance between performer and audience—either by spatial integration or by provocative addresses. In the manifesto *Variety Theater* of 1913 Filippo Tommaso Marinetti made several suggestions concerning the physical involvement of the audience: "The Variety Theater is alone in seeking the audience's collaboration. It doesn't remain static like a stupid voyeur, but joins noisily in the action, in the singing, accompanying the orchestra, communicating with the actors in surprising actions and bizarre dialogues."[2]

Whereas the Futurists limited their call for participation mainly to stagelike performances, in 1920 Max Ernst introduced the possibility of audience participation in exhibitions. At the second Dada exhibition in the backyard of the Brauhaus Winter in Cologne, where works by Max Ernst, Jean Arp, and Johannes Theodor Baargeld were shown, Ernst placed an ax next to one of his works, to be used by the visitors in case they did not like the object.[3] Using the ax, which was meant to provoke the audience into actively stating its opinions, remained an imaginary possibility, since the object elicited the trained response of detached contemplation. There was another explicit invitation in this exhibition to intervene in the presentation of a work which the visitors actually made use of. A critic for the *Kölnische Volkszeitung* wrote: "One of the incomprehensible 'drawings' left a lot of space on the paper and beneath it are written the words: 'Any visitor of this exhibition is entitled to insert a Dadaistic or anti-Dadaistic aphorism in this drawing. No prosecution.'"[4]

In 1938 Marcel Duchamp developed and reinterpreted Ernst's challenge to the audience. In the exhibition *Exposition internationale du surréalisme,* in the Galerie des Beaux-Arts in Paris, he wanted to illuminate the paintings with a light that would only switch itself on when the visitors activated a light sensor. The organizers—including André Breton, Paul Éluard, Salvador Dali, Max Ernst, and Man Ray as "illuminator in chief"—eventually had to abandon this project because of technical difficulties; however, they provided the visitors with lamps so that they could illuminate the paintings themselves. After all the lamps were stolen, the organizers returned to traditional illumination.

In the end Duchamp's staging left the "envisioning" of images to the viewer. Like Max Ernst, Duchamp put in perspective the active role of the artist as well as the status of the "sacrosanct" work of art. Unlike Ernst, however, Duchamp placed the main emphasis on the technical transfer of perception, which he further developed in his Rotoreliefs: though the spatial image of the spiral completes itself in the viewer's perception, the activity that makes this perceptual process possible is not performed solely by the beholder but also by the motion of the Rotorelief. Artist and artwork share their former authoritative position not only with the beholder but with the machinery as well, which in the end is the precondition for the altered perception. This is the reason why some of the artists who worked on the interplay of "art and technology" in the sixties took Duchamp as their paragon. Duchamp himself had a rather indifferent attitude toward the role given to him. "They [the artists who work with technological systems] have to get somebody as progenitor so as not to look as though they invent all by themselves. Makes a better package. But technology: art will be sunk or drowned by technology."[5]

Happenings

In the early fifties John Cage took up Duchamp's ready-made concept and separated it from its object fixation. This was accomplished not only by a transformation into sound processes but also by transferring responsibility to the viewer. In Cage's case, however, the spectator's responsibility is not linked to an active participation. Here Cage's events and the later Fluxus events, which often took place in a stage-like situation, differ from the Happenings of Allan Kaprow, who was a student of Cage at the New School for Social Research in New York. By presenting Happenings in garages, in the streets, or in shops, Kaprow (and also Wolf Vostell) abolished the exclusivity of the usual exhibition venues in the sixties. Although Kaprow chose the term "Happening" to avoid any connotation with the world of art, the press and some New York galleries still regarded Happenings as a new form of art.[6] Thus they contributed, like Duchamp's ready-mades, to the reinterpretation and extension in form of the concept of art, not to its abolishment.

The redefinition of the audience in Happenings and participatory art forms has led some authors to seek the traditions of interactive art there. Regina Cornwell draws a plausible line from exemplary work of Allan Kaprow (Happening) via that of Robert Rauschenberg (reactive environment), Yoko Ono (participatory event), and Valie Export (closed-circuit installation) to interactive art, but she does not elaborate the differences.[7] Erkki Huhtamo, too, sees the roots of interactive art in the participatory art of the sixties: "The roots of interactive media art are to be found in the 1960's. . . . The expansion of the traditional field of art, the dream about 'Total Art,' the annihilation of the barrier between life and art, the 'dematerialization of the art object' (Lucy Lippard), process art, participation art, concept art, Fluxus, the Happening movement and Situationism, 'Art and Technology,' kinetic art, 'cybernetic art' (Jack Burnham), closed- circuit video installations—these phenomena may be heterogeneous, but they are part of one and the same process which had a profound effect on the relationship between art and its audience."[8]

The references to participatory art forms of the late fifties and sixties are not only to be found in the history of art, they are also reflected in the biographies of some interactive artists: in the oeuvre of Jeffrey Shaw and Lynn Hershman Leeson, interactive works have their origins in participatory art forms like performances, Happenings, and site-specific works. This development characterizes the oeuvre of Peter Weibel and Bill Seaman as well. However, the technology-oriented method of Myron Krueger and David Rokeby as well as video art have equally important significance for the development of interactive art and constitute evidence for a heterogeneity of approach rather than for a homogeneous tradition.

The linear tradition postulated by Regina Cornwell, Erkki Huhtamo, and other authors must be differentiated,[9] as it does not allow detailed statements about the characteristics of interactive art—characteristics that spring from parallels with other art forms but especially from the differences. It is primarily the differences that show the significance of interactivity for contemporary culture. Therefore, in the following discussion the decisive developments toward interactive art will be examined not only for parallels but for qualitative inconsistencies.

Audience participation is the essential criterion for the comparability of interactive art and art of the sixties. Allan Kaprow is considered an important exponent of participation efforts. He defined Happenings as big "environment-like, non-theatrical exhibitions that turn to the public in an increased degree."[10] In his solo exhibition in New York's Hansa Gallery in 1958 visitors could explore a mazelike room while being confronted with unexpected things. However, the audience's possibilities of intervening in his Happenings remained limited. Johannes Schröder summed up in his analysis of *The Spring Happening:* "Under this condition [of absolute control by the organizer] the Happening does not seem to be a step toward viewer participation, but a precisely elaborated artistic act that guarantees the integration of the participants as a material."[11] Neither in Cage's "idea" Happenings nor in most of Kaprow's "participation" Happenings did the participation of an unprepared audience take place. Instructions or scripts (even minimal ones) were always present and controlled the performers' behavior. Happenings that refrain from explicit instructions have been realized in Europe chiefly in politically motivated street actions.

Kaprow's Happenings make abundantly clear that not every form of participation per se implies a higher responsibility for the visitor and thus a less authoritarian role of the artist. Rather, participation is located along a fragile border between emancipatory act and manipulation. The decisive factor in judging the receptive situation is how active the unprepared viewer becomes within a certain framework of action and without specific instructions. Furthermore, it is important to differentiate between nontechnical participation and technically mediated participation. At about the same time as Happenings, reactive kinetic art evolved, replacing instructions given by the leader of the Happening with technically communicated and preprogrammed participation.

Cyborg Art

The employment of partly simple, partly complex technical strategies in the mid-sixties allowed the development of an art form generally described as "reactive," "cybernetic," or "responsive."[12] Its origins, however, go back to the fifties. Norbert Wiener's popular description of cybernetics, in which he made his 1948 theory available to a larger audience, apparently had a strong influence on the development of reactive art and its theory.[13] After Roy Ascott in 1966 showed the implications of an art concept shaped by cybernetics,[14] Jack Burnham introduced the term "cyborg art" into art theory discussions two years later. He used this term to describe electromechanical systems with a lifelike behavior as well as man-machine systems that take on some of the features of biological organisms by means of feedback.[15]

In cooperation with the composer Pierre Henry and the Philips Company, Nicolas Schöffer produced as early as 1954 a "cybernetic sculpture," which belongs to the first group defined by Burnham. It produces sound, dependent upon environmental influences, but the relation between cause and effect remains deliberately uncertain.[16] Two years later *CYSP 1* (cybernetic-spatiodynamic) was created, a "timid" sculpture that becomes active in darkness and silence, and remains motionless in brightness and noise. Unlike Schöffer's first sculpture, *CYSP 1* shows a causal connection between stimulation and reaction. Thus a personality, a sort of being, is attributed to the sculpture. In *CYSP 1* this anthropomorphization—determined in traditional sculpture by visual mimetic processes—is shifted to the sculpture's ability to react, which is anchored in its program.

The series of "cysp"sculptures, created in the following years, is only one element in Schöffer's conception of the impact of technology on society. The plans for a cybernetic city, presented in 1965 in a joint exhibition of Schöffer and Jean Tinguely at the Jewish Museum in New York, demonstrated that for Schöffer the ability to program not only sculpture but the whole urban area offers the chance to create a dialogue between technology and environment.[17] With Schöffer, however, the historically rooted antagonism between nature and technology is strangely paradoxical: the development of technology appears to be predetermined and capable of being influenced at the same time. This paradox constitutes a fundamental conflict within the technology discussion of postindustrial societies.

Art and Technology in New York

The fundamentally optimistic attitude toward technology shaped both reactive art and the American movement of Art and Technology in the late sixties, thus continuing the traditions of the Russian Constructivists, the Italian Futurists, and the Bauhaus artists. In the sixties as well as the twenties, these attempts at a reunion of art and technology, however heterogeneous they may have been in their respective attitudes, all aimed at renewal of art. The modern progressive technology was played off against an antiquated, manually produced art. In 1967 Rauschenberg stated provocatively, when Henry Liebermann of the *New York Times* asked him the reason for his commitment to the Art and Technology movement: "If you don't accept technology, you better go to another place because no place here is safe. . . . Nobody wants to paint rotten oranges anymore."[18] Most important is the notion that an art that excludes modern technologies will lose its social relevance. In the sixties technology was used provocatively against an art establishment that clung to an object-oriented and handicraft art. A glorification of technology, as came about in the Constructivist and Futurist art of the twenties, was almost nonexistent in the sixties. It was replaced by the realization of cooperation between artists and engineers, with the aim of promoting their mutual understanding.

After Robert Rauschenberg met the engineer Johan Wilhelm (Billy) Klüver in 1960 during his preparations for Jean Tinguely's self-destroying machine *Hommage à New York,* a close cooperation between the two developed. John Cage, who worked with Rauschenberg as early as 1952 at his Black Mountain College event—the forerunner of the Happening—also cooperated with Klüver. In the performance *Variations V* (1965) Cage and Merce Cunningham employed a sound system by Klüver that reacted via photoelectric cells and microphones to sounds, to the movements of dancers, and to the projections of a film by Stan Vanderbeek and video images by Nam June Paik.[19] By using the system in such a way, the functional principle of computer-controlled interaction between live actions and sound effects—to be used artistically only later—had been anticipated.

Nine Evenings: Theater and Engineering

One year later the opportunity arose to develop these projects further. Ten New York artists—among them John Cage, Merce Cunningham, Lucinda Childs, Deborah Hay, Robert Rauschenberg—prepared a contribution to the Stockholm Festival of Art and Technology. Although in the end the artists did not participate in the Stockholm event, they created a series of performances that were held in October 1966 in the Armory Hall under the title *Nine Evenings: Theater and Engineering.*[20] A wireless system was the central technical element of the events. This system was composed of transportable electronic units that could function without cables and be operated by remote control. Cage used the wireless system for switching on and off loudspeakers, which reacted to movement via photocells. In *Variations VII* (1966) Cage also used contact microphones, making body functions that normally cannot be heard—like heartbeat and noises from the stomach and lungs—audible. Apart from the wireless system Cage used 20 radios, 2 television monitors, and 15 telephones around which the performers moved.[21]

The performances of *Nine Evenings* presented not only the principle of auditory feedback but that of visual feedback as well. The visual closed-circuit principle—which at that time had been barely claimed for artistic use—was employed after Rauschenberg's performance *Open Score (Bong).* Five hundred people were on a stage in utter darkness, performing simple actions. Their image was recorded by infrared cameras and projected on a screen so that the audience could reconstruct the situation on the stage only on the basis of the projected image. When the light went on again, the actors had disappeared.

The Reactive Environment

While Cage in *Variations V* and *Variations VII*—which led to the sı sequent interactive performances—kept to a performance without audience participation, in 1968 Rauschenberg developed a visual reactive environment that involved the nonspecialist, unprepared visitor.[22] Rauschenberg conceived *Soundings* in close collaboration with the engineers of EAT (Experiments in Art and Technology), a New York–based organization he founded with Billy Klüver in 1967 to support interdisciplinary projects between artists and engineers.

Soundings consisted of three sheets of Plexiglas, placed one after the other. The front sheet (approximately 11 by 2.5 centimeters) had a mirror on one side, and the two smaller sheets presented different silkscreened views of a chair. If visitors kept quiet in the exhibition space they would only see their mirror images—an effect that also plays a part in Rauschenberg's *White Paintings*. But as soon as somebody spoke or made a noise, lights were activated that made visible different views of the chair. This effect was described by Robby Robinson, who worked on *Soundings* together with Rauschenberg: "We started to tune the circuits, and then I saw the effect he was after, these chairs tumbling around in a random way . . . in an optical illusion."[23] The visible image of the chair varied according to the pitch of the voice or the noise.

While Happenings imply a stage situation and are bound to a fixed, limited performance time, reactive environments address the exhibition situation in galleries and museums. They assume that an unprepared visitor will move through the exhibition space with heightened attention. Although *Soundings* distinguished itself from other environments by the fact that it did not occupy a whole room, it can still be described as "environmental," because it opened up to the visitor by its ability to react. With the technically conveyed involvement of visitors in a visual and/or auditory electronic process within the context of an exhibition space (museum, gallery, or festival), the essential preconditions for interactive environments and installations have been created. A series of works created in the midsixties that allowed for different kinds of viewer participation can be divided into reactive environments, reactive sculptures (cybernetic sculptures), and their intermediate forms. Of the latter, Rauschenberg's *Soundings* blazed the trail for the subsequent development of interactive environments, because unprepared visitors were involved in a dialogue-like relation by means of hidden technological devices.

Another important factor for the development of interactive art is the principle of the visual closed-circuit installation, which was introduced in the late sixties not only at stage performances such as *Nine Evenings* but also in the context of exhibitions.

Closed-Circuit Installations

Two closed-circuit installations could be seen in the first video group exhibition, *TV as a Creative Medium,* in New York's Howard Wise Gallery in 1969: *Participation TV II* (1969) by Nam June Paik and *Wipe Cycle* (1969) by Ira Schneider and Frank Gillette.[24] Paik started to experiment with the functions of the TV set as sculptural material in the early sixties. Together with engineers he developed modulations that created nonrepresentational electronic images and used sound waves to change the images on the monitor.[25] Those attempts led to *Participation TV I* (1963–66), in which visitors talked into two microphones or produced other sounds and subsequently watched the effects of the sound waves on the monitor.

In *Participation TV II* Paik used visual feedback. The work consisted of three or four color monitors and three cameras aimed at a monitor, resulting in an endless feedback. If visitors stepped between camera and monitor their images appeared on the monitor as colored, overlapping, almost abstract shapes. *Participation TV II* reflected on the principle of feedback in its original technical meaning, that is, part of the original impulse was returned to affect the further course of events. *Participation TV II* did not serve the self-reflection of visitors, since in contrast to other closed-circuits they were not "reflected" on the monitor. Instead, their images were refracted and distorted by the effects of the feedback. As soon as visitors stepped between camera and monitor they saw their outlines from behind, seemingly fading away in the endlessly scaled space of the feedback image.

While Paik's *Participation TV II* made visible the entry of the visitor into the closed-circuit arrangement as a feedback effect on the monitor, thus illustrating the unity of the technical cycle, *Wipe Cycle* by Frank Gillette and Ira Schneider confronted visitors with their own images "on television." On nine monitors the recorded images of visitors were juxtaposed with images from a TV program, previously recorded footage, and time-delayed live images. Taken to the center of the nine monitors the (TV) viewers became aware that they were elements of recordings of varied and partly nonreconstructable origin and temporality.

In closed-circuit installations visitors are often unintentionally or at least unconsciously confronted with images of themselves on a monitor. The use of cameras implies at the same time the possibility of being observed by others. This situation causes a tension between uncertainty and exhibitionism. The visitor can either get away from this situation and leave the visual field covered by the camera or accept the new context. In both cases the possibility of intervention or action is limited. Closed-circuit installations are not so much about providing the visitors with the opportunity to act creatively but about showing them their situation within a system determined by automated surveillance technology.

Review: Comparison of Reception Situations

The connections between Happenings, reactive art, closed-circuit installations, and interactive art result primarily from their intermediary nature. Dick Higgins uses the term "intermedia" to describe artistic forms of expression that cannot be attributed to a certain genre.[26] In contrast to Happenings, which are defined by their distance from dramatic performances of the classical theater and are sometimes characterized as "new theater," interactive art does not have any direct forerunners in the traditional art genres. Its precursors are rather those forms that already follow the enlarged notion of art in the twentieth century and are directed against the established art system.

The involvement of the audience in interactive art goes beyond the approach of the "classic" New York Happenings. The visitors are not only integrated spacially and addressed "in an increased degree" (Kaprow), but they are involved in a close dialogical relation. This dialogue constitutes the *artistic material.* Similar to Happenings, the free space that the program allows the users-players will vary.

In interactive art the artist only rarely takes on the leadership of the event, as is the case in most Happenings. The interactive system takes the place of the authorial leader.[27] Conceptually, the artist delegates his role to the program and withdraws from the action. The receiver later realizes the program. In this way the plot directions of the classic Happening, written down or passed on verbally, will be automatized. The introduction of technical means of control in art marks a turning point in the participatory Happening and performance art because it is the precondition for the automatization of participation. First steps toward this automatization were already made by Duchamp's Rotoreliefs, reactive art, and the closed-circuit installations.

Happenings and performances are generally characterized by the impulse of bringing art and life closer together, and this fundamental approach also applies to interactive art, even though there is a significant difference with an inherent shift of meaning: "life" is not primarily associated with human substantiality or with the immediate experience of everyday life; it is linked to media-based, automated events. The programmatic fight against the alienation of art from everyday life was a central topic of the late sixties. Happenings and performances dealt with a social situation in which new forms of political participation in decision making were widely discussed.

This situation has now changed. Essential aspects of social life no longer take place in the urban space. Thus street action only has a limited public effect. Instead, essential aspects of work and leisure have shifted to communication with and by electronic and digital media. Interactive art discusses the arising social manners formed by digital technology. It transfers aspects of technology-dominated daily life to internal concepts of art. The motto "art and life" is being transformed into "art and technology." This process of transformation started in the sixties, and it has reached a peak today with the terms "life" and "technology" becoming increasingly congruent.

The widespread judgment that interactive intercourse with computer systems prepares the ground for an emancipation from the media context, via the development from "passive" to "active" reception, is being euphorically defended by referring to the participatory art of the sixties.[28] But the role of the performers and the leader of Happenings has also shown that neither the authoritative role of the artist nor the notion of work has been abandoned completely. These concepts will remain a principle in interactive art, too. They are delegated to the program and automatized. The *artistic material* of interactive art is the *automatized dialogue* between program and user.

Interactive artworks provide a critical analysis of the automatized communication that is replacing interhuman relationships in more and more social fields. Thus the distribution of power between user and system is not just a technological issue but a social and political one as well.

Dionysus in Wonderland

A Few Musical Metaphors in Techno-Culture

Jean Gagnon
Translated by Gisèle Cervisi

I recently participated in a meeting that brought together speakers on the arts, culture, and telecommunications of the Ottawa-Carleton region, among them the National Gallery of Canada, the National Art Center, the Art Council of Canada, Carleton University, and representatives from Stentor, Bell Canada, and Ottawa Carleton Research Institute, the latter being responsible for establishing the information superhighway in the area. The industry that controls and implements the technology wanted to approach cultural and artistic institutions as suppliers of "content," while surrounding itself with beautiful, enthusiastic, and soaring speeches on a "paradigm shift" that would transform not only the exchange, dissemination, and usage of the information, but also the very relationship of the cultural industry with art and the artists, with culture and the cultural producers. "Paradigm shift," a convenient expression, is in fact used here to cut through the discussion ideologically so that it does not bear too much on the economic aspect. On the whole, whenever we explained the meaning of artistic production through new technologies in telecommunications and information, we were always reminded of the notion of profitability so dear to the cultural industry, *Jurassic Park* being given as an example. In other words, the highly promising paradigm shift gets lost in the same circulation of capital, for the same entertainment objectives, the same teleology of amusement, that are conveyed by the Hollywood model of production and diffusion of cultural productions.

Even though the cultural industry, and those I call cultural producers, who provide this industry with standardized programs, do not burden themselves with such considerations, it is still important to take the expression "paradigm shift" very seriously, because a paradigm establishes the parameters and the nodes through which the thought develops; these points are precisely mnemonic anchors, unconscious or rational, determined by an epistemological-historical concept. In other words, the paradigms of knowledge are formed by the technological parameters of an era, based on the available scientific knowledge, corresponding to the rationality and finalities of societies, as well as by the terms set by the ideology of an epoch that rests on and is embodied in the techno-media complex.

The paradigms governing both common sense and specialized learning are structures of knowledge and systems of expectations that make up a horizon beyond which it is difficult to explain the world. The possible horizons set the parameters by which the perceptions of reality are filtered through thought processes that rely on articulated values from the paradigmatic notion itself. There is no doubt that the human world is a world of valuation, and as such every paradigm is intrinsically closed off, locked in the order of self-valuation. Thus we must consider, following James M. Curtis in *Culture as Polyphony*, that paradigms are related in a complex manner and that in the course of history they fluctuate in their relationships with one another.[1]

In a manner particularly interesting for my exploration of the musical metaphor in relation to digital and electronic technologies, Curtis sets apart essentially linear and nonlinear paradigms and associates the former with the visual and the latter with aurality. Linearity is characterized by its tendency to create dichotomies (good and evil, the rational and the irrational) while attributing a judgment of implicit value to one of the two terms. This type of thought, which has dominated modernism since the Renaissance, also has certain similarities to the classical philosophy of Plato, and we should remember that the myth of the cave is a cinematographic device representing a cognitive model based on sight and vision. As for nonlinearity, it is characterized by a binary system in which a function mediates between the members of the pair, creating a dynamic (structure/discontinuity, organism/environment). The difference between the two types of paradigms resides in the fact that the former rests on static separations and hierarchized values, while the latter is moved by dynamic unities. Whereas linear figuration would be a continuous line formed by individual points, nonlinearity would be rather a set of points with possible connections between all the points and in all directions. But this would still be a visual representation of nonlinearity, which should be described in aural terms instead, that is to say, as demonstrating the notion that the process is an energetic transformation. A visual metaphor is substituted for an aural, resounding, musical metaphor calling for the idea of moving the content through the fluctuating form. In fact, Curtis concludes:

> In esthetics, this means a resolution of a dichotomy between the work of art and the spectator who contemplates it disinterested. In a nonlinear paradigm, the work of art and the spectator interact; the art work affects the perception of the spectator, whose reaction may affect the artist's subsequent work.[2]

Even though it would be possible to articulate this in terms of Jauss's concept of an aesthetic of reception,[3] it should be noted that the linearity affecting the "succession" of the works contradicts Curtis's nonlinear argument. But this idea of an interactive reception of the work of art modifying perceptions and values, looking on the work of art and on technology as cognitive forms, as forms of cognition, is an important idea in aesthetic thought of the twentieth century. Moreover, Curtis's book leans toward Marshall McLuhan's *Understanding Media* as a nonlinear concept of the media and mediatized society. McLuhan is represented at the turning point between modernism and postmodernism. Thus interactivity comes to characterize reception in a nonlinear horizon of expectations, and with the interactivity of computers, this takes on a concrete form, more pressing every day. McLuhan, like other twentieth-century thinkers such as Bergson, does not use the classic dichotomy between free will and determinism, but instead he conceives of technology as an extension of man, a concept derived from the binary pair organism/environment. This systemic concept echoes cybernetics and finds a sort of creativity in the media, as in language, myth, or art—art itself being conceived as a cognitive form. In McLuhan, forms of knowledge stem from three types of historical comprehension: an un-perspective world, as can be found in the pre-Socratics so dear to Nietzsche; the perspective world of the Renaissance, where linearity is embodied in the printed written word; and finally the a-perspective world brought about by electricity—the electronic media—where postliterary oral form predominates.

The a-perspective world is the one where time and space are engulfed in the fluctuating dynamics of telecommunications.

The aural or musical metaphor for the nonlinear paradigm is of great importance here because in a discussion of the aesthetic concerns of the media arts—artistic forms using electronic and digital media—these metaphors are constantly employed or, better still, the intrinsic "musicality" of the electronic media is highlighted. Bill Viola writes in "The Sound of One Line Scanning": "All video has its roots in the live. The vibrational acoustic character of video as a virtual image is the essence of its 'liveness.' Technologically, video has evolved out of sound."[4]

It is not so much this metaphor, musical or even aural, that preoccupies Viola, but rather the reference to electronic and digital technologies through which sounds and images together become malleable, a wave. Instead, it is the "live" that is metaphorically combined with "the vibrational acoustic character of video."

Moreover, it should be noted that the notion of noise has preoccupied many artists and practitioners of electroacoustics throughout our century, beginning with *The Art of Noises* by Luigi Russolo, and Dziga Vertov's ideas in phonography, or even John Cage, for whom all sounds become musical inasmuch as the listener is receptive to them. Located at the heart of the electronic creative work, at the junction of several fields of investigation, the notion of noise belongs to the constellation of terms associated with aural metaphors. Diversely valorized depending on the approach and the particular field, it became perceptible and pertinent when technology made sound recording and reproduction possible toward the end of the nineteenth century and, later in our century, took on an increasing importance in information theories in which noises represent the level of a system's entropy.

Frances Dyson, in a recent article, stresses the aural nature of electronic media. According to her, "aurality" refers to the phenomenal and discursive field of sound. She contends that the image has suffered a loss of credibility in the twentieth century, while sound has maintained a stability suggesting the veracity of *presence*. She writes:

> Being both heard outside and felt within, sound blurs the distinction between the interior and the exterior of the body,

> annihilating distance between subject and object, self and other. This immersive quality, together with the physiology of the ear, destabilizes the subjectivity of the subject.[5]

Once again we see the concepts stemming from visual statics (subject/object, form/content, rational/irrational) and those coming from aural dynamics which I refer to here as musicality (structure/discontinuity, organism/environment, energetic content/ form of interaction). It is not surprising that works characterized as immersive in virtual reality evoke, through their fluidity and simultaneity, "spiritual" notions of transcending bodily limits and spatiotemporal limits of experience through telepresence.

A work by Char Davies presented recently at the Museum of Contemporary Art of Montreal (August 19–October 1, 1995) bears the very appropriate title *Osmosis.* The artist wrote in an unpublished document dated June 1995 that "'OSMOSIS' is about our relationship with Nature in its most primary sense. Osmosis: a biological process involving the passage from one side of a membrane to another. Osmosis as metaphor: transcendence of difference through mutual absorption, dissolution of boundaries between inner and outer, intermingling of self and world, longing for the Other."

This notion of presence has been deconstructed by Jacques Derrida as deriving from the idea that the utterance of the spoken word showed the sincerity and truth of the being and subject in western metaphysics. Writing becomes the medium that leads to falsification, duplicity, fabrication—in brief, to falsehood—in contrast with the authentic self-presence of the thinking subject in the spoken word. But in other respects, writing is a mnemotechnical process—language itself being a medium for the subject in dialogic intersubjectivity—that allows memory and history. In the same way, media technologies are means of falsification as well as instruments of memory. The notion of presence always comes from metaphysics, whereas the idea that art and technology as support of falsification and artifice opens the way to hermeneutics, in which the temporal idea of the present replaces the spacial idea of presence. In this sense Paul Ricoeur talks of the present as being threefold: a present for things anticipated in the future, a present for things filtered through memories, and a present for things occurring through untimely actions.[6] We should then speak of the presenting of presence and conceive the use of media as a highly symbolic action. But this would amount to engaging in discursive analyses beyond the scope of this text, which is of a more general nature.

Finally, the history of the development of technologies to record and reproduce images and sounds can be traced to the constant search for a new synaesthetic relation between the senses, particularly hearing and vision.[7] Here, too, one finds a characteristic tendency of the nonlinear paradigm to melt categories together, to decompartmentalize perceptions, to abolish dichotomies.

Apollo and Dionysus

Le retour de Dionysos (The Return of Dionysus) by Jean Brun at once puts the realm of Dionysus into the category of nonlinear paradigms. He announces that our epoch defines cognizance according to separate fields of knowledge, themselves associated with the field of history, and in doing so he brings out the dispersal of the subject, the dissolution of the individual consciousness in "an epistemological-historical field that is in a state of perpetual reshuffling, endlessly re-creating those who have the illusion of being able to define it."[8] Similarly, he further states that the unconscious in subjective dynamics constitutes another field that causes the subject to move, to be moved—that is, a field of the self by which the driving force divides the subject. He can then advance the idea that man devoid of his interiority becomes "a known being, possessed by the id and the it."[9]

About the same time *Le retour de Dionysos* came out in 1969, several authors published works that exhibit a remarkable community of spirit in spite of different starting points and divergent paths for each: *La société du spectacle (The Society of the Spectacle)* by Guy Debord in 1967; *Pour comprendre les médias (Understanding Media)* by Marshall McLuhan, which came out in French translation in 1968; *Le système des objets (The System of Objects)* by which Jean Baudrillard was being discovered; *De la grammatologie (On Grammatology)* by Jacques Derrida; and the journal *Tel quel (As Is)*, with contributors such as Roland Barthes, Julia Kristeva, and Philippe Sollers. Together they represent a quite amazing union of ideas, which has the power to provoke thought about the artistic challenges of postindustrial society. *Le retour de Dionysos* is a most astonishing work, although very little discussed since it was published. It deals with the relationship between technology, art, and culture in general, as does another book by Jean Brun entitled *Les masques du désir (The Masks of Desire).*[10] What is surprising about the book is that it ex-presses another version of the often rehashed transition from modernism to postmodernism, which implicitly preoccupies all these authors to various degrees. The book is especially astounding in that it associates the character of Dionysus with technology, whereas tradition associates him with ecstasy produced by the fruit of the vine.

The figure of Dionysus reveals the process whereby art has met technology since the mid-nineteenth century: the encounter between the artistic creation and photomechanical, electrical, electronic, and digital technologies. In the current discourse of the industry in search of artistic or cultural content, as well as in the discourse of a few intellectual circles dealing with media art, there is talk of a paradigmatic shift, of a more or less abrupt change in paradigm. However, when concentrating on the notion of a paradigm of knowledge with the help of the figure of Dionysus as the key to this discussion, I realized that the paradigmatic changes are unveiled in their aesthetic resonance. For Dionysus is also the god of ecstasy brought about by music; he is related to what Nietzsche calls, after Schopenhauer, "the spirit of music," and to the ecstatic and emotional agitation provoked by sounds. By 1872, with the publication of *The Birth of Tragedy*, Nietzsche pointed out a crucial aesthetic concern that would be borne by the society he could already anticipate in his time, that is, the relationship of music with image and concept.[11]

Whereas one of the main flaws of Jean Brun's book is his total neglect of the figure of Apollo, for Nietzsche, the figures of both Apollo and Dionysus are inseparable. In fact, the encounter between the Dionysian and Apollonian figures is what makes Attic tragedy. It is true that Nietzsche is concerned with what constitutes the tragic, while Brun intends to show how the technique is Dionysian. Neglecting the Apollonian figure leads him, however, to attribute to Dionysus characteristics that are, in my opinion, of an Apollonian nature. Jean Brun thus affirms that "the wave of formalization, which [pervades] little by little all the areas" corresponds in the myth of the god to the episode of Dionysus's laceration, and this coincides with the fashion for logistics that has presided over the development of the computer.[12]

Nietzsche, however, sees an Apollonian tendency in such a logical schematism.[13]

In Nietzsche, the coexistence of the two figures represents the deep spirit and nature of Greek civilization and art, whereas a 1893–94 work on Dionysianism by his great friend Erwin Rohde did better in making allowances for the difference between a primordial, fundamentally Apollonian Hellenism and the alteration of this character by the introduction of the cult of a barbaric god, for Dionysus is not Greek. In any case, regardless of the scientific veracity of Nietzsche's and Rohde's positions, the figures of Dionysus and Apollo stand as figures that symbolize divergent tendencies.

In Nietzsche's aesthetic, two worlds confront each other: the Apollonian world of dreams and the Dionysian world of ecstasy. Thus Apollo is the god who presides over the visible world, who watches over the borders of dreams and hallucinations, who functions according to a principle of individualization, and who is also the god of prophecies and moderation, therefore of planning. He is linked to the "wisdom of appearance," in the ethical concept of moderation, while Dionysus is the bearer of the immoderation of ecstasy, and his action leads to the splitting of the subject's appearance, to its dismantling and dispersal, whereby it rejoins the fluctuating nature of life. If I wanted to stress the difference in a way that would probably be too simplistic, I would say that Apollo is a form and Dionysus an energy. Nietzsche does not fail to associate Dionysianism with the notion of a will to live, the notion of will, which I would replace with the idea of vital energy, or even with something more familiar since Freud—the field of drives, of the energy of impulses, of the semiotic in Kristeva.

If Apollo is associated with plastic arts and epic poetry, Dionysus is associated with "the spirit of music." For Nietzsche, music is different in character and origin from all other arts because it does not represent an image of the world but an image of the very will that moves and shakes the world, and this is why music moves us in such a powerful manner. Apollo and Dionysus are thus divergent figures in their essence: one is linked to the principle of individualization by which the "redemption in the appearance" operates, whereas the other is a "jubilation" breaking the "prison of individualization" for direct connections with the mobility of things.

While Jean Brun totally ignores the dynamics brought forward by Nietzsche between Apollo and Dionysus in Attic tragedy, the figure of Apollo appears to me in a mediatized world as the lord of the society of the spectacle. Apollo goes through a mutation by assuming some of Narcissus's features. Jean Brun is not wrong to see, in what he called ultra-media back in 1969, Dionysian instruments producing combinations and syntaxes, couplings and mixings. He is also right when he touches upon the notion of paradigm in discussing "the Model as an aspect of Moderation" in Plato, and in criticizing the verticality that goes from the copy to the (transcendent) model, to the benefit of the combinative function of the model that "establishes relations in the heart of a system." But he fails to place his notion of spectacle under the rule of Apollo when he declares that the man of today "is literally invaded by the image and becomes, so to speak, the spectacle that surrounds and haunts him."[14] Furthermore, he does not conceive that in the reign of spectacular appearances the image has an identity function and that the subject finds himself individualized in the reflection of images.

Guy Debord, in the fourth aphorism of his book *La société du spectacle* writes that "the spectacle is not a set of images, but a social relationship between people, mediatized by images."[15] Although originally written in 1967, these lines could account for certain dimensions exhibited by the exchanges occurring on today's computer networks of the Internet and the World Wide Web. And yet the category of spectacle in Debord confines itself in a modernist dichotomy, that of authenticity versus duplicity, the opposite of what he calls "life" or "social life" compared to the alienation experienced in the society of the spectacle.

In this brief portrait several issues can be extrapolated and examined: the god of individualization and appropriation of the subject by the visible is strongly linked to Narcissus, whereas the god of the splitting up of the individual is associated with Eros in order to abolish separations. Apollo is then the one through whom we are granted repose in the appearance, the form of the individual based on self-knowledge, rationality, and ethics, and benefiting from the identity function of the image, while inversely Dionysus disperses this individualization, projects the single subject (Kristeva) outside its imaginary stases, by musical *ex-stases.*

Composition

While images and electronic sounds are associated with a "musicality" that is still very metaphorical, they are linked to the score or musical composition as soon as they become digital. An image and a sound created digitally consist above all of binary mathematical operations structured by a code (software, operating system), which, just like the musical score, finds its value in its execution. This value of execution, when transposed to the area of interactive multimedia, shows that computer software is similar to the score, and the work is embodied in the execution of the program according to a given form of interaction, through the performance of the interactivity of the work. Contrary to those who see in digital processing a process free of all values—but contrary also to those who, while wishing to oppose this ideological standpoint, stress the power of control and monitoring in the field of digital simulation—one should see in cybernetic systems and digital simulation a domain highly governed by valorization and that the message of the work can be found in the structures and dynamics of the interface.

The idea that the musical score or composition is similar to work done with sounds and digital images had already been suggested by Gene Youngblood in 1983. Computer-assisted editing seemed to him particularly close to a score, and he does not hesitate to refer to "operatic cinema" when talking about the work of the video artist Ernest Gusella. One should also remember that Sergei Eisenstein conceived editing according to musical parameters, the audiovisual counterpoint, where each and all elements, from photogram to color, from music to the force of the movements of the camera and the rhythm of the editing, interpenetrate in a temporal and emotional conception requiring musicality. Thus the software of digital editing increases tenfold the precision and possibilities of musical couplings.

Works of art realized with digital and interactive technologies allow the participants to play and execute a piece according to the parameters of the score (software) in the reconfiguration of the information, permitting whoever receives the work to determine the content by the given form of his interaction, by which the subject himself becomes involved in the composition. Jacques Attali provides a framework for discussing this idea of composition in his study entitled *Bruits (Noises)* on the political economy of music.[16] Moreover, this notion is associated with the figure of Dionysus in Jean Brun.

For Jacques Attali, the economy of music distinguishes between four historical networks or situations. These networks explain the transformations of connections between music and social and political integration. Inasmuch as its social function is to channel noise, music will be sacrificial ritual in the first network, representation in the second, ritual of repetition in the third, and composition in the fourth. From this perspective it is worth studying electronic arts (video art, audio art, electroacoustics, computerized media) since they stem from both the network of repetition and that of composition, in a difficult dialogue between what technology provides as cultural forms (images/sounds and technoscientific knowledge) and what it allows the composer to do. For Attali, repetition is engendered by a society where the technocratic language generates "a more efficient channeling of the production of the imaginary, forming the elements of a code of cybernetic repetition—of a meaningless, repetitious society."[17] The loss of meaning in the repetition is embodied in the spread of technologies that allow recorded sounds to be stored like electronic images. Those sounds that we consume in solitude no longer have the socializing function of the opportunities for encounters offered by the network of presentation (concert, theater, film), but constitute "the tool for an incredible access to an individualized storage of music,"[18] films on videocassettes, video games, and so on.

In Attali, the network of repetition corresponds definitely to Debord's notion of spectacle, and when the latter writes that "any separated power has then been spectacular,"[19] it implies that Attali's repetition is the spectacular dimension of the diffuse power of transnational capitalism in the postindustrial economy. In fact, with the information superhighway in its spectacular dimension as Debord could see it, one should consider that postmodern goods (information) become the whole occupation of social life. In Baudrillardian terms, the spectacle indeed become a simulacrum and a simulation, a seduction by signs rather than by the "commodity form," a seduction by signs which Jean Brun pinpoints as another characteristic of Dionysus and which I would rather associate with the nature of Apollo.

Debord also writes with regard to technology: "The economic system based on isolation is a circular production of isolation. Isolation creates technique, and in turn the technical process isolates."[20] This circularity then operates according to the repetition in which the lonely individual sees his individuality reinforced in solitude. Thus Apollo reigns over the society of spectacle and, with Narcissus, provides the models of identity images as a refuge, rather than as repose, in appearance. As for Dionysus, he dances elsewhere in the composition.

Attali sees in the composition another possible network sketched as an exit from the repetitious spectacular and the circular isolation. In the loss of meaning of the repetition of the spectacle and simulations, the work of artists, with the technologies and instruments they sometimes develop outside of commercial circuits, starts from cultural and technical gains of repetition in an effort to compose, which Attali defines as follows:

> Rapture of the musician, communication with himself, with no finality other than his own enjoyment, fundamentally exterior to all communications, surpassing of oneself, a solitary, selfish, non-commercial act. . . . Composition then proposes a radical social model, where the body is presumed to be not only capable of production, consumption, or even relationships with others, but also of autonomous enjoyment.[21]

Why can an act as solitary as the composition described above break up the circularity of the repetitious spectacular? Because it is part of Dionysus's dance! One cannot approach the notion of enjoyment without looking back at Julia Kristeva's theses from the early 1970s in which enjoyment is linked to nonsense and loss. In her analysis of the work of Georges Bataille, Kristeva states that his experience is always a contradiction between the presence of the subject and his willful loss, his decentralization caused by desire, but his renewal in the representation of desire through fiction. Even more pertinent to this discussion of the idea of enjoyment, she stresses that "if enjoyment is to affect a subject, it must contain the existence of knowledge with which the subject fulfills himself; and for the sake of solidarity, so that knowledge does not constitute an exercise of power but a performance, he must discover in its logic the enjoyment that constitutes it."[22] Kristeva conceives of enjoyment as closely related to the existence of knowledge, the subject being constituted in the symbolic, in other words, with the narration as semiotic structure that corresponds to the unification of the subject in spite of his willful loss. The enjoyment would also be associated with what Kristeva calls the spectacular, formed by the distribution of semiotic processes in the symbolic functioning of the subject; in the case of cinematographic language, this would mean movements, condensations, tones, rhythms, and colors, figures "always in excess compared to what is represented, what is signified."[23]

In Kristeva, it is the articulation of the two orders, one semiotic, the other symbolic, that presides over the process of the subject's stases and *ex-stases.* The symbolic order includes that which in the language includes the notions of sign, signification, denotation of an "object," representation, and image; in contrast, the semiotic order is made up of instinctual synapses *(frayages)* and their marks; "it is a temporary articulation, a non-expressive rhythm," not yet formalized. One can find semiotics particularly in the screams, singing, or gestures of a child, but also in the rhythm, prosody, plays on words, laughter, and dance in the adult world. Yet this semiotics is also described in terms drawn from Plato to designate the *chora,* or an "animated receptacle of mixture, contradiction, and movement . . . prior to the constitution of the first measurable bodies." Couldn't we see the field of semiotics as the realm of Dionysus? Nowhere does Kristeva suggest it, except to note that "Dionysus [was] born a second time having had his mother," suggesting primitive, obscure, and presymbolic forces.[24] The fact remains that symbolism corresponds rather well to the reign of Apollo in the vis-ual order, the measure and the Logos, and Dionysus expresses in the intoxication caused by music the stirrings that the semiotic synapses bear upon the subject in the process of signification.

As regards listening, that is, listening not only to sound and music but also to voices and noises, Roland Barthes writes:

> What is listened to here or there (mainly in the field of art whose function is often utopian) is not the occurrence of a signified, an object of recognition or a deciphering, it is the very dispersion, the mirroring of the signifiers, endlessly put back in the course of a listening session that always produces new ones, without ever stopping the meaning: this phenomenon of mirroring is called significance.[25]

For him, in fact, this amounts to a "panic listening" close to the idea Dionysus's followers had. In short, the enjoyment of composing is what creates an excess of meaning, through which are born semiotic synapses in the symbolic order of culture and technology. If the enjoyment of repetition is that experienced by a solitary subject, it is nevertheless expressed through the knowledge that is transmitted by a repetitious society.

Thus specified, enjoyment, the term used by Attali, can henceforth not only produce a unitary subject withdrawn from the commercial diffusion of the spectacle, but it can also articulate semiotics in terms of a significant practice. The material used in composition together with the instruments that allow it are themselves part of the existing symbolic order. But one does not come happily out of repetition, and composition works on the symbolic by digging into an open and dynamic field of impulses. The sociality of solitary reception, repetition, and technical reproduction still surrounds the subject—the artist in this case. In the composer's enjoyment the body comes into play as well as Dionysian violence, the breaking up of identity in the fluctuating time and space of telemedia. Dionysus represents the principle of collective dissolution of the individual, but at the time of repetition and "personal media," can this dissolution escape spectacular isolation? Because the enjoyment of the composer, of the player with technology, operates from the very simulacra of the media in a kind of disconnection of the real (the simulacrum being a copy without origin), because this symbolic background of the technological environment is characterized by the vacuity of representations in an era of simulacra and simulation, because media sociality is counted at the level of the solitary reception of images and sounds—if this enjoyment is autonomous, it also involves suffering from dissolution and can be resolved in violence and death, in the dismantling of the body.

In the present state of social relationships, violence and the imaginary can thus be assumed individually, in the enjoyment of an action, a poiesis articulating enjoyment by the Dionysian dismantling, body and soul—split up, torn, a suffering body. This at any rate is what would be indicated by some works that confront the technological and its Dionysian component. The performances of someone like Stelarc stand as the most concrete illustration, while a videotape by Neam Cathod in the National Gallery of Canada's collection entitled *Danlkû* (1989) demonstrates the importance of symbolic blockage at work in our culture, where it is difficult for the enjoyment of dissolution to symbolically reformulate the location of the subject.

Digitalian Treasures, or Glimpses of Art on the CD-ROM Frontier

Erkki Huhtamo

The 1990s, it seems, is witnessing another phase in the continuing love affair between art and technology. A multitude of catchwords have been coined: interactive art, cyber-art, online art, multimedia art, CD-ROM art—the list could be continued. Although most of these concepts will not live long enough to make a lasting imprint on "artspeak" (not to mention common parlance), a mere discursive explosion is a noteworthy phenomenon, a token of a burst of creativity looking for an outlet. Where such earlier "technological" genres as video art have attained an established role in the art world, being frequently featured in major international exhibitions and collected by respected art institutions, the position of "cyber-artworks" and other such creations is often precarious. They are looking for their identity somewhere between the art world, the marketplace, the "private," and perhaps some other territory currently in the making. The situation raises important questions about the role of art and creativity in the context of the "media" and "techno" saturated culture of the 1990s; it also raises questions about the context itself. I will face some of these issues by focusing on one aspect of the current multimedia spectrum: CD-ROM as a possibility for art.

It is a truism that digital technology has expanded tremendously since the 1980s. Technologies that were discrete until recently have begun to converge. Little round disks may contain whole encyclopedias with words, images, and sounds. Digitized moving images can now be exchanged in real time over computer networks that few people outside professional communities had even heard about three years ago. All this has been seen since the development of the personal computer. Once a device used mainly for game playing, word processing, and perhaps compiling a private electronic cookbook, the personal computer is rapidly emerging as a powerful and multi-functional domestic media center, providing both online and off-line access to enormous clusters of audiovisual data. At the same time it is becoming (potentially, if rarely in practice) an authorial environment for "homebrew" multimedia products.

Features of the Medium

Of the currently available "packaged," or off-line, multimedia formats, the CD-ROM, in spite of its apparent technical deficiencies, has the best chance to make an impact on the mass market.[1] Although the CD-ROM is technically far from ideal as a storage and distribution medium for multimedia (it is plagued by incompatibility problems, slow retrieval of information, and poor motion video quality), it seems the best compromise between the available hardware, the price/performance ratio, and the expectations of consumers.[2] The CD-ROM drive is rapidly becoming a standard feature of any Power Mac or multimedia PC. CD-ROM disks carry graphics, text, still images, sounds, and even moving images in easily accessible configurations. So does video, but the procedures of reception and information retrieval are different. With its stop, rewind, and forward functions, videotape can be characterized as a "corrected" linear medium. Sequences can be repeated and the tape stopped at will, but most of the time a video program has to be consumed "passively," watching the images flow in front of one's eyes.[3]

A CD-ROM application, however, creates an interactive relationship between the user and the work. Although much hyped, the concept of "interactivity" on the most basic level simply refers to the need for constant mental-physical activity and a "conversational" attitude toward the application. A linear "movie mode" can be included as one of the options of a CD-ROM product, but normally the user operates the work by constantly "pointing and clicking" certain "hot spots" (marked or hidden), responding to responses from the system, and so on. Often one can also arrange elements on the screen, type in simple messages, or make drawings. This happens, however, within the preprogrammed confines of the system. Contrary to videotape, which always has the recording option, the CD-ROM is strictly a "read-only" medium.

Typical metaphors for describing the experience of using a CD-ROM are "traveling" or "navigating." They refer to a spatial experience, an interactive journey of discovery into the virtual world "hidden" on the disk, supposedly beyond the interface. Another set of metaphors refers to reading, conceiving of the CD-ROM as a kind of electronic book. All these metaphors are in line with the underlying "rhizomatic" (Gilles Deleuze) way of organizing information. The basic architectural "grid" of most CD-ROM works is spatial and conforms to the idea of the hypertext.[4] The hypertextual structure offers an alternative to continuous linear progression, at least seeming to give users degrees of freedom to choose their own paths, to negotiate the experience.

The Rush to the Market

The media industries are currently making haste to conquer their share of the consumer market for multimedia. Their rage seems to have been spurred by the sense of vacuum that reigned just a few years ago. Although video games and home-oriented videotape sales and rentals played a significant role in the domestic market in the 1980s, by the end of the decade there was a widespread sense of disorientation. No practicable new media (notwithstanding the hardly viable promises of virtual reality or interactive television) were on the horizon. Commercial network services and multimedia products like the CD-ROM almost overnight have been harnessed to fill the vacuum. Yet the sense of disorientation has not disappeared. According to Michael Punt, the trade press "barely conceals a downbeat disappointment with a thin veneer of euphoria and marketing jargon."[5] About the only thing industry observers seem to agree on is the conviction that the transition from analog to digital media is laying the foundation for a far-ranging reorganization of media culture.[6] In spite of the optimistic tone of the copy, not even the future horizon of the digital multimedia is very clear.[7]

An assiduous, and strategically well-positioned, observer could still master the range of the CD-ROM production in 1993; since then, however, it has become impossible for any human being to have had firsthand experience with everything. Yet in spite of the impressive proliferation of titles, the general impression is curiously flat. There are plenty of genres—reference works, encyclopedias, self-help manuals, interactive pornography, histories of anything, games, "edutainment" and "infotainment" titles, interactive "books," and software packages. There is, however, a clear contradiction between the declared urge to explore a new and unforeseen medium and the simultaneous reluctance to venture into truly daring experimental projects. Although occasional efforts in formal innovation (primarily in interface design) can be found, most commercial products fit easily within familiar product categories adapted from the traditional fields of publishing or mass media such as film and television. Alternatively, CD-ROM products appropriate strategies from already established, commercially successful interactive genres, such as video games.[8]

Although such a state of things may seem normal when a new medium is only looking for its identity, it can just as easily be interpreted as an echo of the growing uniformity of the media industry, keen on coupling new products with existing entertainment "supersystems," product lines, and brand names—and on making sure of the profit from an investment in advance.[9] It is as if the CD-ROM-based multimedia were tamed at the very moment of birth, without having a chance to grow wild first. The potential that interactivity offers—a personalized, active, and intimate relationship with media, an associative coupling of different sensory registers, multiform retrieval of information—has been harnessed into the service of ideologically guaranteed and commercially calculated formulas.

There are exceptions, but, significantly enough, most of them are products for children. "Childware" obviously both allows and requires a wider margin for experimentation than "serious" products for grown-ups. Today's children are growing up with video games anyway. Products like Viacom's *Director's Lab,* which allows the child to create quite complex multimedia products by working in virtual production studios, or Voyager's *P.A.W.S.,* a "dog simulator" with surprising modes of interaction and perception, center on the user and his or her own curiosity and creativity instead of merely repackaging pre-existing content and formulas.[10] No doubt there is much potential for fresh insights and nonconformist ideas. Producing innovative multimedia prototypes is possible even without expensive hardware and a high budget. It seems that the crucial challenge is to find a publisher and a channel of distribution without compromising one's intentions and ideas.

Merging Boundaries

There is already a small but growing body of work that could be loosely identified as the initial corpus of "CD-ROM art."[11] What do we mean by this—CD-ROM works by artists who have already attained an established position in the exclusive value system of the art world? A handful of works, such as Laurie Anderson's *Puppet Motel* (1995), might fit into such a definition, but such works are a minority. It could therefore be claimed that the art world is *not* the common denominator or the primary point of origin of the works in question. In spite of the art world's occasional attempts to prove it is abreast of the times—for example, by organizing special events dedicated to virtual reality, cyberspace, the Internet, and other hip ideas—its relationship with technology remains constrained and retrograde.[12]

So how does one define a CD-ROM artwork without resorting to the convenient semiotic markers used by the various agents of the art world (critics, curators, gallery owners, art dealers) to label something as art and to show it into its own niche? All we can do is to identify innovative works that fulfill a couple of conditions: they stand out from the mainstream, explore the potential of the medium, don't serve a practical (sales) function, at least as their primary concern. As might be expected, such a necessarily subjective sampling gives us a heterogeneous body of work by makers who come from different backgrounds: visual artists, computer artists (who seldom enjoy a high status in the art world), graphic designers, photographers, composers, rock musicians, writers, video makers, computer nerds. Their creations are just as varied, ranging from dreamy audiovisual meditations and autobiographical "archives" to loud satire and outright "antiroms."[13] Such variety could be explained as somehow reflecting the widening availability of multimedia tools and the enthusiastic pioneer spirit raised by the appearance of digital multimedia. It may, however, also be related to the cultural context.

The blurring of boundaries between high and low culture, which began in the 1960s but intensified only in the 1980s, has shaken ideas about creativity, authorship, and "aesthetic purity." The hybridization of the cultural production with commerce has manifested itself, for example, in the music video, postmodern advertising and design, and the video game industry. The idea of vertical product development (as in the design *Gesamtkunstwerk* created around the Pet Shop Boys, or in the entertainment supersystems surrounding Super Mario or Sonic the Hedgehog) has prepared the ground for multimedia. The computer workstation has become one of the most important production tools for industries that attract those young talents who might earlier have opted for careers as video artists. Most of them don't seem to need to justify their position by differentiating themselves from the system they are part of, and instead accommodate themselves comfortably in a world drawn by the market forces. Parallel with this a new market has developed, one that is responsive to popular trends and fashions, but that also develops forms of connoisseurship, requesting more quality, complexity, and the aesthetic "elevation" of prevailing stylistic, generic, and commercial formulas.

*Myst*ifying Multimedia

From this fruitful breeding ground is emerging a new kind of multimedia product that purports to combine commercial ambitions with more cultural and artistic aspirations. Perhaps the best example is the phenomenally successful *Myst* (1993), a mystery game created by brothers Rand and Robyn Miller.[14] Instead of resorting to shooting, virtual jumping, high-speed driving, or any other customary mode of interaction used in countless computer and video games, *Myst* sends the user to explore a mysterious and imaginatively designed virtual world. The user proceeds by entering new spaces and solving puzzles, which lead him or her to reconstruct the hidden scenario behind the work. There is ample time for meditation and appreciation of the virtual scenery.

The Miller brothers have already been surrounded with a mythical aura as prophets of the multimedia to come.[15] Commenting on an article published in *Wired*, John Simmons pays attention to the biblical overtones used in the panegyric. He also remarks about the tendency to elevate *Myst* to the status of art: "The insistence on beauty and art is significant. *Myst* is not an excitement generator so much as something that adumbrates a new art form, or wants to."[16] Surely the attention around *Myst* can be read, at least partly, as an attempt by the industry and its hangers-on to raise the social respectability of the dubitable game market (this reading seems to be proven by the fact that many hard-core gamers dismiss *Myst* as a nongame). Such efforts are particularly evident in the United States, where the rising tide of conservatism carries a risk of state intervention in the form of censorship.[17]

Another attempt to provide commercial multimedia with artistic elevation are the interactive music videos released as CD-ROMs. For example, Peter Gabriel's *Xplora 1: Peter Gabriel's Secret World* (1993) and David Bowie's *Jump* (1994) are curious "play stations" or conglomerations of elements which the music industry usually releases along parallel and interconnected but distinct product lines: compact disks, music videos on TV, video cassettes, posters, concert tours, ephemera for the fans, and so on. These eclectic creations are tied together by the star's image and elements from other genres of multimedia, primarily games. These products purport to enhance the intimacy of the star-fan relationship while keeping one aware of the superhuman range of interests of a Gabriel or a Bowie. Such products are also loaded with "serious" cultural and aesthetic references to provide them respectability and to extend their audience.[18] Gabriel's CD-ROM, for example, includes sections on WOMAD (World of Music, Arts, and Dance) and Amnesty International in addition to many "cultured" connotations.

Most interactive music videos have been little more than loose collections of trivia. The two major exceptions are the Residents' *Freak Show* (1992)[19] and Laurie Anderson's *Puppet Motel.* Both works try to integrate the music and the references to the artist's profile into a more elaborate and uniform setting. *Freak Show,* easily the more successful of the two, presents the fantastic and melancholy virtual world of a circus freak show that the user explores, discovering all kinds of bizarre but strangely touching details as she or he proceeds.[20] The work could also be called an interactive movie, but it has no linear story line or final mystery to be solved; there is just a setting pregnant with little story capsules and submerged musical fragments. Although this work springs from the peculiar icono-audiography created by the Residents, it could be enjoyed without any information about their earlier work.

For Laurie Anderson's *Puppet Motel* to be fully grasped, however, the user must have an earlier knowledge of her art, above all her stage performances. In spite of the virtual "set" created by Huang Hsin-Chien which serves as the access point to everything else, the work is still a rather fragmentary collection of separate pieces (disguised as rooms), connected by Anderson's implied presence. Contextually *Puppet Motel* is interesting because of the position Anderson has established for herself between the art world and the commercial music industry. She is one of the few figures who have been accepted to the

"A Lists" of both worlds. Like her albums, music videos, and stage performances, *Puppet Motel* situates itself on the divide between postmodern avant-garde (a contradictory term) and "quality" pop culture. The reactions raised by *Myst*, however, prove that even after so many years of postmodern rhetoric about breaking boundaries, some boundaries exist. Game culture seems to be one of those fields of cultural production that is still waiting to be elevated to the canon of late-twentieth-century culture. Whether this is needed or not, I see the appearance of products like *Myst* as welcome. *Myst*'s ingenious concept and its overall quality push the limits of multimedia. Whether we call it art is another thing.

Problems of Distribution

In terms of distribution the CD-ROM certainly has some similarities with the videotape. The compact disk is even more "compact" than a VHS video cassette and can easily be distributed via similar channels, even by mail order. CD-ROMs are regularly sold as bonuses for magazines, and the specialized magazines on CD-ROM that are popping up are inheritors of the video cassette magazines that were introduced in the 1980s. The CD-ROM is also quite naturally associated with the audio compact disk, its technical origin. This association could help the distribution of CD-ROMs, at least in certain sectors of the market, for example, those related to the music industry. CD-ROM clubs modeled on mail-order music clubs already exist. Even though personal computers with CD-ROM drives are still far less common than VCRs, this early distribution may presage the transformation of the CD-ROM into a mass-marketed consumer item.

Independent producers of CD-ROMs, including artists, will certainly face problems in the increasingly competitive and commercial media culture of the 1990s. Publishers and distributors avoid risks and try to ensure their profit by intensive market research. Product lines are connected with guaranteed brand names and genres. Concern over censorship and copyright issues is also increasing. Although mainstream products may occasionally seem to push the limits, they will not go beyond what is commonly considered acceptable. What role will there be for works that are emphatically noncommercial and even subversive, such as Linda Dement's *Cyberflesh Girlmonster* (1995) or VNS Matrix's *All New Gen* (1994), or for self-reflective and potentially self-destructive works such as Andy Cameron's *Antirom* (1995)?[21] Will they be doomed to the margin, or will some new and effective distribution channels be created, perhaps with the help of the Internet?[22]

The trade press has already coined a concept to cope with creations like these: "fringeware."[23] While this term could be seen as a negative recognition, it can also be read as a way of neutralizing a phenomenon that potentially disturbs the calculated balance and glitzy surface of the industrial CD-ROM market. The industry, of course, knows how to deal with fringeware: ignore it or co-opt the errant young talent. Nonconformist ideas and solutions have always been vital to the idea of product differentiation which forms the flip side of product standardization in corporate strategies. The video game industry (and the computer industry in general) offers many examples of reformed crackers and computer nerds forming the backbone of its research and development faculties. Even formerly independent computer graphic artists, such as Rebecca Allen and Jane Veeder, have recently been recruited as producers and designers by the video game industry.

Some of the greatest successes of the video game market have been created by cottage industries formed by games enthusiasts, rather than by artificially created "supergroups" or "dream teams," such as the hyped Rocket Science.[24] In addition to *Doom* (by Id Software, a small company created by computer nerds John Romero and Jay Wilbur), which was originally distributed as shareware, the successful *Myst* has done much to send the industry looking for talent among the fringeware makers.[25] The cases of *Doom* and *Myst* prove that one can use ordinary multimedia authoring tools to create products that make money, earn glory, and give a strong feedback for the audience, without resorting to too many compromises. Whether something similar could and should happen in the case of multimedia artists is a more complicated question. With its expansion, the market will certainly accommodate more nonconformist work, but on whose terms and under what conditions remains to be seen.

Is CD-ROM Art Needed?

One of the wittiest independent CD-ROM artworks is *BAR-MIN-SKI: Consumer Product* (1994) by Bill Barminski, Webster Lewin, and

Jerry Hesketh.[26] *BAR-MIN-SKI* is an "art gallery" seemingly presenting the retrospective exhibition of Barminski, an underground artist and creator of the iconoclastic Tex Hitler comic strips. On another level the gallery hilariously appropriates the idea of an interactive shopping mall (and makes therefore a great pair with *2Market,* the *serious* cyber-mall on CD-ROM and the Net!). The makers thus poke fun at both the contemporary art market and the consumer-oriented cyber-culture by depicting them as identical. With its ironical choice of title, *BAR-MIN-SKI: Consumer Product* also points to the multimedia's—and, one could claim, the media culture's—orientation toward producing packaged consumer products.

Judging from the evidence, it could be claimed that by means of the co-opted CD-ROM platform artwork is being reinvented as a marketable product, and not only within the confines of the art world. According to this scenario, contemporary electronic art could be experienced on the desktop at home, or anywhere. Of course, interactive museum catalogues on CD-ROM such as *Le Louvre: Palais et peintures* (Montparnasse Multimedia, 1994) have already taken a step in this direction. Yet instead of becoming another medium for delivering art reproductions, CD-ROM artworks would deliver the Real Thing, to be experienced exactly as in an art institution, but without the disturbing factors of the public viewing situation. The quest is highly commendable, but it will have to surmount many obstacles.

In spite of the official optimism, there are no guarantees that the CD-ROM is going to develop into an important mass-market item, comparable to video game cartridges, for example. Even if it did, who would buy CD-ROM artworks? The situation could be compared with video cassette rentals and sales for the domestic market. This market has been highly successful for certain genres such as feature films, pornography, and aerobic tapes. Packaged video art, however, has remained marginal, although a relatively wide selection of titles has been available, by mail order, if not on the shelves of the local video store. Why would CD-ROM art fare any better? Perhaps it would succeed with a little help from the kind of cross-breeding of art and popular culture already evident in *Myst* or *Freak Show.*

Mike Punt has recently suggested that a system of CD-ROM rentals would consolidate the market.[27] This might be worth considering, especially in the face of the increasing influence of the Net.

Indeed, there are those who see the CD-ROM merely as a transitory medium, needed only until the audiovisual capabilities of network communication are improved to support high quality multimedia. As the Macromedia Corporation did before him, Marc Canter, the founder of the Media Band, an experimental audiovisual multimedia group, has urged artists to create multimedia artworks that are too big for the CD-ROM.[28] For him, the CD-ROM is only good as a kind of demo medium on the way toward the *big* thing, a kind of interactive MTV, an artistic orgy on the Net.

Canter's points are well in line with the current merging of (techno-)cultural boundaries, but they are saturated by Western techno-hubris. They bypass the fact that in spite of its massive growth the Internet will be an elitist and far from universal medium for years to come. There will still be many uses for the CD-ROM—aside from being hybridized with the Net, it has a *potential* to reach audiences who still live outside the "wired" world.[29] Unfortunately, even the CD-ROM is only operational within the confines of Digitalia, the would-be but not-quite universe. The need for the artistic and ideological exploration of the CD-ROM is constantly increasing because of its rapid spread and commercialization. Pushing the technological limits, filling more disk space, and making money may seem important, but they are not everything. It is still content, emphasis, and motivation that *should* matter.

CD-ROM Works Consulted

Because some of these works have several creators, they have been listed in alphabetical order.

All New Gen. Created by VNS Matrix. Produced by VNS Matrix, Australia, 1994. Macintosh.

Ambitious Bitch. Created by Marita Liulia. Published by EDITA, Finland, 1996. Macintosh and PC.

An Anecdoted Archive from the Cold War. Created by George Legrady. Produced by George Legrady, USA, 1994.

Antirom: The Antidote to Multi-mediocrity. Collective work directed by Andy Cameron. Produced by SASS/Antirom, England, 1995.

ArtIntact: CD-ROMagazin interaktiver Kunst (Artists' Interactive CD-ROMagazine). Published by Cantz Verlag, Ostfildern, Germany, 1994 (vol. 1), 1995 (vol. 2).

BAR-MIN-SKI: Consumer Product. Created by Bill Barminski, Webster Lewin, and Jerry Hesketh. Produced by De-Lux'O Consumer Productions, USA, 1994.

Biomorph Encyclopedia: Muybridge. Created by Nobuhiro Shibayama. Produced by 4. Dimension, Japan, 1994.

Coacerwater: Artificial Life Creation. Created by Yoichiro Kawaguchi. Published by NTT Publishing Co., Japan, 1994.

Cyberflesh Girlmonster. Created by Linda Dement. Produced by Linda Dement, Australia, 1995.

Freak Show. Created by Jim Ludtke. Published by Voyager, USA, 1992.

Good Daughter, Bad Mother, Good Mother, Bad Daughter: Catharsis and Continuum. Created by Susan Metros. Produced by Susan Metros, USA, 1994.

Jump. Created by David Bowie. ION, 1994.

Meet the Media Band. Created by the Media Band. Produced by Canter Technology, USA, 1994.

Mistaken Identities. Created by Christine Tamblyn with Paul Tompkins. Produced by Christine Tamblyn. To be published by Voyager, USA, 1995.

Myst. Created by Rand and Robyn Miller. Produced by Cyan, Inc. Published by Brøderbund, USA, 1993.

New Voices, New Visions 1994. Anthology from the Competition. Published by Voyager, USA, 1995.

Puppet Motel. Created by Laurie Anderson with Huang Hsin-Chien. Published by Voyager, USA, 1995.

ScruTiny in the Great Round. Created by Tennessee Rice Dixon and Jim Gasperini. Music by Charlie Morrow. Produced by ScruTiny Associates. Published by Cassiope Media, USA, 1995.

She Loves It, She Loves It Not: Women and Technology. Created by Christine Tamblyn with Marjorie Franklin and Paul Tompkins. Produced by Christine Tamblyn, USA, 1993.

The ToyBox. Anthology with interactive artworks by 20 artists. Produced by Moviola, England, 1995.

Truth & Fictions/Verdades y Fictiones. Created by Pedro Meyer. Published by Voyager, USA, 1995.

Die Veteranen: So nutzlos wie eine Fuge von Bach. Created by Micha Touma, Stefan Eichhorn, KP Ludwig John, and Tjark Ihmels. Published by Systhema Verlag, Germany, 1995.

Xplora 1: Peter Gabriel's Secret World. Created by Steve Nelson. Published by Real World Multi Media Ltd. and Brilliant Media Inc., USA, 1993.

Multimedia, CD-ROM, and the Net

Simon Biggs

Analogs and Languages

With fully digital media the underlying materials on which products are distributed and received become less and less relevant to the specifics and characteristics of the product itself. While recognizing that the medium still has important characteristics that inform the manner in which we experience information, the medium, in the sense that McLuhan conceived it, is no longer the primary message.

With analog media such as film or video the relationships between the raw information, the means by which it is "written," and the means by which it is accessed (film projector, VCR, et cetera) are more or less inextricable. The information is the product of all its physical components. In the case of film an optical device records light to a material itself composed from various optical characteristics which is then "played" through another optical device.

With video this relationship between the components of the media is not quite as direct, but remains close. An optical device converts information to a continuous and infinitely variable analog signal on magnetic tape. The relationship between this signal and the original data is directly analogous, a one-to-one mapping. Another device reads this information and thus drives an optical display device (a CRT).

With digital technology these isomorphic patterns or analogical relationships are lost. The digital data that describes a picture is entirely abstract. Without the correct decoding "key" the information is useless. In this sense digital data is symbolic in the same sense as written language. It is like a Rosetta stone without any means of translation available, sharing with other linguistic forms the implicit complexities involved in reading and writing. Its meaning remains inaccessible until it is passed through a decoding procedure that releases what was originally encoded in it. The analysis of digital information is best undertaken not by physicists or engineers but by linguists and semioticians.

As with any medium, but perhaps more explicitly so for the reasons above, digital media exist in and of a social context. Digital information is produced, encoded, and interpreted entirely within the social environment from which it takes its form and meaning. Before all else, it is an idea. We can establish four aspects in dealing with digital media which reflect on this condition and assist us in its analysis: hardware, software, artware, and wetware.

Hardware and Software

The media to be discussed here are the CD-ROM and the Internet, the most rapidly developing distribution technologies available today for interactive multimedia products. This is not to say that they are the best or that they will last. Nevertheless, each has its unique characteristics which for one reason or another appear at this time to be leading to rapid and sustained growth.

Media such as CD-ROM and the Internet function to allow digital data to be moved cheaply and efficiently from one place to another. Before saying anything about that data, let us look at the physical media themselves.

CD-ROM's primary value seems to be the cost/data equation. With a capacity of up to 600 megabytes (allowing high bandwidth data such as video or sound to be stored) and with access times similar to that of a computer's internal hard disk (enabling interactive documents to function satisfactorily), CD-ROM immediately has an important role. Given its very cheap production costs (as little as one dollar per unit) and its small, light, and easily packaged nature, CD-ROM becomes irresistible and, not surprisingly, has moved to take a large market share in only a few years. By the end of the decade it may become the dominant means of distribution for electronic cultural product, whether games, movies, educational material, dictionaries, or artworks.

The Internet has some similar and some quite different characteristics. Like CD-ROM it is a very cheap means of access to data (the cost of a local telephone call); the material costs of publication are very low; and it is very portable. In fact, the Internet is so portable that the notion of place is lost altogether, since what is being "ported" is not the data but the user. When "surfing on the Net" it is quite common to move from city to city, country to country, continent to continent, in seconds. "Net surfers" are hardly aware of "where" they are. Most likely they don't even bother to keep track of their "virtual" geographic whereabouts. Notions of space as we have understood them collapse.

This is where the Internet differs most radically from CD-ROM, or any other medium that exists as a physical object. In a sense the Internet has something in common with broadcast technologies such as radio and television; however, its high levels of interactivity mean that the information is not so much received by the viewer but rather entered by the user. One can see the Internet as one giant computer that is everywhere and nowhere at the same time. The user enters this nonspace and becomes similarly dematerialized.

This brings us to what makes these two media common, what could be seen as the real "metamedium" behind them—the computers that have ubiquitously invaded our desktops, offices, studios, bedrooms, and living rooms and that move data to and from these places. These machines both produce the material we experience and allow us access to it.

The computer is a language machine. It is defined by linguistic, programmable forms and is optimized for storing and processing linguistic material (here I am using the term "language" in its broadest sense, to include images, sounds—in fact, any symbolic or symbolically describable phenomena). As such, it is an abstract machine. Nothing in its definition, as originally proposed by Alan Turing during the Second World War, implies that it must have any physical existence or any particular function. Turing simply defined the computer as a machine that could be any machine. It could be this because it was programmable—as such, operating symbolically upon symbolic things.

This universe of symbolic forms includes the computer itself, and the recursive aspect of the medium is what lends it real technological, and therefore social, power. It is this aspect that places the computer less as a medium and more as a metamedium. To paraphrase Turing, the computer is the medium that can be any medium. From this definition we can see the rapid development of the computer as the means for what has come to be called "multimedia," although perhaps the term "metamedia" would be more appropriate.

Thus while the discussion here focuses on the production of and access to computer-based multimedia products via two of the most popular contemporary means of distribution—CD-ROM and the Internet—in reality the underlying media (which is also at the heart of any questions about CD-ROM and the Internet) is the computer itself, as both a physical and social artifact.

Given this fact, and that the future of a medium like CD-ROM appears good but not necessarily assured (as what has happened to video surely tells us), our attention is directed not only to the specifics of these media but also to the underlying principles of digital technologies so that the discourse explored and extrapolated will remain valid beyond the lifetime of specific distribution technologies.

Artware and Wetware

CD-ROM and the Internet are relatively new, at least for artists, and it is clear that there is a conspicuous lack of "artware." The technologies in question have been available for some years, but with recent drastic cuts in costs (prices falling as much as 80 percent in the last two or three years) artists and others who tend to work independently can only now afford to access them. If we look at the impact of the music CD on the music scene, with the rise of small independent producers encouraged by the low mass-production costs involved, we can get some idea of the possibilities the medium presents to practitioners who are familiar with counting copies of their videotapes on their fingers rather than in the thousands on their calculators.

Education has been critical in this process. Art schools over the past few years have invested relatively heavily in new technologies, and this has led to the emergence of a new generation of artists who are familiar with computers and peripheral systems. These artists have also developed their work within a social context that regards technology as an almost natural phenomenon. Entertainment technologies such as computer games have contributed to the development of what some are now calling cyber-culture.

Because of this background these artists have a distinct attitude toward their audience. They expect their audience to be involved in the work, to take on the role of a protagonist in the interactive processes of interpretation, making problematic the whole process of reading and writing. This is something explicit in all interactive technology, but also a major factor in the psychological makeup of today's youth culture. Computer games have shifted forever our expectations of media and our role relative to them. The passivity of cinema, video, and television is being transformed into an entirely different media culture.

The Internet has been around since the 1950s, but artists have only now begun to consider its attractions for artistic production and distribution. The reasons for this are much the same as for CD-ROM: the problems of access to technology, the difficulty of acquiring the skills to work with computers and similar advanced technologies, and the lack of a social context within which to engage meaningfully with the technology.

This situation is rapidly changing. Internet usage is increasing exponentially. During 1994 there was an increase of 20 percent each month in the number of people on the Net. Nobody has any idea of how many people use the Net, but it is perhaps in the area of 30,000,000, and doubling every six months.

One can see the Internet as one giant distributed computer, which is everywhere and nowhere at the same time. The user enters this nonspace and becomes similarly dematerialized. In this sense the user becomes a linguistic node, another simulation among a "universe" of simulations, a "packet" of information constantly moving from one server to another. When on the Net one feels not only disembodied and displaced but also transformed.

With the Internet we can see the possibility for artists, who once may have considered broadcast technologies as an appropriate medium for their work, to shift their means of production from the linear to the interactive, and their means of dissemination from fixed broadcast to customized narrow access.

Artists' use of TV has been sparse and generally unsuccessful. Why? We know it is expensive and politically difficult to access, but perhaps the determining reason is that to use broadcast media requires an entirely different approach from that of traditional art. It's not that you can't make art on TV; it's just that to do it well, you have to shift your practice, intentions, and definitions so far that the result doesn't really resemble art anymore, at least as we generally accept it. The same holds true for attempts at cultural intervention or subversion. As Saturn consumed his children, broadcast media consume difference. Can something remain radical and continue to function as different if it is culturally shared on the scale that broadcast allows?

New York–based artist Paul Garrin made his reputation partly with hard-hitting broadcast interventions. Like other artists around the world who consider themselves part of the media underground, Garrin, in collaboration with Nam June Paik and several ex-Fluxus artists, has recently moved to the Internet as a means of achieving his ends. Apparently Garrin sees the future of disruptive underground practice as being outside of the broadcast context. Whether this is a forward step into a new media world of fragmentation or a regressive step brought about by the apparent paradoxes involved in artists' engagement with mass media is a question that remains open.

Certainly the Internet is distinct from broadcast. Perhaps the greatest distinction lies in the relationship between medium and "audience" (a difficult concept in reference to the Internet). While broadcast functions to deliver a shared cultural experience to the maximum number of people, the Internet is all about subcultural production and experience in its most extreme form. In contrast to broadcast viewers, who more or less passively accept a paradigm, Internet users choose to enter a cultural context, which they know they are sharing with others who have similar reasons for being there. As more users opt for such inclusion within various subcultural milieus, the disruptive and subversive nature of the Internet becomes apparent—not in how it may intervene in our televisual flow, but in how it may change our whole rela-tionship with information media and cultural experience.

One problem here is the status of art and the artist. New media always offer the chance to short-circuit notions of what art and culture are, and thus encourage the emergence of new ways of working, of seeing, of being seen. The emergence of both photography and the cinema functioned in this way. If artists are less concerned about something being art, then perhaps they are free to be more creative with their ideas, the form of their work, and their relationships with the audience/viewer/user.

This idea can be seen to inform much of the emerging practice. A perfect example is the Digitale Stad (Digital City) project by a group of artists and social theorists in Amsterdam. It involves the creation of a parallel but virtual city where participants can choose to live virtually, parallel to their normal existence in the real city they inhabit. The intention is not to create an ideal or utopian city, nor to establish it as a metaphorical-critical space. Their agenda is not specific in any of the ways that such objectives would suggest. Rather, the Digital City exists as a potential space where individuals and groups may invent their own shared experience in a form that is totally open-ended and unstructured. As such, perhaps it can be seen as a utopian space if one sees the creation of a discontinuous and fragmentary space occupied by diverse subcultures as an objective worth seeking. Regardless, we should recognize that much of the intrinsic value of this type of work is in its differences rather than its similarities with more traditional art forms and modes of cultural expression.

Some multimedia work may resemble games, "edutainment," or computer simulation. Hopefully, some work looks like nothing we have ever seen before, evading definition. Our criteria should be founded on notions of creativity in its widest (and wildest) sense, rather than on ideas of what is or is not art. As has already been argued above, at this point it seems both retrograde and limiting to confine one's interest to works that are very obviously artistic, especially when considering media forms that in their very nature bring into question the whole notion of the artist and authorship.

Romancing the Anti-Body

Lust and Longing in (Cyber)space

Lynn Hershman Leeson

Many artists have attempted to reauthenticate reality by dissolving the boundaries between art and life. Their efforts effectively succeeded in reducing illusion into yet a sheerer veil of enigmatic invisibility.

Prior to this decade, there has been no medium available to render ideas about the "edge of life" as effectively and instantly as cyberspace. Dissolutions related to time and space in computer-mediated communications (termed CMC by Howard Rheingold) not only erase social boundaries but irrevocably alter identity itself.

Before being truly plugged into or grounded in cyberspace, a person must create a mask. It becomes a signature, a thumbprint, a shadow, a means of recognition. The justification for this disguise is similar to that for tribal coverings: masks camouflage the body, and in doing so liberate and give voice to virtual selves. As personal truth is released, the fragile and tenuous face of vulnerability is protected. Giving one reason for this in his book *The Virtual Community: Homesteading on the Electronic Frontier,* Howard Rheingold notes that people seem to need depersonalized modes of communication to get personal with each other—it is a way to connect.[1]

Masks and self-disclosures are part of the grammar of cyberspace. They are the syntax of the culture of computer-mediated identity, which can include simultaneous multiple identities or identities that abridge and dislocate gender and age. One of the more diabolical elements of entering CMC or virtual reality is that people can only recognize each other when they are electronically disguised. Truth is precisely based on the inauthentic!

Identity is the first thing you create when you log on to a computer service. By defining yourself in some way, whether through a name, a personal profile, an icon, or a mask, you also define your audience, space, and territory. In the architecture of networks, geography shifts as readily as time. Communities are defined by software and hardware access. Anatomy can be readily reconstituted.

Masking through computer-mediated communication is read differently than in real life. You can be anything you can imagine, instantly, with very few props or prompts. Self-created alternative identities become guides with which to navigate deeper into the Internet. You do not need a body to do this.

Not only do you not need a body, but entering cyberspace encourages a disembodied body language. "Posing" and "emoting" are some of the terms for phantom gestures that can be read through words, or seen in special video programs through simple movements such as waves. Codes of gestures can be read by attachments on the computer that articulate hidden meanings of voiceless and mute speech.

Actions are constantly under surveillance—tracked, traced, digitized, and stored. The disguises used today are especially important because they may determine an archetype for the ephemeral nature of a future society geared toward image manipulation and self-recreation.

In the search for contact, computer-mediated communications solicit dialogues that require mutual narrative s(t)imulations. While these dialogues are often subliminally fulfilling and inherently full of amorous potential, some recent incidents have caused disturbances.

Let me describe three famous case studies in the cyber-world annals.

Case One

A classic example is "The Strange Case of the Electronic Lover," by Lindsay Van Gelder, which was published in *Ms.* magazine in October 1985.

Van Gelder met "Joan" on CompuServe and began to chat. Joan was said to be a neuropsychologist in her late twenties, living in New York, who had been disabled—crippled and left mute—by an automobile accident involving a drunken driver. Joan's mentor, so the story went, had given her a computer, modem, and subscription to CompuServe, where Joan blossomed into a celebrity. Her wit and warmth extended to many people.

Eventually, however, Joan was unmasked . . . defrocked (so to speak), and it was discovered that she was not disabled, disfigured, mute, or female. Joan was in real life a New York psychiatrist, Alex, who had become obsessed with his own experiments in being treated as a female.

The shock in the electronic world has a higher voltage than anywhere else. This assault of a discovery was coupled with the fact that Joan had achieved an intimacy with many people who trusted her. Joan's very skeleton was based on pure deception. Van Gelder says that "through this experience, those who knew Joan lost their innocence."[2]

In the real world, the incident could be thought of as a kind of rape, a deep penetration by a masked stranger. Questions of ethics and behavior ensued in an attempt to avoid further incidents of "net-sleazing" and other repulsive forms of bad netiquette.

Alex had cleverly called upon the icons and codes of a society that has learned to fantasize media-produced females in a particular way. He chose to be a woman, a gender marginalized in technology. Most people logging on are men. When Joan logged on, it was 1986, and it was unusual for women to chat. It is still so unusual that even today whenever someone logs on as a woman, there is a barrage of questions to determine whether the person really is a woman, or someone just trying on a new sex for size. People logging on as men or animals do not experience this kind of harassment.

Alex chose to make Joan the epitome of vulnerability, perhaps whetting desires even more by making her paralyzed and mute. The fictional presumption was that in real life she had lost her body, yet she could still be seductive. She could even lure her responders, like the Sirens calling Odysseus, into lustful responses to her nonbody.

Case Two

In February 1993 an at-home mother signed up for a computer service to access information and make friends. She found she was able to form online relationships that quickly became intense. Such close connections were hard to achieve in the busy world of real life. Very quickly, however, "she found herself the target of an invisible high-tech predator who threatened to become an all-too-real menace to her children."[3]

She began to receive vile, unsolicited messages from someone known as Vito. She had no idea if Vito was a man or a woman, a friend of her family or a psychotic maniac. Vito was able to tap into all of her messages, get a bit-by-bit profile of her, and post messages to the whole Internet. She complained that it was like rape, again without a body.

The woman sought out a computer crimes detective. Vito became well known, even infamous. Many people claimed to be him, just as many people claim to have committed the crimes of Ted Bundy.

When a suspect was finally arrested, the district attorney was forced to release him because of insufficient evidence. The case raised the question of how to bring law and order to the information superhighway, a place where villains are invisible and users become unwitting victims in crimes of the nonbody.

The Electronic Frontier Foundation is attempting to answer this question. A self-sponsored group that has been enormously effective since its creation, this hacker posse rounds up, captures, and holds virtual vigilantes accountable. The group not only focuses on hackers, it has also questioned the computer and privacy invasions launched by the U.S. government. New users are forming the largest immigration in history. What happens to this population's nonbody is of critical importance.

Case Three

About 1990, Tom Ray created a virtual reality system in which creatures evolved. As Kevin Kelly notes in his book *Out of Control,* "Beginning with a single creature, programmed by hand, this 80 byte creature began to reproduce by finding empty RAM blocks 80 bytes big and then copying itself. Within minutes, the RAM was saturated with replicas. By allowing his program to occasionally scramble digital bits during copying, some had priority. This introduced the idea of variation and death and natural selection, and an ecology of new creatures with computer life cycles emerged. The bodies of these creatures consisted of program memory and space. A parasite, this creature could borrow what it needed in the RAM to survive."[4]

Furthermore, to everyone's astonishment, these creatures very quickly created their version of sex—even without programming! Sometimes in Terra (which is what Ray called this system) a parasite would be in the middle of asexual reproduction (as in genetic recombination), but if the host was killed midway, the parasite would assimilate not only that creature's space but also part of the dead creature's interrupted reproduction function. The resultant junior mutant was a wild new recombination created without deliberate mutation, a kind of inbred vampiric progeny, an unrestrained strain.

Body-less sex, in an anti-body ecosystem for co-evolution, cultured in the digital pool—what could be more appealing?

Don't Byte Off More Than You Can Eschew

Getting back to the rational nonreality we have learned to love and trust—in other words, the real world—it becomes all too clear that much of what is considered groundbreaking is not really new, and that each perspective we have today derives from many years earlier. Consider, for example, the rules for one-point perspective, written by Leone Battista Alberti 500 years ago. His mathematical metaphor was first applied to painting and drawing and promulgated an age of exquisite illusionism. Artists who used his theories could paint windows onto imagined vistas with such precision that viewers were impressively deceived. Was this ethical? What implications did it have? Did Raphael or Vermeer question the vistas of voyeurism their windows would invite?

In an effort to eschew illusion, Marcel Duchamp investigated the essentials of art production, including selfhood and the uncontrolled idiosyncratic inner impulses. The sine qua non of art, according to Duchamp, is not some essence or quality residing in the final work, but rather an infinitely subtle shifting of the artist's intent. In Duchamp's works such as *Rrose Sélavy,* the intent and body of the artist are the essentials of artistic practice. Rrose was a nonbody through which Duchamp could escape fixed identity, in the process becoming an "other"—something defined by what it is not.[5]

This preramble leads to the development of my own oeuvre of nonbody and anti-body work produced in the past three decades. I divide my work into two categories, B.C. and A.D., or Before Computers and After Digital. One begets the other.

Early B.C. Nonbody Works

From 1960 to 1970 I created various wax masks that talked to viewers through audiotapes, or dissolved, extinguished by fire. In 1972 I created my first nonbody work in a room in the Dante Hotel. The identity of an absent person was surrounded by the objects that defined her taste and background. In painting, the nonbody might be called negative space. Books, glasses, cosmetics, and clothing were selected to reflect the education, personality, and socioeconomic background of the provisional identities. Pink and yellow lightbulbs cast shadows, and audiotapes of breathing emitted a persistent counterpoint to the local news playing on the radio.

Thus my path to nonbody works and interactivity began not with technology but with installations and performances. Visitors entered the hotel, signed in at the desk, and received the key to room 47. Residents of the transient hotel became "curators" and cared for the exhibition. I intended to keep the room permanently accessible, letting it gather dust and be naturally changed through the shifting flow of viewers. But "real life" intervened. Nine months later, a man named Owen Moore came to see the room at 3:00 a.m. and phoned the police. They came to the hotel, confiscated the elements, and took them to central headquarters where they are still waiting to be claimed. It was, I thought, an appropriate narrative closure.

Despite its tenuous and short-lived existence, *The Dante Hotel*[6] became one of the first alternative space or public artworks produced in the United States that used a "site-specific" space, four years before the term was coined. The identity of the nonbody inside was formed by what was absent.

The drive to alter "found environments" that existed in real life persisted. Eventually I installed temporary works in such unlikely places as casinos in Las Vegas, store windows in New York, even the walls of San Quentin Prison. In each the idea was the same: to transform what already existed through an interactive negotiation of simulated or "virtual" reality, and to define the "identity" of each context in terms of the Other, or what was not there.

Inside the Dante Hotel room 47 was the "essence" of an identity. When the room closed, it seemed important to liberate the essence of the person who might have lived there, to flesh out experience through real life. This led to a 10-year project titled *Roberta Breitmore,* a private performance of a simulated persona. In an era of alternatives, she became an objectified, disembodied, alternative personality.

Roberta was at once artificial and real. She was a nonperson, the gene of the anti-body. Roberta's first live action was to place an ad in a local newspaper for a roommate. People who answered the ad became participants in her adventure. As she became part of their reality, they became part of her fiction.

I wanted Roberta to extend beyond appearance into a symbol that used gesture and expression to reveal the basic truth of character. She had credit cards, checking accounts, and more credit than I had (still have). Roberta was an interactive vehicle with which to analyze culture. Her profile was animated through cosmetics applied to her face as if it were a canvas, and her experience reflected the values of her society. Roberta participated in trends such as est and Weight Watchers, saw a psychiatrist, had her own language, speech pattern, handwriting, apartment, clothing, gestures, and moods. Most significantly, she witnessed and documented the resonant nuances of her culture's alienation.

Over time Roberta accumulated 43 letters from individuals answering her ads, and she experienced 27 independent adventures. Her most difficult test was staying in character during psychiatric sessions, and her most dangerous was being asked to join a prostitution ring.

Roberta's manipulated reality became a model for a private system of interactive performances. Instead of being kept on a disk or hardware, her records were stored as photographs and texts that could be viewed without predetermined sequences. This allowed viewers to become voyeurs into Roberta's history. Their interpretations shifted depending on the perspective and order of the viewing.

In her fifth year of life, Roberta began to have such archetypically victimized adventures that I created multiples. Even with four different characters assuming her identity, the pattern of her interactions remained constant and negative. After zipping themselves into Roberta's clothing, the multiples began to have Roberta-like experiences. Perhaps they were like Tom Ray's computer parasites, filling the RAM space of real life, taking with them the genetic codes of Roberta's nonembodiment.

Many people assumed I was Roberta. Although I denied it at the time and insisted that she was "her own woman," with defined needs, ambitions, and instincts, in retrospect, I feel we were linked. Roberta represented part of me as surely as we all have within us an underside, a dark, shadowy cadaver that we try with pathetic illusion to camouflage. Roberta's traumas became my own haunting memories. They would surface with no warning, with no relief. She was buried deep within me, a skin closer to my heart. The negativity in her life affected my own decisions. As a "cure," Roberta was exorcised.

The exorcism took place in Lucrezia Borgia's crypt in Ferrara, Italy. Before the ceremony, Roberta had been a sculptural life/theater performance, a sociopsychological portrait of culture seen through an individual woman who metaphorically became everywoman. The exorcism and subsequent transformation through fire, water, air, and earth, incorporating the alchemical colors from white to red to gray to black, and her rebirth out of ashes represented a symbolic emergence from powerlessness. In completing the ritual, Roberta's nonbody disintegrated, slowly dissolving into the smoke of her reincarnation.

Roberta was not my only work with alternative nonbody images. Jerry Rubin had visited the Dante Hotel, knew about Roberta, and asked me to work with him on creating the visual elements of his public identity. With elements similar to those used in Roberta's deconstruction, his reconstruction was a kind of nonbody image cannibalization.

Roberta's exorcism took place in 1979. When the smoke cleared, it was 1980. That year I picked up my first video camera. Video and interactive systems became tools for retracing the body of my personal history. It was a fortunate coincidence that as video was defining its language, I was finding my voice.

In each of the 53 videotapes I have completed since Roberta's exorcism, the idea of "site" or medium is part of the content. Though each is quite different in external appearance and content, many of the tapes are about surveillance, voyeurism, and the inherent dangers of technological systems and media-based reality in which identity is threatened.

In *Longshot* (1989), for instance, a video editor, Dennis, obsessively pursues the image of a woman whose identity is fleeting and fragmentary. As Dennis tries to edit together Lian's reality, it becomes more fractured and fragile. Lian is a nonperson, marginalized in her culture. The romance begins without her, and the seduction continues on the tape, without her corporeal presence, in Dennis's editing room.

Seeing Is Believing (1991) is about a 13-year-old girl who uses a video camera to search for her missing father and lapsed history. Eventually she finds both, but through the process dissolves her "essence" into the "negatives" of the film itself.

In *Desire Incorporated* (1990) seduction ads were aired on television. Those who responded were eventually interviewed as to why they wanted to meet a fantasy or artificial person. The answers were woven into a videotape about desire.

Virtual Love (1993) is about a shy woman, Valerie, who, discouraged with her own real body, implants someone else's image into the computers of identical twins, one of whom (Barry) she is infatuated with. This surrogate nonbody, Marie, causes Barry to fight with his girlfriend and to reach into the system to find his perfect simulated, virus-free mate.

Seduction of a Cyborg (1994) is about technology infecting the body, and the addiction this causes. In this video the female central character eventually becomes part of the technology, seduced into cyborg-hood, where she both participates and witnesses the pollution of history. The effects were designed from digitized and manipulated images of computer chips.

Twists of the Cord (1994) is about the history of the telephone. In the story Michelle becomes involved in a phantom or virtual relationship with R.U. Sirius. Both have sex with nonbodies, using the screen as a simultaneous condom and connection.

Double Cross Click Click (1995) is about the ramifications of cross-dressing on the Internet.

The Electronic Diary (1984–95), a personal work, deals with the relationship of an invisible body and a "talking head." Often the body fractures or ruptures in the process of coming to self-understanding.

Phantom Limbs, Interactivity, and Disappearances

For the past decade I have been creating a series of photographs known as *Phantom Limbs.* Each articulates mutations of the female body through the seduction of media. Reproductive technological parts sprout from the image of the female, creating a cyborgian reformation as parts of the real body disappear.

While video is like a reflection that does not talk back, interactive works are like a trick two-way mirror that allows you to have a dialogue with the other side. I find this deeply subversive!

I consider *Lorna* (1984), the first interactive artist videodisk, to be my entrance into electronics. Unlike Roberta, who existed in the world, Lorna never left her one-room apartment. The objects in her room were very much like those in the Dante Hotel, except that there was a television set. As Lorna watched the news and ads, she became fearful, afraid to leave her tiny room. Viewers were invited to liberate Lorna from her web of fears by accessing buttons on their remote control unit that corresponded to numbers placed on the items in her room. Instead of being passive, the viewers had the action literally in their hands. Every object in Lorna's room contained a number and became a chapter in her life that opened into branching sequences.

The viewer-participant accessed information about Lorna's past, future, and personal conflicts via these objects. Many images on the screen were of the remote control device Lorna used to change television channels. Because the viewer-participant used a nearly identical unit to direct the disk action, a metaphorical link or point of identification was established and surrogate decisions were made for Lorna.

The telephone was Lorna's link to the outside world. Viewer-participants chose voyeuristically to overhear conversations of different contexts as they trespassed the cyberspace of her hard-pressed life. There were three endings: Lorna shot her television set, committed suicide, or—what we Northern Californians consider the worst of all—moved to Los Angeles.

The plot had multiple variations that included being caught in repeating dream sequences or using multiple soundtracks, and could be seen backward, forward, at increased or decreased speeds, and from several points of view. There was no hierarchy in the ordering of decisions, and many of the icons were made of cut-off and dislocated body parts, such as a mouth or an eye.

Once *Lorna* was released, I wanted to create a work that more directly involved the body of both the viewer-participant and the computer. Five years later, *Deep Contact* (1989)[7] was completed, and participants were required to touch the screen, penetrate it, or do both. Viewers choreographed their own encounters in the vista of voyeurism by putting their hands on a touch-sensitive screen. This interactive videodisk installation compared intimacy with reproductive technology, and allowed viewers to have adventures that changed their sex, age, and personality.

Participants were invited to follow their instincts as they were instructed to touch their "guide" Marion on any part of her body. Adventures developed depending upon which body part was touched. The leather-clad protagonist invited "extensions" into the screen—the screen became an extension of the viewer-participant's hand, similar to a prosthesis. Touching the screen encouraged the sprouting of phantom limbs that became virtual connections between the viewer and the image.

At certain instances viewers could see, close-up, what they had just passed. For example, Marion ran past a bush that, examined closely, revealed a spider weaving a web. In some instances words were flashed on the screen for just three frames, forcing the viewer to go back and, frame by frame, see what had been written. At other points the Zen Master spoke his lines backward, forcing the viewer to play the disk in reverse to understand what he said. A surveillance camera was programmed to be switched on when a cameraman's shadow was seen. The viewer's image instantaneously appeared on the screen, displacing and replacing the image. This suggested "transgressing the screen," being transported into "virtual reality."

Room of One's Own (1993),[8] my third interactive computer-based installation, allowed the viewers' eyes to enter the actual space of a tiny articulated interactive electronic peep show. A stainless-steel box placed at eye level, with a movable periscopic viewing device, turned the viewer into a voyeur in a miniature bedroom scene. Within this room were several objects, similar to those in the Dante Hotel and Lorna's room. The very act of looking initiated the action.

The voyeurs' eyes, positioned as they were in the small video monitor, became a simultaneous virtual participant in the scene being seen. All the while, the protagonist (the same one in *Deep Contact*, but now a bit older) chided the viewers for their persistent gaze. This work was not only about voyeurism and a feminist deconstruction of the "media gaze," but also about the explosive effects attached to media representations of female identity. Furthermore, it repositioned the viewer into the victim.

Real-Time Virtuality

In 1888 Etienne-Jules Maray perfected a gun that substituted film for bullets. This camera-gun has a direct relationship not only to the history of film and to the eroticization of female imagery in photography and pornography, but also to the horrors of our century perpetrated by weapons and translated into images by cameras.

For example, many serial killers photograph their victims, as if to capture and possess them. The associative notions of guns/camera/

trigger link all electronic media representations to lethal weapons. *America's Finest* (1992–1995),[9] an interactive M16 rifle, addressed these issues. Action was directly instigated through the trigger itself, which, when pulled, placed the viewer-participant within the gunsight (this time the entire body, holding the gun). Viewers saw themselves fade under horrible scenarios in which the M16 was used, and if they waited, ghosts of the cycling images dissolved into the present. As in *Room of One's Own,* the aggressor became the victim. Through their complete immersion, viewers again lost control of their images and became floating nonbodies.

Paranoid Mirror (1995) was inspired by the paintings of Jan van Eyck, in particular *Giovanni Arnolfini and His Wife.* This piece used reflection as a means of portraiture and reflected self-portraiture. Though obscured and distanced, the artist's reflection watched from behind the central figures. *Paranoid Mirror* engaged ideas of reflection, tracking, surveillance, and voyeurism and used the viewer as a direct interface. Sensors strategically placed on the floor caused the still image in a gold frame to activate, turn around, and dissolve between sequences of reflection into the viewer or other women in the videodisk sequences. In some instances, a switcher placed the viewer's back into the frame, countering the direct reflection into the scrimlike layers of the images.

The back of an older woman's head was seen when the piece was inactive. The suggestion of difficulties with eyesight underscored the paranoiac fear of being watched as well as the relationship of paranoia to voyeurism and surveillance. Accompanying this piece were four photographs from the filmed sequences. These images were framed so as to obscure the image. Appearances therefore, are often reflective illusions and projections of the observer.

Birth of the Anti-Body

The work in which I am presently engaged is the creation of a fictional persona, designed as an updated Roberta, who is navigating the Internet.[10] Surveillance, capture, and tracking are the DNA of her inherently digital anatomy. They form the underpinning of her portrait.

The persona has her own home page on the World Wide Web and is involved with chat lines, bulletin boards, and other computer-mediated communications. She is different from the nonbody works of the 1970s and 1980s in that the veil of her illusion—the computer screen—is sheerer than ever.

I refer to her as an anti-body because of the way she was cultured. Biological antibodies produce systems of immunity from toxins in their environment. This persona will function as a benevolent virus that will roam the breathing form of the Internet, randomly accessing herself into unknown home sites. Interestingly enough, terms for new technologies have ramifications in the language and time of AIDS. In reaction to an unhealthy natural environment, she rejects what exists and, in order to survive, forms another environment.

This Internet-linked, plugged-in anti-body is a transitory construction of time, circumstances, and technology, a newly issued prescription of earlier impulses. She has chosen to negate the selfhood into which she was born. Instead, she shows a marked preference for the artifice of technology.

Like Botticelli's Venus she is forward-looking and seductive. She is also optimistic and cyborgian. A purebred anti-body of the 1990s, she moves through time and electronic geographies of space, discreetly challenging privacy, voyeurism, and surveillance in her own imitable, mutable, and inauthentic revolutionary fashion.

The obsession to alter environments found in both physical and electronic life persists as a principle in work I produce. The seductive challenge is to continually subvert presumptions and look through the reflections of what already exists, into the still invisible potential that lurks just beneath the peeling surface we call reality. By doing this, perhaps we can embrace the illusion that this elusive and sheer separation, like death, might somehow eventually be erased.

7 Items on the Net

Siegfried Zielinski

1.

Now and again unforeseen events burst into the telematic Net. In the December 15, 1994, issue of the magazine *Fineart: Art and Technology Netnews*, Jeremy Grainger broke the AP news story via Fringeware that Guy-Ernst Debord had committed suicide. The report was terse: "He was 62. . . . Little known outside France, Debord denounced what he called 'the show-biz society' and declared that performing arts should be based on powerful emotions, passions, and sexual desire. His ideas were influential among theoreticians and essayists who achieved prominence in the May 1968 student-led cultural revolt that shook French society." That was it. That the cofounder of the Situationist International movement—who in *Society of the Spectacle* had diagnosed more than 20 years ago that all direct experience had given way to representation, who in the same book had attested that telecommunication "reunites the separate but reunites it as separate"—had died by his own hand did not affect by one pixel the tidily arranged symbols on the Net, nor their author. In 1952, at the age of 23, Guy Debord made a film with dialogue seemingly organized on random principles. The title was *Howlings in Favour of Sade.* At one point the second voice says, "The perfection of suicide is in ambiguity." In the script this is followed by a stage direction: "5 minutes' silence during which the screen remains dark."

2.

The way language is used on the Net is most affirmative of life. As a rule, the language is positive, animated, apologetic, smart. It bristles with energy. It is an electronic fountain of youth. The computers, their technical designers, and the connections set up, enable, facilitate, and support—nature, for example. Programs lead and organize and select. Landscapes are created, as are populations or generations, that even develop dynamically and unfold freely in (self-)organization. The interfaces must be interactive and empathic (in the

Aristotelian sense) or even biocybernetically interactive—that is, they have to organize something alive within the closed circuit. Their secret agents don't have trench coats with turned-up collars to hide their faces; they're not up to anything, and you will search in vain for them in the underground. They are tourist guides standing in the spotlights, inviting us to leisurely surf. Many decades after their discovery by theoretical physicists between the wars, the waves of possibilities in which quantum truths are now formulated exclude the violence of contexts/connections; they are waves neither of pain nor of ecstasy. "The linking of sensor data with parameters of user interaction permits meaningful correlations over and above various output modalities."[1]

In Chris Marker's *Sans Soleil,* inspired by the music of Mussorgsky, we encounter a Japanese man who is always making lists of things, for example, of things that make the heart beat faster. I started to make a list of phenomena, phantoms, and modi that I miss on the Net, and the columns of speech on the subject are getting longer by the minute. Here are some of my favorite substantives:

ambiguity
anger
attack
collapse
crime
cruelty
danger
dark anguish of spaces
daze
death
deviance
discomfort
discongruence
doubt
drive
ecstasy
eczema
evil
excess
hysteria
incest
interruption
irritant
lust
macrogenetosomia praecox
monster
neurosis
obsession
passion
pathology
risk
scream
seduction
uneasiness
yearning

3.

Although many differences existed between, for example, Artaud, Bataille, Duchamp, and Leiris, the dissidents of the Surrealist movement had a common focal point from which they developed their relationship to the (intellectual and art) world: they disrupted their own marginal tributary as well as the larger mainstream because of their rejection of any kind of functionalized ethics, their resistance to one-dimensional rationality, their celebration of unrepressed pleasure, and their aesthetic development of desire as an existential mode. To them, it was of imperative significance that their thinking be far removed from any hierarchical structures and that their aesthetic practices be immanently and wildly heterogeneous juxtapositionings (philosophy and cultural critique took over these paradigms at a much later date, notably with the work of the duo Deleuze/Guattari). Particularly for characters of a passionate and tortured or suffering disposition, like Antonin Artaud, the focal point of artistic praxis was the undispersed duality of experience and sensation (with a radicalness comparable only to Bataille's work in literature), which he confronted with the pure praxis of the concept. Indeed, this also essentially shaped the work of Duchamp, for all his extravagances and eccentricities. On what does the hyperrealistic avant-garde orientate itself? What orientation is it capable of elaborating and capturing for itself? The unconscious appears to have been consciously written to death after Freud and Lacan (who neglected to adhere to his own dictum that "there are problems one must decide to abandon without having found a solution"), and, above all, after their innumerable adepts and interpreters. In the 1950s and 1960s, activists, Situationists, and performance artists threw their own bodies into the fray, to the point of (self-)mutilation and (self-)immolation, against the discourse and direction of power. So, will there now be a reorientation toward concepts, toward the natural and life sciences, toward the illusion of a continuity, a flow, a beautiful order in chaos? Or will new, artificial bodies be created in the form of bodies of knowledge, and their mise-en-scène in the form of aesthetically experienced volumes in the tele-age, moving and ephemeral artifacts in antiquated space?

4.

The experimental work of the group Knowbotic Research suggests one possible avenue: their creations and workshop processes are factional; that is, they are extracted both from empirical data and from the realm of fiction, to which they always seem to want to return. In the circensic Net they strive to direct visualization (knowledge and its organization) while at the same time hinting at a seduction, without which art as a sensitizing terrain for the experience of the enigma is (no)thing at all. In order to develop this character of the double agent, the "Knowbots" have been assigned a second mode of existence that can assume form outside of the Net: in the event, in the once-removed setting of publicly accessible space, they once again become empirical bodies, sensations.

5.

The most complex mysticism praxis with the most complex language that I know of is the theoretical Cabala: "a technique for exercising reason or, instructions for use of the human intellect . . . it is said, that angels gave the Cabala to Adam after being expelled from the Garden of Eden as a means whereby to return there."[2] The 10 *sephirah* with their 22 connecting pathways constitute a sheer, inexhaustible, networklike reservoir of associations, connections, punctuations; its construction principle is binary, and it is built of the basic tensions of theoretical reason *(chockmah)* and the power to concretize, to form *(binah)*. The only meaningful mode in which the Cabala can be read and rerevealed over and over again is that of interpretation. In this, the Cabala and art are akin.

Edmond Jabes's texts are philosophical poems. In a discussion with Marcel Cohen about the unreadable, he was asked what he meant by the "subversion" of a text, to which he replied by referring to the beginning of each and every subversion: disruption/interference. The paradox, that he himself operates with grammatically correct sentences and words that retain their connotative meanings, he resolves cabalistically:

> I have not attempted to ruin the meaning of the sentence nor of the metaphor: on the contrary, I have tried to make them stronger. It is only in the continuity of the sentence that they destroy themselves, the image, the sentence, and its meaning when they are confronted with an image, a sentence, a meaning, that I consider to be just as strong. To attack the meaning by rebelling against the sentence does not mean that it is destroyed. On the contrary: it is preserved because a path to another meaning has been opened up. All this appears to me as though I were confronted by two opposing discourses that are equally persuasive. This results in the impossibility of privileging one over the other which, in turn, constantly defers the control of the meaning over the sentence. Perhaps the unthinkable is just simply the mutual suspension of two opposite and ultimate thoughts.[3]

There might be a key here to how aesthetic action within orders and structures might unfold, between Pentagon, academe, and the market which afford only slim possibilities for temporary interference, the filigree weaving of labilities.

6.

On the Net, there is no art of this kind, yet; it has had no time to develop a notion of the Other, the vanishing point of which would be death. The model for Net culture is life, and because there it has relinquished its unique existence, it easily and usually becomes a model. The algorithms used by the engineers and artists who are working more or less secretly on the orders of the Circe Telecom have been copied from (bio)logical life form(ula)s translated into mathematics. Genetic algorithms are useful and fascinating because of their proximity to this life. They are bursting with strength and confidence. For art, it would be worthwhile to attempt to invent algorithms of (self-)squandering, of faltering, of ecstasy, and of (self-)destruction as an experiment. In full recognition and acceptance of the risk that perhaps there would not be much to see or hear, these algorithms would be transformed into sounds and images. In the universal shadow, in the dark halo, where the strong, light bodies of knowledge of

Knowbotic Research move, but are prevented from dispersing, there is a presentiment of this secret.

7.

When art becomes independent, represents its world in dazzling colors, a moment of life has grown old, and it cannot be rejuvenated with dazzling colors. It can only be evoked in remembrance. The greatness of art only begins to appear at the dusk of life.[4]

—Guy Debord

Radical Software Redux

David A. Ross

In the early seventies, the video revolution seemed a relatively radical place. A little comfortable, perhaps, but nevertheless a place where central questions of postmodernity could be addressed directly. During an openly political moment in American history, television was curiously relevant to a wide range of artists, and appropriately hard to marginalize. But if video was seen as a relevant art form, it was also part of the arcane avant-garde, and as such, not much of a threat. Since most people didn't connect the word (or idea of) video with anything remotely important (it was a term known mostly as a technical description of the television picture signal), it went virtually ignored in the mainstream press.

Even to connect the word "video" with art seemed ludicrous to many—it confounded even many liberal open-minded folks within the arts. But as it was a time of triumphant late conceptualism—and on a certain grassroots level conceptualism meant do whatever you want and call it art—video art nestled itself quickly though uncomfortably into the art world.

In fact, the idea of artists challenging the hegemony of the corporate interests that controlled mass communications was anything but a silly variation of art-is-what-you-can-get-away-with-ism. Quite the contrary: for independent artists to question the validity of the mass identity proposed by commercial broadcast television was a powerful ambition then, and still seems powerful 25 years later. Radical hardware had arrived, but what about the radical software? Douglas Davis's attack on the core concept of mass audience, and Gene Youngblood's call for an "inversion" of the hierarchy of media control and a reversal of the roles of consumer and producer may have a quaint ring in the mid-nineties, but you have to admit, it still has a certain resonance.

Of course, video godfather Nam June Paik's pioneering mid-seventies conception of an information superhighway was framed within a rather heady moment. Blue sky predictions were the currency of much of the video literature. And the Raindance group, Ira Schneider,

Frank Gillette, Beryl Korot, and their circle, had a pretty good notion that what they were proposing in their short-lived publication *Radical Software* was nothing short of a revolution in art and communications. New communities would form around the simple yet profound idea of taking active responsibility for communication systems, seen as a primary aspect of community. Nothing short of a near Blakean transformation of consciousness was predicted by visionary writers like Paul Ryan. And though the word "video" now functions as a verb, noun, and adjective in the lingua franca of the late century, it must be admitted that video art still remains safely (and now quite comfortably) ensconced within the sheltering confines of the art world.

From today's hindsight vantage it seems that the problem was that videotape was the wrong medium and cable television was the wrong delivery system. As it turned out, this was a pretty big problem, though it wasn't that simple. Plainly stated, the issue was more likely that several complex systems were developing in and out of synch with each other, and all were struggling within an economic framework of capital enterprise we now recognize by names like Viacom and Time Warner. But this has little to do with the indisputable fact that many important works of art were produced by those artists, musicians, poets, and media activists concerned with transforming television into (or perhaps merely using television as) a creative medium. In fact, extraordinary works that were created with the tools of television production redefined, and in a fashion redirected, the technical development of the medium itself, and helped redefine its grammar. Television was bent and stretched in the service of aesthetic innovation. Even television's inherent passivity was questioned and aesthetically toyed with, though these experiments could only go so far.

For this reason, the fact that Bill Viola was the American artist at the 1995 Venice Biennale is, in itself, rather unremarkable—even though the work he created for the American pavilion was in fact very strong and beautiful. A quick survey of major art museum programs, film festivals, and similar large-scale survey exhibitions makes it clear that video art is now considered fully within the mainstream, and that it no longer signifies any particular ideological direction or political attitude. Video has become, as John Baldessari once predicted, like a pencil.

Of course, a major problem with video is that it continues to resist interactivity, but, more important, that video remains firmly rooted in an economy of scarcity—an economy that limited the future of the medium to the hyper-entrepreneurial. The commodity value of television remains measured in blocks of time, and as the poet David Antin once noted, much video art unthinkingly adopted this basic measure, one he termed the money metric. Video artists sidestep the problem when they work within the gallery-bound world of installation sculpture, or the cinema-like screening room. But as strong as these works may be—and some are indeed sublimely beautiful—the conventions of traditional architectural space also rob video art of its potential to unite remote and dispersed communities. It was specifically this capacity that fueled so much of the speculation surrounding alternative video and the early days of cable television.

When Nam June Paik in a 1973 collage asked when artists would have their own television channels, he wasn't mocking postwar consumer advertising as much as he was pointing toward the situation we find ourselves in 20 years later, created by the greening of the Internet. For the first time in the postmechanical image age, the individual artist has been significantly empowered by a singularly elegant set of tools. Not only can each artist chose to function as an independent distribution agency, but the resultant need for mediating institutions has been dramatically undermined as well. As a result, the individual artist is functionally the equal of any group or organization. That is quite a powerful change, the impact of which has yet to be properly predicted, let alone measured.

Simply stated, these new tools have developed within an economy of abundance. They have been taken up rapidly by an alienated and deeply cynical generation of media artists, schooled and engaged in the postmodern, postideological politics of identity and suspicious of all institutions, including their own. Having gone well beyond the publishing of desktop 'zines, this generation is more than computer-literate; they are computer-comfortable. Their hypertext worldview is international, unbound by local cultural conventions, functionally interactive, absolutely instantaneous, and completely untethered. Doors open onto open doors. Within the Internet, the vanishing point of traditional space has been eliminated.

Yet some legitimately wonder if what constitutes the Internet can be considered a medium at all. Strictly speaking, and novelty aside, computer art never amounted to very much—what the pundits of General Idea called "pabulum for the pabulum eaters." Cybernetic serendipity often appeared to be a pathetic cutesifying of the computer's frightful power. Complex man-machine interface ignored the fact that all tools are equally dependent on genius and that all genius requires human inspiration and an essential human spirit. Computer-assisted design is precisely that, computer-assisted.

But this isn't computer art. It is quite something else, something still not fully defined or definable. From its relatively obscure origins as the anarchic playground of hackers and Web-heads, the Internet was absorbed quickly by the same corporations that controlled and developed broadcast television and ensured that cable television would remain an essentially commercial service. Yet the Internet remains free and quintessentially anarchic. Formally, the Internet is already more than digital image and hypertext, more than Real Audio sound and Quick Time video imagery, more than edited narrative constructions propelled simultaneously in multiple directions. This new medium has blurred even further boundaries and definitions that have limited the imagination and potential of media artists for far too long.

Complicating matters further, the art world is far different now than it was in the early seventies. Decimated by AIDS, defunded by the conservative tide in American politics, caught as Frank Gillette put it, "between paradigms," shaken by the collapse of the eighties boom market, self-conscious in ways that are not necessarily beneficial to artistic freedom, it is an angry and yet more diffident art world.

And it would be a mistake to overlook the fact that access to computers is far from the near universal access that people now have to television. The disparity of haves and have-nots is even greater in this exotic world of privilege. And though video was distinctly different from television, people had an idea of the medium after tens of thousands of hours of mind-numbing exposure. Regardless of whether the high-speed Internet or cable television emerges as the primary distribution structure, the linkage of personal computers to wired communications systems is still a remote and frightening concept, even for those who can afford to participate. In an almost knee-jerk fashion, many fear that this form of communication will further alienate people from one another, leading to greater social anomie rather than establishing valuable new forms of community and communion.

What remains to be seen is whether the artists who so actively defended the idea of video as an aesthetic realm will respond not out of the need for novelty, but out of a renewed sense that art can be a transformative force within the world culture. And finally, recalling the ambitions of media artists working a quarter century earlier, several questions loom. Do artists really want this kind of power? That seems obvious. But will artists respond to this unprecedented opportunity? Seems like we need some really radical software, right away.

NOTES

PART THREE NOTES

SHERRY TURKLE, RETHINKING IDENTITY THROUGH VIRTUAL COMMUNITY, PP. 116–22

1. The materials in this paper are reported on more fully in Sherry Turkle, *Life on the Screen: Identity in the Age of the Internet* (New York: Simon and Schuster, 1995).

SADIE PLANT, THE FUTURE LOOMS: WEAVING WOMEN AND CYBERNETICS, PP. 123–35

1. Sophia Frend, quoted in Doris Langley Moore, *Ada, Countess of Lovelace* (London: John Murray, 1977), 44. Ada was Byron's only legitimate daughter and acquired her later surname from her husband, William King, Earl of Lovelace.
2. Ada Lovelace, 14 August 1843.
3. William Gibson and Bruce Sterling, *The Difference Engine* (New York: Bantam, 1992), 89.
4. William Carpenter, quoted in Moore; *Ada, Countess of Lovelace,* 202.
5. Ada Lovelace, 4 July 1843.
6. Ada Lovelace, 4 July 1843.
7. Frend, in Moore; *Ada, Countess of Lovelace,* 229.
8. Ibid., 198.
9. Lady Byron, June 1835.
10. Ada Lovelace, "Sketch of the Analytical Engine Invented by Charles Babbage by L.F. Menabrea. With Notes upon the Memoir by the Translator, Ada Augusta, Countess of Lovelace," in *Charles Babbage and His Calculating Engines, Selected Writings by Charles Babbage and Others,* ed. and introduced by Philip Morrison and Emily Morrison (New York: Dover, 1961), 250.
11. Charles Babbage, "Of the Analytical Engine," in ibid., 56.
12. Ibid., 251.
13. Ibid., 252.
14. Ibid.
15. Lucie Lamy, *Egyptian Mysteries* (New York: Thames and Hudson, 1981), 18.
16. Morrison and Morrison, *Charles Babbage and His Calculating Engines,* xxxiv.
17. Fernand Braudel, *Capitalism and Material Life 1400–1800* (London: Weidenfeld and Nicholson, 1973), 247.
18. Manuel de Landa, *War in the Age of Intelligent Machines* (Cambridge, MA: M.I.T. Press, 1992), 168.
19. Margaret Mead, *Cultural Patterns and Technical Change* (New York: Mentor Books, 1963), 247.
20. Ibid.
21. Sigmund Freud, "On Femininity," *New Introductory Lectures on Psychoanalysis,* The Pelican Freud Library, 2 (London: Viking Penguin, 1977), 166–67.
22. Sigmund Freud, *The Interpretation of Dreams,* The Pelican Freud Library, 4 (London: Viking Penguin, 1985), 388.
23. Lovelace, "Sketch of the Analytical Engine," 281.

24. Ibid., 264.
25. Ibid., 56.
26. Babbage, "Of the Analytical Engine," 53.
27. Ibid., 53.
28. Lovelace, "Sketch of the Analytical Engine," 285.
29. De Landa, *War in the Age of Intelligent Machines,* 162.
30. Allan Newell, in ibid., 63–64.
31. Luce Irigaray, *Marine Lover of Friedrich Nietzsche* (New York: Columbia University Press, 1991), 118.
32. Michael Heim, "The Metaphysics of Virtual Reality," in *Virtual Reality, Theory, Practice, and Promise,* ed. Sandra K. Helsel and Judith Paris Roth (Westport, CT: Meckler, 1991), 31.
33. Luce Irigaray, *Speculum of the Other Woman* (Ithaca, NY: Cornell University Press, 1985), 232.
34. Luce Irigaray, *Marine Lover of Friedrich Nietzsche* (New York: Columbia University Press, 1991), 116.
35. Ibid., 118.
36. Marshall McLuhan and Quentin Fiore, *War and Peace in the Global Village* (New York: Bantam Books, 1968), 89.
37. Irigaray, *Marine Lover of Friedrich Nietzsche,* 39.

John Perry Barlow, Selling Wine Without Bottles: The Economy of Mind on the Global Net, pp. 148–72

1. The thoughts in this essay have not been "mine" alone but have assembled themselves in a field of interaction which has existed between myself and numerous others, to whom I am grateful. They particularly include: Pamela Samuelson, Kevin Kelly, Mitch Kapor, Mike Godwin, Stewart Brand, Mike Holderness, Miriam Barlow, Danny Hillis, Trip Hawkins, and Alvin Toffler.

Guillermo Gómez-Peña, The Virtual Barrio @ the Other Frontier (or The Chicano Interneta), pp. 173–79

1. See www.sfgate.com/foundry/pochanostra.html

Part Four Notes

Lev Manovich, The Labor of Perception, pp. 183–93

1. Walter Benjamin, "On Some Motifs in Baudelaire," in *Illuminations*, ed. Hannah Arendt (New York: Schocken Books, 1969), 175.
2. On the connection between SIMNET and Battletech Center, see Tony Reveaux, "Virtual Reality Gets Real," *New Media* (January 1993), 36–41. On VR entertainment systems in the context of location-based entertainment—arcades and theme parks—see Richard Cook, "Serious Entertainment," *Computer Graphics World* 15, no. 5 (May 1992), 40–48.
3. Alphonse Chapanis, *Man-Machine Engineering* (Belmont, CA: Wadsworth

Publishing Company, Inc., 1965), 16.

4. In his textbook on human-machine systems Chapanis calls an automobile "a first rate example of a true man-machine system . . . a highly complex system in which the operator plays a commanding role or actively intervenes in the system from time to time," ibid.
5. Now, however, these shocks arrive exclusively through the visual channel (dials, computer screen, head-mounted display). Thus of the roles mentioned by Benjamin, the film viewer rather than the assembly line worker directly anticipates the experience of an operator in this type of human-machine situation.
6. Anson Rabinbach, *The Human Motor: Energy, Fatigue, and the Origins of Modernity* (New York: Basic Books, Inc., 1990), 3.
7. Ibid., 10.
8. Ibid., 68.
9. Frederick Winslow Taylor, *The Principles of Scientific Management* (New York: Harper, 1967).
10. William R. Spriegel and Clark E. Myers, eds., *The Writings of the Gilbreths* (Homewood, IL: R.D. Irwin, 1953).
11. Rabinbach, *The Human Motor,* 117, 277.
12. Marta Braun, *Picturing Time: The Work of Etienne-Jules Marey (1830–1904)* (Chicago: The University of Chicago Press, 1992), 337.
13. Quoted in Eliot Hearst, "One Hundred Years: Themes and Perspectives," in *The First Century of Experimental Psychology,* ed. Eliot Hearst (Hillsdale, NJ: Lawrence Erlbaum Associates, Publishers, 1979), 27.
14. Quoted in Douglas Noble, "Mental Materiel: The Militarization of Learning and Intelligence in U.S. Education," in *Cyborg Worlds: The Military Information Society,* ed. Les Levidow and Kevin Robins (London: Free Association Books, 1989), 34.
15. Quoted in ibid., 34–35.
16. Quoted in Rabinbach, *The Human Motor,* 298.
17. Ibid.
18. Morris Viteles, *Industrial Psychology* (New York: W.W. Norton & Company, Inc., 1932), 43.
19. Paul Fitts, "Engineering Psychology and Equipment Design," in *Handbook of Experimental Psychology,* ed. S. S. Stevens (New York and London: John Wiley & Sons, Inc., 1951), 1287–340.
20. Alphonse Chapanis, Wendell R. Garner, and Clifford T. Morgan, *Applied Experimental Psychology* (New York: John Wiley & Sons, Inc., 1949), v.
21. Ibid., 8.
22. William Estes, "Experimental Psychology: An Overview," in *The First Century of Experimental Psychology,* 630.
23. Chapanis, Garner, and Morgan, *Applied Experimental Psychology,* 7–8.
24. As Paul Fitts notes in his 1951 overview of engineering psychology, "Radar operators are often forced to search for weak signals at near-threshold levels." Fitts, "Engineering Psychology and Equipment Design," 1290.
25. Franklin Taylor, "Psychology at the Naval Research Laboratory," *American Psychologist* 2, no. 3 (1947), 87, 91.
26. On NASA/Ames virtual reality research in the 1980s, see Scott S. Fisher, "Virtual Interface Environments," in *The Art of Human-Computer Interface Design,* ed. Brenda Laurel (Reading, MA: Addison-Wesley Publishing Company, 1990), 423–38.

Florian Rötzer, Attack on the Brain: Reflections on Neurotechnology, pp. 194–209

1. Marvin Minsky, "Die Geistesmaschine," in *Chip Inside* (Erstes European Software Festival) (Wuerzburg: Vogel, 1991), 12.
2. Horst Prehn, "Koerperzeichen—Zeichenkoerper," in *Die Zukunft des Koerpers II, Kunstforum International* Bd. 133 (1996), 191f.
3. Filippo Tommaso Marinetti, "Technological Manifesto of Futurist Literature," in *Futurismus,* ed. Hansgeorg Schmidt-Bergmann (Reinbek bei Hamburg: Rowohlt, 1992), 288.
4. Paul Virilio, *Die Eroberung des Koerpers* (Munich: Hanser, 1994), 112.

Diana Gromala, Pain and Subjectivity in Virtual Reality, pp. 222–37

1. The French word *jouissance* may be translated as "extreme pleasure" and generally is connected to the prelinguistic infant or to an experience which defies representation. Sometimes associated with sexual pleasure, it is found in psychoanalytical discourses of D. W. Winnicott, Jacques Lacan, Julia Kristeva, and Luce Irigaray.
2. I refer specifically to American cultural production.
3. Archytas of Tarentim (c. 400–350 B.C.) was reported to have created an automaton in the form of a pigeon, remotely controlled by jets of steam or compressed air. At about the same time, the Chinese were purported to have created a mechanical orchestra controlled by remote operators. M. J. T. Louis, "Gearing in the Ancient World," *Endeavour* 17, no. 3 (September 1993), 110–116; and Larry Stevens, *Virtual Reality Now* (New York: MIS Press, 1994).
4. Donna J. Haraway, "A Cyborg Manifesto: Science, Technology, and Socialist-Feminism in the Late Twentieth Century," in *Simians, Cyborgs, and Women* (New York: Routledge, 1991).
5. Jean Baudrillard, *Simulations,* trans. Paul Foss, Paul Patton, and Philip Beitchman (New York: Semiotext[e], 1983).
6. Paul Virilio, *The Vision Machine* (London: British Film Institute and Bloomington and Indianapolis: Indiana University Press, 1994).
7. Fredric Jameson, "Postmodernism and Consumer Society," in *The Anti-Aesthetic: Essays on Postmodern Culture,* ed. Hal Foster (Seattle: Bay Press, 1983).
8. Gilles Deleuze and Felix Guattari, *A Thousand Plateaus,* trans. Brian Massumi (Minneapolis and London: University of Minnesota Press, 1987).
9. N. Katherine Hayles, "The Seductions of Cyberspace," in *Rethinking Technologies,* ed. Verena Andermatt Conley (Minneapolis and London: University of Minnesota Press, 1993), 174.
10. As Katherine Hayles reminds us, Jaron Lanier's view that VR will supplant language denies the underlying assembly language of VR computation, as well as the formation of our sensibilities through language. Because our sensibilities are formed through language, Hayles continues, language pervades even nonlinguistic domains. Ibid., 190, n. 38.
11. Jean-François Lyotard, *The Postmodern Condition: A Report on Knowledge* (Minneapolis: The University of Minnesota Press, 1988).
12. Haraway, "A Cyborg Manifesto," 181.
13. Hayles, "The Seductions of Cyberspace," 186–88.
14. Avital Ronell, "Our Narcotic Modernity," in *Rethinking Technologies,* ed. Verena Andermatt Conley (Minneapolis and London: University of Minnesota Press, 1993), 61.

15. Elizabeth Grosz, *Volatile Bodies* (Bloomington and Indianapolis: Indiana University Press, 1994), 192. See also Julia Kristeva, *Powers of Horror: An Essay on Abjection,* trans. Leon Roudiez (New York: Columbia University Press, 1982).
16. Elaine Scarry, *The Body in Pain: The Making and Unmaking of the World* (New York and Oxford: Oxford University Press, 1985; rpt. 1987), 5.
17. The discourses to which I refer include those proffered by such authors as William Gibson, O. B. Hardison, Jr., and Hans Moravec, among others. Many media representations of VR are similarly described in these terms. However, significant scholarship calls such a view into question, particularly the work of N. Katherine Hayles, Allucquere Rosanne Stone, and Anne Balsalmo.
18. Allucquere Rosanne Stone, "Virtual Systems," in *Incorporations,* ed. Jonathan Crary and Sanford Kwinter (New York: Zone Books, 1992; distributed by M.I.T. Press).
19. Scarry, *The Body in Pain,* 165.
20. Mircea Eliade, *Shamanism: Archaic Techniques of Ecstasy,* trans. Willard R. Trask (Princeton: Princeton University Press, 1964; rpt. 1972).
21. Scarry, *The Body in Pain,* 307.
22. Ronell, "Our Narcotic Modernity," 62.
23. Haraway, "A Cyborg Manifesto."
24. *Dancing with the Virtual Dervish: Virtual Bodies* was a project in Virtual Environments created by artist Diana Gromala and choreographer Yacov Sharir. It was funded by a major grant from the Canadian Government's Department of Communications and the Banff Centre for the Arts. The author wishes to recognize the computer scientists and engineers who collaborated: John Harrison, Glen Frazier, Graham Lindgren, and Chris Shaw, as well as Raonull Conover, computer artist. *Dancing with the Virtual Dervish: Virtual Bodies* has been performed at numerous international venues, including the Fifth Cyberspace Conference, the Art and Virtual Environments Symposium, the Second Biennial Conference on Art and Technology, and the International Society for Electronic Arts (ISEA).
25. Scarry, *The Body in Pain,* 31.

Catherine Richards, Fungal Intimacy: The Cyborg in Feminism and Media Art, pp. 258–63

1. This essay is based on work undertaken during my fellowship at the Canadian Centre for the Visual Arts, National Gallery of Canada, 1993–94. A longer version was presented to the International Symposium of Electronic Art, Helsinki, Finland, 1994.
2. Recent works include: *Spectral Bodies* (1991), a work with VR technology; *The Virtual Body* (1993), an interactive installation; *Curiosity Cabinet at the End of the Millennium* (1995); forthcoming, *Specimens* (1996), an Internet installation.
3. I followed Scott Fisher's work when he lead NASA's Ames Virtual Environments lab at Moffet Field, California. Consequently I was able to experience VR in the early eighties with the first VR system designed considering civilian use and developed with the glove interface with VPL.
4. From an early working paper of Rosi Braidotti's, later published in *Nomadic Subjects: Embodiment and Sexual Difference in Contemporary Feminist Theory* (New York: Columbia University Press, 1994).
5. Donna Haraway, "A Manifesto for Cyborgs: Science, Technology and Socialist Feminism in the 1980's," *Socialist Review* 80 (1985), 65–107.

6. Marvin Minsky, public presentation during Ars Electronica, Linz, Austria, 1990.
7. William Burroughs, "Is the Body Obsolete?" *Whole Earth Review* (Summer 1989), 54.
8. Jean-François Lyotard, "Designing the Social," in *Virtual Seminar on the Bioapparatus*, ed. Catherine Richards and Nell Tenhaaf (Banff: Banff Centre for the Arts, 1991), 28.
9. From an article by Sadie Plant published in the *Women and New Media* catalog for the Edge Festival.
10. Orlan, public presentation, "New Technology, Art and Gender," Institute of Contemporary Art (ICA), London, England, 1994.
11. Haraway, "A Manifesto for Cyborgs," 65, 67.

Part Five Notes

Rudolf Frieling, Hot Spots: Text in Motion and the Textscape of Electronic Media, pp. 267–78

1. "Mit dem Prinzip des entgrenzten Buches ist das Abenteuer moderner Literatur so tief verknüpft, dass man nicht zu sagen wüsste, was denn ein moderner Text sei, wenn nicht ein solcher, in dem die Zeilen und Seiten mit den Grenzen ihrer eigenen Darstellungskraft zu spielen begonnen haben," in Peter Sloterdijk, *Medien-Zeit* (Stuttgart, 1993), 60.
2. The religious background of condemning the image in Jewish, Protestant or, of course, Islamic traditions is obvious but can't be deepened in this context. It would be interesting, however, to examine how the consequences of interpreting a text of religious authority such as the Bible tend to generate an indefinite overflow of text commentary that bears an affinity to electronic textual processes.
3. Rudi Stern, *Let There Be Neon* (New York: H.N. Abrams, 1979), 132.
4. Quoted in Michael Auping, *Jenny Holzer* (New York: Universe, 1992), 73.
5. Ibid., 95.
6. "Some are very slow, a contrast to the regular MTV programming, and others are frenetic, even psychedelic. For example, there are speeding words with vapor trails going to a vanishing point." Jenny Holzer, quoted in Auping, *Jenny Holzer*, 101–2.
7. Her very first installation was a completely blue room that conveyed a loss of perspective.
8. See also Gary Hill's renowned visualization of the conflict between body and text in his videotape *Incidence of Catastrophe.*
9. Quoted in *Paintings* (Rotterdam: Museum Boymans-van Beuningen, 1989), 136.
10. Jay David Bolter, ed., *Writing Space: The Computer, Hypertext, and the History of Writing* (Hillsdale: L. Erlbaum Assoc., 1991), 60.
11. The term "hypertext" was coined by Ted Nelson in a text from the early seventies entitled "Dream Machines," in Bolter, *Writing Space,* 23.
12. Roland Barthes, *From Work to Text,* cited in Bolter, *Writing Space,* 161.
13. In *The Clearing* George Legrady used the metaphor of the hunter for one of the most coherent CD-ROMs that have been produced in the artistic domain.
14. Bolter, *Writing Space,* 59.
15. For Benjamin, this ambiguity was attached to the introduction of a similar device to annihilate distance: the telephone that was usually installed in the dark halls of the bourgeois apartment.

16. "Electronic writing opposes standardization and unification as well as hierarchy. It offers as a paradigm the text that changes to suit the reader rather than expecting the reader to conform to its standards." Bolter, *Writing Space,* 233.

Söke Dinkla, From Participation to Interaction: Toward the Origins of Interactive Art, pp. 279–90

1. See Regina Cornwell, "Interactive Art: Touching the 'Body in the Mind,'" *Discourse: Berkeley Journal for Theoretical Studies in Media and Culture,* no. 14.2 (Spring 1992), 203–21; Lynn Hershman, "Art-ificial Sub-versions, Inter-action, and the New Reality," *Camerawork: A Journal of Photographic Arts* 20, no. 1 (1993), 20–25. As early as 1966, Roy Ascott described "behavioristic," participative aspects in art from Futurism and Constructivism via kinetic art to Environments, reactive art and Happenings—without referring to interactive art, though. See Roy Ascott, "Behaviourist Art and the Cybernetic Vision," Part I, *Cybernetica: Review of the International Association for Cybernetics* 9, no. 4 (1966), 247–64.
2. Filippo Tommaso Marinetti, "The Variety Theater," in Michael Kirby and Victoria Nes Kirby, *Futurist Performance* (New York: PAJ Publications, 1986), 179–86.
3. See Michael Kirby, *Happenings: An Illustrated Anthology* (New York: Boulevard Books, 1965), 29f. Since a review of the exhibition in the *Kölnische Volkszeitung* of May 1, 1920, does not mention the ax, it can be assumed that the audience did not accept the offer. See Werner Spies, "Max Ernst and Dada in Cologne," *Max Ernst: Collagen* (Cologne: Kunsthalle Tübingen, 1988), 37–78.
4. Spies, *Max Ernst,* 246.
5. Dore Ashton, "An Interview with Marcel Duchamp," *Studio International* 171, no. 878 (June 1966), 244–47.
6. Kaprow was not pleased with the term "Happening": "The name 'Happening' is unfortunate. It was not intended to stand for an art form, originally. It was merely a neutral word that was part of a title of one of my projected ideas in 1958/59." See "A Statement," in Kirby, *Happenings,* 44–52.
7. Cornwell, "Interactive Art," 203–8. In 1983 Myron Krueger spoke of the "responsive environment," which to him is congruent with the term of interactive environment: "The Responsive Environment has closer ties with the Happening of the early 1960s in its attempt to involve the audience, than it does with these conventional modes of art." Myron Krueger, *Artificial Reality* (Reading, MA: Addison-Wesley, 1983), 50.
8. Erkki Huhtamo, "I am Interactive—Therefore—Am I?," in *Interaktiviisen taiteen näyttely* (Exhibition of Interactive Art) (Helsinki: Galerie Otso, Espoo, 1992), 5–7.
9. See, for example, Peter Weibel and Gerhard Johann Lischka, "Polylog für eine interaktive Kunst," *Kunstforum International* 103 (September/October 1989), 65–86; Itsuo Sakane, "Introduction to Interactive Art," in *Wonderland of Science Art: Invitation to Interactive Art* (Kanagawa, Japan: Kanagawa International Art and Science Exhibition, 1989), S.3–8, 38–42; Richard Wright, "Freedom and Interaction in New Media," in *Interactions: Rijksmuseum* (Enschede: Twenthe, 1990), S.24–30; Ann-Sargent Wooster, "Reach Out and Touch Someone: The Romance of Interactivity," in *Illuminating Video: An Essential Guide to Video Art,* ed. Doug Hall and Sally Jo Fifer (New York: Aperture, 1990), 275–303.
10. Allan Kaprow, "Interview with Peter Sager during the Cologne Exhibition Happening and Fluxus," *Kunstwerk,* no. 1 (1971), 5.

11. Johannes Lothar Schröder, *Identität, Überschreitung/Verwandlung: Happenings, Aktionen und Performances von Bildenden Künstlern* (Münster, 1990), 25.
12. For Myron Krueger, the "responsive environment" is a system whose reactions/programming range from simple forms of direct feedback via playful, dialogical involvement of the visitors to the establishment of the visitors as protagonists. See Krueger, *Artificial Reality,* 41–46. Concerning the term "reactive environment," see also James Seawright in Douglas Davis, *Art and the Future: A History-Prophecy of the Collaboration Between Science, Technology and Art* (New York: Praeger, 1973), 156.
13. Norbert Wiener, *The Human Use of Human Beings: Cybernetics and Society* (Boston, Houghton Mifflin: 1950); Norbert Wiener, *Cybernetics, or Control and Communication in the Animal and the Machine* (Cambridge, MA: M.I.T. Press, 1948).
14. Ascott, "Behaviourist Art and the Cybernetic Vision," part 1; also part 2, *Cybernetica: Review of the International Association for Cybernetics* 10, no.1 (1967), 25–56.
15. Jack Burnham, *Beyond Modern Sculpture: The Effects of Science and Technology on the Sculpture of This Century* (New York: G. Braziller, 1969), 332ff, 356. The term "cyborg" is composed of the first syllables of the words "cybernetic" and "organism." In contrast to Burnham, Ascott defines the term "cybernetics" in a broader sense. He does not attribute it to a certain art genre, but sees it as an expression of a general social development. Norbert Wiener defines feedback as "the control of a system by reinserting into the system the results of its performance. . . . In its simplest form, the feedback principle means that behavior is scanned for its results, and that the success or failure of this result modifies future behavior" (*The Human Use of Human Beings* rev. ed.[New York: Da Capo, 1988], 69, 71).
16. See Burnham, *Beyond Modern Sculpture,* 340.
17. Nicolas Schöffer, *La Ville Cybernetique* (Paris: Tchou, 1969).
18. Henry R. Liebermann, "Art and Science Proclaim Alliance in Avant-Garde Loft," *The New York Times,* October 11, 1967, S.49.
19. On *Variations V,* see Davis, *Art and the Future,* 50, 85; Monique Fong, "On Art and Technology," *Studio International* 177, no. 907 (January 1969), 5f.
20. *Nine Evenings: Theater and Engineering* was performed at the 25th Street Armory, New York, on October 13–16, 18–19, 21–23, 1966.
21. Ibid.
22. As early as 1960 Rauschenberg reflected on an environment where temperature, smell, and sound could be influenced by the visitors. See Billy Klüver and Julie Martin, "Four Difficult Pieces," *Art in America* (July 1991), 80–99, 135.
23. Ibid., 86f.
24. *TV as a Creative Medium, 1969* (New York: Whitney Museum of American Art, 1994, brochure on the partial reconstruction of the exhibition of the same name in the Howard Wise Gallery in 1969). The 1969 show was the first exhibition devoted entirely to video art.
25. See Edith Decker, *Paik* (video) (Cologne 1988), 64f, and Nam June Paik in an interview with Douglas Davis, *Art and the Future,* 185.
26. Dick Higgins, "Intermedia," *The Something Else Newsletter* 1, no. 1 (February 1966), reprinted in *Intermedia '93* (Heidelberg: Edition Tangente and AG Kunst am Klausenpfad, 1969), unpag. Higgins was a member of the Fluxus group, which was formed by John Cage's class at the New School for Social Research. Beginning in 1962 the group staged simple nonnarrative forms of action with its "Fluxcelebrations."

27. See Thomas Dreher, "Après John Cage, Zeit in der Kunst der sechziger Jahre—von Fluxus-Events zu interaktiven Multi-Monitor-Installationen," in *Kunst als Grenzbeschreitung: John Cage und die Moderne* (Munich: Bayerische Staatsgemäldesammlungen, Neue Pinakothek, 1991), 57–74, 86.
28. Weibel and Lischka, "Polylog für eine interaktive Kunst," and Peter Weibel, "Momente der Interaktivität," *Kunstforum International* 103 (September/October 1989), 87f.

JEAN GAGNON, DIONYSUS IN WONDERLAND: A FEW MUSICAL METAPHORS IN TECHNO-CULTURE, PP. 291–305

1. James M. Curtis, *Culture as Polyphony: An Essay on the Nature of Paradigms* (Columbia and London: Missouri University Press, 1978).
2. Ibid., 39.
3. Hans Robert Jauss, *Pour une esthétique de la réception (For an Aesthetic of Reception)* (Paris: Gallimard, 1978).
4. Bill Viola, "The Sound of One Line Scanning," in *Sound by Artists*, ed. Dan Lander and Micah Lexier (Banff: Walter Phillips Gallery; Toronto: Art Metropole, 1990), 44.
5. Frances Dyson, "In/Quest of Presence: Virtuality, Aurality, and Television's Gulf War," in *Critical Issues in Electronic Media*, ed. Simon Penny (Albany: State University of New York Press, 1995).
6. See Paul Ricoeur in *Temps et récit (Time and Narration)*, 3 vols. (Paris: Éditions du Seuil, 1983–85).
7. See *Eigenwelt der Apparate-Welt: Pioneers of Electronic Art*, catalogue published by David Dunn for an exhibition organized by Woody and Steina Vazulka (Linz, Austria, 1992).
8. Jean Brun, *Le retour de Dionysos (The Return of Dionysus)* (Paris: Desclée, 1969), 112.
9. Ibid., 114.
10. Jean Brun, *Les masques du désir (The Masks of Desire)* (Paris: Buchet/Castel, 1981).
11. Friedrich Nietzsche, *La naissance de la tragédie (The Birth of Tragedy)* (Paris: Denoël/Gonthier, Bibliothèque médiations, 1970), 104.
12. Brun, *Le retour de Dionysos*, 102.
13. Nietzsche, *La naissance de la tragédie*, 93.
14. Brun, *Le retour de Dionysos*, 118, 119, 80.
15. Guy Debord, *La société du spectacle (The Society of the Spectacle)* (Paris: Gallimard, 1993), 4.
16. Jacques Attali, *Bruits: Essai sur l'économie politique de la musique (Noises: Essay on the Political Economy of Music)*, Collection Biblio essais (Paris: PUF, 1977).
17. Ibid., 137.
18. Ibid., 57.
19. Debord, *La société du spectacle*, 13.
20. Ibid., 15, aphorism 28.
21. Attali, *Bruits*, 57.
22. Julia Kristeva, *Polylogue*, Collection Tel quel (Paris: Éditions du Seuil, 1977), 119.
23. Ibid., 374.
24. Ibid., 14, 57, 206.
25. Roland Barthes, *L'obvie et l'obtus: Essais critiques III (The Obvious and the Obtuse: Critical Essays III)*, Collection Tel quel (Paris: Éditions du Seuil, 1977), 229.

ERKKI HUHTAMO, DIGITALIAN TREASURES, OR GLIMPSES OF ART ON THE CD-ROM FRONTIER, PP. 306–17

1. This statement excludes, of course, different video game cartridge formats, which are closed systems for a particular purpose. The CD-ROM was announced by Sony and Philips in 1983, as a further development of the research that led to the introduction of the CD-Digital Audio the year before. This explains some of the problems the format has: as an extension of the CD-DA, the CD-ROM was originally meant for data publishing and archival purposes, not for consumer-oriented multimedia (see David Rosen, "Multimedia and Future Media," *Multimedia: Gateway to the Next Millennium,* ed. Robert Aston and Joyce Schwartz [Cambridge, MA: AP Professional, 1994], 230, 235). A draft standard for encoding information on the CD-ROM was accepted in 1985, and an international standard in 1987. CD-ROM products began to appear on the market at the end of the 1980s (see Roy Rada, *Interactive Media* [New York: Springer-Verlag, 1995], 65).
2. The situation will improve in the coming years with the introduction of high-density CDs and new digital video standards (see Hal Glatzer, "High-Density CDs Set for Showdown," *New Media* [June 1995], 17–18).
3. This is true even in the case of video artworks that combine material from different sources, abandoning the linear structuring of commercial film and television to pursue a more metaphorical approach. However, even then the nonlinearity remains subordinate to the "flow," not fully supported by the (delivery) medium.
4. George P. Landow, *Hypertext: The Convergence of Contemporary Critical Theory and Technology* (Baltimore: The Johns Hopkins University Press, 1992).
5. Michael Punt, "CD-ROM: Radical Nostalgia? Cinema History, Cinema Theory, and New Technology," *Leonardo* 28, no. 5 (1995), 388.
6. Frank Ricketts states, "There is overwhelming evidence that all-digital media will predominate in the interactive technologies of the future. . . . The implications of this move away from analogue are enormous" ("Multimedia," in *Future Visions: New Technologies of the Screen,* ed. Philip Hayward and Tana Wollen [London: BFI, 1993], 74). Marketing consultant David Rosen speculates, "While it is dangerous to prognosticate on the future, it seems clear from today's vantage point that the media world beyond 2001 will likely witness the expanded performance capabilities of digital media. Going further, it seems that this media will likely be transformed into an increasingly 'plastic' media, fostering a communications experience that aspires to become quasi-organic in form and function" ("Multimedia and Future Media," in *Multimedia: Gateway to the Next Millennium,* 230).
7. Although the first CD-ROM products and commercial online services came into existence in the late 1980s, the real rush into these markets began around 1993. The rapidity of change can be proven by looking at back issues of *Wired* magazine from 1993 on. Take, for example, the prediction in vol. 2, no. 10 (October 1994), 13: "Don't look now, but Prodigy, AOL, and CompuServe are all suddenly obsolete—and Mosaic is well on its way to becoming the world's standard interface to electronic information." I can almost imagine a Netscape user asking, perplexed: "What was Mosaic?" *Wired's* spectacular growth in only two years into the most widely circulated and influential mainstream vehicle for the American technoculture (with circulation well over 100,000) is in itself interesting, and will make *Wired* one of the main sources for the mentalities of the 1990s. *Wired's* rise to fame, fortune, and power has also raised criticism and hostility, even among its former supporters. After all, *Mondo 2000* hasn't changed much over the years, to say nothing about the *Whole Earth Review* . . .

8. This impression is echoed in Marie d'Amico's instructions for a beginning multimedia developer: "You can choose a content provider from the film, music, radio, or television industries. Or you can align yourself with those who have withstood market onslaughts from others and diagnoses of doom for 50 years—book publishers" (Marie d'Amico, "Developing Interactive Books: Using Pre-made Content to Save Time and Money," *InterActivity* [September/October 1995], 22).
9. About the notion of "entertainment supersystem," see Marsha Kinder, *Playing with Power in Movies, Television, and Video Games* (Berkeley: University of California Press, 1991), 3. Kinder's main example is the supersystem constructed around Teenage Mutant Ninja Turtles.
10. The Voyager Company was founded in 1984 by Robert Stein, Aleen Stein, William Becker, and Jonathan Turell as a joint venture between Voyager Press and Janus Films. The company originally produced video laserdisks. It published their first CD-ROM title in 1989. Another well-known Voyager product is their Expanded Books series released on floppy disks.
11. See the list of the CD-ROM works at the end of the article.
12. About the art world's uneasy relationship with digital art, see Daniel Pinchbeck, "State of the Art," *Wired* 2, no.12 (December 1994), 156–59, 206–8. In Pinchbeck's article David Ross, the director of the Whitney Museum of American Art, makes a revealing comment: "We are going to commission artists to create works for the Whitney [Web] site, the 'A list' of artists you might want to see in this medium, from Laurie Anderson to Robert Rauschenberg." Pinchbeck's comment is worth quoting: "Although Ross's engagement with the medium demonstrates courage and foresight, it will be a shame if the Whitney resorts to his 'A list,' which will only further centralize power around a few 'art stars.' Art-world politics might force places like the Whitney to promote the same old celebrity system. But the almost unlimited distribution power of the Internet could give artists a chance to reach a vast new audience, if they take matters into their own hands."
13. Among my favorites are Jim Gasperini's, Tennessee Rice Dixon's, and Charlie Morrow's poetic and dreamy interactive "book" *ScruTiny in the Great Round* (1995) and George Legrady's independently produced *An Anecdoted Archive from the Cold War* (1994), a "memory archive," which allows the user to explore the intertwining histories of Communist Hungary and the fates of the artist's expatriate family.
14. Significantly, the Millers learned their trade by designing children's multimedia titles, such as *Cosmic Osmo.*
15. *Wired* made a major contribution to their mythologization with a cover feature by Jon Carroll, "Guerrillas in the Myst," *Wired* 2, no. 8 (August 1994), 69–73. On the article's opening page the brothers were shown standing in the midst of clouds in the sky, in a setting familiar from Christian iconography. Self-conscious and ironic, sure. But then again . . .
16. John Simmons, "Sade and Cyberspace," in *Resisting the Virtual Life: The Culture and Politics of Information,* ed. James Brook and Iain A. Boal (San Francisco: City Lights, 1995), 155.
17. It is tempting to relate the "transfiguration" of *Myst* to the early attempts to raise the "moving pictures" to the status of art at the beginning of the twentieth century (most emphatically by the Film d'Art movement, which began in 1908 in France and soon spread to other countries). It is clear now that the cultural pretensions behind Film d'Art were mainly motivated by the young industry's need

to extend its audience to the wealthy middle classes. The difference lies, of course, in the fact that where Film d'Art recruited the famous actress Sarah Bernhardt to convince the bourgeoisie of its cultural value, the Miller brothers have appeared practically out of the blue, certainly without high cultural pretensions. Perhaps another kind of American myth, that of the self-made man, has been activated here (this was, in fact, also D. W. Griffith's background). About Film d'Art, see Davide Turconi: "From Stage to Screen," in *Sulla via di Hollywood 1911–1920, a cura di Paolo Cherchi Usai & Lorenzo Codelli* (Pordenone: Edizioni Biblioteca dell'Immagine, 1988), 16–32. The cultural pretensions were personified in the development of D. W. Griffith. See Larry May, *Screening Out the Past: The Birth of Mass Culture and the Motion Picture Industry* (Chicago: Oxford University Press, 1980), chap. IV.

18. Interestingly, less than covert references to *Myst* were used to provide this dimension of quality in the interactive music video released by The Artist Formerly Known as Prince (Time Warner Interactive, 1994), but with little success.
19. *The Freak Show* was directed by Jim Ludtke. See Gaye L. Graves, "Jim Ludtke: Multimedia Surrealist," *New Media* (June 1995), 99–100.
20. See Lynn Ginsburg, "Twin Peaks Meets SimCity," *Wired* 3, no. 9 (September 1995), 110–21. Ludtke and the Residents have since realized a new CD-ROM called *Bad Day on the Midway*. After *The Freak Show* the group released an "enhanced" CD called *Gingerbread Man* (Voyager, 1994), with some interactive audiovisual material.
21. *All New Gen* deconstructs the ideology underlying the video game culture, identifying it as the embodiment of the male dominion in global capitalism. VNS Matrix does this by appropriating the form of a Nintendo video game and producing its own détourned "game-girl" version. Linda Dement has produced a female "monster" from image-processed representations of "donated" female body parts. *Cyberflesh Girlmonster* brings into light the darker, "monstrous" side of femininity.
22. Artist and critic Christine Tamblyn printed her CD-ROM *She Loves It, She Loves It Not: Women and Technology* (1993) privately and sold it directly from her bag. This curiously recalls Maya Deren renting her early avant-garde films from her own flat in New York in the 1940s.
23. Mikki Halpin, "Fringeware: Our Guide to Weird, Offbeat, and Underground Electronic Publishing," *CD-ROM Power* 1, no. 2 (March/April 1995), 96–97.
24. The Rocket Science hype was "officially" launched by *Wired* magazine in its cover feature "Rocket Science," by Burr Snider, *Wired* 2, no. 11 (November 1994), 108–13, 159–62. Snider used the expression "the first digital supergroup."
25. Ted Nelson has connected the success of *Doom* to the hacker tradition, which produced Apple Computer. He sees "3-D engines like *Doom*" as challenges to the industry-produced, expensive high-end visualization software. "Nobody thought shareware could work in the big-time entertainment world. They were wrong." (Ted Nelson, "Doomsday 3-D's Here to Stay," *New Media* [January 1995], 16).
26. See Mikki Halpin, "Consumer Product: Political Art Comes to CD-ROM," *CD-ROM Power* 1, no. 1 (February 1995), 23–28.
27. Michael Punt, "CD-ROM: Radical Nostalgia?" *Leonardo* 28, no. 5 (1995), 338.
28. The members of the Media Band are Marc Canter, Jim Collins, Stuart Sharpe, Kelley Gabriel, Chris Watkins, John Sanborn, Mark Shephard, Allison Prince, and Michael Kaplan. Their first product was the CD-ROM *Meet the Media Band*

(1994). John Sanborn, one of the most renowned video artists of the 1980s, forms a bridge into the interactive multimedia of the 1990s. Sanborn has also produced his first interactive CD-ROM.

29. For an overview of online CD-ROM hybrid systems, see Domenic Stansberry, "Going Hybrid: The Online/CD-ROM Connection," *New Media* (June 1995), 34–40. See also Jeffrey Adam Young, "Interactive World's Fair: The Internet's First Theme Park," *CD-ROM Power* 1, no. 2 (March/April 1995), 24–28.

LYNN HERSHMAN LEESON, ROMANCING THE ANTI-BODY: LUST AND LONGING IN (CYBER)SPACE, PP. 325–37

1. Howard Rheingold, *The Virtual Community: Homesteading on the Electronic Frontier* (New York: Harper Perennial, 1994), 165.
2. Quoted in ibid.
3. Mark Stuart Gill, "Terror On Line," *Vogue* (January 1995), 163–65.
4. Kevin Kelley, *Out of Control* (Reading, MA: Addison-Wesley Publishing, 1994), 286–88.
5. There is a relationship between Duchamp and his contemporary, Werner Heisenberg. Heisenberg's theories in quantum mechanics of the observer affecting what is observed metaphorically reflects Duchamp's "experiments" regarding randomness and chance. They were traveling to the same place, but on different roads. Wayne Black, unpublished essay, "We Are All Roberta Breitmore: A Post Mortem on Modernism," 1994.
6. *The Dante Hotel* was created with Eleanor Coppola.
7. *Deep Contact* was created with Sara Roberts and Jim Crutchfield.
8. *Room of One's Own* was created with Sara Roberts and Palle Henchel.
9. *America's Finest* was created with Paul Tompkins and Mat Heckert.
10. *The Internet Project* is being created with Fred Dust.

SIEGFRIED ZIELINSKI, 7 ITEMS ON THE NET, PP. 338–43

1. Dave Warner et al., "Biokybernetik-Eine biologisch gesteuerte interaktive Schnittstelle," in *Ars Electronica Catalogue* (Linz, Austria, 1994), 200.
2. Katja Wolff, *Der Kabbalistische Baum: Adams Schlüssel zum Paradies* (Munich: Knaut, 1989), 10.
3. Edmond Jabes, in *Die Schrift der Wuste,* ed. F. P. Ingold (Berlin: Merve, 1989), 69f.
4. Guy Debord, *The Society of the Spectacle* (London: Rebel Press, 1992), 71.

Contributors

JOHN PERRY BARLOW is a cofounder and the current vice chairman of the Electronic Frontier Foundation. He is a recognized commentator on virtual reality, digitized intellectual property, computer security, and the social and legal conditions arising from the global network of digital devices. Barlow is a contributing editor to numerous publications, including *Communications of the ACM*, *Microtimes*, and *MONDO 2000*, and writes for *Wired*.

SIMON BIGGS creates interactive installations, prints, and animations. He studied electronic and computer music and continues to work with composers. With his father, a computer scientist, Biggs developed a graphics-dedicated computer system in 1979. His early paintings focused on conceptual and formal concerns about language and systems of control. His current work, which is metaphorical, symbolic, poetic, and often text-based, falls between the genres of experimental installation art, video art, traditional animation, and computer art.

SÖKE DINKLA is an art critic and curator in the field of new media. She studied art history, biology, and German literature and ethnology at the Universities of Kiel, Hamburg, and Bielefeld. She received an M.A. in 1992 and has completed her Ph.D. thesis at the University of Hamburg. Dinkla has written articles on interactive art, design, and holography for European magazines and has lectured at international conferences such as the International Symposium on Electronic Art in Helsinki and the 28th International Congress for the History of Art in Berlin.

RUDOLF FRIELING is the video curator at the Center for Art and Media, Karlsruhe, Germany. He studied literature, social sciences, and art history at the Free University of Berlin. From 1988 to 1994 he was curator of the International VideoFest Berlin, associated with the Berlin Film Festival. Since 1990 he has contributed as a freelance critic of art and video to various newspapers and magazines. In 1992 he was co-editor of *Scope*, a European magazine of media art.

JEAN GAGNON is the associate curator of media arts at the National Gallery of Canada, where he is responsible for the exhibition and acquisition of film, video, and new media. He has taught courses on interactivity and the media at institutions such as Carleton University, Ottawa; Concordia University, Montreal; and the Université du Québec, Montreal.

GUILLERMO GÓMEZ-PEÑA is an interdisciplinary artist and writer. He was born and raised in Mexico City and came to the United States in 1978. Gómez-Peña explores cross-cultural issues and north-south relations through performance, bilingual poetry, journalism, video, radio, and installation art. He has contributed to the national radio programs *Crossroads* and *Latino USA*, and is a contributing editor to *High Performance* and *The Drama Review*. Gómez-Peña is a 1991 recipient of the MacArthur Fellowship. He is the author of *Warrior for Gringostroika* (Gray Wolf Press, 1993) and *The New World Border* (City Lights, 1996).

DIANA GROMALA is an assistant professor at the University of Washington in Seattle, where she founded and directs the New Media Research Laboratory. She also conducts research at the university's Human Interface Technology Laboratory. A former art director and interface designer at Apple Computer and a current Fulbright scholar, Gromala studies the relationships among virtual environments, media studies, and interface design. She frequently lectures at international conferences and symposia for organizations such as the National Endowment for the Arts. Her work in virtual environments has been presented at venues in Canada, the United States, Europe, and the Middle East and has been aired on the Discovery Channel. Her forthcoming book is entitled *Recombinant Devices: Ideologies of Virtual Design*.

LYNN HERSHMAN LEESON is an artist who works in diverse media, including photography, film, video, installation, and computers. She created the first interactive artwork, *Lorna*. Her work has been awarded prizes at many international film festivals, and she was the first woman and electronic artist to receive a retrospective at the San Francisco International Film Festival. She is the recipient of a

National Endowment for the Arts Grant for New Genres, the ZKM Media Art Award, the WDR Cyberstar Award, and the Seattle Art Museum's Ann Gerber Award. She has had over 150 one-person shows in museums throughout the world, has made 52 videotapes and films, and has written for numerous publications. Her current projects are a feature film for German and French television and a commission for the opening of the Mediamuseum in Karlsruhe, Germany. Hershman Leeson is a professor of electronic art at the University of California, Davis.

ERKKI HUHTAMO is a media researcher, educator, and curator. Between 1994 and 1996 he was professor of media studies, University of Lapland, Finland. He has published widely on the aesthetics and development of media art and on media archaeology. He has also served on several international juries, such as Interactive Media Festival (L.A., 1995) and Portraits in Cyberspace (M.I.T. Media Laboratory, 1995), and curated several international art exhibitions. He has scripted and directed three television series on media culture for Finnish television.

JOICHI ITO is a bi-cultural entrepreneur and writer who divides his time between Japan and the United States. Currently he is president of the Shima Media Network and Open Doors.

MIZUKO ITO is an advanced doctoral student at the Stanford School of Education and Department of Anthropology. As a researcher at the Institute for Research on Learning, Palo Alto, she is studying simulation games, Internet systems, and virtual reality. Her past work includes ethnographic user studies and field research for a computer-based math curriculum. Her interests include the multiple identities of Internet users, the technical and social apparatuses undergirding the Internet, participatory issues in the design of the Internet, and the use of new simulation technologies by children and teens.

ARTHUR AND MARILOUISE KROKER are internationally recognized writers and lecturers in the areas of technology and contemporary culture. Their extensive writings, published by St. Martin's Press, include *Spasm* (1993), *Data Trash* (1994), and *Hacking the Future*

(1996). They have co-edited the Culture Texts series and a trilogy of books on contemporary feminist theory: *Body Invaders* (1987–88), *The Hysterical Male* (1991), and *The Last Sex* (1993). They also co-edit the electronic journal *CTHEORY.*

JARON LANIER, a computer scientist, composer, and author, is best known for his work in virtual reality. He coined the term, co-invented fundamental components, and founded the industry by starting VPL Research, Inc. As a computer scientist, Lanier is a pioneer in the field of visual programming. He has been a composer and performer in the world of new classical music since the late seventies, performing with artists such as Philip Glass and Ornette Coleman. Two books by Lanier are forthcoming from Harcourt Brace and M.I.T. Press. He is currently a visiting scholar at Columbia University and the Tisch School of the Arts, New York University.

ARTHUR H. LESTER practices law and medicine in Fort Walton Beach, Florida. He has published articles on the ethics of conception and birth, assisted suicide, and physician-patient confidentiality. In addition to presenting seminars on risk management for nurses and physicians and acting as a senior seminarian on health law at Florida State University, Lester serves on the bio-ethics and credentials committees of Fort Walton Beach Medical Center, and on the risk management committee of the health law section of the Florida Bar Association.

MARK LUDWIG is a graduate of Caltech and the University of Arizona, and holds a Ph.D. in theoretical physics. He is the author of *The Little Black Book of Computer Viruses* (1991), *The Giant Black Book of Computer Viruses* (1995), and *Computer Viruses, Artificial Life and Evolution.* He owns a small publishing company, American Eagle Publications, Inc., in Show Low, Arizona, which publishes books about computers, science, and history.

PATTIE MAES is an associate professor at the M.I.T. Media Laboratory, where she holds the Sony Career Development chair. Previously, she was visiting professor and research scientist at the M.I.T. Artificial Intelligence Laboratory. From 1983 to 1989 she was a research scientist for the Belgian National Science Foundation. Maes has authored numerous articles on autonomous interactive agents and has edited four books, among them *Designing Autonomous Agents: Theory and Practice from Biology to Engineering and Back* (M.I.T. Press, 1990). She is one of the project leaders for the award-winning Artificial Life Interactive Video Environment system.

LEV MANOVICH is a theorist and critic of new media. He has lectured widely at major international festivals and symposia on electronic art, and his writings have been published in seven countries. Trained in fine arts and computer science, he also holds an M.A. in experimental psychology and a Ph.D. in visual and cultural studies. Since 1993 he has been an assistant professor at the University of Maryland, where he teaches the theory and history of media, computer graphics, and computer animation. Currently he is a Mellon Fellow in Art Criticism at the California Institute of the Arts. He is working on a book entitled *The Engineering of Vision from Constructivism to Virtual Reality*, a collection of essays on digital realism, and a CD-ROM on the archaeology of digital media.

CHRISTIAN MÖLLER is the director of Archimedia, a new center for architecture and media in Linz, Austria. He studied architecture in Frankfurt and was a postgraduate at the Academy of Fine Arts in Vienna with Gustav Peichl. After working with the firm Behnisch and Partner, he established an architectural office that incorporated a laboratory for electronic media and software development. Möller has been an associate at the Institute for New Media at the Städelschule in Frankfurt since 1991.

SADIE PLANT has recently become a research fellow in cybernetic culture at the University of Warwick, England. Her book *The Most Radical Gesture: The Situationist International in a Postmodern Age* was published by Routledge in 1992.

SHELDON RENAN is best known for his work with advanced-technology audience environments and interactive pavilions and entertainment centers. He has worked extensively for technology companies such as Xerox, Sony, IBM, and Apple. After graduating from Yale University, Renan wrote television commercials while finishing *Introduction to the American Underground Film* (Dutton, 1967). He founded the Pacific Film Archive at the University of California, Berkeley. Renan also writes scripts for popular entertainment and has directed English language versions of foreign films. His company Renan/Margolis, in Santa Monica, produces videos, conferences, and events for Fortune 100 companies.

CATHERINE RICHARDS is a visual artist whose work explores new technologies' simulation of the body and subjectivity. Her award-winning pieces *Spectral Bodies*, *The Virtual Body*, and *Curiosity Cabinet at the End of the Millennium* have been shown at international museums and media festivals. Richards has initiated events investigating the relation of postmodern and cultural theory to new imaging technologies. She co-directed Bioapparatus, an artists' residency and publication of the Banff Centre for the Arts, Alberta. In 1993–95 she was awarded fellowships at the National Gallery of Canada. She is currently an artist-in-residence at the National Gallery and at Xerox Palo Alto Research Center.

DAVID A. ROSS has been the director of the Whitney Museum of American Art, New York, since 1991. Previously he was the director of the Institute of Contemporary Art, Boston (1982–91); founding master of F.A.C.I.E. (Federal Advisory Commission on Major International Exhibitions (1987–91); chief curator and assistant director for collections and programs at the University Art Museum, University of California, Berkeley (1977–82); and deputy director and chief curator of Long Beach Museum of Art, California (1971–74). Ross has taught and lectured at colleges and universities, including the San Francisco Art Institute; the University of California, San Diego; and Harvard University. He has also contributed to numerous publications and journals.

FLORIAN RÖTZER is a freelance writer and journalist living in Munich. He has written extensively about philosophy, science, technology, and art in the digital culture. He has conceptualized, organized, and edited several catalogues for conferences: *Strategies of Fiction* (Frankfurt, 1990), *Cyberspace—on the Way to the Digital Oeuvre* (Munich, 1991), *From Simulation to Stimulation* (Graz, 1993),

Artificial Games (Munich, 1993), *Illusion and Simulation* (Munich, 1994), and *The Evil* (Bonn, 1994). His recent work includes the publication *Future of the Body*, an exhibition about digital photography, and *Telepolis*, an exhibition, catalogue, and conference about the colonization of cyberspace and its impact on real cities.

R.U. SIRIUS is the cofounder and former editor-in-chief of *MONDO 2000*, the original cyber-culture magazine. He is co-author of *MONDO 2000: A User's Guide to the New Edge* (HarperCollins, 1991), *Cyberpunk Handbook: The Real Cyberpunk Fakebook* (Random House, 1995), and *How to Mutate and Take Over the World* (Ballantine Books, 1996). He is a regular columnist for *Artforum International*, *Japan Esquire*, *Wave*, and *21C* and a contributing editor for *Wired* and *bOING bOING.*

ALLUCQUERE ROSANNE (SANDY) STONE is assistant professor in the Department of Radio-TV-Film and director of the Advanced Communication Technologies Laboratory at the University of Texas at Austin. She is director of the Group for the Study of Virtual Systems at the Center for Cultural Studies, University of California, Santa Cruz. In recent years she has served on the program committee for the annual International Conference on Cyberspace. In addition to numerous articles and essays, she wrote *The War of Desire* and *Technology at the Close of the Mechanical Age* (M.I.T. Press, 1995). Her recent work includes *The Gaze of the Vampire: Tales from the Edges of Identity.*

METTE STRØMFELDT is completing her Ph.D. at the University of Copenhagen. She writes both fiction and nonfiction, works with hypermedia, and has authored experimental video with grants from Danish film and video workshops and the Danish Government Film Office. She co-edited The Copenhagen Film + Video Workshop Festival 1990.

SHERRY TURKLE is a professor of sociology at M.I.T. She has a joint doctorate in sociology and personality psychology from Harvard University. Her extensive writings on psychoanalysis and the cultural impact of the computer include *Psychoanalytic Politics: Jacques Lacan and Freud's French Revolution* (rev. ed., Guilford Press, 1992), *The Second Self: Computers and the Human Spirit* (Simon and Schuster, 1984), and *Life on the Screen: Identity in the Age of the Internet* (Simon and Schuster, 1995). She has received support for her research from the National Science Foundation and the MacArthur, Guggenheim, and Rockefeller Foundations. Her work has been widely written about in both the academic and popular press, and she has been a guest on numerous radio and television shows.

SIEGFRIED ZIELINSKI is the director of the Institute for Multimedia Research at the University of Cologne. He has written numerous books in the areas of art, philosophy, and communications, including *Audiovisions: Film and Television as an Interlude in History* (Hamburg, 1989).

Credits

"Multimedia, CD-ROM, and the Net," by Simon Biggs, was originally published under the title "Sentient Selves," in the 1995 Berlin Videofest catalogue, as part of the multimedia program, of which the writer was the director.

"A Plain Text on Crypto-Policy," by John Perry Barlow, was originally published in *Communications of the ACM* 36, no. 11 (November 1993).

"From Participation to Interaction: Toward the Origins of Interactive Art," by Söke Dinkla, was originally published in German in *Interferenzen* 6, no. 1–2 (1995), and in English in the catalogue of the European Media Art Festival, ed. H. Nöring, A. Rotert, R. Sausmikat (Osnabrück, 1995).

"Code Warriors: Bunkering In and Dumbing Down," by Arthur and Marilouise Kroker, is an excerpt from *Hacking the Future* (New York: St. Martin's Press, 1996).

"Romancing the Anti-Body: Lust and Longing in (Cyber)space," by Lynn Hershman Leeson, is reprinted from the ZKM Medienprize catalog, May 1995.

"Artificial Life Meets Entertainment: Lifelike Autonomous Agents," by Pattie Maes, was originally published in Special Issue on Novel Applications of AI, *Communications of the ACM*, 1995.

"The Labor of Perception" ("Die Arbeit der Wahrnehmung"), by Lev Manovich, was originally published in *Scöne neue Welten?*, ed. Florian Rötzer (Munich: Klaus Boer Verlag, 1995).

"The Future Looms: Weaving Women and Cybernetics," by Sadie Plant, was originally published in *Broadsheet Adelaide.*

"Fungal Intimacy: The Cyborg in Feminism and Media Art," by Catherine Richards, was originally published in *Fractal Dreams* (London: Lawrence & Wishart, 1995).

"7 Items on the Net," by Siegfried Zielinski, first appeared in the journal *CTHEORY* on the Internet.

Illustration Credits

Page 2: Lynn Hershman Leeson

Page 40: Lynn Hershman Leeson

Page 70: Lynn Hershman Leeson

Page 139: Christian Möller

Page 180: Lynn Hershman Leeson

Page 211: Dimitri Terzopoulos

Page 212: Naoko Tosa

Page 213: Pattie Maes

Page 214: Dialogue for Julia, autonomous conversing agent, copyright 1990 by Ashne

Page 216: Pattie Maes

Page 234: Diana Gromala

Page 236: Diana Gromala

Page 264: Lynn Hershman Leeson

Also of Interest from Bay Press

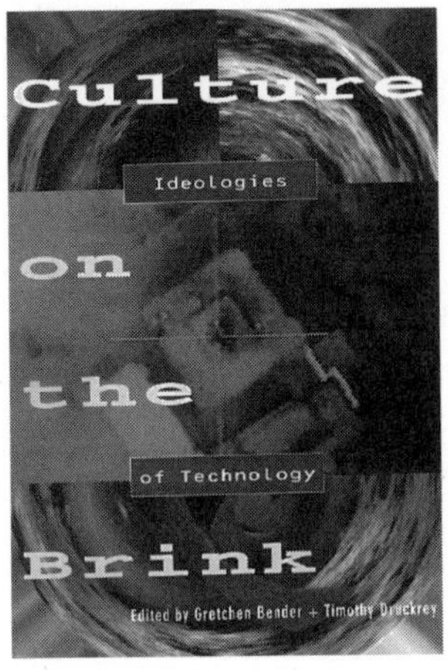

Culture on the Brink: Ideologies of Technology

Discussions in Contemporary Culture #9

Edited by Gretchen Bender and Timothy Druckrey

Technology forms the core of the cultural transformations that are generating startling changes in virtually every cultural and political activity of our time. Not a handbook for technologists, this is an engaging examination of some of the most critical questions facing society's infrastructure and soul. These compelling essays by cultural critics, scientists, and artists reinforce how the effects of technoculture must be contended with if we are to understand and actively participate in the sweeping changes our society faces today. The issues covered, among them technology and the new world order, information, artificiality and science, and politics of the body and identity, are each directly relevant to the experience of modern culture.

The offerings are in fact satisfyingly diverse in topic and approach. The best contributors . . . bend the distinction between the critical and the creative. —Artforum/Bookforum

Worth hunting down. —The Observer (London)

Twenty-two contributors offer their views on culture and our relationship with the emerging technology. . . . Deep thoughts, challenging reading.

—NAPRA Trade Journal

We are on the threshold of a new techno-cultural condition, and this book assesses the implications of current trends. —*Camerawork*

Culture on the Brink contains the best collection of advanced and stimulating essays on the meaning of technology now available. —*Neil Postman, author of* Technopoly

The Contributors: Laurie Anderson, Stanley Aronowitz, Gary Chapman, James Der Derian, Evelyn Fox Keller, Billy Kluver, Les Levidow, R. C. Lewontin, Joan Marks, Margaret Morse, Simon Penny, Kevin Robins, Avital Ronell, Tricia Rose, Andrew Ross, Elaine Scarry, Herbert Schiller, Wolfgang Schirmacher, Paula Treichler, Langdon Winner, Kathleen Woodward

1994 376 pages, illustrated $18.95 softcover

CUSTOMER NOTE

This complimentary CD-ROM artwork contains files that illustrate visually the issues discussed in the accompanying book. By opening the package, you are agreeing to be bound by the following agreement:

This CD-ROM product is sold as is without warranty of any kind, either expressed or implied, including but not limited to the implied warranty of merchantability and fitness for a particular purpose. Neither Bay Press nor its dealers or distributors assumes any liability of any alleged or actual damages arising from the use of or the inability to use this software.

Windows and Macintosh versions of QuickTime 2.x appear on the *Clicking On* CD-ROM. Windows users should ignore the installation instructions in the Windows README file. Instead, double-click QT16INST.EXE to install QuickTime to your local drive.

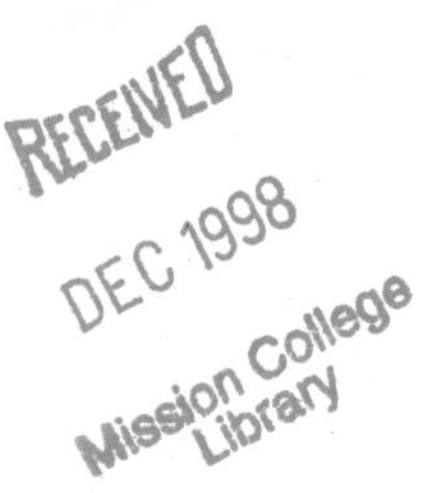